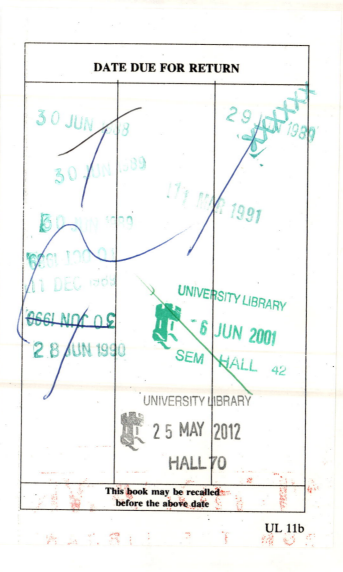

THE POLITICS OF INFORMAL JUSTICE

VOLUME 1

The American Experience

STUDIES ON LAW AND SOCIAL CONTROL

DONALD BLACK *Series Editor*

Center for Criminal Justice
Harvard Law School
Cambridge, Massachusetts 02138

P. H. Gulliver. Disputes and Negotiations:
A Cross-Cultural Perspective

Sandra B. Burman and Barbara E. Harrell-Bond
(Editors). The Imposition of Law

Cathie J. Witty. Mediation and Society:
Conflict Management in Lebanon

Francis G. Snyder. Capitalism and Legal Change:
An African Transformation

Richard L. Abel (Editor). The Politics of Informal Justice, Vol. 1:
The American Experience

In preparation

Allan V. Horwitz. The Social Control of Mental Illness

Richard L. Abel (Editor). The Politics of Informal Justice, Vol 2:
Comparative Studies

THE POLITICS OF INFORMAL JUSTICE

VOLUME 1

The American Experience

Edited by

RICHARD L. ABEL

School of Law
University of California, Los Angeles
Los Angeles, California

ACADEMIC PRESS
A Subsidiary of Harcourt Brace Jovanovich, Publishers
New York   London   Toronto   Sydney   San Francisco

ACADEMIC PRESS, INC.
111 Fifth Avenue, New York, New York 10003

United Kingdom Edition published by
ACADEMIC PRESS, INC. (LONDON) LTD.
24/28 Oval Road, London NW1 7DX

Library of Congress Cataloging in Publication Data
Main entry under title:

The Politics of informal justice.

  (Studies on law and social control)
  Includes bibliographies.
  Contents: v. 1. The American experience.
v. 2. Comparative studies.
  1. Justice, Administration of. 2. Justice,
Administration of--United States. I. Abel,
Richard L. II. Series.
K559.P64   347   81-14920
ISBN 0-12-041501-1 (v. 1) / 342.7 AACR2

0144682

Contents

3   CHRISTINE B. HARRINGTON
Delegalization Reform Movements:
A Historical Analysis   35

II

CONTEMPORARY EXPERIMENTS

4   PAUL WAHRHAFTIG
An Overview of Community-Oriented
Citizen Dispute Resolution Programs
in the United States   75

5   ANDREW SCULL
Community Corrections:
Panacea, Progress, or Pretense?   99

III

THEORETICAL PERSPECTIVES

List of Contributors

Numbers in parentheses indicate the pages on which the authors' contributions begin.

Richard L. Abel (1, 267), School of Law, University of California, Los Angeles, Los Angeles, California 90024

Jonathan Garlock (17), Rochester/Genesee Valley History Project, Monroe Community College, Rochester, New York 14623

Christine B. Harrington (35), Department of Political Science, Rutgers University, New Brunswick, New Jersey 08903

Richard Hofrichter (207), Committee on Behavioral and Social Aspects of Energy Consumption and Production, National Academy of Sciences, Washington, D.C. 20418

Mark Lazerson (119), Department of Sociology, University of Wisconsin–Madison, Madison, Wisconsin 53706

Andrew Scull (99), Department of Sociology, University of California, San Diego, La Jolla, California 92093

Boaventura de Sousa Santos (249), Faculdade de Economia, Universidade de Coimbra, Coimbra, Portugal

Steven Spitzer (167), Department of Sociology, Suffolk University, Beacon Hill, Boston, Massachusetts 02114

Paul Wahrhaftig (75), Divorce and Separation Mediation Center, Pittsburgh, Pennsylvania 15218

THE POLITICS OF INFORMAL JUSTICE

VOLUME 1

The American Experience

1

Introduction

RICHARD L. ABEL

We are presently experiencing what may well be a major transformation of our legal system. Recent years have witnessed repeated tirades against the expansion of substantive and procedural rights, the delivery of more professional legal services, and the proliferation of formal legal institutions (courts, regulatory agencies, etc.) that have characterized the present century. At this early stage the contours of the change are uncertain and its significance ambiguous. Do the following phenomena have anything in common: the attack on professionals, the state, and bureaucracy; calls to deregulate the economy; the advocacy of decentralization; demands for the decriminalization and delegalization of private behavior (drug use, divorce); deinstitutionalization (in education, care of the mentally ill, restraint and punishment of the delinquent and criminal); the preference for informality in hearing complaints and processing disputes? What is it that is really changing: ideology, substantive norms, processes, or institutions? Is the ambit of state control contracting or expanding? What impact will these changes have on fundamental social, economic, and political structures? Or is it all a lot of talk, with minimal significance for anyone except those who manage the legal system?

1

The chapters in this and the companion volume *(Comparative Studies)* attempt to answer those questions. The project grows out of a panel discussion at the second national Conference on Critical Legal Studies, held in Madison, Wisconsin, on November 10–12, 1978,[1] at which drafts of several of these essays were presented and in which the authors of others participated. The companion volume explores the phenomenon of informalism in a wide variety of social contexts: in non-Western, nonindustrial societies, as an aspect of the rise of fascism, in present-day Europe (both capitalist and social democratic), and in the transition to socialism. This volume focuses on the contemporary United States, although it also searches for historical antecedents and tries to situate what we are now experiencing in a larger theoretical perspective. This introduction identifies some of the themes that unite the wide-ranging essays. First, I will review the explanations offered for the movement toward informalism. Should we see it as simply another temporary oscillation in an endless cycle of formalism and informalism? What is the role of legal professionals? Then I will turn to the significance of these changes. What is the relationship between the official justifications for informalism and its actual consequences? How should we assess and compare the political meaning of formal and informal legal institutions? And how should we shape informal legal institutions and processes in order to maximize their contribution to social justice?

Although it is clearly necessary to have some working concept of informal justice, its boundaries must remain quite fluid. A central question, after all, is whether the numerous observable changes in the legal system are actually interrelated, and if so how. Furthermore, whatever unity the movement may possess is derived more from the sense of a common enemy—formalism—than from any clearly shared goal. The following will therefore have to suffice. We are concerned here with *legal* phenomena, i.e., with institutions that declare, modify, and apply norms in the process of controlling conduct and handling conflict. Such institutions are informal to the extent that they are nonbureaucratic in structure and relatively undifferentiated from the larger society, minimize the use of professionals, and eschew official law in favor of substantive and procedural norms that are vague, unwritten, commonsensical, flexible, ad hoc, and particularistic. Every instance of informal justice will exhibit some of these characteristics to some degree, though in none will all of them be fully developed.

[1]The Conference on Critical Legal Studies is an organization of several hundred law teachers, social scientists, students, and legal workers committed to the exploration of the relationship between legal theory and practice and the struggle for the creation of a more humane and just society. It was founded in Madison, Wisconsin, in 1977 and since then has held conferences in Boston, San Francisco, Buffalo, and Minneapolis. Although most of the contributors to these volumes are members of CCLS, each essay expresses the views of its author alone, and these volumes are not an official publication of the Conference.

These essays offer a variety of explanations for the rejection of formal legal institutions, rights, and processes. Some stress the power of ideas: disappointment in the capacity of the state to effect social change, hostility to bureaucrats and professionals, disillusionment with therapy and rehabilitation, the belief that institutionalization has failed. Yet though all of these intellectual currents are indubitably present, this approach encounters problems. First, for every critic of formalism there is usually an apologist. There are still many who believe that the state can and must manage society (e.g., "cure" inflation), advocate further expansion and reorganization of public and private bureaucracies, or propose the creation of new professions. Faith in science (e.g., psychotherapy, behavioral conditioning) as a solution to social problems constantly survives disconfirmation. Second (as Scull notes), the intellectual critique of formalism has been voiced many times in the past two centuries. Therefore the idealist analysis, though helpful, leaves two questions unanswered: Why have one set of ideas proved persuasive rather than another, and why have they done so now when they did not convince in the past?

Other explanations are more or less explicitly materialist. Informal mechanisms of social control express the needs of capital to discipline labor, control surplus populations, and manage class struggle. Furthermore, whereas competitive capital required the predictability assured by formal legal institutions, monopoly capital not only can dispense with formal law but also finds it an obstacle to planning rather than an aid. Greater flexibility is needed in order to cope with two sets of contradictions: those between labor and capital and those among capitalists. Capital seeks to socialize the cost of resolving these contradictions (as it tries to externalize all costs) by transferring them to the state, which heavily subsidizes the institutions that resolve disputes among capitalists and exercise social control over workers. But even the state must pay for these non-productive activities and can do so only by raising taxes, which are resented by the public and resisted by corporations (often successfully). The result is the fiscal crisis of the state, which responds by reducing the cost of certain operations and unburdening itself of other responsibilities. Informal justice may perform both of these functions. But the materialist explanation, though powerful, is incomplete. The movement toward informalism can be detected at other historical periods that exhibit very different economic and class configurations. And the fiscal crisis of the state does not tell us which duties will be abdicated or which expenditures reduced.

A third mode of explanation emphasizes political forces. The present legal retrenchment is seen as a reaction to the progressive victories of the 1960s and early 1970s. The state, at the behest of capital, is seeking to dampen "inflated" expectations, to defuse protest. Law, which had been heavily politicized, must now be "depoliticized"—which actually means that its conservative political content must be hidden. The mechanism for doing so is disorganization: Individual demands are satisfied in order to forestall their aggregation—a micropolitical tactic that imitates the macropolitical style of the 1980s, in which fragmented single-issue campaigns defy unification into a comprehensive program. In this view the state, aware that its repressive resources are limited, regroups its forces and concentrates them on the primary loci of dissent, using less expensive, less coercive methods of control for malcontent that is peripheral (geographically and functionally). This theory explains the opposed (and superficially contradictory) movements toward neoclassicism in penal policy (severe punishment for a limited number of clearly defined crimes) and neopositivism in neighborhood justice ("helping" everyone who has a grievance or problem or is involved in conflict). Yet this explanation simply pushes the question back one step: Why are the progressive forces presently so weak that they can be deprived of recent gains? And, like so many theories of legitimation, it tends to be circular: The greater or lesser need for state control is measured by the quantity of state resources devoted to that project.

A fourth approach emphasizes the role of professionals in the movement toward informalism—for one if its ironies is that there are even professionals at informalism. Although legal professionals are certainly not wholly autonomous in shaping the institutions within which they work, theoretical traditions as divergent as those of Engels and Weber acknowledge their considerable influence. For a variety of reasons, many of the central actors in formal legal institutions are interested in finding somewhere to send portions of their caseload. First, lawyers, like all professionals, seek intrinsic rewards from their work, but many struggle with a case overload that tends to rob them of these rewards. Second, judges, prosecutors, lawyers, and police all have their "junk" cases: matters that do not call for their technical skills, that appear substantively unimportant, or that involve parties of much lower status. The social status of professionals, even more than that of others in contemporary America, tends to be a function of the power they exercise over people and resources. Third, professionals have other reasons for wanting to move cases, such as pressure from a bureaucratic superior or economic interest in maximizing profit per case. None of these factors, by itself, is sufficient to explain the present tendency to create informal alternatives rather than to increase the number of judges, lawyers, etc.—although the activities of "professional" reformers (often legal academics) may be relevant. But once the alternatives are in business, their staff develop a "professional" stake in increasing caseload, expanding jurisdiction, fostering dependence by the lay public, exaggerating the level of their own technical skills, limiting membership, etc.

It is not just the movement *toward* informalism that requires explanation; we must also understand the reciprocal movement *away* from it. The notion of cycles has been justly criticized: Not only is it narrowly idealist but also the end point of each oscillation is necessarily different from the starting point. Nevertheless, there is ample evidence—historical, comparative, and contemporary—of formalist reactions against informalism. Each of the approaches discussed earlier may also help to illuminate that shift. The professional staff in informal institutions may seek to enhance their status and authority by adopting the trappings of formalism: dress and address, procedures, power, etc. (although we must also ask why formality confers higher status). Preserving informalism in an environment where formal legal institutions predominate is a little like trying to build socialism in one country—it is always being undermined politically. On the one hand, informalism depends on levels of moral enthusiasm, consensus, and suasion that are very difficult to sustain; rather than constantly struggling to revivify commitment, legal institutions may fall back on more coercive, hierarchical means of social control and dispute settlement. On the other hand, the state may feel threatened by the existence of autonomous informal institutions and actively suppress them, as Garlock demonstrates and colonial legal history confirms. Informalism may be curtailed for economic reasons. The institutions themselves may be criticized as wasteful and efforts made to "rationalize" them by increasing caseload, expanding jurisdiction, abbreviating hearings, training personnel, etc. Or they may be repudiated as inadequate to the economic tasks confronting the society and displaced in favor of more disciplined processes of social organization, as Spitzer suggests has happened in China. Finally, the influence of ideas should not be overlooked: Informalism will inevitably be perceived—correctly—as a form of coercive control; there will then be demands for procedural protections that necessarily reintroduce formality into the process. This is surely part of the reason for the recent retreat from rehabilitation and therapy in criminal justice.

The explanations for changes in the structure of dispute processing and social control, just reviewed, necessarily imply judgments about the significance of those changes. But it is essential to explore that significance more thoroughly, even if our conclusions must remain highly tentative at this early stage in the transformation. Informal processes appear to be less expensive to operate than formal, since the costs of legal institutions are largely attributable to personnel and informal institutions replace highly paid professionals with low-paid or volunteer lay persons or paraprofessionals. They thus appear to alleviate the fiscal crisis of the state. Yet this outcome is highly problematic. First, the cheapness of informal processes also permits an enormous expansion of the apparatus of mediation and control. Second, although the cost of individual staff may be lower, the staff itself may grow larger and the amount of time each member must expend on a case may be greater. Third, informal institutions supplement, rather than displace, their formal counterparts. If any of these assessments is correct—and especially if they all are—then informalism will aggravate the fiscal crisis rather than relieve it. All proponents of informalism therefore recognize that cost reduction must be a secondary goal, though they vary in the emphasis they give it.

The primary business of informal institutions is social control. Consequently, the central question must be: Do they expand or reduce state control? The authors in this volume agree with Foucault that informal justice increases state power. Informal institutions allow state control to escape the walls of those highly visible centers of coercion—court, prison, mental hospital, school—and permeate society. In place of mechanisms of confinement and exclusion (which, by definition, are spatially delimited) they substitute processes of penetration and integration that are dispersed and all-encompassing. They extend control temporally—beyond the civil judgment, the criminal sentence, the school term, the period of confinement in a mental institution—so that supervision and review never end. They increase the variety of behavior that can be controlled by diversifying and individualizing the remedial apparatus so as to transcend the limited repertoire of prison, fine, and money damages. Where formal institutions are largely passive and reactive, informal institutions can be purposive and proactive. They obliterate the fundamental liberal distinctions between public and private, state and civil society, what is forbidden and what is allowed. In order to facilitate this expansion, they carefully cultivate the appearance of being noncoercive. Thus the retraction of the overtly coercive aspects of state control (the rise of neoclassicism in penology) is not inconsistent with but is rather a necessary complement of the expansion of less obviously coercive mechanisms: The state sheathes its claws while extending a helping hand to the troubled individual. Fewer are categorized as "bad" so that everyone can be seen as "mad." Therapy is eliminated in the prison (and even curtailed within the mental institution) so that it will be less threatening as it percolates throughout society. If coercion is effectively masked, then control can be drained of all political, legal, and ethical content and freed to become pure psychological manipulation. When all are guiltless, all, by the same reasoning, are equally guilty: "*Tout comprendre, c'est tout condamner.*"

But it is possible—and essential—to penetrate the comforting facade of informalism and begin to reveal its political meaning. Informalism is a mechanism by which the state extends its control so as to manage capital accumulation and defuse the resistance this engenders. Its objects are not randomly distributed but rather are concentrated within the dominated categories of contemporary capitalism: workers, the poor, ethnic minorities, and women. This is not accidental (or easily remedied). Although informal institutions seek to appear noncoercive, they typically rely on the criminal justice system for most of their cases, and the grist of that system (both accused and victims) is the oppressed. Furthermore, informal institutions offer help in resolving conflict and solving individual problems. Help is always extended downwards—the very relationship of helping is inherently unequal. Because the personnel of informal institutions are of relatively low status, those whom they help must be even lower.

Informal institutions control by disorganizing grievants, trivializing grievances, frustrating collective responses. Their very creation proclaims the message that social problems can be resolved by fiddling with the control apparatus once more, that it is unnecessary to question basic social structures. But informal institutions also foster disorganization much more directly, by instructing each party that he can, and must, resolve the controversy alone. The way in which the external environment of informal institutions measures their success imposes an incentive structure that reinforces these features: Evaluations are couched in terms of the number of cases handled and the satisfaction of individual parties, not in terms of the impact on groups, the contribution to community, or the attainment of any other substantive goal. It is just because individuation is the primary function of informal institutions that they can accomplish their purpose using staff who possess little or no training, operate with minimal supervision, and are bound by few rules. The precise response to any given dispute or deviant act is unimportant. The goal is not regimentation but disaggregation. Informal institutions produce this result by treating all conflict as individually caused and amenable to individual solutions.

In seeking to understand the significance of informalism it is essential to confront the claims of its proponents. These attempt to distract attention from the fact that the liberal promises of the 1960s were betrayed by the unwillingness or inability of the state to expend sufficient economic or political resources (e.g., to eliminate poverty, racism, sexism) and the inadequacy of the means used (e.g., the grant of due process rights to welfare recipients). The ideology of informalism often resembles Orwellian newspeak: Political choice is portrayed as blind necessity, the interests of dominant groups are dressed up as the wishes of the dominated, and informal processes appear as their mirror images—a form of doublethink strongly reminiscent of the 1984 that is almost upon us.

Informal institutions are said to be a necessary response to inexorable economic forces. The courts are "overcrowded," there is "too much" litigation, crime rates are rising, the prisons are full. Yet even were this conceded (and the ostensibly factual characterization must actually be a value judgment—how crowded is overcrowded? how much is too much?), it would not dictate the response. The courts could be relieved of their congestion instantaneously if they expelled all corporate plaintiffs or prohibited the government from litigating. The prisons could virtually be emptied if they released all drug offenders and persons convicted of property crimes. Informalists therefore speak of cases being "appropriate" for the courts—glossing over the implicit decision to move certain matters to alternative institutions rather than adapt existing courts to handle them. Some forms of litigation are described as luxuries—class actions, prisoners' rights, appeals concerning social security and veterans' benefits—whereas others —such as corporate proxy fights—are assumed to be necessities. The current gloomy economic situation is then invoked as conclusive evidence that we can no longer afford to enforce certain rights in court. Indeed, the very attempt to do so—the insistence on procedural due process—is said to be the cause of the crisis of the courts.

It is a familiar argument—blame the victim for his plight: People are on welfare because they are lazy, central city housing stock is deteriorating because of rent control and housing code enforcement, banks are failing because of truth-in-lending and equal credit legislation (*Los Angeles Times*, October 15, 1980: pt. 4, p. 1). Yet its familiarity should not blind us to its falsity. The dominant classes do not object to litigation—they want the courts to themselves. Corporations do not oppose regulation, they simply want to dictate its content: Look at the demand by automobile manufacturers for import controls or by other domestic industries for antidumping laws; consider the desperate fights by banks, airlines, railroads, the trucking industry, the professions, etc., to preserve anti-competitive restraints. It is simply untrue that we cannot design and operate a court that efficiently enforces a high volume of rights: Look at the way housing courts process evictions or small claims courts attach wages to pay debts! Furthermore, such a court need not be a fiscal burden on the state—housing courts (like the primary courts of colonial Africa and India) actually make money. In weighing the protests of the dominant classes that certain formal legal institutions, rights, and procedures are too expensive, or inappropriate, or cumbersome, it is useful to keep in mind the institutions those classes demand for their own purposes—and get—to compare, for instance, the level of expenditure on the federal courts (which are used largely by business and the state) with the amounts spent on informal institutions.

A second line of argument in favor of informalism is that the people want it. They are said to be dissatisfied with the courts and to prefer institutions that are speedy, cheap, and more approachable. Yet public mistrust of the courts has been a constant for at least a century: People have long perceived—correctly—that courts serve corporate, not individual, interests. The creation of informal alternatives merely accentuates this segregation. Furthermore, although applicants certainly want cheap, speedy justice, justice may be more important to them than speed—and they may be willing to pay for it. Finally, there is considerable evidence that people want authority rather than informality: They want the leverage of state power to obtain the redress they believe is theirs by right, not a compromise that purports to restore a social peace that never existed. The negligible caseloads of those informal institutions that are truly powerless strongly evidence such a preference. Informalism represents an attempt by the dominant classes to impute wishes to the dominated so that the *former* can enjoy speedy, inexpensive access to authoritative courts from which the *latter* have been excluded. And it is hypocritical for state officials, corporate leaders, and legal reformers to mourn the passing of traditional informal institutions when it was they who killed them in the first place, as Garlock and Harrington both demonstrate.

The third element in the ideology of informalism consists of a set of buzz words that evoke a favorable reaction by disguising the true nature of the phenomenon. Although the institutions are said to be informal, they are actually created and constrained by highly formal rules and lines of authority. Although they are said to be decentralized, their very decentralization is centrally controlled. They are said to be noncoercive, but this is true only in the sense that personnel managers use nonauthoritarian techniques to manipulate workers, or that the function of the police is "to protect and serve," as patrol cars in Los Angeles and other American cities frequently proclaim. Informal justice claims to be a "community" institution, but the residential community it serves is usually just the figment of some reformer's imagination. Indeed, by individualizing conflict and facilitating exit from relationships, informal institutions undermine community rather than create or preserve it. They are said to entertain a broader range of issues than would a court. But though mediators may be more tolerant than judges about letting disputants ramble on, they ultimately resolve only a narrow set of issues: those that divide the two parties to the immediate dispute and can be handled at a superficial level. Informal institutions are said to be more accessible, but this may become an excuse for allowing courts to remain inaccessible or even for curtailing judicial access by requiring potential litigants to exhaust informal alternatives. Informal institutions claim to render parties more autonomous when they actually engage in more subtle manipulation; they purport to eliminate professional representatives when they simply create a new category of paraprofessionals, thereby increasing the dependence of lay persons. They speak the language of libertarianism while augmenting state power and preach the laissez-faire gospel while constraining choice. They claim to be neutral and to favor compromise, concealing the fact that "neutrality" always expresses values and confirms existing advantages and that compromise between unequals is necessarily biased. Finally, they stress superficial stylistic differences between informal and formal institutions—dress, manner, speech, location, hours—in order to conceal the fundamental similarities of substance.

A fourth rhetorical device employed by the advocates of informalism is the invocation of false comparisons. Community corrections are portrayed as less coercive and oppressive than prisons. That is true but incomplete—for most of the people they process would otherwise have been released unconditionally. Mediation is compared with adjudication, which is more expensive and less accessible, but most mediated cases would have been handled by negotiation.

There are good reasons for our difficulties in explaining informalism, assessing its significance, and seeing through the claims of its proponents. Formalism and informalism, both as modes of state power and as forms of resistance to it, possess fundamental, inherent political ambiguities. It is not possible to determine, in the abstract, which is preferable. Each must be situated historically in a concrete social context. I argued in the previous section that it is not always desirable to increase the speed and lower the cost of processes of adjudication and social control—it depends on who is mobilizing what against whom. Even reforms that appear to reduce state authority often have inadvertent consequences: liberalization of the grounds of divorce, for instance, has encouraged many more people to seek state approval for their most intimate relationships; the transformation of a criminal prosecution into a civil dispute means that state authority judges, and may sanction, the conduct of the complainant as well as that of the accused. Ultimately, the evaluation of both formalism and informalism turns on the observer's social position and his consequent moral assessment of the relationship between state power and civil society at the particular historical moment.

That legal formalism has, at times, been a revolutionary force is dramatically demonstrated by its association with the rise of capitalism. Formal rights, procedures, and institutions offered the bourgeoisie protection against feudal oppression and monarchical absolutism and gave entrepreneurs the means to acquire land and natural resources, exploit labor, and expand capital. But the fact that formalism once played such a pivotal role should not mislead us into assuming that it always enhances liberty, equality, and community, for the same triumph of capitalism also institutionalized exploitation of the proletariat.

The moral valuation of contemporary legal formalism and informalism is confusing, at best. As a sword, formality can frequently be a useful weapon for the powerless. It can justify the demand for equality across lines of race, religion, gender, and even class. Adherence to formal procedures can help to legitimate radical social change, as the Allende regime in Chile sought to demonstrate. Substantive goals that might elicit violent opposition can hide behind a procedural facade. And yet formalism has numerous drawbacks as a strategy for progressive politics. The concept of formal equality in liberal legalism is sharply dissociated from *substantive* equality in the control over or enjoyment of economic resources. Indeed, capitalists are extraordinarily adept at using the ostensible neutrality of formal procedures to advance their selfish economic and political goals. And there clearly are limits to the capacity of the powerless to use formal procedures to achieve social change: Consider the outcomes of the campaigns to improve conditions in prisons or mental hospitals or to integrate the schools through litigation. Indeed, it is precisely these limitations of formalism that are often said to explain the inability of the liberal state to fulfill its promises to the powerless, and thus to account for the proliferation of (informal) administrative agencies—the hallmark of the welfare state.

As a shield, formalism is just as ambiguous. Without question, it remains an essential defense of the powerless, a bourgeois invention that, as Marx noted, can be turned against the bourgeoisie by workers and other oppressed groups. E. P.

Thompson has properly reminded us that revolutionaries should be the last to discard the hard-won gains of prior revolutions, of which formal legal rights are some of the most important. If prisoners have been unable to humanize the prisons, formal rights have certainly helped them resist further degradation. Although formal procedures, like all law, can be subverted, sometimes they are virtually self-enforcing: The requirement that the accused be represented by counsel in most criminal prosecutions has clearly inhibited state control, a point on which conservatives and liberals agree. And Lazerson describes the dramatic way in which legal services lawyers were able to use procedural formalism to enhance the bargaining position of tenants in housing court—and outside it. These examples should alert us to the fact that every procedure, no matter how trivial it may appear, has some impact on the relative power of adversaries. But formalism not only protects the powerless; it also allows the powerful to resist state control. Opposition to the New Deal, twenty-five years of successful foot-dragging in response to orders to integrate the schools, defeat in battle after battle to preserve the environment and to protect the health and safety of workers—the examples are endless. Furthermore, formal rights and procedures unsupported by organized power quickly deteriorate into formalistic rituals, as anyone can see who observes the daily operation of our criminal courts or the process of civil commitment to mental institutions.

If the bottom line of the balance sheet on formalism is uncertain, so is the verdict on informalism, with which we have much less experience. Surely the first question must be whether informal processes have been imposed externally from the top down or created autonomously from the bottom up, whether they extend state control or facilitate interaction in civil society. Labor–management arbitration within the terms of a collectively bargained contract and commercial arbitration between business enterprises in an ongoing relationship are often held out as laudable examples of informalism (although it is questionable whether either is particularly informal). But each is praiseworthy only to the extent that the process of dispute resolution has been created (or at least freely chosen) by two relatively equal parties. The results are not nearly so attractive when the parties are grossly unequal. Informalism in the criminal process, where the state confronts the individual, almost always increases oppression—witness the dismal history of therapy, rehabilitation, and the juvenile court. And the same is true where the state establishes informal institutions for civil contests between un-equals: Landlord domination of the housing court simply replays creditor domination of the small claims court—and industry domination of administrative agencies.

The political significance of informal institutions turns not only on who uses them but also on the total social environment in which they operate. If it is true that informal institutions express and can help to build community, then it is critically important to investigate the qualities of the community they foster.

Community, after all, is itself morally ambiguous: We do not want to support the old boy networks that cement elite communities, the informal blacklisting that the entertainment industry used against radicals, or the racial, religious, and gender segregation perpetuated by private clubs. What kind of community *should* we be striving for in advanced capitalism? Should it be based upon residential neighborhoods, ethnic enclaves, class solidarity, ideological homogeneity? And how should we view the authority exercised by informal institutions? Is it preferable to control through violence and bureaucracy? Before answering this question we should remember that rhetorical persuasion can be as oppressive and manipulative as any other form of authority.

I do not want to end this brief overview of the issues on a negative note, for the moral ambiguity of informalism must mean that it can liberate as well as oppress. As Santos argues, the enthusiasm it inspires among liberal reformers can be explained only by the fact that it expresses certain fundamental values; rapid and thorough airing of controversies, participation by the disputants in resolving their own conflicts, reduction of dependence on professionals, greater involvement of citizens in an essential aspect of democratic governance. The efforts by state and capital to suppress or coopt informal institutions—the Knights of Labor in the nineteenth century, neighborhood justice today—are further evidence of their revolutionary potential.

No legal institution, formal or informal, can successfully depoliticize conflict. Surely that is the inescapable lesson to be drawn from the last two centuries of liberal capitalism. Institutions that attempt to do so will either become instruments of resistance to oppression or atrophy and die. If informal institutions tend to individualize grievances, they can also allow grievants to see their common problems. But the true significance of informal institutions for conflict resolution and social control is that they empower those who create and operate them. Their instrumental contribution to internal discipline and the resolution of intraclass dissension seems to me less important than their function as symbol of the autonomy and authority of the social unit (however defined). There is ample historical evidence that competition over legal jurisdiction has repeatedly played a central role in the struggle for political domination: Consider the battles between king and feudal lords in medieval England, between the colonial regime and tribal rulers in Africa, or between federal and state governments in the United States. Resolving disputes and applying norms necessarily empowers those who do so: It gives them authority, publicity, patronage, prestige, and often economic resources as well. How else can we explain the contrast between efforts by the capitalist state to destroy union self-governance and its hands-off policy toward the internal affairs of corporations?

But if the assertion of authority to resolve disputes and control behavior has the potential to contribute to the creation of a countervailing power that can oppose both state and capital, it can do so only as part of a broad social movement. This is the experience of the Knights of Labor (as narrated by Garlock), and of German workers at the turn of the century, Chilean *campamentos* under Allende, the Portugese people during the 1974 revolution, and the Mozambican struggle against imperialism (described in the companion volume). Such a movement is essential to informal institutions in two ways. First, it alone can create the community base that allows informal institutions to function by giving people incentives to resolve conflict rather than sever relations and by conferring authority to examine behavior, intervene in conflict, and enforce decisions. Second, legal institutions can gain broad significance only if they are integrated in the pursuit of social, economic, and political objectives. Informalism, thus, is not an end in itself, but it can be a very important means in the struggle for justice.

I

Historical Antecedents

The Knights of Labor Courts:
A Case Study of Popular Justice*

JONATHAN GARLOCK

> *The efficiency of industry requires the strictest discipline in the army of labor, but the claim of the workman to just and considerate treatment is backed by the whole power of the nation.*
>
> (EDWARD BELLAMY, *Looking Backward* [1888: Ch. 19])

INTRODUCTION

Recognizing that "the alarming development and aggressiveness of great capitalists and corporations, unless checked, will inevitably lead to the pauperization and hopeless degradation of the toiling masses," ("Preamble," 1886: 7), a group of Philadelphia workingmen founded the Noble Order of the Knights of Labor in 1869. Unlike trade unions, which organized workers along occupational lines or within particular industries, the Order sought to unite "all those who obey the divine injunction, 'In the sweat of thy face shalt thou eat bread'" (*Ibid.*). They therefore had a heterogeneous membership that included workers of all skills and crafts, on farms and in factories, men and women, and whites, blacks and ethnic minorities.

The goals of the Order reflected its producing class membership and ideology: "To make industrial and moral worth, not wealth, the true standard of individual

---

*An earlier version of this chapter was presented at the Third Annual Meeting of the Social Science History Association at Columbus, Ohio, in November 1978.

17

and national greatness" and "To secure for workers the full enjoyment of the wealth they create" (*Ibid.*). These aims were pursued through both political reform and direct action. The Order's political program focused on securing a wide range of legislation: recognition of worker organizations, improved health and safety standards, access to public lands, mandatory arbitration of labor disputes, protective lien laws, elimination of convict and child labor, collection of labor statistics, imposition of a graduated income tax, implementation of postal savings exchanges, and the nationalization of transport and communications. At the same time, the Order used strikes and boycotts to back its demands for an eight-hour day and equal pay for equal work. Ultimately, it hoped to replace the wage system with a "cooperative industrial system" through the creation of producers' and consumers' cooperatives.

The wide appeal of this program was attested by the Order's extraordinary organizational achievement. Beginning as a secret society confined to a few industrial centers and major coalfields, it spread and grew rapidly between 1869 and 1896, establishing over 12,000 Local Assemblies (LAs) in 5000 communities throughout the nation (Garlock, 1974). During this period perhaps as many as three million workers joined the Order; reported membership stood at 730,000 in the peak year of 1886.

Although administrative affairs were entrusted to an Executive Board elected at annual meetings of a representative General Assembly, the pulse of the organization beat most strongly at the local level. To begin with, it was here that workers chartered themselves as Local Assemblies—*trade* assemblies if a single occupation was represented by ten or more members, *mixed* if either no trade or at least two trades had ten or more members. Local Assemblies considered the economic and political issues of the day, discussed articles published in the labor and radical press, especially the Order's official *Journal of United Labor,* heard invited speakers, organized strikes and boycotts, sang and recited poetry, initiated members and conducted fraternal rituals, and managed the affairs of their own cooperatives. And these Local Assemblies developed and dispensed an important form of popular justice by interpreting and enforcing the laws governing the conduct of members.

EVOLUTION AND STRUCTURE OF
THE KNIGHTS OF LABOR COURTS

The judicial system was established at the outset in the Order's secret work, the *Adelphon Kruptos.* Each Local Assembly was to have a court consisting of a judge, judge advocate, and clerk, elected annually. Where possible, judges were to settle grievances amicably; this failing, they were to order indictments, convene their courts, impartially hear evidence, and render binding decisions. Judge

advocates, prosecuting attorneys, prepared written indictments, issued summonses, and attended all court sessions. Clerks served summonses, attended all
sittings, and recorded court proceedings. Members were guaranteed the right of
appeal. In LAs attached to District Assemblies (DAs), appeal lay to DA courts; in
LAs attached directly to the General Assembly, members appealed to Courts in
Banc, composed of the judges of the three nearest LAs.

Although the *Adelphon Kruptos* articulated the Order's rules and established
the functions of court officers, it ignored many operational details, failed to
specify trial procedures, and was vague with respect to jurisdiction. It thus fell to
the executive officers and the General Assembly to clarify and elaborate judicial
procedures. In 1879 the General Assembly ratified earlier decisions by Uriah
Stephens, the Order's first Master Workman: LA courts were to be "Oyer and
Terminer," their findings "certified to the Local and by them executed without
vote or ballot"; juries were explicitly rejected, as were grievance committees for
disputes between members of LAs (although grievances of all sorts could be heard
at the national level by a committee of the General Assembly); a written summons had to bear the initials of the court officers and the LA seal; DA courts were
empowered to try LAs; and "Officers of Court, who may be interested or implicated in a case, [were] disqualified" (*Proceedings*, 1879: 145–149). However, as
Stephens concluded in his annual report, " The law regulating the proceedings
of the Court needs some further rules... especially that governing appeals"
(*Ibid.*: 100); consequently, the General Assembly approved a number of recommendations made by the Committee on Laws. DA courts were defined for the
first time: They were to consist of three judges (chosen annually by each District
Assembly), a judge advocate, and a clerk; they were to review and determine all
cases appealed from LA courts, trying them de novo; and they were to supersede
Courts in Banc. Local Assembly officers could be required to vacate their offices
while charges were pending against them. And the General Assembly agreed to
adopt laws governing the reinstatement of expelled members (*Ibid.*: 125, 139).

Terence Powderly, Master Workman of the Order from 1879 through 1893,
not only played a major role in guiding its growth and consolidation but, through
a number of important decisions, also defined the courts and articulated their
procedures. A key Powderly decision was that members could be expelled from
the Order only after a fair and impartial trial or by unanimous LA vote (in the
presence and without the objection of court officers) recorded as a "Finding of
Court" (*Proceedings*, 1880: 257–263). By placing LA courts at the center of all
serious discipline, this decision not only safeguarded members' rights but also
established the importance of the courts themselves. Other Powderly rulings
contributed to the development of the courts: District Assembly court verdicts
had to be reached by a full bench; a suspended or expelled member might testify
on appeal although banned from the assembly; court clerks had to turn over to
their LAs all evidence taken during trials; defendants could be required to pay

bers upon initiation. Like the rules of early English trade unions and American fraternal societies, those of the Knights stressed secrecy, obedience, and mutual aid. Members were never to reveal the Order's signs, activities, plans, or membership. Knights were to obey the Order's laws and to

> defend the life, interest, reputation and family of all true members . . . help and assist all employed and unemployed, unfortunate or distressed members to procure employ and secure just remuneration; relieve their distress and counsel others to aid them, so that they and theirs may receive and enjoy the just fruits of their labor and exercise of their art [*Adelphon Kruptos*, 1886: 28].

Given this detailed list of obligations and prohibitions, it is not difficult to conjecture the sorts of misconduct characterized in 70 percent of the expulsions simply as "violation of obligation," "conduct unbecoming a Knight," or both. And it is clear that other expulsions, in which the cause was specified, also involved what may be classed as offenses against the Order (see Table 2.1).

Many of these offenses impaired the Order's capacity to function: improperly issuing or obtaining traveling cards, divulging the Order's secrets or business, insubordination, or working against the Order (such as the two carpet weavers who signed affidavits that the Knights were "injurious to both employer and employee") (*Journal*, March 1885: 936). Offenses such as drunkenness, immorality, becoming a gambler or liquor seller, keeping a disorderly house, slandering the Order or its members, and swearing violated the ethical standards expected of members.

Other offenses against the Order involved contempt of LA or DA courts or perjury before them. Although some Knights simply disregarded the summons of the Order's courts or failed to appear at trial, others manifested their contempt more dramatically. One LA Master Workman, a miner, was expelled not only for the initial offense of swearing while occupying the chair but also for "unjustly accusing the court of his local with unfairness while trying him for swearing, and for drawing a revolver and attempting to shoot" court officers (*Ibid.*, July 1880: 35). Such cases reveal the environment within which the Order's courts operated.

In a different category, however, were expulsions for actions punishable not only by the Order's courts but also by the state (see Table 2.2). Most of these offenses involved peculation of one sort or another—embezzlement, defalcation, and misappropriation of funds—often committed by LA officers whose responsibilities offered the greatest opportunity to betray the trust of members. The range of temptation was extensive. Funds might be pocketed: One member was expelled for appropriating a candidate's proposition fee and another for "inducing a number of colored men to form a temporary organization for the purpose of being founded as an LA," appropriating the charter fee and "utterly refusing to make any restitution" (*Ibid.*, July 1883: 525). Defense funds could find their way into the wrong hands: Two members appropriated to their own use funds collected

TABLE 2.1
Offenses against the Order

Offense	Number expelled
Abusing and/or injuring members	4
Becoming a gambler	2
Contempt of LA and/or DA court	78
Dishonesty	20
Disorderly conduct [in LA]	1
Divulging business of Order	6
Divulging secrets of Order	40
Drunkenness	25
Illegal membership	2
Immorality	1
Insubordination	18
Insulting members and/or wives	2
Issuing cards to brothers not in good standing	1
Joining "Improved K. of L."	4
Joining Order under assumed name	3
Keeping a disorderly house	1
Malfeasance in office	1
Nonpayment of dues	5
Obtaining grip and password by fraud	1
Obtaining traveling card under false pretenses	1
Obtaining traveling card when not in good standing	1
Perjury in LA and/or DA court	4
Reprehensible and/or unworthy conduct	5
Revealing brothers' names	5
Selling liquor	7
Slandering brothers	8
Slandering Order	8
Swearing	1
Working against Order	13

for striking miners under false pretense; a member of a committee collecting subscriptions for Hocking Valley miners appropriated funds to his own use; another member absconded with $500 raised by his fellow workmen to defend him and other members in a lawsuit (*Ibid.*, June 1884: 732; June 1885: 1007; May 1885: 995). Special events also offered opportunities: Members were expelled for keeping money received from selling picnic tickets, refusing to account for ball committee funds, defrauding an LA of festival money, and keeping receipts of fair tickets (*Ibid.*, February 1882: 196; November 1882: 345; May 1884: 693; August 1886: 2143).

Knights found still other ways of getting at and retaining LA funds. Some

TABLE 2.2
Violations of Statute Law

Offense	Number expelled
Absconding with LA funds	14
Adultery	1
Appropriating LA funds	42
Assault	5
Bigamy	1
Blackmail	2
Burglary	3
Cheating brothers	7
Conviction for crime	2
Criminal conduct	2
Defalcation	5
Defaulting with LA funds	1
Defrauding LA	26
Defrauding members	62
Desertion and/or family abuse	15
Embezzlement	113
Embezzling LA funds	82
Extortion	1
Failure to pay board bills	5
Failure to repay debt	1
Forgery	5
Fraud	2
Grand larceny	1
Larceny	1
Misappropriating LA funds	15
Misdemeanor	2
Murder	3
Obtaining goods under false pretenses	1
Obtaining money under false pretenses	23
Petty larceny	2
Rape	1
Robbery	5
Stealing	19
Swindling brothers	4
Swindling LA	1
Theft	8
Withholding LA books	2
Withholding LA funds	8

embezzled from their cooperative stores; one kept money donated to build a new assembly hall; another defrauded the Order's Insurance Association, perhaps by filing a false benefits claim; another absconded with his LA's funds when it lapsed; still others embezzled district funds and special assessments. One even made off with funds collected for the widow of a deceased member (*Ibid.*, May 1884: 693; January 1886: 1176; May 1885: 995; October 1880: 62; November 1885: 1139; September 1884: 788; October 1884: 825).

Not all statutory offenses for which members were expelled were committed against their assemblies or fellow Knights. Two glass blowers were expelled for stealing rollers from their employer ("among window glass blowers . . . [this was] considered worse even than black-legging during a strike"); others were expelled for leaving unpaid board bills, defrauding creditors, bigamy, and deserting their wives (*Ibid.*, May 1881: 117; May 1883: 471; June 1886: 2096; May 1883: 470; September 1883: 561).

It is impossible to determine how often LAs or individual Knights appealed to the state in addition to prosecuting the offender within the Order. Such cases were probably rare, not only because of workers' attitudes toward the legal apparatus of the state but also because a large portion of these offenders left "for parts unknown." That a remedy at law might be sought on occasion is evident from the plea of one LA that was clearly not satisfied with expelling a member for default: "If any of our [*Journal*] readers should come across him they will send word to the above A., who will have him arrested at any cost" (*Ibid.*, January 1885: 888). In a few cases members were expelled who were also convicted in criminal courts for murder, bigamy, and other serious offenses (*Ibid.*, October 1883: 575; May 1884: 693; October 1886: 2189; May 1882: 232; April 1883: 446; January 1885: 887).

A third category of expulsions includes actions such as scabbing or blacklegging, refusing to quit work when ordered out, and returning to work before a strike was ended (see Table 2.3). Though clearly violations of obligation, such actions also threatened class solidarity. Breaking ranks and strikebreaking directly injured working people; the other offenses discussed earlier primarily affected the Order's capacity to govern and impinged only incidentally on the membership as a whole.

The collective nature of these offenses is underscored by the fact that whereas embezzlement, fraud, assault, and offenses against the rules of the Order were generally committed by individual Knights and only rarely by more than a few together, half the cases of scabbing and blacklegging led to the expulsion of several members of an LA at once. For example, during the great Southwest rail strike of 1885 several LAs of mixed railroad employees expelled whole groups, including fifty-two members of one local for "scabbing in the D. & R.G. [Denver and Rio Grande] shops while members of the Assembly were on strike" (*Ibid.*, August 1885: 1066). The largest of these mass trials expelled fifty-four cigarette factory girls in Rochester, New York, for violating their obligation by

returning to work . . . after all members of the Order had been ordered out by DA 44, pending the settlement of the difficulty caused . . . in locking out the cigarette makers. . . . They returned to

TABLE 2.3
Offenses against Class Solidarity

Offense	Number expelled
Blacklegging	63
Blacksheeping	2
Causing brothers to be victimized	3
Employing convict labor	1
Going foul on the trade	1
Instructing boys	3
Refusing to quit work (when ordered out)	2
Returning to work (before strike is over)	57
Scabbing	259
Taking strikers' place	30
Working during a strike	2
Working in a scab shop	4
Working on boycotted job with convicts	1
Working under price	12

that factory when it was their duty to remain out, and by their action prolonged a difficulty that might have been amicably settled long ago. In this labor struggle there should be no excuse for treachery on the part of men or women [*Ibid.*, July 1883: 531].

It is significant that nearly half the Knights expelled for scabbing or blacklegging belonged to mixed LAs and that a third of the LAs that expelled members for these offenses were mixed. Workers in a single trade could be expected to react strongly against actions that threatened strikes in which they were engaged, but those in diverse occupations would have less of a stake. True, the dichotomy between mixed and trade LAs is not complete: many trade assemblies included workers of different crafts, and the members of many mixed assemblies were engaged in only a few trades or, as in the case of the railroad shop employees, constituted industrial locals. Nevertheless, that mixed assemblies often expelled scabs and blacklegs suggests that many Knights were strongly committed to principles of class solidarity, since direct self-interest cannot have operated in most instances.

Useful as these expulsion data are in establishing that courts were active throughout the Order and in providing insight into the nature of cases brought before them, they say little about the historical significance of the courts. After all, adherence to rules and established standards of conduct had characterized many of the antecedents of the Knights of Labor: English friendly societies and trade unions, American fraternal orders and churches. These bodies expelled members for many of the offenses detailed in the preceding discussion (Harris,

1884: 132–136; Gist, 1940: 138–139; Aspinall, 1949: 86–88; Thompson, 1963: 419; Hobsbawm, 1965: 192) and employed similar judicial procedures (Harris, 1884: 139–143; Sickels, 1886: 393–407; Kiddier, 1930: 220–221; Gist, 1940: 139–140). Indeed, the Order's chief procedural innovation appears to have been the role of the court's presiding officer as an advocate representing the organization, which Powderly held to be "an exact copy of a military court martial" (*Journal*, January 1883: 382).

However, the importance of the Knights of Labor courts lies less in their procedure and purview than in their role in the resistance of American workers to the legal apparatus of the state.

THE KNIGHTS OF LABOR COURTS
AND POPULAR JUSTICE

Among the demands included in the Order's original political program was "the abrogation of all laws that do not bear equally upon capital and labor, and the removal of unjust technicalities, delays, and discrimination in the administration of justice" (*"Preamble,"* 1886: 8). This was not rhetorical posturing but the expression of a deep-seated belief that the law served nonproducers as an instrument of class oppression through daily harassment and the suppression of struggles over working conditions.

During this period the only time most American workers encountered the legal machinery of the state was when they were arraigned before the local courts of magistrates, aldermen, and justices of the peace. As the Pittsburgh Survey concluded, the alderman's office was "to the vast majority of alien wage-earners . . . their only place of contact with American law and judicial procedure. For them it was the court of the people" (Blaxter and Kerr, 1914: 139). Officials of these courts were generally unsalaried; their services were paid by fees and fines. Such a system readily lent itself to corruption and victimization: mass arrests of innocent poor and working people, who were then fined for trivial offenses or incarcerated in workhouses if they could not pay.

Investigations of these courts revealed the extent to which they engaged in systematic harassment and intimidation. Abolition of the fee system in proceedings before Baltimore magistrates, for instance, reduced arrests from 12,000 to 7000 in 1882, cutting them by almost half within a single year (Altgeld, 1890: 196). Fully a third of those arrested and jailed by the constables of Chicago magistrates in the 1880s were discharged without trial—a total of 40,000 in the years 1882, 1884, and 1888 alone (*Ibid.*: 197, 275, 286–287). 80 percent of the arraignments before two Pittsburgh aldermen were dismissed and another 9 percent were thrown out by grand juries (Blaxter and Kerr, 1914: 147). And in Scranton local magistrates collected and kept thousands of dollars in fines paid by "poor men whose misfortune rather than criminal instinct threw them into the clutches of the fining power"; drunks in that city were usually fined "about as much as the magistrate could find in [their] clothes" (Powderly, 1940: 86).

As mayor of Scranton from 1878 to 1884, Terence Powderly did what he could to mitigate such abuses. Instead of having offenders brought through the streets to his office, he held court in the lockup, thereby sparing prisoners public display and humiliation. He heard the cases of juvenile offenders privately and made no docket entries unless the offenses were serious enough to deprive him of jurisdiction. He believed that a male judge should not try women for first offenses and apparently arranged for a woman to hear such cases. Wherever possible he settled disputes amicably, managing cases "on a plan not laid down in the statute or court rules." And rather than fine men for being drunk or disorderly, he kept their money in sealed envelopes until they returned with their wives, to whom he entrusted it (*Ibid.*: 81–87).

Although the day-to-day harassment of poor and working people by local courts was serious, it was neither the only unequal application of the law nor the most egregious form of intimidation. While magistrates' courts persecuted workers individually, the criminal courts threatened working people as a class. Two of the most important attacks were the trials of the Molly Maguires (1876–1877) and the Haymarket anarchists (1886). By allowing undercover agents to testify about criminal acts they either incited or failed to prevent, the first encouraged surveillance of the internal affairs of unions and opened an era of widespread industrial espionage. The Haymarket trial extended the doctrine of conspiracy to advocacy itself, making workers who advised violence generally responsible for particular acts of violence "without reference to the object of a particular crime, or the time, place or manner of the crime" (David, 1963: 262), thereby setting the stage for a wave of repression against workers and their organizations.

As late as 1886 only two states had specifically legalized trade unions and only three had exempted strikes from prosecution for conspiracy. In thirty-five states workers acting together were subject to conspiracy acts or common law rules against combinations. In the wake of Haymarket, Illinois promptly passed an anti-boycott law as well as a new conspiracy law that, the Chicago Knights of Labor noted, made all members of a union accessories to any violence committed in a labor dispute. Employers in other states also successfully attacked the widening use of boycotts by branding them as conspiracies.

The Knights of Labor were so concerned about these developments that they created a special Committee on Conspiracy Laws. In its comprehensive survey of state and federal laws regarding conspiracy, the committee noted that though the past century had seen "a general relaxation . . . of the rigid, unreasonable and tyrannical rules respecting combinations of laborers to better their material conditions . . . yet, under the influence of a baleful popular excitement, there have been unfortunately retrograde steps taken" (*Proceedings*, 1887: 1668). The committee astutely remarked that blacklists, lockouts, commodity speculation, employers' associations, and monopolies—indeed, most business activity—represented conspiracies among capitalists, and it reached the ironic conclusion that what was wanted was not the reform of conspiracy laws but their equal application to capital. But the committee was not sanguine about this possibility: "The wage earners of the country are not represented at court; their rights, in a majority of instances, owing to the persuasive blandishments of wealth, are compromised, and it seldom happens that they are fought and contested for to the bitter end" (*Ibid.*: 1667).

Master Workman Powderly, keenly aware of the systematic judicial bias and doubtful about the prospects for reform, recommended that working people institute popular justice as an alternative to the legal machinery of the state:

> The workingmen are learning to despise lawyers and advocates, and to eliminate law courts by establishing courts of their own. They have long perceived that at the hands of advocates, justices and police, they get an immense amount of *law*, but no *justice*; that justice and law have become merely merchandise in the hands of the "authorities," which is sold to the highest bidder; and that as it is the rich who have the most money they can always purchase legal decisions; and therefore in the courts of "law" there is not "justice" for the poor. It is for this very potent reason that the patrons of husbandry, better known as the grangers, the sovereigns of industry, and many other organizations instituted by workingmen, have made it a cardinal feature of their associations to settle all differences which may arise among their members without any appeal whatever to advocates, lawyers, judges, or courts of so-called justice, and in so doing they have shown great wisdom [*Journal*, November 1885: 1111].

Thus it was the nature of class relations that transformed the Knights of Labor courts into a powerful experiment in popular justice. Just as ruling class domination of the political process in this period stimulated workingmen's parties, and capitalist domination of production generated producers' and consumers' cooperatives as well as strikes and boycotts, so bias within the legal machinery of the state led workers to elaborate judicial structures originally intended merely to enforce organizational rules into an alternative judicial system.

To be sure, the rise of mass organizations among working people facilitated this transformation. But the success of the Knights of Labor, the Patrons of Husbandry, the Sovereigns of Industry, the Wheel, and the several Farmers' Alliances was itself attributable to the increasing exploitation of producers—agricultural and industrial workers alike—by the ruling class. The participation of several million working men and women in thousands of local branches throughout the nation, as well as increasing collaboration among the several organizations, lent credibility to their experiments with alternative politics, economics, and justice, culminating in the populist vision of a cooperative commonwealth.

The ramifications of vast numbers of workers promulgating, interpreting, and enforcing their own rules of conduct and settling their differences without appeal to the "courts of so-called justice" did not escape notice, and it was scarcely coincidental that the state directed its attack on workers at the judicial processes of their organizations.

An early case in which the courts intervened in matters of union discipline—described by Clyde Summers (1960: 178) as "the criminal law of union government"—was *People* ex rel *Deverell* v. *Musical Mutual Protection Union*. There the New York Court of Appeals invalidated the expulsion of a union member on the ground that the board of directors had violated the union's procedural requirements by improperly notifying the accused of the charges. Finding that the union had not acquired jurisdiction over Deverell and had therefore expelled him improperly, the court held that he was entitled to reinstatement without fine (since union reinstatement procedures applied only to legitimate expulsions) and awarded him damages for the discharge that followed his expulsion (118 N.Y. 101, 1889).

Two years later the same court struck at the Knights of Labor itself. In *Wicks* v. *Monihan* it held that members of a lapsed Local Assembly in Amsterdam were not required to surrender the LA's property as required by a provision of the Order's constitution that made it "the duty of the district recording secretary to collect and take charge of the charter, seals, books, money and other property of any Locals attached to the District Assembly that may lapse" (130 N.Y. 232, 236, 1891). Basing its decision on a precedent established in a similar case involving the Independent Order of Odd Fellows, the court specifically attacked the Knights' authority to establish or enforce such rules:

> The property of Local Assembly No. 4119 was not derived from the General Assembly, but was contributed and owned by the associated members . . . and held by an absolute title. . . . To hold that the General Assembly can by a decree divest the title to property and vest it in itself, is giving to it a power which is forbidden to be exercised by congress, or by the legislature of any state. Bills confiscating the property of citizens, or of associations, without judicial process, are forbidden by the Constitution [130 N.Y. 232, 238, 1891].

These cases were among the first in what Summers has described as more than sixty years of state court adjudication of internal union disputes. In summarizing this history of intervention he notes that "the underlying legal theory defining the role of the court in internal union affairs is that the constitution is a contract between the union and its members" and that judicial review of union discipline is predicated on the court's responsibility to enforce that contract (Summers, 1960: 179).

Under this rationale state courts were able to repudiate provisions in union constitutions (as in the *Wicks* case), interpret matters not covered by the constitution, review evidence taken at union trials, void disiplinary action (as in the *Deverell* case), determine whether union disciplinary procedures constituted due process, decide whether or not unions adhered to their procedures, and respond with judicial remedies. The courts could be wildly inconsistent: On one occasion a court ordered a member reinstated because he had been tried by a special committee in order to avoid trial by the executive committee, one of whose officers he had accused of mishandling union funds; yet in a later case the same court held that "where a member was tried by an executive committee which included officers whom he had accused of misconduct, the proceedings were void for bias" (*Ibid.*: 194).

Although courts did not insist on formal legal procedures and recognized that union structures varied, still, as Summers observes, "the judges look not to union practices and traditions but to the court's own traditional notions of the essential elements of a fair hearing" (*Ibid.*: 201). The discrepancy between the views of due process held by workers and judges is succinctly revealed in a case involving the disciplinary procedures of a waiters' union whose rules required the accused to wait outside during the testimony of prosecution witnesses and then be called in, told the evidence, and given the opportunity to question those witnesses or offer other evidence. According to union officers, "The procedure is based on a long and sad experience of the past. We are waiters, not lawyers" (*Ibid.*). But the court rejected this argument, demanding that the union institute hearings at which the accused might be present when the accusation was made.

Considering the record of state intrusion into the internal affairs of unions, culminating in the Labor–Management Reporting and Disclosure Act of 1959, it is not surprising that when the U.S. Department of Labor (1963) conducted a comprehensive survey of disciplinary powers and procedures in unions it found that they generally complied with legal due process. Significantly, though all union constitutions provided for discipline on general grounds and most did so on grounds of loyalty, job discipline, and fiscal misconduct, few authorized discipline for behavior "that was not criminal, yet morally offensive." "Union constitutions did not undertake to regulate ethical or moral behavior. Of the 156 constitutions providing for trial, only 37 . . . explicitly authorized punishment for immoral behavior" (*Ibid.*: 34).

A comparison of the expulsions by the Knights of Labor courts with the provisions for discipline found in the Labor Department's survey of union constitutions in the 1960s reveals the former as unique in the range of offenses for which they punished members. Yet in the face of pressure from the state, it is doubtful that the Order could have maintained its judicial procedures and disciplinary policies intact. Had members appealed expulsions to the state courts, many constitutional provisions might have been rejected. Had the state, rather than the General Assembly, settled disputes over jury trials and a national court, the very basis of the order's judicial structure might have been found to infringe the rights of members to a fair trial and a full appeal. Finally, judicial review of the administration of justice within the Order would have undermined the authority of the latter's courts. Had the Knights of Labor survived, their courts would probably have been eviscerated.

Yet the ability of the state to impose its will on the judicial processes of American workers—to reshape disciplinary procedures and define union membership as a property right—did not derive solely from its own power. Although the state had its own reasons for suppressing alternative, popular systems of justice and asserting judicial control over worker conduct, the failure of the programs of producing class associations, the disappearance of the Knights of Labor, and the emergence of trade unionism as the dominant form of worker organization signaled a major shift in the attitudes of American working people, which contributed greatly to the substitution of *discipline* for *justice.*

A key to this shift is the difference between violation of *contract* and violation of *obligation.* Just as the program of the Order expressed the whole constellation of aspirations for social change embraced by nineteenth-century producers, so the obligations imposed by the Order on its members were inspired by the values of social justice. Yet these values and aspirations were undermined by the transformation of the processes and relations of production. By the turn of the century, American workers had become an agricultural and industrial proletariat. The hope of every worker that he might someday own his own farm or become his own employer had faded. As the vision of a cooperative commonwealth dimmed and the wage system came to be accepted as the battleground of worker struggles, campaigns for general reform gave way to sorties against specific employers, and the strategies of the producing class were replaced with the tactics of the working class. The secret society, dependent on "the reciprocal *confidence* of its members" (Simmel, 1906: 471), was succeeded by the open union, dependent on member discipline. The moral brotherhood of all producers was replaced by contractual brotherhoods of workers in specific trades.

Yet for a quarter of a century the Knights of Labor had conducted an important experiment in popular justice. Eight thousand courts or more in 3000 communities had settled differences among working people—blacks and whites, women and men, skilled and unskilled. The sophistication of their judicial process and the range of their concerns were remarkable. As an organized response to unequal justice under law, the courts of the Knights of Labor represented both an index of the values and consciousness of American workers during the critical phase of industrialization and a challenge to the moral authority of the state.

That such courts no longer exist and that workers now repeatedly ask the courts of the state to intervene in disciplinary proceedings to protect them from the excesses of union power is a comment on the complexity of justice and the vicissitudes of class struggle.

REFERENCES

Adelphon Kruptos (1886) in *Knights of Labor Illustrated*, pp. 21–55. Chicago: Ezra Cook.

Altgeld, John Peter (1890) "Our Penal Machinery and Its Victims," in *Live Questions*, pp. 135–296. Chicago: Donohue & Henneberry.

Aspinall, Arthur (1949) *The Early English Trade Unions*. London: Batchworth Press.

Baker, L. C. (1887) *Revised Forms of Knights of Labor Courts*. Independence, [W. Va.]: n.p.

Bellamy, Edward (1888) *Looking Backward*. Cambridge, Mass.: Riverside Press.

Blaxter, H. V. and Allen H. Kerr (1914) "The Aldermen and Their Courts," in P. Kellogg (ed.) *The Pittsburgh Survey*, Volume 5 *The Pittsburgh District: Civic Frontage*. Philadelphia: William F. Fell.

Correspondence of Terence V. Powderly ["Letterbooks"] (1975) in John A. Turcheneske, Jr. (ed.) *Terence V. Powderly Papers and John William Hayes Papers*. Glen Rock, N.J.: Microfilming Corporation of America.

David, Henry (1958) *The History of the Haymarket Affair*. New York: Russell & Russell.

Garlock, Jonathan (1974) *A Structural Analysis of the Knights of Labor: A Prolegomenon to the History of the Producing Classes*. Ph.D. Dissertation, Department of History, University of Rochester.

Gist, Noel P. (1940) "Secret Societies: A Cultural Study of Fraternalism in the United States," 15(4) *University of Missouri Studies* 9 (October).

Harris, Bishop (1884) *The Doctrines and Discipline of the Methodist Episcopal Church*. New York: n.p.

Hines, Thomas R. (1887) *The Anachists' Conspiracy, or the Blight of 3770*. Boston: n.p.

Hobsbawm, E. J. (1965) *Primitive Rebels: Studies in Archaic Forms of Social Movement in the 19th and 20th Centuries*. New York: Norton.

Journal of United Labor (1880–1896). Official organ of the Knights of Labor.

Kiddier, William (1930) *The Old Trade Unions*. London: G. Allen & Unwin.

Powderly, Terence V. (1940) *The Path I Trod*. New York: Columbia University Press.

"Preamble and Declaration of Principles of the Knights of Labor of America" (1886) in *Knights of Labor Illustrated*, Chicago: Ezra Cook.

Proceedings of the General Assembly (1878–1896). Published by the Knights of Labor.

Sickels, Daniel (1866) *The General Ahiman Rezon and Freemason's Guide*. New York: n.p.

Simmel, Georg (1906) "The Sociology of Secret Societies," 11 *American Journal of Sociology* 441.

Summers, Clyde W. (1960) "The Law of Union Discipline: What the Courts Do in Fact," 70 *Yale Law Journal* 175.

Thompson, E. P. (1963) *The Making of the English Working Class*. New York: Vintage.

United States Department of Labor (1963) Bulletin No. 1350, "Disciplinary Powers and Procedures in Union Constitutions." Washington, D.C.: Government Printing Office.

Delegalization Reform Movements: A Historical Analysis*

CHRISTINE B. HARRINGTON

INTRODUCTION

Recent scholarship on dispute processing has concentrated on the relationship between forms of decision making (mediation, arbitration, and adjudication)[1] and the types of social conflict they manage. Scholars have once again questioned the appropriateness of formal adjudication for resolving minor disputes and distributing mass justice. Theoretical attacks on formalism (Nonet and Selz-

*I wish to thank Rick Abel for his careful reading and helpful suggestions. Murray Edelman, Malcolm Feeley, Joel Grossman, Richard Hofrichter, Austin Sarat and David Trubek contributed insightful comments and criticism. I am grateful to the American Judicature Society, in particular Chuck Grau and Jim Alfini, for supporting this research.

[1]See Lon Fuller's discussion of the "mixed form of social ordering involving adjudication" (1978: 405–409).; see also Sarat and Grossman's discussion of the characteristics that distinguish adjudicative institutions (1975).

THE POLITICS OF INFORMAL JUSTICE
Volume 1

nick, 1978) and programmatic development of "informal" dispute resolution[2] are both part of a larger reform wave that advocates "deinstitutionalization" (see Scull, 1977). The recent development of tribunals for minor disputes between parties in on-going relationships (e.g., domestic, neighborhood, consumer–merchant, landlord–tenant, employment) is one expression of the movement for less formal methods of dispute processing.

Neither the discontent with the relationship between types of dispute and adjudication style nor the concern with reorganizing the judicial management of minor conflict is new. Indeed, the contemporary movement displays parallels with reforms proposed and instituted between 1900 and 1930. Such reforms were based on sociological jurisprudence, an ideology that was also hostile to legal formalism. Roscoe Pound's famous critique (1906) voiced his distaste for the "sporting theory of justice." He argued that legal formalism encouraged the instrumental use of law because it failed to produce a compromise based on a consensus concerning underlying values.

> The effect of our exaggerated contentious procedure is not only to irritate parties, witnesses and jurors in particular cases, but to give to the whole community a *false notion of the purpose* and end of law.... If the law is a mere game, neither the players who take part in it nor the public who witness it can be expected to yield to its spirit when their interests are served by evading it.... Thus the courts, instituted to administer justice according to law, are made agents or abetters of lawlessness [1906: 406; emphasis added].

Seventy years later Nonet and Selznick agree.

> A formalist, rule-bound institution is ill equipped to recognize what is really at stake in its conflicts with the environment. It is likely to adapt opportunistically because it lacks criteria for rational reconstruction of outmoded or inappropriate policies.... The idea of legality needs to be conceived more generally and to be cured of formalism [1978: 77, 108].

The principal objection to legal formalism advanced at both points in time is that the substantive ideals invoked on behalf of *legality* in a liberal democracy (equality, justice, and liberty) come into conflict with *legalization* (the extension of procedural rules governing the processing of disputes). Such a view opposes the extension of legal rights on the ground that formal rationality, the necessary basis of legal legitimacy, fails to provide substantive justice. Consequently, the reform movement favors delegalization. The classic tension within liberal legalism between procedural and substantive rationality is revealed during these reform periods (Abel, 1979). Advocates of delegalization justify their proposals as reconciling, harmonizing, and balancing formal and social justice. The task of orchestrating a system for adjudicating conflict that questions the utility of formalism calls for different principles of legitimacy *and* the reorganization of a

---

[2]Delegalization reformers have suggested that informal dispute processing actually resolves disputes because the underlying sources of conflict are more easily dealt with in mediation and arbitration. Since this has not yet been demonstrated, I will use the term dispute processing to refer to informal mechanisms for handling minor disputes.

legal consensus. The legitimacy of delegalization reforms is still grounded in procedure, but, in contrast to legal formalism, these procedures are characterized as "informal alternatives" (Aaronson *et al.*, 1977; Garth, 1982).

It would be misleading to suggest that the delegalization reform movements throughout this century have sought to *replace* the legalistic paradigm of dispute processing (Shklar, 1964). On the contrary, they tend to complement the existing mechanisms of adjudication rather than to displace them or to challenge them fundamentally. Furthermore, delegalization reforms have generally been limited to minor disputes or what might be called order maintenance problems.[3] Although the criticism of formality voiced by Progressives and contemporary scholars could be applied more broadly, delegalization movements have instead been directed toward constructing tribunals for managing everyday disputes. One reason for this focus is that the "sporting theory of justice" is particularly flawed in petty causes. The expense to both the parties and the state of observing procedural rights in the adjudication of minor claims is so prohibitive that formality frustrates the exercise of individual rights and the effective management of conflict by criminal and civil courts. Although the significance of financial barriers has always been recognized, these two periods of reform are distinct in responding to the problem by seeking to *channel* and *absorb* minor conflict into specialized forums.

The intention of this chapter is neither to determine whether delegalization reforms have adequately resolved the problems identified with legal formalism nor to contribute to the literature that advances "informalism" as a universal value and searches for models that can implement it. Rather, I will argue that the delegalization of minor dispute processing occurs within the context of a broader social reform: the construction and reconstruction of a rationality for judicial management of lower court organization and for intervention in everyday conflicts in capitalist society. Although strategies of judicial management may not be coherent, "uni-directional," or "uni-dimensional" (Heydebrand, 1979: 30), they do reflect a mode of rationalization for both the work process and the adjudication process in courts.[4] Specifically, the mode of rationalization associated with delegalization reforms is an administrative–technocratic approach to the organization of the judicial work process and the management of order maintenance problems in urban poor and working-class communities. I will examine the

---

[3]"Order maintenance" refers to discretionary intervention by officials (usually without making an arrest) in minor disputes such as disorderly conduct, disturbing the peace, or simple assault and battery. See Wilson (1968) and Goldstein (1977) for discussions of the distinction between law enforcement and order maintenance.

[4]I am not using organization theory (Feeley, 1973; Eisenstein and Jacob, 1977) or systems theory (Nimmer, 1978); nor am I viewing courts as bureaucracies (Blumberg, 1967). Rather I am interested in examining the models that reformers have used for the management of lower courts because these structure the type of transformation that occurs. We can identify the mode of rationalization associated with reform models by studying two related court processes: the organization of court personnel (the judicial work process) and procedures for processing disputes (the adjudication process).

politics of delegalization from a historical standpoint, focusing on the relationship between judicial management and delegalization reforms.

It is necessary to begin by noting some limitations of the historical literature
and clarifying the different perspective adopted in this chapter. Preoccupied with
their debates about the Progressive period, historians have given scant attention
to court reform that had an explicit delegalization ideology. Nevertheless, those
debates have still influenced analysis of delegalization. For example, a dominant
approach has been to examine the rhetoric of Progressive reformers and contrast
it with the reality of the institutions they developed. Two accounts attribute the
failure of the juvenile court to the optimism of Progressive reform (Ryerson,
1978; Rothman, 1980). Noting the tension within the Progressive platform between humane ideals and the desire for an administratively efficient mechanism
for handling juveniles, both authors emphasize the "gap" between the reform
model and the juvenile courts. Informal procedures are idealized as nonadversarial, rehabilitative, and preventive methods of dispute processing. The reform
goal—informalism—is treated as nonproblematic. Instead of focusing on the
politics of this reform, the analysis centers on barriers to implementing the goal.

Similarly, Barbara Yngvesson and Patricia Hennessey conclude from their
review of the small claims court literature that reformers failed in their missions
to create a truly nonadversarial dispute process because they did not question
"the *kind* of process through which small claims—whether those of rich or
poor—are being handled, and thus have left intact a cornerstone of the small
claims hearing, the adversary process" (1975: 263). They correctly attribute this
oversight to the "cross-cutting interests" of the legal profession. But once again
the analysis employs the goals of informalism as the standard for evaluating the
success or failure of the reform movement.[5] The object of analysis—
informalism—becomes the criterion for judging historical events. The approach
offers a predictable and unilluminating analysis of the politics of informalism.
That the juvenile and small claims court movements did not institutionalize the
ideals of informalism does not mean they were simply failed reforms. Both clearly
have had significant consequences for lower courts as well as for the people who
use them.

Samuel Walker's history of criminal justice administration begins with a similarly idealized conception of the Progressive period (1980). Borrowing Herbert
Packer's categories, Walker argues that tensions within the Progressive movement were the result of a conflict between an "efficiency-oriented crime-control"
model and a "due-process orientation." Yet he argues that "both shared a 'system' approach to the administration of criminal justice, and for both sides, the

---

This approach begs the question of what explains the rise of particular forms of judicial management.
Richard Hofrichter (1982) has attempted to link legal changes to economic and political constraints
on the state; see also Hirschhorn (1978) and O'Connor (1973: Ch 2, 5, 6).

[5]See Feeley (1976) for a discussion of the problems with gap studies. For a recent "gap" analysis of
the neighborhood justice movement, see Tomasic (1980).

system perspective fostered the nationalization of crime control" (*Ibid.*: 128). His book escapes the dominant tendency to reduce tensions or contradictions within reform movements to static and often dualistic concepts (adversarial and nonadversarial, formal and informal). Walker is thus able to explain the transformation in the administration of criminal justice—the developement of a systems approach—as an outcome of these contradictions, instead of merely concluding that all Progressive reforms were "failures" like the juvenile courts were.

Another dominant approach to analyzing informal procedures emphasizes the *type* of dispute as the unit of analysis. For example, historical commentaries on the juvenile court movement are primarily concerned with the relationship between Progressive ideology and adolescent socialization (see Platt, 1969; Fox, 1970; Mannel, 1973; Schultz, 1973; Faust and Brantingham, 1974; Ryerson, 1978; Rothman, 1980). Youth became a new object of social attention during this period, meriting closer scrutiny by the courts and requiring a distinct legal environment. Such studies suggest that the particular kind of conflict (juvenile) is the major determinant of dispute processing styles. However, the application of informal procedures during this period was hardly limited to the juvenile, nor did Progressive reformers believe that such procedures were uniquely suitable for juvenile cases. Without belittling the importance of justifications for adopting informal procedures in juvenile cases, I suggest that we also need to consider the impact of organizational and structural constraints, such as judicial management, on the form of dispute processing for particular types of cases.

The politics of delegalization cannot be uncovered by contrasting practice with idealized categories for describing forms of adjudication, by using "informalism" as a standard for evaluating the reform. Nor can we understand the politics of delegalization by simply focusing on the type of disputes that are diverted to informal tribunals. The reform goal of informalism is itself problematic. An alternative approach for studying the politics of delegalization is to examine the historical development of organizational structures that mediate the political tensions and contradictory aspects of the reform movement.

THE "CRISIS" OF THE COURTS AND
THE MANAGERIAL PERSPECTIVE ON
ACCESS TO JUSTICE

Progressive reformers argued that lower courts required "business-like" management in order to defuse criticism of the law by the public[6] as well as by private

[6]Historians have given considerable attention to the question of who supported Progressivism. Samuel Hays notes that "reformers maintained that their movement rested on a wave of popular demands, calling their gatherings of business and professional leaders 'mass meetings,' . . . [and describing] their reforms as 'part of a world-wide trend toward popular government" (1964: 167; see also Hofstadter, 1955: Chs. 4–7; Lasch, 1965: Ch. 6; Wiebe, 1967). Similarly, Progressives characterized reforms proposed by bar and trade associations as expressions of popular discontent.

commercial groups. Progressive New York City Court Judge William Ransom, commenting on public opinion in general and the views of business groups in particular, said with disapproval: "Instead of bringing methods for ascertaining facts and determining controversies, public opinion took the performance of essentially judicial functions away from the courts" (1917a: 145).[7] Eleven years earlier Pound made a similar observation in his famous speech on the causes of popular dissatisfactions with the administration of justice:

> Public opinion must affect the administration of justice through the rules by which justice is administered rather than through the direct administration. All interference with the uniform and automatic application of these rules, when actual controversies arise introduces an anti-legal element which becomes intolerable [1906: 400].

What were the sources of "anti-legal" criticism of the courts? How did delegalization reformers characterize the "crisis" of courts? And what were the consequences of adapting "business-like" management for the adjudication of minor disputes?

The growth in the early 1880s of arbitration tribunals independent of the courts notified reformers that business had a strong aversion to courts. Progressives argued that the failure of legislatures to enact provisions creating simplified judicial procedures for handling commercial disputes led to the expansion of private arbitration tribunals. Delay, congestion, and "formality" in procedures were continually cited as the reasons why conservative, law-abiding businessmen were "ready to 'settle for fifty percent' of the amount in dispute rather than be subject to 'a law suit,' even in a court which has been considered peculiarly the 'business man's court' in the metropolis" (Ransom, 1917b: 199). Ransom believed that courts were out of tune with business practices.

> In the past fifty years we have revolutionized our methods of the conduct of private business, and largely also the conduct of public business; our methods are more direct, exact, and to the point; they minimize the possibility of error, eliminate "lost motion" and cut "red tape." Yet to all this improvement in method our judicial procedure has paid substantially no heed [*Ibid.*: 199].

Reformers viewed the disjunction between commercial methods and judicial administration as a "crisis" for courts. Lacking adequate procedures for intervening in commercial disputes in a manner acceptable to business interests, the judiciary was handicapped in shaping economic relations during the transition from merchant to corporate capitalism.[8] On another level, lower courts were

---

[7]Ransom was referring to the development of public service commissions, commerce commissions, and railroad commissions. Most historical work on this period is concerned with the legal profession rather than courts or private arbitration tribunals.

[8]For general surveys of legal developments in this period, see Hurst (1956) and Horwitz (1977). Wolfe (1977: Ch. 3–4) offers an excellent summary of the impact of the economic transition from merchant to corporate capitalism on the development of the state.

isolated from everyday life (the mass of small transactions), by what reformers called the "doctrine of contentious procedure" (Harley, 1911; Hurst, 1953). Reformers believed that the legitimacy of courts suffered as a result of delay in processing claims (court congestion) and that the situation might become intolerable if left unremedied.

Percy Werner, a member of the Missouri bar, argued that although lawyers had "instinctively turned against this method [arbitration] of disposing of private differences, as being unscientific, as an adjudication by non-experts must be," yet they should not oppose *all* arbitration (1914: 278). Private arbitration tribunals might be considered symbols of an "anti-legal" bias, but judges and lawyers dedicated to professionalization could still endorse constitutional amendments and statutory provisions establishing judicial arbitration. Many state and local bar associations began to pass resolutions in the early 1900s encouraging "the bar and business men generally to pull together in each locality for the prevention of unnecessary litigation" by providing information about ways to prevent disputes from arising (JAJS, 1919b: 158). Werner proposed that "voluntary tribunals" be established by the bar, with lawyers serving as arbitrators (1914: 279). The Joint Committee of the Chamber of Commerce Committee on Arbitration of the State of New York and the New York State Bar Association Committee on Prevention of Unnecessary Litigation was formed in 1916. "Backed by the brains of the New York bar and the money of the New York merchant," they drafted a proposal for judicial arbitration of commercial disputes (Robbins, 1916: 280). Disputes concerning contracts, wills, licenses, and insurance policies were all designated as appropriate for arbitration. Other commercial arbitration boards, such as those promoted by the Chicago Association of Credit Men, were established with either the assistance or approval of the bar (JAJS, 1918a). The Association of the Bar of the City of New York was active in supporting the creation of the Arbitration Society of America in 1922, described by the American Judicature Society as comprised of "men prominent on the bench, at the bar and in the business world unite[d] to promote voluntary adjudication under arbitration statutes" (JAJS, 1922a: 59). In addition, many states passed arbitration statutes modelled on the commercial arbitration proposals drafted by the American Judicature Society (see Willoughby, 1929: 64–75).

These reforms were part of a strategy to "re-establish" the lost jurisdiction and credibility of courts (Potter, 1922). Unable to keep pace with the changing needs of commercial interests, the judicial method itself became the target for critics. Ransom observed that "business men go to arbitration to avoid legal *procedure* and not legal principles" (1917b: 201). Procedural formality, according to the Progressives, was the primary source of "anti-legal" criticism by the private sector. Proposals for judicial arbitration were offered by the organized bar as a means of preserving legal principles while avoiding the problems of legalization.

The "crisis" of the courts was characterized as judicial inaction. Reformers argued that judicial nonintervention, resulting from the doctrine of contentious procedure, prevented courts from affirming the principles of legality. They believed that courts, by failing to sustain institutional legitimacy on procedural grounds (the essence of formal rationality), faced a "crisis" of legitimacy. The *form* of judicial intervention, therefore, became the central issue of the delegalization movement.

The organization of a new legal consensus encompassed more than the advocacy of an ideology of judicial intervention through informal methods. It also required the creation of institutional structures to implement informal dispute processing. Arbitration, supervised by the legal profession and sanctioned by state institutions and laws, was the form of intervention by which reformers proposed to rebuild the legitimacy of a legal consensus and expand jurisdiction over everyday commercial disputes.

The principles that structured this form of judicial intervention were largely derived from the influential model of scientific management developed by industrial organizations. The American Judicature Society, state and local bar associations, and private trade associations all agreed on the importance of the scientific model of efficiency. Frederick Taylor's theory of scientific management (1911) was explicitly adopted in early reorganization proposals as *the* cure for the "crisis" of the courts. In one of their debates on judicial reform, a group of New York City lawyers, the Phi Delta Phi Club's Committee of Nine, proposed that courts be organized and managed like any other business.

> Treating the system of administrating justice as if it were a great machine, it is obvious that if the courts are to be regulated by the same theories of efficiency as any other administrative business or organization, what we desire must be a frictionless movement of a well-lubricated machine in which all the parts cooperate to produce the desired result. "Peace" in its last analysis is frictionless activity, not inaction of human life . . . (it is) the ultimate desired condition of the administration of justice, in spite of the fact that the administration of justice relates itself to the settlement of contentious disputes [Jessup, 1917: 4].

Just as the principles of scientific management transformed commercial dispute processing, so too the principles of legal efficiency transformed the meaning of access to justice for minor criminal and civil disputes. Joined by the legal aid societies, Progressives attacking the doctrine of contentious procedure applied the principles of legal efficiency to the management and organization of forces that generated the second "crisis" of the courts: the growth of urban immigrant workers and poor. The problems of public order in the new urban economy were met with managerial solutions.

Reformers maintained that there was no justice for the poor in either the inferior courts or the rural justice of the peace courts. The former were depicted as too expensive, dilatory, and remote from the problems of the new urban working class. The latter were condemned as corrupt, arbitrary, and lawless (Smith, 1919a; Scott, 1923; Maguire, 1926). Yet Progressives continually drew attention to the massive number of "petty," urban conflicts that were ignored by the judiciary:

> Claims of this sort are often contemptuously spoken of as "petty litigation." But it is in this very field that the courts have their greatest political effect. In every urban community these are the cases of the large majority of citizens. As they are treated well or ill, so they form their opinion of American judicial institutions [Smith, 1919a: 42].

Pound argued for the "socialization of law" in order to "secure social interests in the modern city" (1913: 311). By this he meant that laws had to be created by society to "protect men from themselves, to regulate housing, to enforce sanitation, to inspect the supply of milk, to prevent imposition upon ignorant and credulous immigrants" (*Ibid.*). This was true whether the problems involved wage claims by workers or the "relations of family life, where conditions of crowded urban life and economic pressure threaten the security of the social institutions of marriage and the family" (*Ibid.*: 323). The scope of judicial administration would be enlarged by the "socialization of law."

An example of the socialization of law was the campaign to "Americanize" the immigrant and rehabilitate the delinquent, the deviant, and the discontent (Smith, 1919a). One of the first active Americanizing groups, the North American Civil League for Immigrants (1907), focused public attention on the political significance of "petty litigation" and the role of courts in processing such conflict. The league was a private philanthropic organization formed to represent Northeastern conservative economic interests (Hartmann, 1948: 38). In 1908 Frances Kellor, a member of the league, was appointed to the New York State Immigration Commission by Governor Charles Evans Hughes and charged with directing research on the relationship of immigrants to criminal and civil law. As a result of its study the commission established the New York State Bureau of Industries and Immigration (1910). Kellor described this bureau as an "immigrants court" (1914: 168), yet unlike the inferior courts, this government agency served as "mediator in bringing together the disputants in cases concerning immigrants" and was "authorized to publish and distribute information which would faciliate assimilation" (Hartmann, 1948: 70). Other private organizations, such as the Charity Organization Society of New York City, established joint committees with government agencies to investigate and recommend legislation on dispute processing and the Americanization of the immigrant (Paddon, 1920).

Remarking on the 1915 reform of the magistrates' courts in New York City, a Philadelphia lawyer described their socializing influence:

> Due regard has been had for the psychological value of a proper setting for such courts, in giving the magistrates dignified and sanitary courtrooms or buildings. In this way the value of these

magistrates' courts as an Americanizing influence over the foreign elements—of many races and nationalities—in New York City popuation, is fairly well secured [Shick, 1926: 116].

Reformers concerned with legal aid for the poor shared this perspective. Reginald Heber Smith, reporting to the Conference of Bar Association Delegates in 1924 on the work of the Committee on Small Claims and Conciliation, hailed small claims courts as socialization agents worth more to the cause of Americanization than any amount of talk (1924a: 14). Similarly, juvenile and family courts were developed to stabilize the family and, through that essential institution, integrate the immigrant into a middle-class American life (see Paddon, 1920; Roberts 1920; Hartmann, 1948). In addition to being part of the policy for the *socialization* of law, informal dispute processing also was perceived as a socializing force.

To provide access to justice, the barrier of cost had to be overcome. At the same time, the reformers needed a forum that could draw legitimacy from the law but remain sufficiently flexible to absorb minor social conflict in a new urban economy. The Progressives were convinced that the problems they faced in designing an urban judicial system for absorbing such conflict were essentially managerial. Commenting on the virtues of informal procedures, Judge Manuel Levine of the Conciliation Court of Cleveland expressed support for this perspective:

> One thing is certain: we cannot even hope to render justice without first having a clear conception as to what justice means. There are many classical definitions, but it took a commercial age to discover that in the main it is merely a problem of correct bookkeeping. We have come to realize, in both the criminal as well as the civil work of courts, that justice is the art or science of obtaining human or social balances [1918: 11].

The justifications for the socialization of law through informal dispute processing were based on two conceptions of access to justice that reinforced this managerial perspective while simultaneously seeking to legitimize the form of judicial intervention. One concept of access to justice was explicitly based on an administrative rationale. Reformers maintained that by streamlining both institutions and procedures administrative efficiencies would provide greater access to justice. The familiar phrase "justice delayed is justice denied" and the characterization of justice as "the frictionless movement of a well-lubricated machine" reflect this administrative perspective on access to justice. The second concept also shares this administrative rationale but to legitimize judicial intervention in a liberal democracy, reformers also appealed to participatory ideals. Progressives believed that law would be a more effective socializing agent if citizens participated more directly in informal proceedings.

Both concepts of access to justice are important for analyzing the transformation in minor dispute processing in the Progressive period and in the contemporary delegalization movement. The principles that structure these transformations provide a key for understanding the content and politics of delegalization movements. The following sections focus on the relationship between these concepts of access to justice and judicial management theories and their implications for both the internal administration of justice in lower courts and, more generally, the role of minor dispute processing in order maintenance.

THE RISE OF JUDICIAL MANAGEMENT AND INFORMAL DISPUTE PROCESSES

The judicial reorganization movement beginning in the late 1880s furnished the environment for experimentation with informal procedures for handling minor disputes. It may seem ironic that the same group of Progressive reformers who led the battle against justice of the peace (JP) courts advocated the use of simplified procedures, arbitration, and conciliation for processing minor disputes. The "khadi-justice" of the justices courts was transformed under the Progressive movement into "socialized law." What accounts for the simultaneous hostility toward JP courts and zealous support of informal procedures?

It is difficult to discuss the caseload and dispositions of justice of the peace courts between 1890 and 1930 because their jurisdictions were so diverse; most were not courts of record, and researchers did not use uniform methods to collect and report data. Nonetheless, the literature is replete with generalizations: that 80 percent of the cases were default judgments, that the court's nickname—"judgment for the plaintiff"—was a consequence of the fee system (Schramm, 1928; Keebler, 1930; Douglass, 1932; Howard, 1935; Blackburn, 1935; Vanlandingham, 1964; Ireland, 1972). It is striking, however, that most of the research focuses on the organization of these courts rather than on the type of cases they heard or the procedures they followed. The irregularity of these courts is attributed to their decentralized organization. Herbert Harley, founder and secretary of the American Judicature Society (1913), described the evils of decentralization.

> Our present inferior court systems exemplify our powerful inclination toward decentralization. They are courts of and for the people living in town and country. The fact that they are democratic is no valid excuse for inefficiency. It is an unfriendly ideal of democracy which excludes *efficient service*. Democracy like every other ideal, must justify itself by its works [1917a: 190; emphasis added].

Reformers such as Harley believed the justice of the peace courts failed to provide an efficient service not so much because summary procedures and informal negotiations predominated, but because they lacked administration.[9]

[9]Many statutes required that justice of the peace courts be audited annually, but this provision was rarely done (Silverstein, 1955: 245).

Those calling for the abolition of the JP courts objected to their decentralized organization, the high degree of local autonomy, and the unchecked expansion of their jurisdiction by the legislature (Strasburger, 1915; Wickersham Commission, 1974). At first, Harley criticized the lack of administrative control rather than the qualifications of the personnel: "The fact that he [the justice of the peace] is a layman will be no objection [under the unified court proposal] because he will be guided by his responsible superior" (1917a: 190).

As the movement to organize municipal courts grew and attacks on law justices of the peace intensified, the lack of *supervision* remained a principal argument against these courts. But the call for greater supervision came to include a demand for professional training.

> Argument against an inferior class of judges to serve at a lower salary has been submitted. There are certain duties, however, more administrative than judicial, which can properly be performed by an official of lower salary under the direction of a judge. To meet this need the act should provide for a certain number of masters, and fix their compensation. The powers which they shall exercise should be determined by the judicial council. Genuine judicial talent is too rare and too valuable to be permitted to wear itself out on details which can as well be done by an assistant. Masters may become highly expert, and as long as they are directed, may prove economical from more than the mere financial standpoint [Harley, 1915a: 513].

During this period of the institutional transformation and growth of the legal profession, the duties of justices of the peace were often described as administrative functions in contrast to judicial tasks. This perspective led to the later stratification of judicial decision making into administrative and judicial categories that corresponded to the jurisdictions of specialized tribunals.

Charges that justice of the peace courts were corrupt stemmed in large part from the fact that the justices were paid a proportion of the fines they collected (Kogan, 1974: 110). Following the Supreme Court's decision in *Tumey* v. *Ohio* (273 U.S. 510, 1927) that the fee system was unconstitutional in criminal cases, reformers hoped the JP courts would be abolished. In many states, however, that required a constitutional amendment. To avoid this lengthy and difficult procedure, reformers passed legislation giving the newly formed municipal courts the same jurisdiction as the justice of the peace courts. But this strategy had no impact in rural areas, and in some urban areas it also proved ineffective (Douglass, 1932). Although all reformers clearly felt that the more serious disputes were denied justice in JP courts because formal rules were not applied, Pound (1913) and others argued that the "petty litigants" were also hurt. Pound contended that eliminating pleadings and rules of evidence and allowing disputants to submit their responses by mail would permit access to a higher quality of justice. The American Bar Association Special Committee to Suggest Remedies and Formulate Proposed Laws to Prevent Delay and Unnecessary Cost in Litigation wrote about the Chicago Municipal Court: "It is perfectly feasible to administer a much *higher grade of justice* in petty causes than that dispensed by the justice of the peace without resort to the cumbrous and expensive machinery of our superior courts of record" (American Bar Association, 1909: 591; emphasis added).

Professionalism served to justify supervision of minor dispute processing by expanding the definition of what was "professional" to include administrative tasks. Terence Halliday's history of the Chicago Bar Association demonstrates that professional expansionism depended upon "the capacity of the profession to exert control over its primary sphere of institutional activity and to extend its influence into various secondary spheres" (1979: 13). This capacity is a "direct result of a profession's accomplishments in dressing its normative contributions to change in technical clothes" (*Ibid.*). Similarly, professionals sought to supplant the justice of the peace courts by presenting the managerial solution to the problem of lower court organization as a process of democratization.

Whether the ideology of "efficient service" and access to justice under the supervision of professionals represented an increase in democracy has been a subject of much debate among historians. The more interesting point, however, is a central paradox of this period of municipal reform: "the ideology of an extension of political control and the practice of its concentration" (Hays, 1964: 167). The municipal court movement (1904–1930), like the pervasive municipal reform movement, expanded the role of experts in the delivery of state services as well as the scope of those services (see Schiessel, 1977). This required the reorganization and stratification of the judicial work process, which affected the methods of decision making. The principles of scientific management, first developed in factories (Braverman, 1974; Burawoy, 1979; Clawson, 1980), were understood by court reformers as "capable of being applied to any given form of human activity" (Jessup, 1917: 4). Pound asserted that the concept of efficiency was necessary "in a modern court no less than in a modern factory" (1940b: 286). The application of scientific management to the judicial work process increased centralization and specialization. Court unification was the instrument through which the principles of scientific management were implemented. Thus in court reform as in municipal reform power was concentrated through the unification of the courts, and the ideology of "efficient service" suggested that access to justice was being extended to those who most frequently came in contact with lower courts—the powerless.

THE UNIFICATION OF THE JUDICIAL SYSTEM

Pound was the first American to advocate a unified judicial system on the ground that the prevailing decentralized structure could not respond to the demands of a growing industrialized urban population. Relying on the English model of unification developed in 1873, he called for the consolidation of all state appellate and trial courts into a single structure with two layers (1906). In 1940 he modified this model by including an additional tier of minor trial courts (Ashman and Parness, 1974; Berkson and Carbon, 1978). An ABA report (1909) outlined principles of unification similar to those suggested by Pound. In 1920, at the request of the American Judicature Society, the National Municipal League drafted a model state judicial unification proposal (see Berkson and Carbon, 1978: 5). The National Economic League of Boston and the Phi Delta Phi Club of New York City (a group of lawyers studying professional problems) were some of the other groups urging the adoption of a unified court organization (Jessup, 1917). All of these proposals concerned the organization of entire state judicial systems, but the reforms in management and procedure directly affected the operation of lower courts (see generally Vanderbilt, 1955; Elliott, 1959; Galub, 1968). Indeed, when Pound announced his unification proposal (1906) he applauded the first municipal court (Chicago, 1904) for adopting managerial and procedural innovations together with the principles of unification.

Before I examine the application of these principles in the municipal court movement and their impact on the establishment of specific tribunals, a brief overview of the management concepts and procedural reforms associated with the early unification models helps to reveal the relationship between court reorganization and the implementation of informal procedures. The most significant development was the centralization of management through the creation of a presiding judge in the municipal court. This established a single judicial officer empowered to supervise record keeping, control caseload, and "clerical subordinates" (Cohen, 1917; JAJS, 1928; Willoughby, 1929: 339–340). The introduction of a unified calendar regulating caseload enhanced the administrative power of the presiding judge. Earlier attempts to control local courts through reorganization alone failed because of the "political power of clerks and marshalls" (JAJS, 1928: 117). Reformers had always viewed clerks as "partially independent functionaries over whom courts [had] little real control" (American Bar Association, 1909: 591). It was not until 1928 that the presiding judges in most municipal courts were given the authority to manage their staffs and control calendars.

The calendar system of caseload management also introduced specialization. Even before judges came to view themselves as specialists, dockets were specialized to maximize the efficiency of each judge. Specialized tribunals—small claims, domestic relations—were also developed as branches of the municipal court. Describing the virtues of specialized tribunals, Harley compared the management of courts with business principles of management:

> Not to have specialization and direction would be equivalent, in the business world, to employing fifty or one hundred clerks for a department store and allowing them to do any part of the work which they might, at any time, prefer to do.... In commercial terms, our judicial business is done at a number of small and disassociated shops [1915a: 516].

Each branch was headed by a presiding judge who performed management tasks similar to those of the judge.

Although reformers adopted specialization as a strategy for rationalizing organization, they did so cautiously. Harley warned: "Specialization is the demand of the times, but *unification should precede specialization*. Without an overhead organization specialization means a new form of waste" (1917b: 23). Unification antedated specialization, introducing principles of efficiency into both the work process of courts and dispute resolution procedures. To respond to the lack of coordination resulting from the growth of specialization, reformers argued that courts needed greater authority to regulate these developments. Proposals for judicial rule-making and for allowing municipal court judges to create specialized tribunals expanded judicial autonomy. At the same time that the bar was proposing judicial self-regulation as an alternative to the recall of judges (see Cohen, 1917; Potter, 1922: 166; McKean, 1963: Ch. 5; Kogan, 1974), lawyers argued that greater judicial autonomy from legislative oversight would lead to the adoption of efficient administration and the virtues of scientific management.

On the one hand, this expansion of judicial autonomy legitimated the exercise of discretion by lower court judges, who could now establish specialized tribunals and adopt informal procedures through judicial rule-making. On the other hand, the rise of court management stratified judicial personnel, creating management posts and dividing work into specialized calendars and tribunals. Power was thus centralized and decentralized at the same time. Within this context the adjudication process was rationalized. In a letter proposing the organization of what would later become the American Judicature Society, Harley wrote; "We may beneficially modify our doctrine of contentious procedure by increasing discretion and responsibility of the court and thus relatively decreasing the importance of advocacy. A trend in this direction appears inevitable" (1912: 8).

THE MUNICIPAL COURT MOVEMENT

The Chicago Municipal Court served as *the* model for reforming the "old" municipal courts [10] and establishing unified city courts. Through the work of a committee, headed by the mayor and two leading industrialists,[11] the Municipal Court Act was drafted and the Illinois constitution amended, and the municipal court opened in 1906 (Gilbert, 1928; Kogan, 1974). The same constitutional

[10]In 1866 the Boston Municipal Court was established to assume the jurisdiction of the JP courts (civil) and the Boston Police Court (criminal). A municipal court was established in New York City in 1898. These were both considered "old" municipal courts because they lacked an administrative structure (see Roesch, 1904; Greene, 1910).

[11]B. E. Sunny, president of the Chicago Telephone Company, and Bernard Eckhart, described by Harley as a "wealthy miller and grain dealer" (1917b: 4; see also Gilbert, 1928; Kogan, 1974: Ch. 1).

amendment abolished the justice of the peace courts, but most municipal courts were created by legislation, which often meant that the municipal and JP courts had overlapping jurisdictions. Where the legislature could restrict the jurisdiction of the latter (as in Columbus, Ohio, and Philadelphia, in 1913) they transferred it to the municipal courts. With few exceptions (such as Kansas City), most municipal courts established between 1904 and 1922 assumed the jurisdiction of police courts over misdemeanors and the arraignment of felonies. Their civil jurisdiction included tort claims under $1000 and unlimited jurisdiction over contract claims (see Anderson, 1916).

Although reformers agreed that the "modern" city court should be unified, there was some conflict over the scope of unification and the extent of professional control. The most common criticism was that some municipal courts lacked complete jurisdiction over criminal cases. According to the 1917 report on "Unification of Local Government in Chicago" by the Chicago Bureau of Public Efficiency, the most serious shortcoming of the municipal court was the failure to establish a "single court to have general charge of the administration of justice" (Willoughby, 1929: 287). Efforts to expand the jurisdiction of the municipal court consolidating city and county courts were turned down by Chicago voters in 1922. The Detroit Records Court (1920) was praised as the first successful integration of all criminal jurisdiction in a single court.

Most municipal court judges had to be members of the bar, usually for five years, and a resident of the city. The first requirement enhanced the control of the relatively young local bar associations over who would be nominated (Kogan, 1974). Despite heated debates over the virtues of appointed judges, most municipal judges were elected on nonpartisan ballots.

Chicago also provided the model for the creation of branches within the municipal court. Six were established between 1911 and 1916: the Court of Domestic Relations, Speeder's Branch, Morals Court, Boys Court, Small Claims Court, and the Psychopathic Laboratory. These increased specialization and the division of labor. Harley commented:

> They [branches] succeed because the age demands economical production, and has no reverence for empty formalism, the kind exhibited when a supreme court writes *finis* on a cause after all the original litigants are dead. These new tribunals throw to the wind the rules of evidence, because under our jury and appellate system the knotty subject refuses to be reformed [1917b: 25].

The application of criteria of efficiency to the reorganization of tribunals for minor disputes under a unified administrative system produced the municipal court and its specialized branches. These courts were designed to respond to two demands: efficient production and legal socialization. The relationship between the rationalization of judicial organization and the rationalization of procedures for handling minor disputes will now be examined more closely.

THE SOCIALIZED COURTS

The domestic relations, small claims, and conciliation courts were called "socialized courts" in the sense that their 'procedures and remedies focused on diagnosis, prevention, cure, education" (Hurst, 1953: 5). Progressives claimed that the specialized tribunals provided "social justice" in contrast with "legal justice," or the denial of justice that occurred if there was no judicial intervention. It was in this sense that the reformers saw informal procedures as delegalizing minor dispute processing.

The idea of socialized courts was introduced in the late 1880s by the juvenile court movement (Faust and Brantingham, 1974: 145-149). Juvenile courts developed investigative mechanisms to identify social facts about an individual and apply them in the adjudication process. Probation and parole officers, social workers, and psychopathic clinics were used to diagnose the cause of delinquency. Individuals' dossiers served as the basis for a treatment-oriented disposition. "The end sought [must be the] adjustment of a social difficulty rather than the punishment or penalization of the defendant" (Willoughby, 1929: 325).

The juvenile court movement was "anti-legal" in the sense that it "encouraged minimum procedural formality and maximum dependency on extra-legal resources" (Platt, 1969: 141). The juvenile court was more than an instrument for assigning guilt; it was conceptualized as part of a social process capable of adjudicating, preventing, and resolving conflict.

The use of "unofficial" dockets in juvenile courts reflected the belief that children could be treated more effectively through informal dispositions (Ryerson, 1978: 93; Rothman, 1980: 249-260). There were two main consequences of such "unofficial" treatment. First, judicial supervision of children expanded. By deemphasizing issues of guilt and innocence, the category of disputes heard in the juvenile court was broadened. "Pre-delinquent" children formed a new group as a result of the blurring of the distinction between dependent, delinquent, and neglected children (Fox, 1970; Ryerson, 1978: 45-46). Second, the "policing machinery" of unofficial treatment "removed many distinctions between the enforcement and adjudication of laws" (Platt, 1969: 140). Social workers and psychologists provided new resources for handling juveniles and linked courts to social agencies.[12] The state, represented by probation and parole officers, was cast in the role of "friend," helping poor and working-class immigrant children to become socialized or "Americanized" (*Ibid.*: 139). Both developments rendered the courts more interventionist.

Prior to the establishment of domestic relations courts, police and legal aid

[12]Ryerson (1978) provides an excellent discussion of the relationship between the creation of a new stratum of court officials and developments occurring within the social sciences. I am grateful to Austin Sarat for directing my attention to this work. See also Rothman (1980: Ch. 3).

have extended the use of conciliation to the civil proceedings of divorce and separate support [1919b: 81].

Other accounts of domestic relations courts confirm Smith's observation that conciliation was used as a preliminary procedure, particularly during the initial interviews with the parties. But it is apparent that reformers defined conciliation as almost any attempt by a court official (clerk, prosecutor, judge) to get the parties to resolve their differences, whether at the filing of the complaint, the interviews, or the informal hearing.

This broad definition of conciliation reflected the view that court personnel should play a proactive role in the socialized courts. Situations for exercising discretion became opportunities for reconciling disputants on the premise that the objectives of conciliation were "spreading the practice of peaceful settlement of disputes and . . . aiding in overcoming the delays of the law" (Lauer, 1929: 4). In many respects, "conciliation" became a shibboleth to justify the exercise of discretion. Reformers idealized the role of the judge adjudicating minor disputes in lower courts as one of "umpire," although studies of these lower courts reveal a very different picture (Wickersham Commission, 1974). The judge in the socialized courts was to be an "impartial investigator into the truth. He is not a passive agent waiting for objections, he is in affirmative control of the whole proceedings . . . [he] is equipped and empowered not only to prevent injustice but to do justice" (Committee on Small Claims and Conciliation Procedure of the Conference of Bar Association Delegates, quoted in Willoughby, 1929: 317).

Reformers defined the boundaries of delegalization not by articulating the fine lines between conciliation, mediation, arbitration, and litigation, but by establishing different institutions for minor disputes.[15] They were less explicit about the appropriate tribunal for minor criminal cases because they did not question the basic structure of the criminal court. We can obtain a clearer understanding of the boundaries of delegalization by examining the debate among reformers over small claims courts and conciliation tribunals.

SMALL CLAIMS COURTS AND CONCILIATION TRIBUNALS

The first small claims court was created in 1913 as a result of what Judge Manuel Levine of Cleveland characterized as the success of earlier experiments

[15]The actors in this reform movement were a highly unified group, made up of trade associations of lawyers and judges, such as the American Judicature Society. But though (Yngvesson and Hennessey, 1975: 225) there was considerable unity of opinion, reformers did disagree about particular types of informal tribunals.

with conciliation in the police prosecutors' office.[16] The small claims court was established by a rule of the Cleveland Municipal Court, which provided in very general language that the "judge shall endeavor to effect an amicable adjustment" (Smith, 1919b: 63). In practice, the clerk for the Conciliation Branch initiated the process, offering a settlement to the defendant by either telephone or mail. If that attempt failed, the case would then go before a legally trained judge in the Conciliation Branch. The original rule required the clerk to place all cases involving claims under $35 on the docket of the Conciliation Branch, but this was amended to give discretion to the plaintiff. In 1914, 42 percent of the cases docketed were settled by conciliation, and 23 percent in 1915. In the remainder of the cases, the Conciliation Branch rendered a judgment (Smith, 1919b: 63). The court process used simplified procedures, required no pleadings, and cost only a nominal fee of seventy-five cents. Lawyers were discouraged from participating, but not excluded.

Most of the city-wide small claims courts were modeled after Cleveland: Chicago (1916), Minneapolis (1917), New York (1917), and Philadelphia (1920). All were branches of the municipal court, created by a court rule, and their jurisdiction was subject to regulation by the municipal judges. The Kansas legislature, by contrast, created Small Debtors' Courts in Topeka, Levenworth, and Kansas City in 1913. The act provided that the "board of county commissioners or mayor [select] as judge some reputable resident citizen of approved integrity who is sympathetically inclined to consider the situation of the poor, friendless and misfortunate" (Smith, 1919b: 44). The lay judge served without pay and was free to hold court in his own home or place of business, or in a location specified by those who appointed him. The court's jurisdiction was limited to claims under $20 and the law provided that the judge and the defendant should work together to arrange for the payment of the judgment (Edholm, 1915: 30).

This type of conciliation tribunal was attacked as representing too "violent" a reaction to the problems of formality that plagued traditional procedures (Smith, 1919b: 44). Smith and other prominent reformers opposed the Small Debtors' Court because it subverted the principle of a unified judicial system. The Kansas court was criticized on three grounds. First, instead of being organized and supervised by the municipal court, it was independent. Reformers argued that the jurisdiction of the small claims courts had to be supervised by the judiciary rather than by the legislature to ensure sufficient flexibility and planning. Second, reformers objected to the lay judge who provided "justice according to individual conscience after the manner of an Eastern Cadi" (*Ibid.*: 45). Pound also rejected

[16]The first experiment with conciliation that reformers discuss in any detail occurred in the police prosecutor's office in Cleveland in 1904. Under the Municipal Court Act, parties in minor criminal cases who were unable to pay for counsel would meet with the deputy clerk, selected by the municipal judge, and he would assist them in reaching an out-of-court settlement (Levine, 1915).

the lay justice in Small Debtors' Court: "The old idea of justice without law administered on the basis of sympathy repeated a feature of the system which failed to be justified by experience. There were no provisions for effective control over the supervision of the tribunal" (1940b: 268). [17] Finally, reformers criticized the statute for prohibiting attorneys from "intermeddl[ing]" in the process. William Willoughby, director of the Institute for Government Research, commented:

> To prohibit the attorney by absolute fiat we consider a mistake. While reiterating the proposition that in most small claims court cases the attorney has no function to perform, we believe that there are likely to be some cases where a party is ignorant, or frightened, or unfamiliar with our language, so that an attorney (the attorney of a legal aid society, for e. g.) might assist the court and facilitate the hearing [1929: 319].

In 1919, after the establishment of municipal small claims courts, the American Judicature Society drafted a model bill to create statewide courts. Although the bill was designed to address the "failures" of the only existing statewide law (North Dakota, 1913), it expressed a general program for the delegalization of minor dispute processing. Two of its central features became the major issues of debate in this period of reform: delegating supervision of the conciliation boards to the trial judge and fixing the jurisdiction of the board. Any voter was eligible to become a conciliator, even a lawyer, although legal training was not required. The American Judicature Society believed that eligibility criteria should be flexible to give the supervising judges maximum discretion. Therefore, they had authority to delay a court hearing in any civil action until the parties tried to reach a settlement with the assistance of a conciliator. If they were unable to do so, the case would proceed to a court hearing, although instead the conciliator could arbitrate with the written consent of the parties (JAJS, 1919a).

Both of these features—supervision by the District Court and compulsory conciliation followed by the "option" of arbitration—were consistent with the fundamental principle: centralized supervision of decentralized specialized branches. The original 1895 North Dakota law (as amended in 1913) limited conciliation to cases pending in court in which both parties agreed to the process (Smith, 1924: 17). The first state to adopt a state-wide small claims court act was Massachusetts. The 1920 act was praised for making the "small claims court an integral part of the judicial system" and leaving wide discretion to the courts to adopt and modify rules in an experimental fashion (Willoughby, 1929: 315). The act did not create a new court, but instead required that every lower court judge

[17]It is interesting to note that the bar, the Association of Credit Men, the Chamber of Commerce, and the other influential advocates of small claims courts did not support religious tribunals such as the Baltimore Jewish Court of Arbitration, in which three lay persons presided, lawyers were not allowed to participate in any way, and the parties had to agree to arbitration (See Hartogensis, 1929).

establish special sessions and procedures for hearing all claims under $35. California and South Dakota (1921) and Nevada and Idaho (1923) were among the states that created similar institutions. The North Dakota structure—supervision over small claims proceedings by the District Court judge—was found to be less desirable because the latter did not adequately oversee the conciliation boards.

In contrast to most states, Iowa made conciliation optional with the judge (1923). The American Judicature Society called this a "conservative experiment" (JAJS, 1923: 15; Harley 1926), objecting to the exclusion of lawyers and the absence of a record. Furthermore, they found that after two years of experimentation there had been "no instance of any judge electing to give the plan a trial" (Harley, 1926: 96). Reformers preferred mandatory procedures to increase the use of conciliation and closer supervision in accordance with the principle of unification.

Reformers consistently urged the reduction of litigation through conciliation and called for more compulsion to achieve this goal. They proposed that lower courts adopt rules requiring parties to try conciliation before their dispute would be placed on the court calendar (JAJS, 1918c; Lauer, 1928).

Conciliation procedures, such as the Rules on Conciliation of the New York City Municipal Court, 1917, were also criticized for failing to ensure the enforceability of agreements. Two separate but related issues were involved in the question of the "legality" of conciliation agreements. First, should parties be required to submit disputes involving certain amounts of money to conciliation; and second, should conciliation agreements be enforceable. On the one hand, Smith criticized "pure conciliation," exemplified by the Kansas Small Debtors' Court, because it was "entirely detached from the regular administration of justice, [and therefore] seems to defeat its own ends" (1924a: 2). He argued that conciliation tribunals, in contrast with small claims courts, lacked compulsory jurisdiction and the power to enforce agreements and therefore failed to satisfy the goal of providing access to justice for the petty litigant. He recommended, instead, that conciliation procedures be adopted by regular courts and not relegated to "extra-legal" tribunals (1924a: 3). On the other hand, Smith acknowledged that "compulsion exercised to force a settlement is, of course, not conciliation at all, but unless an agreement can be enforced, the door is left open for fraud by refusal to abide by the adjustment, so that the proceeding merely results in loss of time and disappointment" (1919b: 64). Smith resolved this conflict by encouraging the use of arbitration to supplement conciliation.

The Kansas Small Debtors' Courts, the Iowa Conciliation Boards, and the New York City conciliation calendar were considered conciliation tribunals rather than small claims courts. Reformers associated such experiments with conciliation in Norway and Denmark because the tribunals were somewhat independent of the court system and conciliation was optional with either the parties or the judge (Grevstad, 1918; Smith, 1926). Reformers not only criticized these tribunals because they were unsupervised but also dismissed them as failures. We have little information about who used conciliation and why, but it appears that disputants preferred small claims courts to voluntary conciliation. The New York Law Review reported in 1925 that the New York City Municipal Court conciliation calendar was a failure because few parties would agree to submit their disputes since the resulting agreements were not enforceable. Willoughby's survey of conciliation tribunals concluded that voluntary conciliation "rarely occur[s] unless careful provision has been made for the establishment of a system of conciliation . . . as an integral feature of the judicial system and this system has received at least legal recognition" (1929: 40).

In summary, reformers supported those conciliation experiments that required participation and operated within the context of a unified court system. Both minor criminal and civil disputes were handled by procedures located within existing institutions. Informal procedures complemented conventional adjudication in two respects. First, the flexibility of investigatory proceedings, characteristic of conciliation and arbitration, enabled the judiciary to absorb more conflict (both in kind and intensity), thus appearing to respond to social demands without fundamentally altering existing judicial structures. Second, with the growth of specialization in the lower courts, informal procedures served to channel the exercise of discretion within judicial institutions.

Criticism of the socialized courts after 1940 focuses on the fact that they were appendages of traditional judicial institutions rather than genuine alternatives to the adversarial process. The literature on small claims courts takes the position that informal procedures were nothing more than a simplified, streamlined version of conventional adjudication without due process protections (see Yngvesson and Hennessey 1975). The "cross-cutting" interests of judges, who sought to expand their role rather than to relinquish jurisdiction to lay conciliators, is often given as the reason. During this early period of reform the concept of due process was not as developed as we understand it today (see Ryerson, 1978: 57–58, 63), nor was the distinction between proactive judges and proactive courts as clear. Because they failed to distinguish between courts and judges, delegalization reformers established a complementary adjudication process within what they thought would be a unified court system. But contrary to their desire for a lower court *system* in which specialization would be managed by centralized administration, the socialized courts did not complement a unified lower court but rather increased the organizational complexity of the judicial structure (Virtue, 1953; Galub, 1968).

Unification continued to be the dominant management strategy. In 1938 the ABA adopted the Parker–Vanderbilt resolution calling for more unified judicial organization through the establishment of administrative judges, judicial councils to make policy, statistical information systems and, once again, the replacement of the justice of the peace courts by municipal courts. Although scientific management techniques used in the industrial sector had by then been influenced by the human development approach (see Baritz, 1960), the legal order was slow to consider the importance of individual behavior for management. Court unification between the 1940s and 1960s was aimed, instead, at greater centralization and control of the judicial work process (Volcansek, 1977).

For the past seventy years, unification has been the predominant goal in reorganizing decentralized trial courts (Gazell, 1977). But attempts to bring lower courts within a unified system have been hindered by local resistance. The county jurisdiction of local courts has presented political and cultural obstacles to a fully rationalized judicial administration (Gallas, 1976).

COURT REORGANIZATION AND NEIGHBORHOOD
JUSTICE CENTERS: 1970–1980

The unified model has recently been challenged by court reformers who argue that the management and organization of courts must be decentralized to integrate them within the local environment and utilize local resources more effectively.[18] It is argued that less formal, rule-bound instruments of management are essential because the prosecutorial staff, public defender, and probation programs represent "uncontrolled resources" (*Ibid.:* 44). One critic of unification contends that

> . . . the most notable consequence of over-centralizing the judicial system is the resulting diminution of flexibility and responsibility to local environmental demands. Without a large measure of local autonomy, trial level judges and administrators will be incapable of rapidly adjusting their procedures to respond to changes in their immediate environments [Hays, 1977: 130].

Whereas scientific management concentrated on promoting efficient service by minimizing "wasteful human motion," the current interest in integrating court organization with elements indigenous to the environment represents a shift in policy from managing *organizations* to managing organizational *environments*. This reform, however, is a different approach to, rather than a rejection of, the fundamental tenet of unification. Ashman and Parness argue that unification should not be limited to courts, but should be conceptualized more broadly to encompass a unified judicial system (1974: 39).

> Consideration of the concept of a unified judicial system would justify application by the judiciary of the unification principles of centralized supervision to court-related institutions. Court-related

[18]One example of integrating resources from the environment into the court is the Community Resource Program, which is "designed to more fully utilize community resources and probation services by the court, and to provide the court [with] mechanisms to develop resources previously unavailable" (American Judicature Society and Institute for Court Management, 1978: 46–47).

institutions include jails; state prisons; pretrial diversion centers dealing with such matters as rehabilitation of alcoholics, drug addicts, and juvenile offenders or delinquents; probation offices; parole boards; prison disciplinary boards; compulsory and voluntary arbitration panels; conciliation bureaus; pretrial detention centers; and so-called "community moots" [*Ibid.*: 40].

The contemporary movement to decentralize judicial organization is an effort to regulate court-related institutions in their own environment. Reformers maintain that the flexibility associated with decentralized organization and management will allow courts to incorporate the resources of court-related institutions into a unified judicial system while using these resources to expand and integrate services into a system. Management under decentralization is conducted through networks rather than hierarchical structures. Such an approach has correctly been characterized as the simultaneous centralization and decentralization of courts (Heydebrand, 1979: 39–40; Spitzer, 1980: 37–43).

Decentralized court organization allows modification of the decision making process without the chaotic proliferation of specialized tribunals that occurred in the Progressive period. Institutions such as the neighborhood justice centers (NJCs) can develop as a "complementary system, supplementing and in some areas substituting" for existing court services (Danzig, 1973: 7). These new tribunals are specialized (Cappelletti and Garth, 1978), but remain part of a decentralized organization and rely on judicial system personnel to refer cases to them. Unlike the specialized branches of the municipal court, they do not have official jurisdiction over particular cases, but depend on referrals for their cases.[19] This arrangement, reformers speculate, will lead to the development of a network that can become an administrative mechanism for managing the NJC. In addition, the NJCs neither destroy the existing dispute apparatus nor possess sufficient autonomy to become as highly specialized as the branches of the municipal court. The NJC is a fail-safe mechanism because litigants still have recourse to the courts (Danzig, 1973: 8). Decentralized court organization thus encourages the evolution of "appended remedy systems" without disrupting the organization of the "official remedy system" (Galanter, 1974) and increases the capacity of the judiciary to create programs—to become proactive.

The second wave of delegalization reform in minor dispute processing, which we are currently experiencing, coincides with this proposed shift in judicial management. Danzig's proposal (1973) for a decentralized criminal justice system includes a "community moot" that relies heavily upon agents in the criminal justice system for referrals, and other community mediation models are even more dependent upon courts (McGillis and Mullen, 1977). Indeed, the earliest recent experiments with mediation and arbitration of minor criminal and civil disputes were developed by prosecutors and courts (McGillis, 1980; Florida Supreme Court, 1979).

---

[19] Eric Fisher's "community court" (1975) is an example of a minor dispute resolution program with statutory jurisdiction. This model, however, has not been adopted or even discussed seriously.

The principles of judicial management structure minor dispute processing reform today, as they did in the Progressive era. Such reform is occurring within both the judicial work process and the adjudication process. What type of reform is produced by delegalization of minor dispute processing under a decentralized management model?

One consequence of decentralized organization and management has been the rationalization of the judicial work process. The management principle of decentralization is the specialization of tasks and improvement of the "fit between the technical and social subsystems in the organization" (Gallas, 1976: 47). The use of paraprofessionals to organize community resources and mediate minor disputes is far more prevalent today than it was during the Progressive era. It is often associated with deprofessionalizing decision making as well. Yet closer examination of the role of paraprofessionals in a decentralized management model suggests that this is not the case. As one reformer states:

> A key to successful municipal operation of police, courts, and prisons lies in determining which functions already have been professionalized, which may be feasibly and appropriately professionalized in the near future, and which are not easily or should not be professionalized. The latter are ripe for decentralization. Thus formulated, *decentralization becomes not a force in opposition to professionalization*, but rather a force well coordinated with it, a force which in fact speeds professionalization by shaping the role definition the professional is seeking to assume [Danzig, 1973: 9; emphasis added].

Danzig notes that police spend a large percentage of their time performing order maintenance tasks—responding to domestic and neighborhood disturbances—for which "police training and professionalization efforts are least directed" and they exercise wide discretion in these situations (*Ibid.*: 29). Advocates of pretrial diversion similarly criticize the mismatch between the training of prosecutors and judges and the type of discretion they must exercise in handling order maintenance problems. A new stratum of court-related personnel created as paraprofessionals (lay mediators) assume these tasks. In the decentralized model, discretion is exercised within a unified judicial system. As a result, the judicial work process becomes further stratified and rationalized.

The reform objective of efficient service introduced in the Progressive period reemerges in the contemporary delegalization movement, but its application extends beyond a rationale for intervention by courts in order maintenance to a justification for intervention by court-related institutions. The shift from centralized judicial management under unification to decentralized management under a unified judicial system necessitates a broader concept of efficient judicial service. [20] This shift in judicial management strategies resembles the reorganiza-

---

[20]Prevention and rehabilitation have been suggested as two "alternative" criteria for measuring the efficiency of NJC. In the midst of the present urban fiscal crisis it remains to be seen whether these measures will justify continuing financial support. In Kansas City (although funding decisions are not yet finalized), it appears that the city government will not support the NJC to distribute those resources to fire and police services.

tion and rationalization of social services (Hirschhorn, 1978: 68). Notions of efficiency are not limited to simple cost accounting. Although initially some effort was made by the U.S. Justice Department to promote NJCs as cost effective programs (see Law Enforcement Assistance Administration, 1977; 1979: 1), it is clear that they are not cheaper than courts when compared in terms of cost per case (Felstiner and Williams, 1980). Greater emphasis has been placed on expanding access to justice by reorganizing the judicial work process and creating court-related institutions. Efficient service therefore signifies the building of networks to channel social conflict into dispute forums that have the technical expertise to manage minor disputes. Efficiency in the delegalization movement means matching different types of disputes with the appropriate technical skills of judicial system personnel. Thus, the expansion of access to justice coincides with an administrative–technocratic rationalization of the judicial work process.

The contemporary reformers, however, argue that the delegalization of minor dispute processing "promises something deeper than technology" (Cover, 1979: 912), something more substantive than a mere administrative or technocratic remedy to the problems of access to justice for the powerless. In addition to pointing out the internal inefficiencies of court adjudication of minor disputes, reformers once again note the costs of conventional adjudication for disputants. The psychological, economic, and temporal costs together with the linguistic and cultural barriers make courts inefficient mechanisms for processing minor disputes (Galanter, 1974; Johnson, 1978). These barriers limit citizen participation in dispute processing. Reformers argue that informal dispute processing tribunals, such as the neighborhood justice centers, will reduce community alienation from courts and thereby expand access to justice through increased participation. Expanding the role of citizens in dispute resolution is viewed by reformers as a substantive alternative to the problems of access for minor disputes.

Yet within the decentralized management model, minor disputes are channeled into appended tribunals that emphasize therapeutic intervention by trained lay citizens. Individuals, assisted by mediators, seek to reach an agreement on how to restructure their future behavior to avoid or prevent conflict. Disputes such as violence against women, neighborhood quarrels, and landlord–tenant problems are reduced to individual problems. The origins of these disputes are depoliticized or ignored, and the resolutions are internalized by the individualized form of participation. Conflict in this setting is absorbed into a rehabilitative model of minor dispute resolution.

Just as the Progressives advocated socialized law in socialized courts, so too the current delegalization movement seeks to rebuild a legal consensus for judicial intervention through a participatory concept of access to justice. As a result, discretion once exercised by court officals and police officers is formally exercised by mediators and arbitrators in a therapeutic setting. Delegalization in this context serves to rationalize the adjudication process. The form of judicial intervention in specialized tribunals such as the neighborhood justice center expands the scope of dispute processing by the state.

CONCLUSION

Starting from the premise that courts are limited by their structure (formal procedures) and function (determining innocence or guilt on the basis of legally relevant facts), delegalization reformers in both periods have attempted to expand the judicial capacity of courts and court-related institutions to manage minor disputes through the use of informal procedures, mediation, and arbitration. The objectives of the contemporary delegalization movement are efficient dispute processing and expansion of access to justice in minor criminal and civil disputes. Both goals have antecedents in the Progressive reforms. Critics of both sets of reforms have argued that these two objectives are in conflict (Singer, 1979; American Friends Service Committee, 1978–1980). But this historical overview has suggested that by examining these objectives in light of the organizational context from which delegalization programs develop, we find that these objectives are collateral policies of an administrative–technocratic rationale for judicial intervention in order maintenance. It is apparent that dispute processes premised upon a hostility to formality play a significant role in the judicial management strategies of the twentieth century. The expansion of administrative access to justice and the expansion of participatory access to justice under such reforms were facilitated by the rise of judicial management and extended through the contemporary decentralization of judicial management. Both objectives were structured by the politics of judicial management—the concentration of judicial power under an ideology of expanding participation.

REFERENCES

Aaronson, David, Bert H. Hoffa, Peter Jaszi, Nicholas N. Kittrie, and David Saari (1977) *The New Justice: Alternatives to Conventional Criminal Adjudication*. Washington, D.C.: Institute for Advanced Studies in Justice, American University.

Abel, Richard L. (1979) "Delegalization: A Critical Review of Its Ideology, Manifestations, and Social Consequences," in E. Blankenburg, E. Klausa, and H. Rottleuthner (eds.) *Alternative Rechtsformen und Alternativen zum Recht*. Opladen: Westdeutscher Verlag.

Allen, H. K. (1937) "Administration of Minor Justice in Selected Illinois Counties," 31 *Illinois Law Review* 1047.

American Bar Association (1909) "Report of the Special Committee to Suggest Remedies and Formulate Proposed Laws to Prevent Delay and Unnecessary Cost in Litigation," 34 *American Bar Association Journal* 578.

_____ (1923) "Report of the Committee on Legal Aid Work," 48 *American Bar Association Journal* 374.

American Friends Service Committee (1978–1980) *The Mooter*. Pittsburgh.

American Judicature Society and the Institute for Court Management (1978) *Misdemeanor Court Management Research Program*. Washington, D.C.: Law Enforcement Assistance Administration.

Anderson, Claude H. (1916) "Reforms in Legal Systems," 10 *American Political Science Review* 569.

Ashman, Allen and Jeffrey A. Parness (1974) "The Concept of a Limited Court System," 24 *DePaul Law Review* 1.

Auerbach, Jerold (1976) *Unequal Justice*. New York: Oxford University Press.

Aumann, F. R. (1931) "Domestic Relations Courts in Ohio," 15 *Journal of the American Judicature Society* 89.

Baldwin, William H. (1913) "The Court of Domestic Relations of Chicago," 3 *Journal of Criminal Law, Criminology and Police Science* 400.

Baritz, Loren (1960) *The Servants of Power*. Middletown, Conn.: Wesleyan University Press.

Berkson, Larry (1977) "The Emerging Ideal of Court Unification," 60 *Judicature* 372.

Berkson, Larry and Susan Carbon (1978) *Court Unification: History, Politics and Implementation*. Washington, D.C.: National Institute of Law Enforcement and Criminal Justice.

Berkson, Larry, Steven Hays, and Susan Carbon (1977) *Managing the State Courts: Text and Readings*. St. Paul, Minn.: West Publishing Co.

Blackburn, William J. (1935) *The Administration of Criminal Justice in Franklin County Ohio*. Baltimore: Johns Hopkins University Press.

Blumberg, Abraham S. (1967) *Criminal Justice*. New York: New View Points.

Boston, Charles A. (1917) "Some Observations upon the Report of the Committee of the Phi Delta Phi with Special Reference to the Typical Judiciary Article for the Constitution," 73 *Annals of the American Academy of Political and Social Science* 104.

Braverman, Harry (1974) *Labor and Monopoly Capital*. New York: Monthly Review Press.

Bryant, Louise Stevens (1918) "A Department of Diagnosis and Treatment for the Municipal Court," 9 *Journal of Criminal Law and Criminology* 198.

Burawoy, Michael (1979) "Towards a Marxist Theory of the Labor Process: Braverman and Beyond," 8 *Politics and Society* 247.

Burkheimer, Charles L. (1926) "The Advantage of Arbitration Procedure," 125 *Annals of the American Academy of Political and Social Science* 98.

Butts, A. B. (1928) "The Justice of the Peace—Recent Tendencies," 22 *American Political Science Review* 946.

Cady, William G. (1915) "Practical Sides of Local Inferior Courts of Civil Jurisdiction," 22 *Case and Comment* 25.

Cappelletti, Mauro and Bryant Garth (1978) "Access to Justice: The Newest Wave in the World-Wide Movement to Make Rights Effective," 27 *Buffalo Law Review* 181.

Carbon, Susan, Larry Berkson, and Judy Rosenbaum (1978) "Court Reform in the Twentieth Century: A Critique of the Court Unification Controversy," 27 *Emory Law Journal* 559.

Cayton, Nathan (1939) "Small Claims and Conciliation Courts," 205 *Annals of the American Academy of Political and Social Science* 57.

Clawson, Dan (1980) *Bureaucracy in the Labor Process*. New York: Monthly Review Press.

Cobb, W. Bruce (1920) "A Court of Prevention: The Municipal Term Court of the City of New York," 11 *Journal of Criminal Law and Criminology* 47.

Cohen, Julius Henry (1917) "Administration of Business and Discipline by the Courts," 73 *Annals of American Academy of Political and Social Science* 205.

Columbia Journal of Law and Social Problems (1969) "Comment: Small Claims Court: Reform Revisited," 5 *Columbia Journal of Law and Social Problems* 47.

Columbia Law Review (1934) "Small Claims Courts," 34 *Columbia Law Review* 932.

Cover, Robert M. (1979) "Dispute Resolution: A Forward," 88 *Yale Law Journal* 911.

Danzig, Richard (1973) "Toward the Creation of a Complementary Decentralized System of Criminal Justice," 26 *Stanford Law Review* 1.

Danzig, Richard and Michael J. Lowy (1975) "Everyday Disputes and Mediation in the United States: A Reply to Professor Felstiner," 9 *Law & Society Review* 675.

Day, C. B. (1928) "The Development of the Family Court," 136 *Annals of American Academy of Political and Social Sciences* 105.

Dayton, Kenneth (1934) *Report of the Committee on Courts of Limited Jurisdiction.* New York: Association of the Bar of the City of New York (Pamphlet No. 53).

Douglass, Paul F. (1932) *The Justice of the Peace Courts of Hamilton County, Ohio.* Baltimore: Johns Hopkins University Press.

Edholm, Charlton Lawrence (1915) "The Small Debtors' Courts," 22 *Case and Comment* 29.

Eisenstein, James and Herbert Jacob (1977) *Felony Justice.* Boston: Little, Brown.

Elliot, Sheldon D. (1959) *Improving Our Courts.* New York: Oceana Publications.

Faust, Frederick L. and Paul J. Brantingham (1974) *Juvenile Justice Philosophy.* St. Paul, Minn.: West Publishing Co.

Feeley, Malcolm M. (1973) "Two Models of the Criminal Justice System: An Organizational Perspective," 7 *Law & Society Review* 407.

—— (1976) "The Concept of Laws in Social Science: A Critique and Notes on an Expanded View," 10 *Law & Society Review* 497.

Felstiner, William L.F. (1974) "Influences of Social Organization on Dispute Processing," 9 *Law & Society Review* 63.

—— (1975) "Avoidance as Dispute Processing: An Elaboration," 9 *Law & Society Review* 695.

Felstiner, William L. F. and Lynne E. Williams (1980) *Community Mediation in Dorchester, Massachusetts.* Washington, D.C.: U.S. Department of Justice.

Fisher, Eric A. (1975) "Community Courts: An Alternative to Conventional Criminal Adjudication," 24 *American University Law Review* 253.

Florida Supreme Court, Office of the State Court Administrator (1979) *The Citizen Dispute Settlement Process in Florida: A Study of Five Programs.* Tallahassee: Florida Supreme Court.

Fox, Sanford J. (1970) "Juvenile Justice Reform: An Historical Perspective," 22 *Stanford Law Review* 1187.

Friedman, Lawrence M. (1978) "Access to Justice: Social and Historical Context," in M. Cappelletti and J. Weisner (eds.) *Access to Justice*, vol. 2, Book 1. Alphen aan den rijn: Sijthoff and Noordhoff; and Milan: Giuffrè.

Fuller, Lon L. (1978) "The Forms and Limits of Adjudication," 92 *Harvard Law Review* 353.

Galanter, Marc (1974) "Why the 'Haves' Come Out Ahead: Speculations on the Limits of Legal Change," 9 *Law & Society Review* 95.

Gallas, Geoff (1976) "The Conventional Wisdom of State Court Administration: A Critical Assessment and an Alternative Approach," 2 *Justice System Journal* 35.

—— (1979) "Court Reform: Has It Been Built on an Adequate Foundation?" 63 *Judicature* 38.

Galub, Arthur L. (1968) *The Politics of Court Reorganization in New York State*, Ph.D. Dissertation, Department of Political Science, Columbia University.

Garth, Bryant (1982) "The Movement toward Procedural Informalism in North America and Western Europe: A Critical Survey" in R. Abel (ed.) *The Politics of Informal Justice*, vol. 2: *Comparative Studies.* New York: Academic Press.

Gazell, James A. (1974) "Lower-Court Unification in the American States," 1974 *Arizona State Law Journal* 669.

——— (1977) "The Principal Facets and Goals of Court Management: A Sketch," in L. Berkson, S. Hays, and S. Carbon (eds.) *Managing the State Courts*. St. Paul, Minn: West Publishing Co.

Gemmill, William N. (1914) "Chicago Court of Domestic Relations," 52 *Annals of the American Academy of Political and Social Science* 115.

Gilbert, Hiram (1928) *The Municipal Court of Chicago*. Chicago: Author.

Goldstein, Herman (1977) *Policing a Free Society*. Cambridge, Mass.: Ballinger Publishing Co.

Greene, J. Kent (1910) "The Municipal Court of Chicago," 58 *University of Pennsylvania Law Review* 335.

Grevstad, Nicolay (1918) "Norway's Conciliation Tribunals," 2 *Journal of the American Judicature Society* 5.

Halliday, Terence Charles (1979) *Parameters of Professional Influence: Policies and Politics of the Chicago Bar Association, 1945-70*. Ph.D. Dissertation, Department of Sociology, University of Chicago.

Harley, Herbert (1912) "A Circular Letter Concerning the Administration of Justice." Chicago: American Judicature Society Archives.

——— (1912) "The Scientific Attitude toward Reform in Procedure," 75 *Central Law Journal* 147.

——— (1915a) "Court Organization for a Metropolitan District," 9 *American Political Science Review* 507.

——— (1915b) *The Small Claims Branch of the Municipal Court of Chicago*. Chicago: American Judicature Society (Bulletin No. 8).

——— (1915c) "Ultimate Types of Interior Courts and Judges," 22 *Case and Comment* 3.

——— (1917a) "An Efficient County Court System," 73 *Annuals of the American Academy of Political and Social Science* 189.

——— (1917b) "Business Management for the Courts," 5 *Virginia Law Review* 1.

——— (1919) "Justice or Litigation?" 6 *Virginia Law Review* 143.

——— (1920) "Conciliation Is Succeeding," 4 *Journal of the American Judicature Society* 70.

——— (1926) "Conciliation Procedure in Small Claims," 125 *Annals of the American Academy of Political and Social Science* 91.

——— (1928) "Administering Justice in Cities," 136 *Annals of the American Academy of Political and Social Science* 87.

Hartmann, Edward G. (1948) *The Movement to Americanize the Immigrant*. New York: Columbia University Press.

Hartogensis, B. H. (1929) "A Successful Community Court," 12 *Journal of the American Judicature Society* 183.

Hays, Samuel (1964) "Municipal Reform in the Progressive Era: Whose Class Interest?" 55 *Pacific Northwest Quarterly* 157.

Hays, Steven (1977) "Contemporary Trends in Court Unification," in L. Berkson, S. Hays, and S. Carbon (eds.) *Managing the State Courts*. St. Paul, Minn.: West Publishing Co.

Heydebrand, Wolf (1977) "Organizational Contradictions in Public Bureaucracies: Toward a Marxian Theory of Organization," 18 *Sociological Quarterly* 83.

——— (1979) "The Technocratic Administration of Justice," 2 *Research in Law and Sociology* 29.

Hirschhorn, Larry (1978) "The Political Economy of Social Service Rationalization: A Developmental View," 2 *Contemporary Crises* 63.

Hofrichter, Richard (1982) "Neighborhood Justice and the Social Conrrol Problems of American Capitalism: A Perspective," in R. Abel (ed.) *The Politics of Informal Justice*, vol. 1: *The American Experience*. New York: Academic Press.

Hofstadter, Richard (1955) *The Age of Reform*. New York: Knopf.

Horwitz, Morton J. (1977) *The Transformation of American Law, 1780–1860*. Cambridge, Mass.: Harvard University Press.

Howard, T. L. (1935) "The Justice f the Peace System in Tennessee," 13 *Tennessee Law Review* 19.

Hurst, J. Willard (1953) "Changing Popular Views about Law and Lawyers," 287 *Annals of the American Academy of Political and Social Science* 1.

———— (1956) *Law and the Conditions of Freedom*. Madison: University of Wisconsin Press.

Illinois Law Review (1908) "Has Chicago the Best Municipal Justice in the United States?" 3 *Illinois Law Review* 290.

Ireland, Robert M. (1972) *The County Courts in Antebellum Kentucky*. Lexington: University Press of Kentucky.

Jacoby, A. L. (1923) "The Psychopathic Clinic in the Criminal Court: Its Use and Possibilities," 7 *Journal of the American Judicature Society* 21.

Jessup, Henry W. (1917) "The Simplification of the Machinery of Justice with a View to Its Greater Efficiency," 73 *Annals of the American Academy of Political and Social Science* 1.

Johnson, Earl (1978) *Courts and the Community*. Williamsburg, Va.: National Center for State Courts.

Journal of the American Judicature Society (JAJS) (1918a) "Commercial Arbitration," 2 *Journal of the American Judicature Society* 156.

———— (1918b) "Informal Procedure in Chicago," 2 *Journal of the American Judicature Society* 23.

———— (1918c) "Informal Procedure in New York," 2 *Journal of the American Judicature Society* 26.

———— (1919a) "Act to Provide for Conciliation," 2 *Journal of the American Judicature Society* 151.

———— (1919b) "Unnecessary Litigation," 2 *Journal of the American Judicature Society* 158.

———— (1920) "North Dakato Legislature Enacts Law for Conciliation Procedure," 4 *Journal of the American Judicature Society* 165.

———— (1921a) "California Adopts Small Claims Procedures for All Justice of the Peace Courts," 5 *Journal of the American Judicature Society* 29.

———— (1921b) "Conciliation Courts and Procedure Provided for Minnesota Cities," 5 *Journal of the American Judicature Society* 25.

———— (1922a) "Arbitration Society of America," 6 *Journal of the American Judicature Society* 59.

———— (1922b) "Conciliation Law Held Valid," 6 *Journal of the American Judicature Society* 133.

———— (1923) "Try Conciliation in Iowa," 7 *Journal of the American Judicature Society* 15.

———— (1924) "Municipal Court of Chicago a Modern Institution," 8 *Journal of the American Judicature Society* 62.

———— (1928) "Great City Court Given Management," 12 *Journal of the American Judicature Society* 116.

Keebler, Robert S. (1930) "Our Justice of the Peace Courts—A Problem in Justice," 9 *Tennessee Law Review* 1.

Kellor, Frances (1914) "Justice for the Immigrant," 52 *Annals of the American Academy for Political and Social Science* 159.

Kelsey, Carl (1926) "Immigration and Crime," 125 *Annals of the American Academy for Political and Social Science* 165.

Kogan, Herman (1974) *The First Century: The Chicago Bar Association 1874–1974*. Chicago: Rand McNally & Co.

Kronheim, Milton S. (1951) "Does the Small Claims Branch of Our Municipal Court Measure Up to the Standards of the Community?" 18 *Journal of the Bar Association of District of Columbia* 113.

Larson, Magali Sarfatti (1977) *The Rise of Professionalism*. Berkeley: University of California Press.

Lasch, Christopher (1965) *The New Radicalism of America, 1889–1963*. New York: Knopf

Lauer, Edgar J. (1918) "Conciliation and Arbitration in the Municipal Court of the City of New York," 1 *Journal of the American Judicature Society* 153.

———— (1928) "Conciliation—A Cure for the Law's Delay," 136 *Annals of the American Academy for Political and Social Science* 54.

_____ (1929) "Conciliation: A Cure for Congested Court Calendars," 27 *New York Legal Aid Review* 1.

Law Enforcement Assistance Administration (LEAA) (1977) "Grand Application Guidelines and Procedures: Memorandum on Proposed Neighborhood Justice Centers." Washington, D.C.: LEAA.

_____ (1979) "Justice Centers Ease Caseload," 8 (3) *LEAA Newsletter* 1.

Levine, Manuel (1918) "The Conciliation Court of Cleveland," 2 *Journal of the American Judicature Society* 10.

Lowe, Stanley R. (1973) "Unified Courts in America: The Legacy of Roscoe Pound," 55 *Judicature* 316.

Lupe, John J. (1928) "Domestic Relations Branch," 1928 *Annual Report of the Municipal Court of Chicago* 101.

MacChesney, Nathan William (1913) "A Progressive Program for Procedural Reform," 3 *Journal of Criminal Law, Criminology, and Police Science* 528.

McGillis, Daniel (1980) "Recent Developments in Minor Dispute Processing." Cambridge, Mass.: Center for Criminal Justice, Harvard Law School.

McGillis, Daniel and Joan Mullen (1977) *Neighborhood Justice Centers: An Analysis of Potential Models.* Washington, D.C.: National Institute of Law Enforcement and Criminal Justice, LEAA.

McKean, Dayton D. (1963) *The Integrated Bar.* Boston: Houghton Mifflin Co.

Maguire, John MacArthur (1926) "The Model Poor Litigants' Statute," 125 *Annals of the American Academy of Political and Social Science* 84.

Mannel, Robert M. (1973) *Thorns & Thistles: Juvenile Delinquents in the U.S., 1825–1940.* Hanover, N.H.: University Press of New England.

Mariano, John H. (1925) *The Italian Immigrant and Our Courts.* New York: Arno Press.

Nehemkis, Peter R., Jr. (1933) "The Boston Poor Debtor Court—A Study in Collection Procedure," 42 *Yale Law Journal* 561.

New York Law Review (1925) "Do Litigants Want Law and Not Conciliation?" 3 *New York Law Review* 425.

Nimmer, Raymond (1978) *The Nature of System Change.* Chicago: American Bar Foundation.

Nonet, Philippe and Philip Selznick. (1978) *Law and Society in Transition: Toward Responsive Law.* New York: Harper & Row.

Northrop, Everett H. (1940) "Small Claims Courts and Conciliation Tribunals: A Bibliography." 33 *Law Library Journal* 39.

O'Connor, James (1973) *The Fiscal Crisis of the State.* New York: St. Martin's Press.

Paddon, Mary E. (1920) "The Inferior Criminal Courts of New York City," 11 *Journal of Criminal Law, Criminology and Police Science* 8.

Perkins, W. B. (1919) "Family Courts," 3 *Journal of the American Judicature Society* 19.

Platt, Anthony (1969) *The Child Savers.* Chicago: University of Chicago Press.

Potter, William (1922) "Give Judiciary Greater Power," 6 *Journal of the American Judicature Society* 164.

Pound, Roscoe (1906) "The Causes of Popular Dissatisfaction with the Administration of Justice," 29 *American Bar Association Reports* 395.

_____ (1912) "Social Problems and the Courts," 18 *American Journal of Sociology* 331.

_____ (1913) "The Administration of Justice in the Modern City," 26 *Harvard Law Review* 302.

_____ (1928) "Social and Economic Problems of the Law," 136 *Annals of the American Academy of Political and Social Science* 1.

_____ (1940a) *Organization of Courts.* Boston: Little, Brown.

_____ (1940b) "Principles and Outline of a Modern Unified Court Organization," 23 *Journal of the American Judicature Society* 225.

Ransom, William L. (1917a) "The Layman's Demand for Improved Judicial Machinery," 73 *Annals of the American Academy of Political and Social Science* 132.

—————— (1917b) "The Organization of the Courts for the Better Administration of Justice," 2 *Cornell Law Quarterly* 261.

Robbins, A. H. (1916) "Preventing Unnecessary Litigation at the Source," 82 *Central Law Journal* 280.

Roberts, Peter (1920) *The Problem of Americanization*. New York: Macmillan.

Roesch, George F. (1904) "The Municipal Court," 1 *Municipal Court Review* 4.

Root, Elihu (1916) "Public Service by the Bar," 41 *American Bar Association Reports* 355.

Rothman, David J. (1980) *Conscience and Convenience*. Boston: Little, Brown.

Ryerson, Ellen (1978) *The Best-Laid Plans*. New York: Hill and Wang.

Saari, David J. (1976) "Modern Court Management: Trends in Court Organization Concepts— 1976," 2 *Justice System Journal* 19.

Sarat, Austin (1976) "Alternatives in Dispute Processing: Litigation in a Small Claims Court," 10 *Law & Society Review* 339.

Sarat, Austin and Joel Grossman (1975) "Courts and Conflict Resolution: Problems in the Mobilization of Adjudication," 69 *American Political Science Review* 1200.

Schiessel, Martin J. (1977) *The Politics of Efficiency: Municipal Administration and Reform in America: 1880–1920*. Berkeley: University of California Press.

Schramm, Gustav L. (1928) *Piedpoudre Courts: A Study of the Small Claims Litigant in the Pittsburgh District*. Pittsburgh: The Legal Aid Society of Pittsburgh.

Schultz, J. Lawrence (1973) "The Cycle of Juvenile Court History," 17 *Crime and Delinquency* 457.

Scott, Austin W. (1923) "Small Causes and Poor Litigants," 9 *American Bar Association Journal* 457.

Scull, Andrew (1977) *Decarceration: Community Treatment and the Deviant: A Radical View*. Englewood Cliffs, N.J.: Prentice-Hall.

Shelton, Thomas W. (1928) "Greater Efficacy of the Trial of Civil Cases," 136 *Annals of the American Academy of Political and Social Science* 95.

Shick, R. P. (1926) "Simplifying Criminal Procedure in the Lower Courts," 125 *Annals of the American Academy of Political and Social Science* 112.

Shklar, Judith (1964) *Legalism*. Cambridge, Mass.: Harvard University Press.

Silverstein, Lee (1955) "Small Claims Courts versus Justices of the Peace," 58 *West Virginia Law Review* 241.

Simon, William H. (1978) "The Ideology of Advocacy: Procedural Justice and Professional Ethics," 1978 *Wisconsin Law Review* 29.

Singer, Linda (1979) *The Growth of Non-Judicial Dispute Resolution: Speculations on the Effects on Justice for the Poor and on the Role of Legal Services*. Washington, D.C.: Research Institute, Legal Services Corporation.

Smith, Chester H. (1927) "The Justice of the Peace System in the United States," 15 *California Law Review* 118.

Smith, Reginald Heber (1919a) "Denial of Justice," 3 *Journal of the American Judicature Society* 112.

—————— (1919b) *Justice and the Poor*. New York: Charles Scribner's Sons.

—————— (1920) "Small Claims Courts for Massachusetts," 4 *Journal of the American Judicature Society* 183.

—————— (1924a) "Report of the Committee on Small Claims and Conciliation of the ABA," 22 *New York Legal Aid Review* 1.

—————— (1924b) "Small Claims Procedure is Succeeding," 8 *Journal of the American Judicature Society* 1.

_____ (1926) "Simplified Procedure in the Administration of Justice: The Danish Conciliation System," 1926 *Monthly Labor Review* 1 (May).

_____ (1928) "Conciliation and Legal Aid an Opportunity for Pioneering," 136 *Annals of American Academy of Political and Social Science* 80.

Sonsteby, John J. (1932) *Business Methods in Courts*. Chicago: Champlin-Shealey Co.

Spanagel, Robert L. (1939) "Courts—The Justice of the Peace System," 1939 *Wisconsin Law Review* 414.

Spitzer, Steven (1982) "The Dialectics of Formal and Informal Control" in R. Abel (ed.) *The Politics of Informal Justice*, vol. 1: *The American Experience*. New York: Academic Press.

Steele, Eric (1977) "Two Approaches to Contemporary Dispute Behavior and Consumer Problems," 11 *Law & Society Review* 667.

Strasburger, Milton (1915) "A Plea for the Reform of the Inferior Court," 22 *Cases and Comment* 20.

Surrency, Erwin C. (1974) "The Evolution of an Urban Judical System: The Philadelphia Story, 1683 to 1968," 18 *American Journal of Legal History* 95.

Taylor, Frederick W. (1911) *Scientific Management*. New York: Harper & Brothers.

Tomasic, Roman (1980) "Mediation as an Alternative to Adjudication: Rhetoric and Reality in the Neighborhood Justice Movement," Presented at the Annual Meeting of the Law and Society Association and the ISA Research Committee on Sociology of Law, Madison, Wisconsin (June).

United States Department of Justice (1974) *Report of the National Advisory Commission on Criminal Justice Standards and Goals; Courts*. Washington, D.C.: U.S. Department of Justice.

Vance, William (1917) "A Proposed Court of Conciliation," 1 *Minnesota Law Review* 107.

Vanderbilt, Arthur T. (1955) *The Challenge of Law Reform*. Princeton, N.J.: Princeton University Press.

Vanlandingham, Kenneth E. (1964) "The Decline of the Justice of the Peace," 12 *University of Kansas Law Review* 389.

Virtue, Maxine Boord (1953) "Improving the Structure of Courts," 187 *Annals of the American Academy of Political and Social Science* 141.

Volcansek, Mary (1977) "Conventional Wisdom of Court Reform," in L. Berkson, S. Hays, and S. Carbon (eds.) *Managing the State Courts*. St. Paul, Minn.: West Publishing Co.

Walker, Samuel (1977) *A Critical History of Police Reform*. Lexington, Mass.: Lexington.

_____ (1980) *Popular Justice: A History of American Criminal Justice*. New York: Oxford University Press.

Wells, Frederick (1917) "A Justice Factory," 73 *Annals of American Academy of Political and Social Science* 196.

Werner, Percy (1914) "Voluntary Tribunals: A Democratic Ideal," 2 *Virginia Law Review* 276.

_____ (1919) "Voluntary Tribunals: A Democratic Ideal for the Adjudication of Private Differences Which Give Rise to Civil Actions," 3 *Journal of the American Judicature Society* 101.

White, Edward (1972) "From Sociological Jurisprudence to Realism: Jurisprudence and Social Change in Early Twentieth-Century America," 58 *Virginia Law Review* 999.

Wickersham Commission (1974) "Petty Offenses and Inferior Courts," in J. Robertson (ed.) *Rough Justice: Perspectives on Lower Criminal Courts*. Boston: Little, Brown (first published 1931).

Wiebe, Robert H. (1967) *The Search for Order 1877–1920*. New York: Hill and Wang.

Willoughby, W. F. (1929) *Principles of Judicial Administration*. Washington, D.C.: The Brookings Institution.

Wilson, James Q. (1968) *Varieties of Police Behavior*. Cambridge, Mass.: Harvard University Press.

Wolfe, Alan (1977) *The Limits of Legitimacy*. New York: Free Press.

Yngvesson, Barbara and Patricia Hennessey (1975) "Small Claims, Complex Disputes: A Review of the Small Claims Literature," 9 *Law & Society Review* 219.

Zunser, Charles (1926) "The Domestic Relations Courts," 125 *Annals of the American Academy of Political and Social Science* 114.

II

Contemporary Experiments

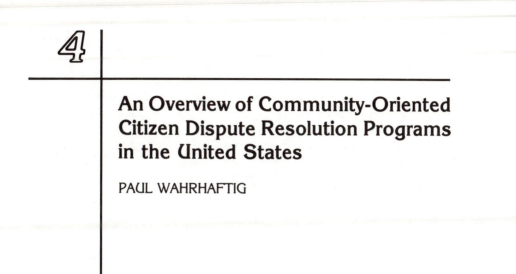

An Overview of Community-Oriented Citizen Dispute Resolution Programs in the United States

PAUL WAHRHAFTIG

INTRODUCTION

In this chapter I seek to provide an overview of citizen dispute resolution programs from a perspective that emphasizes community empowerment. A list of such programs might include hundreds, or only two, depending on how citizen dispute resolution is defined. This introduction explains why I have limited my discussion to the few programs highlighted in this chapter.

I headed the administration of justice programs of the American Friends Service Committee (AFSC) in Pittsburgh from 1969 through 1980. In 1971 the Program Committee of the project was introduced to what we now call citizen dispute resolution by an anthropologist committee member, Michael J. Lowy. After a period of initial skepticism we became excited about Lowy's vision of transplanting to this country the informal tribal moot he had studied in Ghana. The idea of people working together to solve their individual problems within the community, focusing on reconciling the parties rather than on assigning blame, was appealing to a Quaker organization. Also attractive was the idea that the people hearing the dispute, unlike professional judges, would come from the same

75

THE POLITICS OF INFORMAL JUSTICE
Volume 1

neighborhood as the people engaged in the dispute. The mediators, as we called those who listened to the problem, would be familiar with the setting, language, and customs of the neighborhood. It was an exciting idea. But just as we began to feel proud of ourselves for discovering this concept, we found that at least three groups were already using it.

The Community Assistance Project, a small justice program run by the black community in Chester (a city southwest of Philadelphia), had a mediation component: People brought their troubles to a staff member described as "motherly." An imaginative proposal writer called her a "mediator" and received Law Enforcement Assistance Administration (LEAA) funding to underwrite her salary. A few contacts with the court and with justices of the peace assured a more regular flow of cases. But the program never moved beyond that point. When funds were cut and the mediator moved out of town, mediation ended (Wahrhaftig, 1977c).

The American Arbitration Association (AAA) had a few programs in the field. In Philadelphia, AAA handled cases that had been filed in the municipal court and in which the parties had accepted the alternative of arbitration. Hearings were held in AAA's downtown office before trained lay hearing officers from all walks of life and sections of the city. The 4A program (Arbitration as an Alternative) was later placed under the control of the municipal court, was soon emasculated, and withered away (Dunn, 1977). Other American Arbitration Association Programs lasted longer. In early 1979, 4A programs were sprinkled across the country, in such places as Columbus, Akron, and Cleveland, Ohio; Garden City and Rochester, New York; and San Francisco.

We also discovered the Night Prosecutor Program in Columbus, Ohio, which, as its name implies, operated out of the prosecutor's office in the central police station. Private citizen complaints to the police about interpersonal disputes were referred to the project, where an evening or weekend hearing was scheduled. Hearing officers were law students who helped the parties to seek an agreed solution or, if the process broke down, could advise them about filing charges. The Night Prosecutor was chosen as an exemplary program by the National Institute of Law Enforcement and Criminal Justice and retains substantially the same form today (Wahrhaftig and Lowy, 1977).

Thus we discovered at the very beginning of our project that this new mediation service was being packaged in three models that differed in terms of whether it was owned by the community, an existing agency, or the justice system. It became clear to us that more was involved than the efficient delivery of a service. But although we had our biases, we did not have enough information to reject any of those forms as effective vehicles for rendering mediation services. A sensitive director could structure a court, an agency, or a community program in such a way that the participants would feel comfortable, talk freely, and work toward some agreement regarding their future behavior. However, once we analyzed the potential of mediation for community empowerment, we began to see some clear distinction.

We saw that dispute resolution, like any other service, tends to benefit the sponsoring organization. Even if the benefit is only patronage or control of federal funds, AFSC is more comfortable when that is lodged in communities.[1] Further, Community Dispute Resolution (CDR) programs tend to enhance the sponsor's reputation as a problem solver. We were more inclined to enhance the reputation of a community organization than that of a court or outside agency.

We also recognized that the dispute resolution process is capable of generating valuable information. Although the participants perceive their dispute and its solution as unique, in fact it often reflects broader community ills. The organization running a mediation program can draw conclusions from individual disputes about generic problems in its jurisdiction. For example, a number of cases involving vandalism could lead the sponsor to conclude that there is a general juvenile problem in the neighborhood around which resources ought to be mobilized. A court or governmental agency probably would not make this generalized analysis; a nonprofit agency might do so but still not take action. The community affected by the problem, however, is likely not only to make the analysis but also to do something about the problem.

Thus we saw the need to establish a resource center that would encourage community groups to develop citizen dispute resolution programs. The Pittsburgh-based AFSC program informally served that function. The Grassroots Citizen Dispute Resolution Clearinghouse evolved from that base in 1977 as a national center for community groups. I gathered the information in this chapter in my capacity as director of that program. Given this perspective, I offer little information on models sponsored by the justice system but rather focus on agency and, especially, community models.

I am aware that the program analyses presented here rest on insufficient quantitative data. Although LEAA gathers many superficial figures, little significant information is available on dispute resolution projects. Caseload counts cannot tell how a program changes the way in which communities function. Similarly, client-satisfaction questionnaires designed to elicit participant appreciation of the process tell us little about a program's impact on the community. I therefore present an analysis of structure and potential community impact, coupled with impressionistic data. Some of the material comes from records, and some from personal observation. It should serve to indicate the directions in which dispute resolution is moving in this country, as seen from a community-empowerment perspective.

JUSTICE SYSTEM MODELS

The most common dispute resolution projects, as well as the best documented, are those connected with the justice system. The Columbus Night Prosecutor is particularly well known, and in 1974 replication workshops were

[1]See Appendix, "A Note on Community."

held around the country based on that experience.[2] As a result, mediation programs operated out of the prosecutor's office have proliferated, especially in the Midwest.

Court-run programs are probably even more popular, primarily in New Jersey and Florida.[3] Most operate from centralized court buildings, use professional mediators, and serve the entire city or county. In some situations, however, a court-sponsored project can have a neighborhood focus.

The Dorchester Urban Court in Boston was started in 1975 by the Justice Resource Institute (JRI), which is a nonprofit reform agency that, according to the project proposal, seeks to improve the "quality of justice through assisting public agencies in establishing projects like drug diversion, pretrial diversion and service-delivery programs for female offenders." The proposal describes JRI's operating style: "Probably the chief distinguishing feature of JRI's work is its style. JRI is committed to planning and working with those in the system, realizing that reform can be made permanent only if the established bureaucracy feels itself to be part of the process of change" (Justice Resource Institute, 1974: 14).

JRI designed the Urban Court from the start so that it could be incorporated into the budgetary and administrative structure of the Municipal Court in Dorchester, a neighborhood of Boston, and this has since occurred. The Urban Court occupies a store front, uses community mediators, and has a neighborhood advisory committee. But despite these community trappings, control is vested in the chief judge.

However informal and folksy justice system programs may appear, it is clear that they do not advance community empowerment but rather serve the needs of the justice system. These include the orderly and efficient processing of cases and the freeing of resources to handle cases the system defines as serious. Thus Dorchester was able to operate on a community scale only because Boston still has a highly decentralized judicial system. Virtually all other programs sponsored by the justice system serve cases from the entire jurisdiction of the relevant court or grouping of courts—a constituency that is generally too large to have a sense of ownership of the program. For example, the Neighborhood Justice Center (NJC) in Atlanta was established by an "independent" nonprofit agency that was heavily court dominated. It opened in a neighborhood locale with a mandate to develop a program oriented to that neighborhood. But referrals to the program came from courts and police throughout the city of Atlanta. By late 1979 it was receiving 200–300 cases a month. Thus the Atlanta NJC no longer has any connection to the neighborhood in which it is located and receives very few local cases. It is a citywide agency. The probable reason for this development is that justice agencies are not organized to differentiate between cases on the basis of neighborhoods or communities. Some might even argue that such differentiation would

[2]See U.S. Department of Justice (1974) NILECJ (1974), and McGillis and Mullen (1977).
[3]See Office of the State Courts Administrator, Florida (1979).

present equal protection problems. The goal of the justice system is not to enhance community decision making but to allow courts throughout the system to unload categories of cases.

Although Dorchester avoided this problem because of the unique structure of the Boston courts, it shares other problems with justice system programs. For instance, Felstiner and Williams (1978) have observed that sponsorship by the courts may affect the way in which mediators define the real parties in the dispute. Because court records generally list two parties—a complainant and an accused, a plaintiff and a defendant—the whole bureaucratic structure encourages a finding and report to the court in terms of those parties. Thus, in a case in which the dispute was actually between a party and a witness, the mediators dismissed the witness as irrelevant and did not involve him in the process of building a consensus. Their blinders allowed them to handle the problem only as it was defined in court papers.

Finally, the message these programs proclaim to the public is unchanged: If you have a problem that you can not cope with by yourself, bring it to your local justice system (police, prosecutor, or court), and they will handle it. The program may be packaged more informally and staffed by people who speak the same dialect as you, but you are still dependent on the resources of the state.

AGENCY MODEL

An agency program that began with an emphasis upon community is the Institute for Mediation and Conflict Resolution (IMCR) Dispute Center in Manhattan. The idea came from two women, Ann Weisbrod and Sandi (Freinberg) Tamid, who had become frustrated in trying to work for reform within the New York City Department of Corrections. Having learned about citizen dispute resolution from the American Friends Service Committee, they quit their jobs, developed a proposal, and searched for an appropriate agency sponsor. This they found in the IMCR, a private, nonprofit agency with a sound reputation for adapting labor mediation to deal with various forms of community conflict.

Their object was to create a "community-involved" program. They began, however, by organizing from the top down, eliciting the cooperation of the police and courts, and then, using demographic and judicial data, selecting their pilot neighborhood—two police precincts on the edge of Harlem. Then followed the lengthy process of selling the idea to the community and recruiting and training community volunteer mediators.

The program opened in a converted brownstone in Harlem. I visited it soon afterwards, early in 1975, and observed:

A story best illustrates the difference between this community mediation program and the traditional criminal justice system. Sandi Freinberg came home from working her 1 to 9 plus PM shift at the center greatly wrought up. An attempt at mediation of a crucial case had not worked and she felt that one of the reasons was that the atmosphere for the parties was not quite right. Waiting areas are too congested. There is a lot of chaotic movement of mediators, staff and parties in and out of rooms, up and down stairs, and in general the parties were not made to feel properly at ease. [In a sleepless night she developed a solution] which involved moving her office upstairs, which would require her to climb more stairs per day than she would have liked [Wahrhaftig, 1977a].

That emphasis upon keeping the parties at ease in a homelike setting contrasts markedly with what I observed upon revisiting the center in the spring of 1979. It is now run by a second-generation staff in a new location. The Manhattan center (there is also one in Brooklyn) outgrew the old brownstone and relocated in a large building in Harlem that apparently houses many community service agencies. The building looks and feels like the old charity hospital it used to be, and whose name it still bears. One enters past a glassed-in receptionist and takes a cranky elevator to the fourth floor, where an IMCR receptionist sits behind a small desk in the hall. To the right the hall is lined on both sides with plastic chairs on which the disputants sit and wait. There are a number of bare hearing rooms, each painted in institutional pastel colors, with a table and a few chairs. The program now resembles any other big-city charity.

In 1978 the IMCR center handled 2225 cases, of which all but 336 were referred by a criminal justice agency. The cases came from everywhere in Manhattan, and the center extended its jurisdiction to the entire city of New York in June 1979. There are fifty-four volunteer mediators, of whom about thirty-one are active; they receive a nominal stipend that covers only expenses. Each mediator handles an average of 75 cases per year. After four years of funding by the Law Enforcement Assistance Administration the center was incorporated into the New York City budget under the Office of the Mayor. It was immediately required to reduce staff and services.

I asked the director, William Madison, how the community (i. e., Harlem) would be different if the program folded. He answered that the situation would revert to exactly what it had been before IMCR started. There would be chaos in the courts and nowhere for people to find help with conflict resolution. George Nicolau, IMCR vice-president, responded similarly. He pointed out that the center's mission was not to change the way in which a community works but to provide a more humane city service. One might ask what this service will look like in a few years when there are more cutbacks and a civil-service mentality sets in.

A closer look at the IMCR center gives some indication why it, like most agency programs, has not significantly changed the way in which the community functions. In making these comments, I do not mean to denigrate the integrity of IMCR staff or mediators. They are committed people with good insight into the problems they handle and appear to be providing a useful service. My point is rather that the imperatives of the agency structure work against them.

What are the imperatives that prevent an agency-structured mediation center from responding to the disputes as those are defined by neighborhood people and from bringing about a change in the way communities function? First, the program was never "owned" by the community. The idea was developed by outsiders—in this case by people working within the criminal justice system. They designed it on the basis of their perceptions of neighborhood problems, drawn from the cases that surface in courts, police stations, and prosecutors' offices. The package was "sold" first to the criminal justice system, and only then to the community. IMCR was particularly effective in securing community involvement. George Nicolau was the administrator of New York City's Economic Opportunity Agency before he came to IMCR and thus had good contacts with most poverty and social action agencies in the target area. But community people were never involved in the definition of the problems to be addressed or the design of the program. Their input was sought only as participants.

By adopting a perspective that emphasized court reform, IMCR was able to obtain funding for four years from the Law Enforcement Assistance Administration. LEAA is not concerned with either community development or helping people handle disputes that are not likely to burden the courts. Hence, from the beginning IMCR was under pressure to justify its existence to LEAA in terms of the number of cases processed and the impact on the court system. Therefore, although the program was originally designed to serve a neighborhood, it soon turned out that two precincts in Harlem did not generate enough cases to satisfy the criteria of LEAA: It was not cost effective.

The easiest way to increase both caseload and impact on the court system is to make two closely related changes. First, expand geographic jurisdiction. Therefore, the program began handling disputes from all over Manhattan. Second, invoke the help of the criminal justice system. Since word of mouth and community organizing cannot spread the word and stimulate people throughout the city to use the program voluntarily, IMCR concentrated on increasing referrals from many levels of the court system. Permanent staff are now located wherever cases come into the courts. This increased reliance on court referrals further diminishes the community orientation of the program. Centralized courts, as we have seen, are not structured to differentiate between cases by neighborhood. Hence a program dependent on court referrals, like a program sponsored by the court, will inevitably receive cases from throughout the court's geographic jurisdiction.

Thus IMCR became a borough-wide program, and now that it has city funding, it is citywide. Only 10.6 percent of its cases come from the community, and even these so-called walk-ins include referrals from other social service agencies, particularly those in the same building. It is clear, then—and readily acknowledged by IMCR—that it is no longer a neighborhood program.

Orientation toward servicing a court influences process within the program.

The complaint comes to the program only after first going to a justice system agency and then being referred. How does the program get the respondent to appear? Although a few disputants may jump at the chance to talk about their problems, most do not. Absent a reliable neighborhood grapevine supporting the project—such as local leaders doing some gentle persuading—IMCR has only two alternatives. Staff time can be spent on the telephone telling the respondent about the benefits of mediation. Or, better still, the respondent can be persuaded by letter. What will best convince a person to show up across town at an unfamiliar agency? The threat of court action will. The respondent therefore receives a letter on the district attorney's stationery indicating that charges have been filed or will be filed and the respondent will be summoned to court unless he appears at IMCR.

Hence the presence of one party is at least partly attributable to the impression that IMCR's ties with the court threaten some sort of sanction. Upon arrival the parties sign an agreement submitting the case to arbitration which clearly states that if they do not agree, the hearing panel can impose a decision. That option is seldom exercised, but its existence presumably has some effect. Finally, in any referral from a court, charges have already been filed and remain pending until the outcome of the hearing, or even afterwards.

The coercion that anticipates and accompanies the hearing continues when it is over. The "arbitration award" is legally enforceable, although the process is so cumbersome and illsuited to many resolutions that legal action is rarely taken. For example, how would a court enforce an arbitration award requiring one person to play his stereo more quietly and the other to use civil language in addressing the neighbors? However, in a case involving an agreement to make restitution or pay damages, enforcement can be a realistic threat. As a matter of policy, IMCR requests the court to maintain jurisdiction until the respondent has paid off his obligation. William Madison, IMCR Manhattan program director, feels that the threat of returning the case to criminal court is an essential tool in making sure that "awards," as they are called, are complied with.

The coercion involved in the process creates a central problem. One argument for informal dispute settlement is that a mediator who knows the parties, their situation, and the environment is better suited to help them resolve their problems. Program proposals often contrast such an approach with judicial procedures, where a judge hears the cases of people who differ greatly from him in age, gender, education, occupation, race, and culture. As soon as the mediator is given any significant power, however, citizens as well as lawyers balk at using a hearing officer who might be biased. That person is required to be neutral, which is equated with ignorance. Hence any IMCR mediator with direct personal or neighborhood ties to either party is disqualified.

IMCR offers a valuable service that is more humane than the existing court system. But what does the person in the street learn—particularly those in the original Harlem target area? If one has a problem, one seeks a solution from the relevant governmental agency. No one discovers that indigenous community structures or neighbors are useful resources. Even if one's neighbor is a mediator—and IMCR has trained many qualified mediators who live and function in the target neighborhood—one has no access to that neighbor except through existing agency and court channels. By insisting that hearing panelists be neutral and possess no ties to the parties, IMCR prevents people from discovering those neighbors who might be useful mediators.

It is possible, indeed probable, that IMCR mediators use the insight gained from their training and mediation practice in their everyday lives, with the result that their community leadership skills are enhanced. But this is an unplanned, incidental benefit of the program. It happens despite the structure and was not even mentioned by the leadership when I asked what would be different in the community if IMCR disappeared tomorrow.

In short, a program conceived and implemented by an agency is likely to reinforce dependency on agencies as the appropriate mechanisms for handling problems. This is so whether the sponsoring agency is IMCR, the American Arbitration Association, or the Neighborhood Justice Center of Atlanta, Inc.[4]

Is it impossible for an agency-based program to engage in community building? None has done so thus far. One shows some potential, but since the project staff do not share my community perspective, this potential is likely to remain unfulfilled. The Community Mediation Center, (CMC) in Suffolk County, Long Island, is one of the first mediation programs in a suburban setting. Like IMCR, it began with top-down planning. The idea was conceived by a young lawyer, Robert Saperstein, who was active with a justice reform group and became the director of the new program. The assistant director, Ernie Odom, is a former trainer with a narcotics rehabilitation program. They arranged for the YMCA to be the nominal recipient of their LEAA grant and soon developed an independent nonprofit corporation to oversee the program, with a board that includes mediators and blue-ribbon community leadership.

Because a suburban area was thought to be ill suited to a "neighborhood" program, there originally was no such focus. CMC offered to mediate cases that arose anywhere in Suffolk County, using a centralized location in an office building. Mediators are essentially volunteers and receive a stipend of ten dollars

---

[4]In this chapter I have omitted extensive discussion of the various American Arbitration Association programs because their definition of *community* is so much broader than that of IMCR. Whereas IMCR initially concentrated on a geographically bounded neighborhood, from which it drew its mediators, AAA centers tend to be located downtown and to have citywide or county-wide jurisdiction. Mediators are "community" people only in the sense that they are not lawyers, but they are more likely to be affluent professionals than ghetto residents. My assessment of the extent to which IMCR empowers courts, agencies, or community people would also apply to AAA programs, where the influence of the community served is considerably weaker.

per hearing. They were recruited through newspaper, radio, and television announcements.[5] The first generation of mediators was trained by IMCR, and subsequent generations by the program itself.

Although the program receives most of its cases from the justice system, it is more sensitive than IMCR-Manhattan is to issues of coercion. For instance, the program began by writing respondents on the district attorney's letterhead but soon abandoned that practice. The current letter warns that a charge may be filed or processed if the respondent fails to participate, but it does not use the official stationery since it seeks to avoid giving the appearance of being linked to a court.

Only mediation is used. Arbitration, in which the parties empower a third person to make a binding decision, was seen as too coercive. The program does not keep charges open to force compliance. If a case is referred from court and a hearing successfully completed, CMC reports only that fact to the court. The program relies on the ability of the parties to arrive at their own solution by discovering a mutual interest, which then provides the incentive to carry out the agreement.

Because the caseload of CMC, unlike that of IMCR, tends to involve disputes over children and dogs, awards rarely require the payment of damages. Showing more consideration toward one's neighbor or spouse and communicating directly are frequent elements of an agreement. Even in those few cases where resitiution in involved the court does not retain jurisdiction. The parties are informed that the agreement between them is a legally enforceable contract. The program serves as an intermediary in collecting the funds and reminding the party who falls behind in payments. Odom could think of only one case in which payment was not made: The debtor was on drugs and incapable of paying.

In 1978 the Mediation Center opened up two satellite hearing locations, each in a township. Although intake is still centralized and dominated by court referrals, hearings are held in the township when parties from that area are involved. Mediators from that township are used whenever possible, although they are disqualified if they know the parties.

Suppose the center took the additional step of creating advisory committees for each of its decentralized centers, through which to publicize the program in those townships. These centers could then encourage township residents to submit cases directly, could process them locally, and then, in monthly meetings, could discuss the kinds of problems revealed in the hearings. Using that information, they could alert other township organizations to potential problem areas. Each township might be allowed to modify its center to fit local needs while still servicing court-referred cases allocated by the central office. The Centers then might evolve into real neighborhood programs.

---

[5]The mediators mirrored the demographic composition of both the county population and the CMC clientele—mostly middle class, but with a few poor and a few very rich.

CMC staff members are sensitive to other uses for mediation. They are training school authorities to employ mediation in handling vandalism and discipline problems, and some industries have sought their assistance with personnel issues. In its first newsletter CMC highlighted the experiences of one volunteer mediator who applied her skills at her workplace and in voluntary associations.

Although the styles of CMC and IMCR may differ, the general structure is the same. The message remains: Look to the agency for help in resolving problems. Nevertheless, CMC does legitimate mediation as a technique to be used at school, in industry, and in private associations.

Can an agency-based program be a mechanism for community fact-finding? There are a few mediation centers run by human relations commissions that would seem to be ideal for this purpose. Nevertheless, programs sponsored by human relations commissions in Santa Clara County, California, and Portland, Oregon, see themselves solely as a service to individual disputants. Both programs train their mediators to be humble and to recognize that they cannot change the universe. Neither acknowledges that while mediators are performing their valuable role the information they acquire about community problems could be channeled to their parent organizations, which style themselves as action-oriented agencies.

COMMUNITY MODELS

Community-based dispute resolution programs are very much in the minority. It appears to be easier to manipulate bureaucracies and obtain outside funding than to engage in the slow and arduous task of community organizing, using volunteers and relying on minimal funding. The community models that do exist, however, can be divided into three categories, which I will label grass roots, homespun, and middle class dominated.

Middle Class Dominated

The most influential low-budget, middle-class-dominated community program is the Community Dispute Settlement Service of the Friends Suburban Project (FSP) in Delaware County, a suburban–rural setting outside of Philadelphia with a population of 583,000 persons. The roots of the project must be traced through its parent organization, Friends Suburban Project, which was founded soon after black power advocates made it clear to liberal whites that the proper role of the latter was in reforming their own community. The Friends had a project house in Chester, a city near Philadelphia with a substantial poor black population. Blacks seized the building, and the Quakers eventually acquiesced, turning it over to black community control. FSP was then founded in the suburbs and soon concentrated on the criminal justice system. Members became actively involved in court-watching and later engaged in direct action to improve conditions. FSP educated suburban whites and persuaded them to make their property available to a black community organization in Chester so that it could be used as collateral for bail bonds. FSP also founded a Juvenile Advocate group to work with youth in trouble and investigated cases in which citizens had been attacked by police dogs. In 1975 FSP began to explore the concept of mediation, having defined the need through their court-watching project. They were inspired by both the Community Assistance Project (CAP) mediation program in Chester (the same agency that managed the bail fund) and information garnered from the American Friends Service Committee.

In early deliberations, FSP talked of training some of its own liberal white constituency and as many community people as they could reach through the county. They envisioned a network of volunteers and mediation sites linked by a centralized telephone in the FSP office that people could call for assistance. I label this original program "liberal" because it did not envision social structural change but sought to empower residents by exposing them to a better way of problem solving. People whose cases were mediated, as well as the mediators, would learn new skills, which they would then use in everyday life.

The network of mediators turned out to be less broad-based than originally envisioned. Ninety-five percent are white, and most are women, fairly well-off and well educated. While although my initial impression was that this project involved middle-class people helping working-class people resolve their disputes, Deborah Baskin, who is compiling data or the project for her doctoral dissertation at the University of Pennsylvania and who supplied the information in this section, desputes that observation, as do project staff members. They point out that 95 percent of the disputants are also white and tend to be fairly affluent, if less educated than the mediators. The distinction between mediators and disputants, then, is based not on income level but on education and possibly income source.

Cases come from a variety of sources: 55 percent from the court system, frequently the District Justice's Court, 33 percent from other agencies, and 12 percent "self" referrals, many in response to fliers posted in laundromats and supermarkets. The staff stresses that participation is voluntary, even in cases referred from the criminal justice system.

Case load is low. In the eighteen months between March 1977 and October 1979, 160 cases were referred. Many were resolved at intake. Only 44 percent went to a hearing. It is hard to measure the cost effectiveness of the project since paid staff members divide their time between running the mediation project, doing outside training, and running other FSP activities. They estimate annual costs to be around $3500. Perhaps a better index is that the twenty-one mediators have enough work to feel involved but not overwhelmed.

The program strongly stresses informality, communication, and voluntariness. Court jurisdiction is not retained. If restitution is promised but not paid, the defaulting party will be telephoned and the matter talked out. A second session might be scheduled to get at the root of the restitution problem. Agreements always include some mechanism for the parties to discuss disputes that may arise in the future.

When asked to differentiate their program from an agency model, CDS staff responded with four criteria. CDS uses mediation rather than arbitration. Mediation occurs at sites within the community in which the dispute takes place. The hearing is scheduled at a time agreed to by the parties rather than at one imposed by the program. Finally, the agreement is reached through consensus and is written in the parties' own words. Each of these characteristics can be found, alone or in combination, in many agency models. They reflect the sensitivity of FSP staff rather than structural differences. In fact, though the staff is loathe to admit it, CDS is really an agency model. Certainly, that the program need not account to LEAA helps keep it small, informal, and low key. But the question remains: Is the community changed by CDS? The message to the potential user is still that if your own coping skills are inadequate to the situation, you should look to an agency outside of your immediate community.

Does this program have any greater long-term potential? FSP staff agree that their original vision of empowering people to solve their own problems, by teaching them communication skills is not having much impact. They are therefore working with a small group in Landsdown to set up a storefront mediation center that will be run by a local steering committee. It is unclear, however, whether the program will be run by the community served or by a more educated elite.

A second way a community mediation program can promote change is to help the sponsoring agency—in this case the Friends Suburban Project—to document community ills. FSP can then develop new projects or build coalitions around these issues. The FSP orientation and structure would seem ideal for this approach, and staff say it happens, though they offer few concrete examples. Furthermore, they have been struggling with the extent to which the requirements of neutral mediators and confidentiality conflict with follow-up social action. If people identify Citizen Dispute Settlement with Friends Suburban Project, does FSP advocacy undermine the ability of CDS to mediate?

Perhaps the major contribution of FSP to dispute resolution is training other groups in mediation techniques.[6] They assisted a Latino center in the county and have instructed groups in Syracuse and Schenectady, New York, and

---

[6]Acknowledging its Quaker roots, the Community Dispute Settlement Service of FSP in mid-1979 began to offer its services to other Quaker institutions in the hope that mediation skills would help those organizations resolve some of the issues that divide them.

Wilmington, Delaware, that have modeled their programs upon FSP. A Kalamazoo, Michigan, program was also inspired by FSP, although its mediators were trained elsewhere.

I visited the New York programs and found them to have problems similar to those of FSP in its early stages. They are funded by tiny grants—$2000-$3000— from Quaker and church groups. Their directors receive nominal salaries or are CETA workers. They have been largely unsuccessful in enlisting minority participation in their programs and feel uneasy about that. Very few people respond when they solicit cases directly from the community. Criminal justice officials do not have much confidence in small citizen groups and are reluctant to refer cases. Caseload is so low that mediators are frustrated at their inactivity. A similar, though unrelated, project in Chapel Hill, North Carolina, had comparable problems in its first year.

All these programs feel the need for redirection. Some see their first priority as the building of a community base, but no one has the time to invest in such a task. Creating a sense of real community ownership of a program is an exceedingly difficult job. But without the will or the resources to do this, these programs are doomed either to wither away for lack of a sufficient demand for their services or to become dependent on receiving referrals from courts and agencies.

Grass Roots

Some projects have been able to establish a community base on which to build. The most prominent grass roots model of dispute resolution is the Community Boards Program in San Francisco. Since it was planned from the beginning as an experiment in community empowerment, this discussion will focus on it.

But first another well-publicized "grass roots" effort should also be noted. The Neighborhood Justice Center (NJC) in Venice, Los Angeles, is one of three such centers established by the Justice Department in 1977 as alternative pilot projects for a possible nationwide system. Although the Kansas City NJC was viewed as an extension of the criminal justice system, and the Atlanta NJC as a hybrid— location in the community but with strong court sponsorship—Venice was seen as the grass roots program.

I wonder whether Venice might more accurately be called a strawman. Conversations with people associated with the Neighborhood Justice Center effort have convinced me that Attorney General Griffin Bell saw the NJCs as an extension of court services. Even in his public comments (1977a) he defined the problem as increasing access to justice rather than as returning responsibility for dispute settlement to the community.

In many disputes, it costs too much and takes too long to go to court. We are setting up three experimental Neighborhood Justice Centers to develop a mechanism that will provide access to justice for people who are now shut out and to provide relief to our overburdened courts by diverting matters that do not require a full court proceeding.

Bell apparently did not see any role for the community in designing the Neighborhood Justice Centers: "The centers would be developed as pilot projects through the joint efforts of local government, the courts and the bar" (1977b). A grass roots model was included only after protests by community-oriented people. But Venice, when established, was given neither the support nor the resources necessary to become a neighborhood institution.

The Venice NJC was organized from the top down. It was sponsored by the Los Angeles County Bar Association, which still controls its board of directors. Site selection was primarily in the hands of the board. Only later was the community involved in implementing the program. The support of community leaders was solicited, and some became board members. They, in turn, recommended local candidates as mediators and staff. Although the director and research staff do not reside in the Venice–Mar Vista area, many of the front-line staff do. The program has held fiestas, participated in community organizations, and demonstrated mediation through role-playing in order to increase community awareness of the center.

The criteria used to evaluate NJCs reflect their orientation toward the courts (Sheppard *et al.*, 1979). Because this grass roots model generates fewer hearings than the two NJCs that are more directly subordinated to courts, it looks to the evaluators like a more questionable investment. If criteria more related to community development were used, the Venice program might be rated higher. As re-funding of the Venice center has become uncertain, pressure has built to increase its caseload. Originally, all cases were to be referred from the community or from community agencies; now, however, NJC staff are stationed in Small Claims Court in order to identify cases. Even though staff are strongly oriented toward the community, they are constantly under contradictory pressures from the Justice Department.

The San Francisco Community Board Program (CBP), on the other hand, has been able to develop a community model without suffering some of these tensions. Like most of the programs reviewed, Community Boards began as the brain child of someone outside the community who was involved in the criminal justice system. Ray Shonholtz developed the idea while he was clinical associate at the University of San Francisco Law School. From the beginning he saw it as a community-based alternative to the justice system, one in which citizens resolve disputes and complaints in a responsible way. He proposed the CBP as a means by which community people could assess and document structural problems through their experiences in helping to resolve what initially are identified as individual conflicts. Shonholtz has been able to raise funds from private sources.

The program was organized from the bottom up with community people involved in decision making from the beginning. Neighborhoods were not selected on the basis of crime data and the like, although these were considered. Instead, meetings were held in various neighborhoods to sound out reactions to the concept of mediation. The first neighborhood Visitacion Valley, was chosen in 1976. It contains 5000 households with a diverse racial mix of whites, blacks, Latinos, and Asian-Americans, ranging from poor to middle class. Bernal Heights was selected as a second site in December 1977. Two others were chosen in April 1979.

The next step was to involve the community in program planning. Planning committees that included local people modified Shonholtz's original model to increase community involvement. Then followed a lengthy process of building a community base. Virtually every organization, business, and church in the target area was visited. The program was explained and support solicited. Living-room meetings spread the word further. Finally, "panelists" were selected at open neighborhood meetings, usually held in churches, school auditoriums, or community centers. Although CBP literature refers to this selection process as "elections," that appears to be an idealization. In fact, most of the first-generation panelists were drawn into CBP during the organizing period. One might therefore say that they volunteered but that their selection was subsequently ratified by open community meetings.

Since the project does more than simply help individuals to solve their problems, its structure and the function of the panelists differ markedly from those found in an agency program. Panelists sit in groups of three to five to maximize the number of people involved in working out a problem. Hearings are open to the public to enable people to understand what is happening in the neighborhood, although the sessions are not heavily attended. The panelists also meet as a group and serve as a neighborhood steering committee to oversee the program. They discuss the cases they have heard and identify common neighborhood problems. Members of the Visitacion Valley panel were invited to attend a neighborhood coalition meeting to present their views on local problems in light of their experience as mediators. Furthermore, the coalition recognized the value of the panelists' mediation skills by asking them to run small-group workshops at the coalition meeting.

Each CBP neighborhood has a staff of four, which will be reduced to three when the program is stabilized. A central downtown office provides the neighborhood centers with administrative, fund-raising, and public relations skills. The program has a board of directors that includes neighborhood representatives, but the neighborhood panels are given as much autonomy as possible.

CBP seeks to handle cases before they enter the criminal justice system. Its role is preventive. It assumes there are many disputes or problems that are known to friends, neighbors, and school counselors but that are not reported to the authorities until the situation becomes intolerable. The 1978 case log for Visitacion Valley shows that most referrals originated outside the criminal justice system: Leaflets, security guards, school counselors, newsletters, CBP panel members, and other such sources appear frequently. No case is accepted if a warrant or a complaint has been served.

That all hearings are open may be one reason why Community Boards do not attract many disputes between intimates, although such cases are common in other projects. CBP is more likely to handle loitering, fence disputes, school fights, shoplifting from the local mom-and-pop grocery store, and housing problems. CBP hearings tend to involve more parties than do those in other projects since disputes, if fully explored, usually involve clusters of people and not just the two original disputants.

I saw one case involving a housing association president who complained that an owner had not boarded up a burned-out, abandoned house. The latter responded that there were many fires in the subdivision. A member of the audience then produced the missing link between this case and the broader problem. She corroborated the frequency of fires and pointed out that the main problem was the substandard electrical wiring installed by the housing developer twenty years earlier, and she listed its defects. The ensuing conversation explored the role the housing association should take in relation to the larger problem. This redirection of the discussion was strongly supported by one of the panelists, who lives in the subdivision. No specific solution was proposed at the hearing, but the community nature of the problem was acknowledged and the housing association was designated as the appropriate organization to work on it.

Community involvement also helps to explain how CBP, which is so detached from the criminal justice system, persuades respondents to appear. Shonholtz (1977) attributes this to "the involvement of neighborhood-oriented people in the application of personal and collective approval and disapproval mechanisms, as the basis for encouraging people to come to the Community Board, follow through in the Board process, and abide by the Board resolutions."

The use of a carefully constructed community network is illustrated in a case where staff were ultimately unsuccessful in getting one party to appear. An old man fed pigeons from his back porch, an act he felt to be a religious obligation. Neighbors suffered significant property damage from the bird droppings. CBP staff feared that an armed confrontation was near and tried to get the pigeon feeder to participate in a hearing. They visited him once in his home and returned a second time, but he remained adamant. Believing the case to be important, staff learned which church he attended and asked his pastor, a CBP supporter, to intercede. When that failed they went to the Kiwanis lodge, in which he was very active, and its leadership tried to persuade him to attend. After that, the staff felt they had run out of options. The man's reluctance may have been related to his conviction that God had directed him to feed the pigeons. Community pressures are more likely to work when their object is more mundane.

Information about cases of general interest, community problems, and Community Board developments is published in *Community Board News*, which now has a circulation of approximately 22,000. Case volume was very low in the first six months of operation but has begun to pick up. By early 1979 hearings were frequent. Shonholtz stresses the enormous amount of work necessary to create a sense of community ownership sufficient to motivate people to use the project.

Community Boards, then, exemplify the successful effort of a professional to graft the idea of dispute resolution onto a community base. A sense of pride and ownership has developed, and community people have begun to use the program to attack larger issues.

Are there any problems? Two that are closely intertwined may arise soon. First, what happens when the initial source of money dries up? Foundation support was generous when the program began, but the model needs a continuing subsidy of approximately $145,000 per year per neighborhood. No community can generate that amount by itself. Will government fund the boards? That is apparently the hope of CBP staff, who are supporting state and national legislation to fund dispute resolution programs. Second, is government funding consistent with community empowerment, or will CBP find itself under pressure to count heads and process cases in the most "cost effective" way? The future may tell.

What if funding simply disappears? CBP neighborhoods would probably be in a better position than IMCR neighborhoods to regroup and carry on the project. All CBP mediators live in the neighborhood and are known in that role to many neighbors since the process is local and open. Cases always came from the neighborhood and therefore could be processed at least in the interim, by some local agency. Thus, even in the worst situation it is possible that CBP has already brought about lasting change in the way the neighborhood functions.[7]

Had it recruited its panelists by other criteria, CBP might leave a more valuable legacy of dispute processing institutions if funding were eliminated. CBP

[7]When I offer this analysis of what happens when the money runs out, I am generally accused of negativism and of undermining the cause. But in fact I am being realistic. However committed one is to CDR, it is essential to realize that others are equally committed to their own service-rendering, change-oriented, money-saving reforms, and new competitors for the limited funds will arise in the future. CDR advocates should fight for the funds they need but simultaneously plan for the survival of their programs should funding fail. Seymour B. Sarason urges that we look at networks of people and agencies as economic resources for program ideas (e.g., Sarason *et al.*, 1977).

organizers apparently assumed when they began that no indigenous dispute solving institutions existed between the efforts of random individuals and those of formalized agencies. Although this hypothesis may be correct, it was never tested empirically. It is certainly just as plausible that many neighborhood people were already settling disputes in their roles as block association leaders, involved parents, or politicians. Rather than to ask panelists to volunteer or agencies to nominate them, CBP might have tried to identify and involve indigenous problem solvers. Those who volunteered may in fact have been indigenous problem solvers, but no one bothered to find out.

Had CBP employed the strategy just described, it might have taken less time to persuade people to bring their cases to this newfangled project. Community residents would be approaching someone they already knew as a mediator, and that person's skills would be improved. Then, if the funding ended, the community would not have to graft the remnants of the program onto preexisting community structures. This strategy has been tried in Pittsburgh.

Homespun

Community Association for Mediation (CAM) in Pittsburgh has attempted to build the concepts of mediation and community growth found in CBP directly into the fabric of a black neighborhood. Unlike most community dispute resolution project organizers, Gloria Patterson, its originator, is an active community worker in the target area. She was involved in most volunteer groups in her neighborhood and had built a wide range of contacts before becoming a staff member of the AFSC Justice Program. While serving with the latter, she learned about mediation and dispute resolution programs around the country, particularly Community Boards.

Lacking financial backing, she simply identified those people in her community whom she already knew to be problem solvers: agency paraprofessionals, block club leaders, involved parents, and social workers. They met informally in Patterson's home over dinner and talked about mediation. Some discovered that this fancy new label simply described what they were doing already. They saw a need for additional training to enhance their skills and designed a program of continuing education. Concurrently, CAM notified and met with existing community leaders to inform them of the new project. Thus they were able to avoid jurisdictional jealousy and to solicit cooperation.

Although Patterson had envisioned taking the further step of establishing a center, the informal group disagreed. To do this would require a grant, and the grantor would demand reports and records. The group felt that "our people have been recorded and studied enough already." No center was established. Community Association for Mediation persists as a network of people who completed training together. They mediate disputes that come to them primarily through their individual networks of jobs and then meet together biweekly to discuss their experiences. Through occasional radio interviews and similar media exposure their central telephone number is disseminated, but the calls that result represent a distinct minority of the cases.

In the summer of 1979 CAM sought to expand its network. A group of residents in a housing development interviewed their neighbors about the kinds of disputes that occurred and asked to whom they would turn for assistance if they were involved in such a "fuss." CAM hopes to gather better information about what kinds of fusses bother people and whom to involve as additional problem solvers.

It is virtually impossible for an outsider to make any reliable observations about how CAM works. No records are kept. Mediation does not take place in a definable location or at a preappointed time. Members mediate in homes, bars, on the telephone—anywhere and any time. If the program works as I have described it, many of the goals of Community Boards may also be achieved by CAM. The unresolved disputes that fester in the gap between informal dispute resolution resources and formal agencies are handled, and the skills of indigenous mediators are enhanced. Community growth is fostered at the biweekly meetings of mediators, which discuss not only the effectiveness of mediation techniques but also the substantive problems encountered. Mediators are linked with most of the agencies in the target area, so that the information can be channeled to an appropriate body when intervention is necessary. They are part of nonagency community networks that can be mobilized. Thus, in a case that initially involved a confrontation between a neighbor and a young single mother who had left her eighteen-month-old child at home unattended, CAM members were able to integrate the mother with others on her block who could watch her child while she ran down to the grocery store.

CAM thus quietly operates to build a community. It is probably unknown to most people in the local criminal justice system and will never have a demonstrable impact on their caseload. Can it be copied? Is it even capable of surviving in its unfunded ad hoc form? Patterson was thoroughly indoctrinated in mediation through her AFSC employment, but other community activists could also obtain the necessary training. AFSC paid her salary during part of the organizing period; at other stages she received only unemployment insurance. But what will happen if she gets a regular job that takes her out of the neighborhood eight hours a day? Patterson maintains that CAM is designed to be an after-hours operation: All meetings and business take place after work. It therefore should continue.

The conditions that will determine CAM's survival are different from those of funded programs. As long as people see CAM members as viable problem solvers, they will bring cases to them. As long as CAM members feel their efforts are worth while, they will continue to mediate. The cost is volunteer effort.

When the payoff, in terms of dispute settlement and community development, is felt to be less than that cost, CAM will fail. If these are kept in balance, CAM has a chance of survival.

CONCLUSION

This overview of citizen dispute resolution acitvities in the United States is written from a community-empowerment perspective. Most CDR programs now in operation are designed as adjuncts to the existing justice system. Therefore, although they are more informal and humanistic, they preserve the existing relationship between the communities served and the justice system.

A number of agency-sponsored programs exist. They also tend to serve the ends of, and to benefit, their sponsors. Citizens are encouraged to rely on agencies, rather than on the justice system, to solve their problems, and a network of agencies is often strengthened through the development of an inter-locking referral system.

Community-based programs are rare since they require extensive preliminary effort. Few community organizers are able to obtain the resources, both money and people, to perform that task. CDR programs that are truly operated by the community served would appear to have great potential for legitimating and strengthening local problem-solving resources. But it is too early to assess the long range impact of CDR programs on community structure, particularly in light of the meager resources available.

APPENDIX: A NOTE ON COMMUNITY

In this chapter I have avoided defining *community*. It is no easier for those involved in CDR programs to define *community* than it is for criminal justice personnel to define *justice*. In either case the word is a shorthand that allows people of diverse interests to cooperate even though their ultimate goals may differ.

Criminal justice planners often use *community* to mean an identifiable geographical neighborhood that can be outlined on a map. Social action groups such as the American Friends Service Committee tend to use a more political definition: a group of citizens who are oppressed or powerless, such as an ethnic minority community. Another approach is to identify a group of people linked by a network of personal relationships. Such a community might, but need not, be bounded geographically or ethnically.

For example, the Community Assistance Project in Chester, Pennsylvania, covered an identifiable geographical community—one that would be acceptable to courts and LEAA. But the program was actually geared to that half of the approximately 50,000 Chester residents who are black; hence it served a minority community, whose bail project could be supported by Friends Suburban Project. This latter community was so tightly knit that staff people either knew, or knew someone who knew, every black person in the city. This generated remarkable community support for CAP. For instance, when someone stole the program's electric typewriter, the director cornered some addicts she knew. Through them she put out the word that whoever stole the typewriter took it from the community and that it had to be returned that day with apologies. The thief returned the typewriter that afternoon and made his apologies (Wahrhaftig, 1977c).

IMCR, on the other hand, serves a geographical and ethnic community— Harlem—but it is one where such a network of relationships is inconceivable. Many Harlem residents probably go through life without meeting or having any significant contact with neighbors four blocks away. There is no way that a network could link all the inhabitants of Harlem. There is no community of functioning relationships that could support or assert ownership of the IMCR program. Hence, by default, the program is owned by and serves agencies and the courts, whose definitions of community it then must meet.

Visitacion Valley, a CBP site, is a geographical community that can be recognized by funding sources. Its multiethnic residents are relatively powerless and are therefore an appropriate locus for social activism. Is it also a community of relationships? I do not have the data to answer this question. My superficial impression is its 5000 households constitute a neighborhood that is sufficiently small and cohesive to sustain a large number of face-to-face relationships. A Samoan-American from one end of the valley may meet a Mexican-American at their common grocery store, or their brothers may work at the same factory. It is possible that creating a CBP project in an area with potential for further face-to-face relationships could serve as the catalyst to enhance community ties.

In reviewing these CDR projects, I have reached the tentative conclusion that a program can be operated by and benefit a community only where the latter is a network of relationships, regardless of geography, population size, or ethnic composition. Of course, the economic and racial makeup of the community remains relevant to the political question of whether it is one into which the organizer wishes to put his or her efforts. Nor is it necessary that a community be a neighborhood; it could also be a workplace, school, prison, or any other locus where people interact.

Perhaps in the future a person will have the choice between taking a dispute to a CDR program in his residential area, workplace, or even his leisure or religious association. It is likely that such decisions will be made without the theoretical problems that plague law students in conflict of law courses. Since mediation is voluntary, a complainant is likely to choose the forum where he feels most confident and which also inspires the trust, and therefore will secure the appearance, of his respondent— which will probably be the "community" in which both parties interact most regularly.

REFERENCES

Bell, G. B. (1977a) Address to Mexican-American Legal Defense Fund, February 15.
––––––– (1977b) Press Release, July 28.
Dunn, E. (1977) "Arbitration as an Alternative to District Courts," in P. Wahrhaftig (ed.).
Citizen Dispute Resolution Organizer's Handbook. Pittsburgh, Pa: American Friends Service Committee.
Felstiner, W. L. F. and L. A. Williams (1978) "Mediation as an Alternative: Ideology and Limitations," 2 Law and Human Behavior 223.
Justice Resource Institute (1974) "The Urban Court Program: A Proposal" (unpublished).
McGillis, D. and J. Mullen (1977) Neighborhood Justice Centers: An Analysis of Potential Models. Washington, D.C.: National Institute of Law Enforcement and Criminal Justice.
National Institute of Law Enforcement and Criminal Justice (1974) Citizen Dispute Settlement: The Night Prosecutor Program of Columbus, Ohio. Washington, D.C.: National Institute of Law Enforcement and Criminal Justice.
Office of the State Courts Administrator, Florida (1979) The Citizen Dispute Settlement Process in Florida. Tallahassee, Fla.: Office of the State Courts Administrator.
Sarason, S. B., C. Carroll, K. Maton, S. Cohen, and E. Lorentz (1977) Human Services and Resource Networks. San Francisco: Jossey-Bass.
Sheppard, D. I., J. A. Roehl, and R. F. Cook (1979) Neighborhood Justice Centers Field Test: Interim Evaluation Report. Washington, D.C.: U.S. Department of Justice.
Shonholtz, R. (1977) "Quarterly Narrative Report" Mimeographed copy (February 12).
United States Department of Justice (1974) Citizen Dispute Settlement: The Night Prosecutor Program of Columbus, Ohio, Replication Model. Washington, D.C.: Government Printing Office.
Wahrhaftig, P. (ed.) (1977a) Citizen Dispute Resolution Organizer's Handbook. Pittsburgh, Pa.: American Friends Service Committee.
––––––– (1977b) "Community Dispute Center, New York—Some Observations," in Wahrhaftig (1977a).
––––––– (1977c) "Disputes Resolved in the Community, Community Assistance Project," in Wahrhaftig (1977a).
Wahrhaftig, P. and M. J. Lowy (1977) "Mediation at the Police Station: A Dialogue on the Night Prosecutor Program," in Wahrhaftig (1977a).

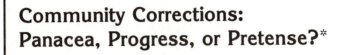

5

Community Corrections: Panacea, Progress, or Pretense?*

ANDREW SCULL

> Get thee glass eyes;
> And, like a scurvy politician, seem
> To see things thou dost not.
>
> (SHAKESPEARE, *King Lear* [Act 4, scene 6, lines 170–172])

In the last few decades we have been witnessing what appear to be the beginnings of a major shift in the ideology and apparatus of social control—a change that may come to rival in importance the early-nineteenth-century shift toward institutionally based modes of segregative control. Like that earlier transformation, the current developments are widely hailed as a beneficent and progressive reform. Like their predecessor, they are accounted the product of humanitarian instincts and our increasing knowledge about the control and rehabilitation of errant human beings. And like that prior episode of "reform," the reality is at once more complex, less benign, and morally more ambiguous than its apologists would have us believe.

Notwithstanding the manifestos of the labeling theorists and the programmatic statements of their conflict-theory critics, the macro-sociology of social control

*I am grateful to Steven Spitzer, Richard Abel, and David Greenberg for their comments on an earlier draft of this chapter. That version was presented to the Panel on Rehabilitative Techniques of the National Academy of Science's Committee on Research on Law Enforcement and Criminal Justice, Woods Hole, Massachusetts, June 11–13, 1979. I should like to thank that audience, too, for their comments and suggestions.

99

ISBN 0-12-041501-1

has been a strangely neglected topic in modern sociology. Much of the most important work in this area has been done by historians (Rothman, 1971; 1980; Hay *et al.*, 1976; Thompson, 1976; Ignatieff, 1978; Katz, 1978) or by others equally marginal to the mainstream of the sociological enterprise (Rusche and Kirchheimer, 1939; Foucault, 1965; 1977), and it is only in the last few years that this defect has begun to be remedied (Cohen, 1977; 1979; Fine, 1977; Rock, 1977; Scull, 1976; 1977a; 1977b; 1979a; Spitzer, 1979; Spitzer and Scull, 1977a; 1977b). Isolated studies of particular prisons, asylums, and reformatories; more or less sensitive discussions of the police and their lot; or even such synoptic works as Goffman's classic essay (1961) on the total institution—none of these have contributed in any marked degree to a portrait of the larger structure that orders these particularities. Still less can we look to the mass of low-level evaluative studies of individual programs—those parodies of "value-free" social science, with their configuration analyses, their Automatic Interaction Detector computer packages, their feedback and cybernetic systems—for any understanding of the broader network of social control. And the ideological proclamations of the proponents of current reforms are about as reliable a guide to the antecedents, characteristics, and significance of what is happening in the real world as the collected works of the brothers Grimm.

The contemporary drive toward decarceration—the emptying of mental hospitals, the advent of community corrections, and their analogues—involves a sustained assault on the intellectual (and to some degree institutional) foundations of a control system whose hegemony has lasted almost two centuries. As I have argued at greater length elsewhere (Spitzer and Scull, 1977a; Scull, 1979a), the central features of this earlier system were (*a*) the substantial involvement of the state and the emergence of a social control apparatus that was highly rationalized and, generally, centrally administered and directed; (*b*) the treatment of many types of deviance in institutions providing a large measure of segregation—both physical and symbolic—from the surrounding community; and (*c*) the careful differentiation of various sorts of deviance and the consignment of each to the ministrations of "experts," with the inevitable corollary of (*d*) the development of professional and semiprofessional "helping occupations." Throughout Western Europe and North America, all these features of the modern social control apparatus were substantially a product of the eighteenth and nineteenth centuries, a period that saw the coincidence of the need and the ability to organize the necessary administrative structures and to raise the substantial sums required to establish an institutionally based control system. Ultimately (though I do not have the space here to analyze these developments) one must view the move toward this type of social control apparatus as a reflection of the underlying transformations of the social structure associated with the maturation of the capitalist market system (Spitzer and Scull, 1977b; Katz, 1978; Scull, 1979a: esp. Ch. 1; 1979b).

Though not immune to criticism, sometimes of a very fundamental sort (Scull, 1977b: Chs. 6 and 7), the basic elements of this nineteenth-century system have proved remarkably resilient. Only in very recent years has its ideological and practical dominance been systematically challenged and undermined. The insurgent movement has attacked on a broad front. Part of the present stress on the "community" clearly draws upon reservoirs of opposition to centralization and state intervention, and certainly the fashionable emphasis on "the limits of benevolence" (Gaylin *et al.*, 1978; cf. Moynihan, 1969) borrows much of its emotional freight from the existence of widespread suspicion of and antagonism toward all forms of bureaucracy and certified expertise.[1] But this, for the most part, is window dressing, glittering phrases designed to dazzle the eye and attract a crowd. It is scarcely surprising that programs developed by the high-level bureaucrats and intellectual experts who are the movement's principal spokesmen continue to rely heavily upon state initiative and sponsorship, and upon the advice and counsel of persons such as themselves.

The central thrust of their critique lies elsewhere, in the contention that the institution is necessarily, always, and absolutely a failure—a colossal mistake whose commission can only be redeemed by its abolition. Drawing particularly upon the work of the labeling theorists, stabilized deviance is seen primarily as a product of the reactions of others and of the control institutions that represent societal reaction in its most crystallized, unambiguous, and pernicious form. Not only does processing by such institutions inflict more visible, organized, and ineradicable stigma than those commonly suffered in informal interaction, but it also exposes the inmate to the powerful socializing impact of institutional existence. And contrary to a century and a half of rhetoric by institutional custodians, the effect of this socialization is not to cure or rehabilitate but to perpetuate and intensify the underlying pathology. Life in the mental hospital tends "inexorably to the attenuation of the spirit, a shrinking of capacity, and slowing of the rhythms of interaction, a kind of atrophy" (Miller, 1974: 54). The same is true of its sister institution, the prison. With its cruelty, brutality, and lawlessness, the exposure of inmates to a society permeated with corruption and domi-

---

[1]It is surely ironic that the proponents of decarceration should rail so loudly against the snares of benevolently intended "humanitarian" reform. Consider David Rothman's (1971: 295) solemn warning that we should possess

an acute nervousness about all social panaceas. Proposals that promise the most grandiose consequences often legitimate the most unsatisfactory developments. And one grows wary about taking reform programs at face value: arrangements designed for the best of motives may have disastrous results.

With the blithe self-assurance so characteristic of reformers, their own activities are somehow exempt from their favorite historical law: Apparently the cautionary lessons of history apply only to one's opponents!

nated by the very worst elements, it must necessarily "teach crime, instill crime, inure men to it, trap men in it as a way of life" (Wills, 1975: 8). Efforts to reform such places are useless. Their defects are not simply the consequence of administrative lapses or the lack of adequate funds, but rather they reflect fundamental and irremediable flaws deeply embedded in their basic structure (for a popularization of these notions, see Mitford, 1973).

The obverse of this profound pessimism concerning the "correctional effects of corrections" has been an equally far-reaching optimism about the merits of the proposed alternative—treatment in the community. Such an approach is said to permit the reintegration of the offender, while "avoiding as much as possible the isolating and labelling effects of commitment to an institution" (President's Commission, 1967: 20). It is both more humane and cheaper. Moreover, the inexpensive redemption the community offers extends not merely to the decarcerated deviant but also in significant measure to all of us.

> The destination is a degree of community participation and effectiveness which has all but departed our lives as people living together. Part of the powerlessness and frustration which so many sense at this juncture will be resolved in this trend, to the benefit not only of inmates or clients or patients or criminals now in institutions—but of the community as a whole [Alper, 1973: viii].

Such idyllic visions are curiously familiar to those acquainted with the history of reform movements. For the *adoption* of the asylum, whose *abolition* is here pictured as having such universally beneficent results, aroused millenial expectations among its advocates that are almost precisely parallel. Furthermore, it is at least mildly curious to portray modern society as a collection of little organic villages, where neighbor will help neighbor and families willingly minister to the needs of their own troublesome members (if only in potentiality), when surrounded by the reality of the increasingly privatized, rationalized, and atomized existence characteristic of late capitalism.

It is significant, I think, that what effort the decarceration movement *has* made to provide some empirical underpinning for its claims has been concentrated on demolishing the pretensions of the institutions that have traditionally processed our deviant populations. In this connection the labeling literature, with its stress on deviance as an ascribed rather than an achieved status, has provided an invaluable ideological account of the failings and ill effects of prisons, mental hospitals, and juvenile reformatories. Coupled with this has been the adoption (from the same source) of the naive, unexamined, and certainly fallacious notion that deviance responds primarily (or even exclusively) to efforts at control, with its corollary that simple changes in the control system can completely alter the nature and quantity of deviance in a society.[2] (Fortunately

[2]For an empirical critique of this claim, confronting what is generally taken to be its strongest

or unfortunately, deviance responds to much else besides.) The offspring of this alliance has been a ready acceptance of the superiority of "radical nonintervention," the sweeping away of well-intended but mischievous controls, the removal of their erstwhile objects from the antitherapeutic environment of the total institution and their consignment to the tender (if unexamined) mercies of the community. For if deviance is the product of formal efforts at control, elimination of control must surely result in improvement—a point so obvious it scarcely requires demonstration. It is this that lends some credence to the claim that "diversion is the practitioner's operationalization of labeling theory" (Klein *et al.*, 1976: 106); for labeling theory has unquestionably smoothed the way toward abandonment, or at least a major modification, of the system of segregative control, and it has allowed this development to be presented as motivated by humanitarian concern for the deviant as well as for the community as a whole.

It is, of course, an "illusion that a specific penal practice is bound up with a specific penal theory, and that it is sufficient to demolish the latter to set the former under way" (Rusche and Kirchheimer, 1939: 141). One may grant the depths of current pessimism in intellectual circles concerning the value of institutional responses to deviance and recognize the degree to which decarceration has consequently been elevated to the status of a new "humanitarian" myth, comparable only with that which attended the birth of the asylum. Yet social policy generally proves only mildly susceptible to shifting intellectual fads and fancies. What, then, accounts for the apparent success of the critics in this instance?

Certainly it is not the originality or forcefulness of their arguments. Almost precisely parallel contentions about the antitherapeutic consequences of confinement were made by several nineteenth-century critics, who drew conclusions remarkably similar to those of their twentieth-century counterparts. Yet such men, despite their unquestionable political skill and influence, had no success in changing existing social policies (Scull, 1977b: Chs. 6 and 7). Analogous criticisms have been repeated insistently ever since with little effect, at least until recently. Quite clearly, receptivity to and application of a given set of findings are dependent more on the temper of the audience to which they are addressed than on the intrinsic merits of the propositions being advanced.

Further, there are serious lacunae in the arguments of contemporary advocates of the community approach. Extraordinary ignorance of the likely effects of such a policy persisted long after it had become official dogma. Among the mentally ill—the first group to "benefit" from this shift in control strategies and the population among whom it has had by far its greatest impact—"the massive

---

evidence—drug addiction—see Scull (1972); for a more wide-ranging dissent from such romantic notions by one who might be seen as their putative father, see Lemert (1972).

release of patients to facilities in residential neighborhoods" *preceeded* "substantial data collection and analysis" concerning the likely effects of this change, (Wolpert and Wolpert, 1974: 19). Deinstitutionalization has accelerated rapidly despite the absence of community after-care facilities, and even though we continue to lack "substantiation that community care is advantageous for clients" (Wolpert and Wolpert, 1976; see also Ahmed, 1974). The movement toward community corrections began much later, has not proceeded nearly as far (though the statistical data remain difficult to obtain and interpret) (Messinger, 1976; Scull, 1977: Ch. 3), and has recently encountered significant opposition, discussed later in this chapter. But here, too, one of the most striking features has been our sheer lack of knowledge concerning the likely effects of decarceration on crime rates or the social order more broadly conceived (Vorenberg and Vorenberg, 1973; Greenberg, 1975).[3] Even those who applaud these developments concede that "there is not a wealth of sound evidence upon which to justify the current effort to deinstitutionalize correctional programs" (Empey, 1973: 37).

Perhaps more serious still, for those who contend that the change reflects our society's newfound humanitarianism, is the accumulating evidence that actual implementation of the policy (in contrast to its rhetorical claims) has had an effect exactly the reverse of humane. Certainly some of those decanted back into our midst have been reabsorbed quietly, if not without cost. This should scarcely be surprising. After all, many of those subjected to processing by the official agencies of social control have been virtually indistinguishable from their neighbors. In this sense Goffman (1961: 135) rightly describes them as victims of "contingencies." They, at least, can be expelled from institutions without appreciable risk. And the burden of care for those released mental patients whose family ties are reasonably intact can be shifted to the shoulders of their relatives, where it becomes largely invisible if nonetheless real (Brown *et al.*, 1966).

But for many others, expecially ex–mental patients, the outcome has been much less favorable. In discussions of deinstitutionalization there is constant reliance upon "boo" words and "hurrah" words (Stevenson, 1944). But the concrete referents of "hurrah" words such as *community care* remain unknown or undiscussed; their desirability is instead suggested by implicit comparison with the nastiness of the institutional alternatives. For ideological purposes, it is just as well that these concepts remain unexamined, for all too often the *community* consists of the social wastelands that form the core of our cities and *care* is another word for malign neglect. Exploratory research in this area has revealed

the growing ghettoization of the returning expatients along with other dependent groups in the population; the growing use of inner city land for institutions providing services to the dependent and needy ... ⟨and⟩ the forced immobility of the chronically disabled within deteriorated urban

---

[3]On the general difficulties associated with measuring the impact of policy changes on criminal behavior, see Nagin (1978).

neighborhoods . . . areas where land-use deterioration has proceeded to such a point that the land market is substantially unaffected by the introduction of community services and their clients [Wolpert and Wolpert, 1976: 37, 39].

In the absence of any expansion of state-provided services for the burgeoning exinmate population, such "social junk" (Spitzer, 1975: 645) has become a commodity from which various professionals and entrepreneurs extract a profit—the basis for a whole emergent industry battening upon derelicts and discharged mental patients. As a result, "deinstitutionalization" for many has meant little more than a transfer from a state to a private institution or quasi-institution where "one form of confinement has been replaced by another and the former patients are just as insulated from community attention and care as they were in the state hospital" (Wolpert and Wolpert, 1974: 61). What has changed is the packaging of their misery, not its reality. My earlier research on this subject (Scull, 1976; 1977a) suggests that both the sources and the outcome of the movement away from segregative institutions can be best understood as a response to broader social structural changes. I shall argue later in this chapter that the picture I drew there now requires some reconsideration and modification, particularly as it applies to the treatment of criminals. But first let me sketch the basic components of my original approach to these issues.

Briefly, the creation and expansion of the welfare state, providing minimum subsistence for elements of the surplus population, generates structural pressures to curtail sharply the costly system of segregative control by creating some viable alternative. The highly restrictive welfare policies characteristic of the United States until well into the present century meant that asylums, prisons, and the like represented one of the few costs of reproduction that were socialized, i.e., administered by the state rather than by the private sector. As a result, fiscal pressures on the state from this source were relatively slight, and the expenses associated with a system of segregative control were readily absorbed. Moreover, there was little or no choice but to keep the chronically insane in the asylum, for though the overwhelming majority were harmless, they could not provide their own subsistence, and no other sources of support were available to sustain them in the outside world.

The advent of a wide range of welfare programs providing just such support sharply increased the opportunity cost of neglecting community care in favor of the institution, which was inevitably far more costly than the most generous scheme of welfare payments.[4] The comparative advantage of the noninstitutional

[4]The origins of the welfare state are, of course, extremely complex. To oversimplify greatly, we may identify one source as the recognition by the more farsighted capitalists that, in an advanced economy, human capital is at least as valuable as other forms of capital and that welfare measures frequently are a cost-effective way to protect and enhance the value of that human capital. But one must not overlook the frequency with which the passage of welfare measures have required extended

approach was further strengthened by the widespread unionization of state employees, for in the mid-1950s the "advent of the eight hour day and forty hour week in state institutions . . . virtually doubled unit costs" (Dingman, 1974: 48). Moreover, greater state expenditures on welfare were only part of a much broader and more massive expansion of the state's role in civil society, engendered by the need of advanced capitalism to socialize more and more of the costs of production (O'Connor, 1973; Braverman, 1974). The fiscal pressures created by this expansion have been intensified by the failure of productivity in the state sector to keep pace with that in the private sector, with the necessary consequence that rising expenditures are required merely to maintain existing levels of activity. The result is persistent efforts at retrenchment in some sectors of the social control apparatus at a time when general expenditures on welfare are expanding rapidly. It is precisely the expansion of the one that makes possible and desirable the contraction of the other.

State hospital populations stabilized and began to decline in the early 1950s, and as welfare programs markedly expanded during the 1960s and 1970s the movement to empty the asylums accelerated. More devices were developed to divert potential inmates away from institutions, and existing ones were applied with greater urgency and effect. With the intensified effort to control soaring costs came the extension of deinstitutionalization to the criminal justice sector, at first in the form of tentative, small-scale, experimental programs but soon on a much wider scale. The growing fascination of criminal justice planners and policymakers with diversionary programs coincided with a declining concern for imprisonment as a means of retribution and deterrence.

At the end of 1975, when I completed my book *Decarceration*, the advocates of deinstitutionalization clearly dominated public debate about the proper approach to the mad and the bad. Opposition, if not silent, was muted and fragmented and often could simply be dismissed as self-interested. Among the public at large it took the form of protest by the residents of particular communities to the placement of exinmates of any kind in *their* neighborhood. Sometimes this involved harassment, threats of vigilante action, even arson, but in the politically more sophisticated and better-organized communities, the favorite tactic was exclusionary zoning (Coates and Miller, 1973: 67; Segal, 1974: 143ff.; Green-

---

political pressure and organization against significant opposition. The second, and perhaps more direct, source of the welfare state has thus been political struggle by the increasingly organized labor movement, particularly during the period since World War Two, when the largely successful pursuit of full-employment policies was reflected in labor's increased bargaining power in the political process. Third, as Piven and Cloward (1971; see also Nicolaus, 1967) have emphasized, welfare payments at a level close to subsistence have been utilized to damp down or head off unrest among the growing class of economically redundant and superfluous people whose lack of marketable skills renders them a virtually permanent surplus population at the margins of the economy.

berg, 1975: 28ff.; Wolpert and Wolpert, 1976). Such particularistic activities were simply designed to protect the parochial concerns of residents who clearly wished to minimize contact with the very deviants they should eagerly be embracing according to the decarceration ideology. Limited opposition of this sort, by its very nature was not likely to coalesce into a more broadly based attack on the policy *tout court*. Provided the burden could be shifted elsewhere, to other less vociferous, less powerful populations, the discontent could readily be defused without serious modification of the underlying program. These complaints just reinforced other pressures to deposit the decarcerated in the poorest, most deteriorated, and least desirable of urban locations.

Attempts to stimulate a general repudiation of the movement were largely the work of state employee unions (e.g., California State Employees Association, 1972; American Federation of State, County, and Municipal Employees, 1975). They sought to create moral panics (Cohen, 1972) among the general population by skilled manipulation of "exemplary tales" concerning the squalor of the conditions in which exinmates were living, the violence to which they were prone, and the deleterious effects of both on property values and public order. But though such efforts were not without success—the most notable being the decision by the Reagan administration in California to modify sharply its plans to eliminate state hospitals for the mentally ill and mentally retarded (Chase, 1973; *Los Angeles Times*, January 29, 1974: pt. 1, p. 16)—they were clearly vulnerable to the accusation that they expressed the vested interests of those with direct responsibility for the shortcomings of the institutional alternative.

Within the last few years, of course, the situation has changed rather markedly. Although the process of emptying mental hospitals continues substantially as before, our jail and prison population has once again increased (to record levels), overcrowding is rife, and old, discarded buildings are being reopened and crammed with prisoners (Flynn, 1978: 131–132). Moreover, a strong conservative backlash urges longer terms of imprisonment, mandatory fixed sentences, and so forth (Van den Haag, 1975: Wilson, 1975; Fogel, 1975; 1978; Von Hirsch, 1976) and finds a pale reflection in the rediscovery by liberals of the virtues of swift and certain punishment (e.g., Martinson, 1974; see generally Greenberg and Humphries, 1979). What are we to make of these developments, and what implications do they have for the future of the decarceration movement?

Let me confess at the outset that they suggest serious limitations to studying prisons and asylums as a unitary phenomenon. It is not that such assimilation is never theoretically or empirically justified or that I feel I was completely wrong in invoking similar imperatives to explain the drive to decarcerate prisoners and patients. But I now recognize how important it is to remain sensitive to crucial differences that may modify policy outcomes (Christie, 1978).

Ironically, the casual dumping of the disoriented and the senile has been made easier by the fact that the measures designed to dispose of them are ostensibly undertaken from a benevolent and humanitarian concern for their welfare. However great the discrepancy between the ideology and the reality of asylum existence—indeed, precisely *because* of the magnitude of that discrepancy (Orlans, 1948)—enormous energy and substantial resources have been devoted for more than a century and a half to elaborating, disseminating, and perpetuating the illusion of concern with the inmate's welfare.[5] As someone who is sick and therefore cannot be held responsible for his condition or situation, the mental patient is the recipient of treatment "for his own good." If it is concluded that traditional approaches are destructive and antitherapeutic, then nonintervention, dressed up as community treatment and promoted in the name of the very virtues once attributed to the asylum, can be advocated on the grounds of its advantages for the client. But prisoners are not clients, and pain, privation, and suffering are seen by many as their just deserts. Because they "chose" to offend, retribution is in order. The "humanity" of community corrections is thus its Achilles heel, precisely the feature most likely to alienate (fiscal) conservatives and indeed the public at large, who might otherwise be attracted by the idea. Criminals recidivate because of an innate or acquired depravity, and if prisons are unpleasant places, that is exactly what they should be.

The social legitimation that punishment derives from the positivist approach and public opposition to whatever smacks of leniency toward criminals clearly delayed and inhibited the expansion of deinstitutionalization to the criminal justice system. (As we shall see, they may also have affected its character.) If the structural pressures I have identified ultimately prompted some movement in this direction, it was inevitable that such efforts would remain more labile and susceptible to retrenchment than their mental health counterparts.

If a public obsessed by crime in the streets has recently demanded that more (lower-class) criminals be locked up (and for longer periods of time), that has not discouraged the more utilitarian students of the criminal justice system. Quite the contrary, the overcrowding, tension, and violence incident to such a reversal of the downward drift of prison populations has led at least some to speculate that

---

[5]That many of those employed to run such places are not hypocrites but true believers does not detract from the falsity of those beliefs. The benefits of such mythologies accrue largely to those who perpetrate them, not to their alleged beneficiaries. Inmates are generally all too aware of the emperor's missing clothes (save where sharing the illusion makes their lives more bearable). Arnold Hauser has pointed out that this is not atypical of ideological constructs.

> What most sharply distinguishes a propagandistic from an ideological presentation and interpretation of the facts is . . . that its falsification and mystification of the truth is always conscious and intentional. Ideology, on the other hand, is mere deception—in essence self-deception—never simply lies and deceit. It obscures truth in order not so much to mislead others as to maintain and increase the self-confidence of those who express and benefit from such deceptions [quoted in Muraskin, 1976: 559].

× Dangerous.

"a trend diametrically opposed to ⟨non-institutional alternatives⟩ may finally force the development and implementation of plans for prison population reduction and de-institutionalization" (Flynn, 1978: 133). The criminologist's task is then the purely technical one of devising the means for "the classification for risk... and the concomitant development of criteria on the basis of which a process of de-institutionalization—or at least a substantial population reduction—can be implemented" (*Ibid.*: 134). Such a "classification system should seek to identify those offenders who commit serious predatory crimes and violence, in order to separate them from offenders who do not represent any serious risk to the safety of the public." The latter should then be "classified out" of the criminal justice system so as to reduce "the social and economic costs of wholesale incarceration" (*Ibid*: 135, 148). The ethical and constitutional objections to such an approach (Greenberg, 1975) and its intensification of the class-biased character of the punitive system are passed over in silence. More cynically (or perhaps just more honestly), Ken Pease, a British criminologist, has proposed that we simply employ a sliding scale of remission for good conduct in prison, varied according to the numbers entering the system and the target for the total prison population—a sort of "hydraulic, cybernetic model of prison life, whereby, if a lot come in this end then a lot go out that end" (Taylor, 1978: 204). Nagin (1978) has presented data that suggest this has been the implicit policy in the United States for several decades.

In all probability, some such techniques will be devised and implemented to keep the lid on the potentially explosive conditions in our jails and penitentiaries and to permit some modest reductions in institutional populations. But the significance of the revolt against excessive "leniency" toward criminals is much broader than this. It affects the very substance of community "alternatives" to imprisonment and impels decarceration to assume a guise quite different from that found in the deinstitutionalization of the mentally disturbed—and one that is much more heavily interventionist in character.

My earlier critique of decarceration's humanitarian claims (Scull, 1977a) rested in large part on evidence that it meant the substitution of a policy of non-intervention that actually amounted to neglect and exploitation and not to the glorious therapeutic alternative its advocates touted. I remain convinced that for the subpopulation of deviants with whom *Decarceration* was primarily concerned—the mentally ill—this is essentially an accurate representation. But further research (and criticism of that book) has made me realize that for other groups, particularly the criminal, the problem is not so simple: Here the humanitarian dangers, though still present, often come from just the opposite direction.

To be sure, deinstitutionalization has indeed meant little more than token efforts at control and "supervision" for many discharged delinquents and criminals. The massive expansion of the population dealt with through noninstitutional dispositions has not been matched by the development of a comparable infrastructure capable of providing community supervision and control, with the result that community treatment is often present in name only. In this situation it would be difficult to contend that the alternative disposition is less humane than the prison (from the offender's viewpoint).[6] Appalling though our ghettoes may be, conditions there still are not as nasty, brutish, and degrading as those in our penitentiaries. But what is generally neglected in such cost–benefit equations is that though community treatment may be more humanitarian to those who are spared incarceration, it clearly is not so to anyone they subsequently victimize. After all, "whatever else it does or does not do, institutionalization does tend to ensure that these persons, anyway, will not visit depradations on the community while they are institutionalized" (Messinger, 1976: 90). And though, given the present state of knowledge about deterrence, "one ⟨can⟩ only speculate about this possibility... to the extent that the effectiveness of a deterrent threat depends on the certainty of punishment... diversion programs at the pre-trial level or non-institutional sentences like probation could well lead to higher crime rates" (Greenberg, 1975: 8).

The problem I now have in mind, however, becomes significant as and when the slogan "community corrections" actually begins to take on substance. It is hinted at by Norval Morris in *The Future of Imprisonment* (1974) and treated more seriously and at greater length in papers by David Greenberg (1975) and Stanley Cohen (1979). Community programs, precisely because of their less overtly punitive content, may become the occasion for significantly widening the reach and scope of the social control apparatus.[7] As Morris (1974: 10) puts it, "We risk substituting more pervasive but less punitive control mechanisms over a vastly greater number of citizens for our present discriminatory and irrational selection of fewer citizens for more punitive and draconian sentences."

Evidence is now accumulating that the development of so-called diversionary programs leads to "a more voracious processing of deviant populations, albeit in new settings and by professionals with different names" (Cohen, 1979: 350; see Cressey and McDermott, 1974; Lerman, 1975; Klein *et al.*, 1976; Rutherford and Bengur, 1976; Messinger, 1976; Blomberg, 1977). This tendency is hardly

---

[6]This assumes, of course, that those "diverted" to the community would otherwise have been institutionalized. Where this is not the case, even the token supervision entailed by probation may be substantially more intrusive than prior dispositions would have been, not to mention that the probationer is now far more vulnerable to serious sanctions in the future. Even from this narrow perspective, therefore, the humanity of community corrections is dubious. I shall discuss this point at greater length later in this chapter.

[7]For analogous criticism of neighborhood justice centers as a source of expanded social control, see Hofrichter (1982).

surprising, for neglect, pure and simple, has clear disadvantages as a social control strategy, at least when dealing with criminals and some delinquents. Although the advocates of diversion consistently ignore or downplay the importance of the deterrent and retributive functions of punishment, to the extent that crime represents a "rational" form of activity the erosion of sanctions threatens to elicit more of it. The crazy and the senile can, by and large, be contained and isolated even while being neglected. Their very lack of resources, immobility, and absence of initiative, reinforced by such practices as exclusionary zoning and the centralization of welfare services, can be exploited to secure their ecological separation into twilight zones where decomposition can proceed without offense to either the sensibilities or the operations of the larger society, subject only to routine and straightforward policing of the boundaries of these human sewers to ensure that their contents do not spill out and become a public nuisance (Bittner, 1967; Aaronson *et al.*, 1978). Even were we to grant the attractions of unpoliced ghettoes, those cannot be secured by releasing criminals, the targets of whose victimization are insufficiently selective and not adequately geographically concentrated or controllable. The pressures thus generated for visible (and perhaps even effective) supervision are further reinforced by public perception of the criminal as someone whose activities are blameworthy and warrant—indeed require—the infliction of pain (cf. Christie, 1978).

The demands this situation creates dovetail nicely, in turn, with the organizational instincts of the correctional bureaucracy for self-preservation and expansion.[8] By playing upon the fears and mobilizing the disquiet of the public, the correctional staff can readily justify a substantial expansion of the amount and intensity of professional involvement and activity. Thus, one may anticipate that

---

[8]Once again, there are important differences here between corrections and mental health. In the former, the careers of even the professional staff remain inextricably linked to servicing a lower-class "clientele", and because correctional bureaucrats lack alternative markets for their skills, they are forced to be highly protective of their state-supported activities. By contrast, the burgeoning movement for community psychiatry and the growing willingness of insurance carriers to provide some coverage for mental disorders (together with the existing private psychiatric sector) mean that the higher-status mental health professionals have ample alternative markets for *their* "skills." Furthermore, those markets offer significant advantages. Though often heavily subsidized by tax dollars (directly or through the medical deduction), they are free of the stigma of publicly provided care; they attract less disturbed, more "treatable" patients; and the social status of the new clients is generally higher (Chu and Trotter, 1974). In terms of prestige, income, and closer assimilation to the patterns of conventional medical practice, these fields are clearly preferable to the meager rewards associated with institutional psychiatry (see also footnote 9, following). Once more articulate and politically influential professionals have been bought off in this fashion, whatever opposition is generated by hospital rundowns naturally comes primarily from low-status workers with few or no transferable skills. And the low status and minimal professional training of the latter serve to discredit much of their opposition in advance.

Lerman's (1975) findings on the way the California Community Treatment Project has been manipulated by and in the interests of the correctional establishment will turn out to be applicable much more generally.

The convergence created by the special problems involved in controlling crime—"the occupational interests of correctional and prison employees and administrators ⟨and⟩ public demands, partly instrumental and partly symbolic, for sterner measures to stop increasing crime" (Greenberg, 1975: 16)—merely reinforces the tendency toward greater intervention already signaled in the pervasive and uncritical stress on rehabilitation so deeply entrenched in the community corrections literature and practice. Battered by assaults on its constitutionality, effectiveness, and moral justification (Leifer, 1969; American Friends Service Committee, 1971; Kittrie, 1972; Gaylin, 1974), the therapeutic ethic now appears to be giving ground in institutional settings.[9] From both right and left there are renewed calls for fixed sentencing based upon deterrent and retributive considerations rather than rehabilitation (Fogel, 1975; Wilson, 1975; Van den Haag, 1975; Von Hirsch, 1976). What seems to be happening, however, is that the self-same therapeutic rationalizations and practices are being reinvoked as the basis for the new community programs.[10]

The discretionary decision making that forms an integral part of any program of coercive "rehabilitation" is a crucial feature of community corrections at all levels of its operation. It is most obvious in decisions about who is eligible for community dispositions in lieu of the harsher sanction of imprisonment. The very sense that the former is less punitive (or even nonpunitive) and can actually prevent more crime diminishes concern with whether the "client" has actually committed the offense that nominally brought him to the attention of the authorities. Instead of an adjudication focused on prior conduct, there is an assessment of whether the accused can benefit from the services provided by the program, a decision that frequently entails intentional avoidance of due process

[9]This argument applies, of course, to institutional settings in general, including those, such as mental hospitals, whose nominal justification is self-consciously therapeutic. The growing willingness of courts to intervene to secure "patients' rights" has necessarily involved considerable legalistic circumscription of the behavior and judgments of therapeutic staff. By thus sharply limiting professional autonomy (Freidson, 1970), "legalization" has made institutional psychiatry even less attractive to professionals. Moreover, by threatening sharp increases in unit costs per inmate, "right to treatment" decisions such as *Wyatt* v. *Stickney* (344 F. Supp. 373, M.D. Ala. 1972) have added to the pressures to deinstitutionalize the control of the mentally sick (cf. Rothman, 1973).

[10]This transfer of the therapeutic rationalization from the sphere of formal incarceration to that of community corrections obviously deserves more extended treatment than I can give it here. One of the most critical questions it raises, of course, is *why* this flip-flop is occurring. Richard Abel (personal communication) has suggested one plausible explanation—that community dispositions are both less visible and, because they are less imbued with state action, less subject to constitutional scrutiny. Elsewhere, he has made an analogous point about the relationship between the distribution of bias in the criminal justice system and the visibility of that bias in the behavior of official agents (Abel, 1978).

and systematic obfuscation of the whole issue of guilt and innocense.[11] The selection of "suitable cases for treatment" relies upon "critical predictor variables": age, prior institutional commitments, institutional adjustment, marital status, type of (unajudicated) current offense, prior record, employment record, family and community ties, and so forth—the intent being to avoid releasing those who are dangerous or might recidivate (Flynn, 1978). As Cohen (1979: 346) comments:

> while the traditional screening mechanism [sic] of the criminal justice system have always been influenced to a lesser or greater degree by non-offense related criteria (race, class, demeanour) the offense was at least considered. Except in the case of wrongful conviction, some law must have been broken. This is no longer clear.

The basic thrust toward making treatment criteria and dispositions independent of legal scrutiny and review is equally evident at later stages in the process. Once placed in a program such as the Manhattan Court Employment Project,

> the recommendation of the project staff is obviously of critical importance to the defendant. The consequences of an unfavorable decision may include not only a resumption of prosecution, but possibly, if convicted, a more serious sentence, since a judge may be reluctant to grant probation to someone whose performance in the community program has been judged inadequate. Yet this decision is left to administrative staff to be made according to extremely subjective criteria. There is no procedure for appealing a negative recommendation, and given the nature of the criteria employed ⟨changes in attitude and lifestyle⟩, it is hard to see how there could be [Greenberg, 1975: 21].

Or again, as Lerman's (1975) study of the California Community Treatment Program has shown, short-term custody, which is so large a part of its procedures, is not governed by legal rules or due process safeguards (just as the other "treatments" within the program are the product of discretionary decisions by program personnel); therefore the lack of accountability, threats to "client" rights, and feelings of injustice and arbitrariness on the part of those manipulated are simply built into the system (see also Boorkman *et al.*, 1976).

In the words of those running the system, even "such relatively non-delinquent offenses as missing a group meeting, 'sassing' a teacher, showing an uncooperative attitude, or the threat of an emotional explosion" could prompt short-term incarceration (project report, cited in Lerman, 1975: 37). Indeed, the

---

[11]Such questions are obviously left unresolved by the wide variety of schemes involving police discretion and pretrial diversion. In addition, the presumption of guilt that is the foundation of the plea bargaining system (Sudnow, 1965) here acquires a different use. For example, those attempting to distinguish the goats who are to be institutionalized from the sheep who will be released are urged to attend closely to the "type of current offense ⟨as⟩ predictive of future criminal behavior," where that offense is not what has been agreed during plea bargaining but rather the "actual behavior [*sic*]" of the offender (Flynn, 1978: 141).

mere *belief* on the part of the staff that a subject might fail to comply with the program's norms could do so. The whole approach thus brings with it the danger "of highly intrusive intervention concerning matters of personal choice that have no direct bearing on criminal activity" (Greenberg, 1975: 6). And to the extent that these features generate further perceptions of injustice or unfairness, the long-run tendency must be for them to undermine further the legitimacy of a criminal justice system already regarded as inequitable and arbitrary.

This outcome is in no sense an aberration. On the contrary, in "corrections" as in other social control systems, the more control comes to be legitimated in terms of diagnosis and treatment rather than rules, responsibility, and punishment, the more likely it is to intrude into the emotions, thought, and behavior of the individual and to be concerned with generalized behavioral "problems" rather than specific acts. The threat thus looms of a massive extension of official intervention into the lives of millions who had previously escaped notice or attention—all under the guise of "helping" them. In fact, "the more benign, attractive and successful the program is defined ⟨as being⟩ . . . the more it will be used and the wider it will cast its net" (Cohen, 1979: 348).

I am not sanguine, therefore, about recent trends toward community corrections or about the likely impact of this movement on efforts to "rehabilitate" offenders. As I suggested earlier, many of the more extravagant claims and expectations advanced by advocates of deinstitutionalization derive from a serious overestimation of the strength of the casual link between crime and the apparatus of repression. *Pace* the assertions of the more starry-eyed devotees of labeling theory, "the amount and structure of criminality is determined by other social forces: the system of crime control plays only a modest role" (Antilla, 1978: 197). As David Greenberg has suggested (1975: 5–6, 25), a serious attack on the "crime problem" would probably involve, at a very minimum, "efforts directed at reducing unemployment, barriers to teen-age entry into the job market, and other structural features of the labor market which impede the pursuit of 'a lawful style of living in the community.'" Even these changes, any one of which is exceedingly unlikely, would probably be insufficient; we may well need, in addition, a broader attack on inequalities in both income and the ownership of productive property. And yet contemporary changes in the political economy of the United States point in precisely the opposite direction (O'Connor, 1973, 1974; Wilson, 1978).

Thus there seem to be few immediate prospects for social change in the direction of increased equity and equality (though I, like most sociologists, am a lousy prophet and so retain some hope that I shall be proved wrong). And without such change, I see little likelihood of anything more than minor incremental gains and further cosmetic "improvements" (that, more often than not, are actually regressive) dressed up as major advances toward a more just and humane criminal justice system. On the whole, though, I think a realistic pessimism is to be preferred to a synthetic comfort built upon baseless fantasies of the dawn of the therapeutic millenium, or even upon more modest illusions about the possibilities of humanizing a fundamentally inhuman system.

Let me conclude by saying that I am well aware of the pressures to be more than "negatively critical." It is not enough, according to the conventional wisdom, to speak harsh words about contemporary institutions. One "should have the decency to provide a detailed blueprint for change and improvement, and should offer his suggestions in the spirit of one who is thankful for our collective blessings and, at all costs, hopeful" (Boyers, 1979:28). This I cannot do, for I lack the necessary faith in the managerial approach to the problem. (Indeed, I question the very legitimacy of the idea, implicit in such terminology, that the problem of crime and imprisonment can be "solved" by internal technical adjustments. The social roots of our difficulties are too deep.) This leaves me in a distinctly uncomfortable position: Only a confirmed Pangloss can view the realities of a traditional penal system with equanimity, but what I have learned about the community corrections movement simply reinforces my conviction that tinkering around with the criminal justice system in a radically unjust society is unlikely to advance us very far toward justice, equity, or (come to that) efficacy. Perhaps the best I can do is to persuade others to share my sense of discomfort.

REFERENCES

Aaronson, D. E., C. T. Dienes, and M. C. Musheno (1978) "Changing the Public Drunkenness Laws: The Impact of Decriminalization," 12 *Law & Society Review* 405.

Abel, R. L. (1978) "From the Editor," 12 *Law & Society Review* 333.

Ahmed, P. (1974) "New Thrusts in Unified Mental Health Care Systems, and the Status of State Mental Hospitals," in *Where Is My Home?* Washington, D.C.: National Technical Information Service.

Alper, B. (1973) "Foreword," in Y. Bakal (ed.) *Closing Correctional Institutions.* Lexington, Mass.: Lexington Books.

American Federation of State, County, and Municipal Employees (1975) *Out of Their Beds and into the Streets.* Washington, D.C.: A.F.S.C.M.E.

American Friends Service Committee (1971) *Struggle for Justice.* Philadelphia: Hill and Wang.

Antilla, I. (1978) "Control without Repression?" in J. Freeman (ed.) *Prisons Past and Future.* London: Heinemann.

Bittner, E. (1967) "Police on Skid Row: A Study of Peace Keeping," 32 *American Sociological Review* 699.

Blomberg, T. (1977) "Diversion and Accelerated Social Control," 68 *Journal of Criminology and Criminal Law* 274.

Boorkman, D., et al. (1976) *An Exemplary Project: Community Based Corrections in Des Moines.* Washington, D.C.: Law Enforcement Assistance Administration.

Boyers, R. (1979) "Review of Christopher Lasch, *Haven in a Heartless World*," New Republic (February 19).

Braverman, H. (1974) *Labor and Monopoly Capital*. New York: Monthly Review Press.

Brown, G. W., *et al.* (1966) *Schizophrenia and Social Care*. London: Oxford University Press.

California State Employees Association (1972) *Where Have All the Patients Gone?* Sacramento: C.S.E.A.

Chase, J. (1973) "Where Have All the Patients Gone?" 2 *Human Behavior* 14 (October).

Christie, N. (1978) "Prisons in Society, or Society as a Prison: A Conceptual Analysis," in J. Freeman (ed.) *Prisons Past and Future*. London: Heinemann.

Chu, F. and S. Trotter (1974) *The Madness Establishment*. New York: Grossman.

Coates, R. B. and A. Miller (1973) "Neutralization of Community Resistance to Group Homes," in Y. Bakal (ed.) *Closing Correctional Institutions*. Lexington, Mass.: Lexington Books.

Cohen, S. (1972) *Folk Devils and Moral Panics*. London: Paladin.

_____ (1977) "Prisons and the Future of Control Systems," in M. Fitzgerald *et al.* (eds.) *Welfare in Action*. London: Routledge and Kegan Paul.

_____ (1979) "The Punitive City: Notes on the Dispersal of Social Control," 3 *Comtemporary Crises* 339.

Cressey, D. and P. McDermott (1974) *Diversion from the Criminal Justice System*. Washington, D.C.: Law Enforcement Assistance Administration.

Dingman, P. R. (1974) "The Case for the State Hospital," in *Where Is My Home?* Washington, D.C.: National Technical Information Service.

Empey, L. T. (1973) "Juvenile Justice Reform: Diversion, Due Process, and Deinstitutioalization," in L. Ohlin (ed.) *Prisoners in America*. Englewood Cliffs, N.J.: Prentice-Hall.

Fine, B. (1977) "Objectification and the Contradictions of Bourgeois Power," 7 *Economy and Society* 408.

Flynn, E. E. (1978) "Classification for Risk and Supervision: A Preliminary Conceptualization," in J. Freeman (ed.) *Prisons Past and Future*. London: Heinemann.

Fogel, D. (1975) *We Are the Living Proof: The Justice Model for Corrections*. Cincinnati: Anderson.

Foucault, M. (1965) *Madness and Civilization*. New York: Mentor.

_____ (1977) *Discipline and Punish*. New York: Pantheon.

Freidson, E. (1970) *Profession of Medicine*. New York: Dodd, Mead.

Gaylin, W. (1974) *Partial Justice*. New York: Knopf.

Gaylin, W., *et al.* (1978) *Doing Good: The Limits of Benevolence*. New York: Pantheon.

Goffman, E. (1961) *Asylums*. Garden City, N.Y.: Doubleday.

Greenberg, D. (1975) "Problems in Community Corrections," 10 *Issues in Criminology* 1.

Greenberg, D. and D. Humphries (1979) "The Cooptation of Fixed Sentencing Reform," 26 *Crime and Delinquency* 206.

Hay, D. *et al.* (1976) *Albion's Fatal Tree*. New York: Pantheon.

Hofrichter, R. (1982) "Neighborhood Justice and the Social Control Problems of American Capitalism: A Perspective," in R. Abel (ed.) *The Politics of Informal Justice, vol. 1: The American Experience*. New York: Academic.

Ignatieff, M. (1978) *A Just Measure of Pain: Penitentiaries and the Industrial Revolution*. New York: Pantheon.

Katz, M. (1978) "Origins of the Institutional State," 4 *Marxist Perspectives* 6.

Kittrie, N. (1972) *The Right To Be Different*. Baltimore: Penguin.

Klein, M. W., *et al.* (1976) "The Explosion in Police Diversion Programs," in M. Klein (ed.) *The Juvenile Justice System*. Beverly Hills, Calif.: Sage Publications.

Leifer, R. (1969) *In the Name of Mental Health*. New York: Aronson.

Lemert, E. (1972) "Social Problems and the Sociology of Deviance," in E. Lemert, *Human Deviance, Social Problems, and Social Control*, 2d ed. Englewood Cliffs, N.J.: Prentice-Hall.

Lerman, P. (1975) *Community Treatment and Social Control*. Chicago: University of Chicago Press.

enson, C. L. (1944) *Ethics and Language*. New Haven, Conn.: Yale University Press.

now, D. (1965) "Normal Crimes," 12 *Social Problems* 255.

or, L. (1978) *"Ethics and Expediency in Penal Practice," in J. Freeman (ed.) Prisons Past and Future*. London: Heinemann.

mpson, E. P. (1976) *Whigs and Hunters*. New York: Pantheon.

den Haag, E. (1975) *Punishing Criminals*. New York: Basic Books.

Hirsch, A. (1976) *Doing Justice*. New York: Hill and Wang.

enberg, E. and J. Vorenberg (1973) "Early Diversion from Criminal Justice: Practice in Search of a Theory," in L. Ohlin (ed.) Prisoners in America. Englewood Cliffs, N.J.: Prentice-Hall.

s, G. (1975) "The Human Sewer," *New York Review of Books* (April 3).

son J. J. (1978) *The Declining Significance of Race*. Chicago: University of Chicago Press.

son, J. Q. (1975) *Thinking about Crime*. New York: Basic Books.

lpert, J. and E. Wolpert (1974) "The Relocation of Released Mental Patients into Residential Communities." Princeton University (unpublished).

___ (1976) "The Relocation of Released Mental Patients into Residential Communities," 7 *Policy Sciences* 31.

Martinson, R. (1974) "What Works? Questions and Answers about Prison F
  Interest* (Spring) 22.
Messinger, S. (1976) "Confinement in the Community," 13 *Journal of I
  Delinquency* 82.
Miller, M. B. (1974) "At Hard Labor: Rediscovering the Nineteenth Centu
  Criminology* 91.
Mitford, J. (1973) *Kind and Usual Punishment*. New York: Knopf.
Morris, N. (1974) *The Future of Imprisonment*. Chicago: University of Chi
Moynihan, Daniel P. (1969) *Maximum Feasible Misunderstanding*. New Y
Muraskin, W. (1976) "The Social Control Theory in American History—A (
  Social History* 559.
Nagin, D. (1978) "Crime Rates, Sanction Levels, and Constraints on Prison F
  Society Review* 341.
Nicolaus, M. (1967) "Proletariat and Middle Class in Marx," 7 *Studies on t
O'Connor, J. (1973) *The Fiscal Crisis of the State*. New York: St. Martin's.
——— (1974) *The Corporations and the State*. New York: Harper & Row.
Orlans, H. (1948) "An American Death Camp," 5 *Politics* 162.
Piven, F. and R. Cloward (1971) *Regulating the Poor*. New York: Pantheon.
President's Commission on Law Enforcement and the Administration of Just
  Report: Corrections*. Washington, D.C.: Government Printing Office.
Rock, P. (1977) "Law, Order, and Power in Late Seventeenth and Early
  England," 16 *International Annals of Criminology* 233.
Rothman, D. (1971) *The Discovery of the Asylum*. Boston: Little, Brown.
——— (1973) "Decarcerating Prisoners and Patients," 1 *Civil Liberties Revie
——— (1980) *Conscience and Convenience: The Asylum and Its Alternatives in
  Boston: Little, Brown.
Rusche, G. and O. Kirchheimer (1939) *Punishment and Social Structure*. N
  University Press.
Rutherford, A. and O. Bengur (1976) *Community Based Alternatives to Ju
  Washington, D.C.: Law Enforcement Assistance Administration.
Scull, A. (1972) "Social Control and the Amplification of Deviance," in R.
  Douglas (eds.) *Theoretical Perspectives on Deviance*. New York: Basic Boc
——— (1976) "The Decarceration of the Mentally Ill: A Critical View," 6 *Politi
——— (1977a) "Madness and Segregative Control: The Rise of the Insane /
  Problems* 337.
——— (1977b) *Decarceration: Community Treatment and the Deviant: A
  glewood Cliffs, N.J.: Prentice-Hall.
——— (1979a) *Museums of Madness: The Social Organization of Insanity in 1
  England*. New York: St. Martin's.
——— (1979b) "Moral Treatment Reconsidered: Some Sociological Comment
  the History of British Psychiatry," 9 *Psychological Medicine* 421.
Segal, S.P. (1974) "Life in Board and Care: Its Political and Social Contex," in \
  Scottsdale, Ariz.: National Technical Information Services.
Spitzer, S. (1975) "Toward a Marxian Theory of Deviance," 22 *Social Problem.
——— (1979) "The Rationalization of Crime Control," 3 *Contemporary Crises
Spitzer, S. and A. Scull (1977a) "Social Control in Historical Perspective: Fron
  Responses to Crime," in D. Greenberg (ed.) *Corrections and Punishment*. B(
  Sage Publications.
——— (1977b) "Privatization and Capitalist Development: The Case of the P
  Social Problems* 18.

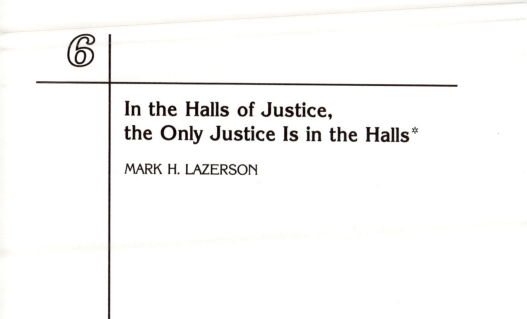

6

In the Halls of Justice,
the Only Justice Is in the Halls*

MARK H. LAZERSON

INTRODUCTION

> If the social interest in rapid, efficient processing is superior to the social interest in carefully individuated justice, it is certainly possible to devise mass production legal methods [Friedman, 1967: 810].

Contrary to the claims of some, American law has not demonstrated that its "paramount concern was with procedural justice" for the lower classes (Cappelletti and Garth, 1978: 240). The advocates of neighborhood justice centers, mediation boards, and other expressions of "informal justice" have constructed a myth of a distant, abstract law, a myth that defies the legal experience of the American underclass. The poor, the dispossessed, the "have-nots" (Galanter, 1974) know a courtroom (Feeley, 1979) that bears little resemblance to the noble promise of due process.

*I wish to give special thanks to Richard L. Abel for first suggesting that I write this chapter and for his skillful editing. My thanks also to Carolyn Kubitschek, Herman Lazerson, Lois Corcoran, Florence Sachs, and Christine Harrington.

119

   Prior to the creation of the Office of Economic Opportunity Legal Services program in the mid-1960s, indigents fared poorly in the courts. Whether pursued by collection agents and landlords or deprived of critical government benefits, the masses of unrepresented poor were unable to take advantage of the procedural and substantive rights available to those wealthy enough to retain lawyers (Auerbach, 1976).

   In recent years a wider range of individuals has been able to obtain legal representation—if sometimes of dubious quality—in part through the Legal Services program and in part because competition has forced the rapidly growing private bar to create legal clinics. As a result, the traditional patrons of the courts find the calendars and courtrooms filled with cases and people undeserving of judicial solicitude and time, and these "hitherto unrepresented, oppressed and inchoate interests . . . are making it more difficult for business to use the system" (Abel, 1979: 30). This development has stimulated a movement to establish new forums to dispose of the myriad problems of the poor that now clutter the civil courts, whose due process rights are viewed as too costly for such trivial matters. By institutionalizing the informal legal practices the courts had followed when the poor were unrepresented, these new forums adopt procedures that undercut the benefits the poor had obtained from legal counsel. Thus many of these reform schemes limit jury trials, pretrial discovery, motion practice, stenographic records, and appeals. Nonjudicial hearing officers, unfamiliar with evidentiary and procedural rules, often preside over trials so brief they can be measured with an egg timer. There has even been a movement to close these forums to legal counsel. Such reforms follow a long tradition of instrumental use of the courts by commercial interests (Horwitz, 1977).

   One example of such a reform is the New York City Housing Court, an institution designed to informalize justice within the existing legal system. I will focus on the Housing Court located in the Bronx, a borough that has become a metaphor for the urban crisis of post-war America (Severo, 1969; 1977).[1] I will begin with a brief exegesis of New York landlord–tenant law and explain why it has traditionally been detrimental to the interests of tenants and incapable of solving the housing crisis. Then I will discuss the legal strategy developed by the Morrisania office of the South Bronx Legal Services Corporation (SBLS) and continued by its replacement, the Landlord–Tenant Office of SBLS (where I practiced as a trial attorney in 1974–1975), in order to shift the balance of advantage in the Bronx Landlord–Tenant Court. The very success of this approach created significant opposition from real estate interests and was one

   ───────────

   [1]One indicator of the gravity of the crisis is a 1969 study by the New York City Medical Examiner's Office of the Hunts Point section of the South Bronx that revealed that its residents have less than one chance in twenty of dying of natural causes (Severo, 1969: 30).

stimulus for the Housing Court legislation. I will contrast the situation before and after the reform to demonstrate how increased institutionalized legal informality eroded the legal position of tenants.

In the summer of 1970 SBLS launched a strategy of using every available procedural technicality and objection as a defense against tenant eviction proceedings. This discouraged landlords from using the courts by transforming an extremely inexpensive and brief legal proceeding into a very costly and time-consuming one. Landlords who had conceded few rights to tenants inhabiting some of the worst housing in the United States[2] were now forced to negotiate settlements that favored tenants. Inside the courtroom, long trials so slowed the movement of cases that few landlords could obtain hearings. Some landlords were effectively deterred from using the courts altogether.

The SBLS strategy was aimed not against informalism as such but against informalism as traditionally practiced by the judges of the Landlord–Tenant Court. Informalism operates against the interests of tenants. Inside the courts, most tenants are unrepresented, whereas most landlords have attorneys; the substantive law requires tenants to pay rent even for a slum dwelling; and hearing officers are often biased against tenants. Outside the court, however, the inequalities between landlord and tenant are considerably reduced, primarily because the tenant cannot be removed without court process. Thus the question that needs to be addressed is not whether informalism is good or bad but which of the two adversaries it will favor.

Most students of the access-to-justice movement completely ignore this critical issue. Which cases should be directed to informal adjudication? Are not the claims of the poor to quality housing, health care, or jobs as deserving of judicial attention as those of the rich? Does the growing movement to transfer the claims of the disadvantaged into new forums express solicitude or hostility?

The New York Housing Court is especially relevant to any discussion of improving "access to justice" for the underprivileged through judicial informality because it is specifically mentioned by Earl Johnson in Mauro Cappelletti's ambitious study of alternatives to traditional adjudication (Johnson, 1978: 945–950). This chapter responds to the call by Cappelletti and Garth (1978: 274) for empirical research on the Housing Court. But it offers little support for their claims that the court "carefully scrutinizes summary eviction proceedings brought by landlords," "uncover[s] tenant defenses based on housing code violations," or " serves to make tenants aware of the new right they have to a certain standard of housing" (*Ibid.*: 275). Instead, I will argue that in-

---

[2]In an extensive study of housing conditions among welfare recipients in New York City, residents of the Bronx expressed the greatest dissatisfaction with their housing conditions (Sternlieb and Indik, 1973: 77).

stitutionalized informal justice subverts the gains that the SBLS had secured for tenants through the development of procedural defenses.

This account of the fight for formal justice in the Landlord–Tenant and Housing Courts also serves to flesh out Abel's theory of a dialectical relationship between legalization and delegalization (Abel, 1979: 43). Such a relationship is found not only in the legislative arena but also within the courtroom, where individuals resolve their differences without direct state interference, under the shadows cast by a highly formalized and exacting legal process (Mnookin and Kornhauser, 1979). If the cost of entry to that process is high and the likelihood of success is low, landlords and tenants will be strongly encouraged to resolve their differences outside of court. But if the courts remove these obstacles, then they will also eliminate the incentive for the parties to create their own informal justice. Efforts by the state that appear to democratize procedures can actually result in an increase in the power of the dominant classes (Hofrichter, 1977). The New York City Housing Court is a prime example.

LANDLORD–TENANT LAW IN NEW YORK

Landlord–tenant disputes in New York usually become a matter for the courts because no tenant may be dispossessed without a judicial determination, nor may any legal papers be issued without the stamp of the Clerk of the Civil Court. But the legal process is abbreviated in order to promote the expeditious removal of tenants.[3] Summary proceedings have little in common with the traditional justice system, which former Attorney General Griffin Bell has accused of being "too slow and costly" for minor disputes (1978: 53). On the contrary, they are quite swift. The tenant must notify the clerk of the court within five days of receiving the petition and request a court date or else the court will enter a default judgment. The clerk, once notified, must schedule a hearing within eight days. If a tenant loses, the landlord receives a money judgment for the back rent and an eviction warrant to reclaim possession of the apartment. A judge is not permitted to stay the warrant more than five days (see Real Prop. Acts. Law § 732, Mckinney 1979).

In fact, because of this law New York City residents have considerably less time to respond to a dispossess petition than tenants elsewhere in the state. A major equal protection and due process attack on these special rules was rebuffed

---

[3]Landlords may use a summary proceeding even when they themselves have delayed for more than a year in issuing a dispossess petition (see *City of New York* v. *Betancourt*). Such a tactic could be used to empty rent-controlled apartments of tenants who have not paid rent for an extended period and cannot possibly obtain the full amount during the brief summary proceeding. One court persuasively made this argument (see *Maxwell* v. *Simons*), but the opinion is no longer good law in light of *Betancourt*.

by the federal courts (*Velazquez* v. *Thompson*). The court held that the summary proceeding assured landlords a quick and inexpensive mechanism for removing nonpaying tenants and that this was a rational legislative response to the critical housing shortage in New York City.

The summary proceeding is also inexpensive. Through most of the 1970s a landlord could purchase a court number for a summary dispossess petition from the clerk of the court for $5 and have it served for an additional $2.50. (In the summer of 1980 the fees increased to $27.50.) Legal representation at that time (including a trial) cost only $25 (now $50).

Indeed, the summary proceeding is probably the greatest legal bargain in a city with some of the highest legal fees in the country. In addition, summary proceedings are extremely profitable for the courts. Today, filing fees amount to over four million dollars, twice the annual estimated budget for Housing Court personnel and related services (Cohen, 1979: 43).

Low fees are a function of the high turnover, made possible by statutes that favor mass processing of summary proceedings. A single telephone call by a landlord to his lawyer's secretary suffices to commence an eviction. The secretary types out the relevant information on a form petition and then affixes the lawyer's name to the verification (a statement swearing that the allegations contained in the legal papers are true). In New York the person with the greatest personal knowledge usually has to verify legal papers. In a landlord–tenant proceeding this would be the landlord or his agent, not the attorney. But in a summary proceeding the attorney verifies "upon information and belief," i.e., he believes the facts to be true, and the basis of such belief is information provided by the landlord. This procedure saves time and expense since the landlord need not sign the petition. After several judges in Manhattan condemned this practice as an attempt to circumvent the object of ensuring honest pleadings, a legislative amendment was quickly passed legalizing it (see *Fisch* v. *Chason*; *New York State Legislative Service Annual*, 1979: 344).

The significance of the verification takes on added importance in light of Real Prop. Acts. Law § 732. Outside of New York City all summary proceedings must be placed on the court calendar by the court clerk. If a tenant does not appear on the hearing date, the judge may enter a default judgment and issue a warrant of eviction. But the judge may also hold an "inquest"—a brief examination of the dispossess petition to see if it satisfies the legal requirements—and may also require the landlord to testify. But because of Real Prop. Acts. Law § 732 a tenant in New York City must first go to the court clerk to have the case placed on the calendar or a default judgment and warrant of eviction will be issued based only on the verification of a lawyer who knows nothing about whether the tenant paid the rent or not. No judicial inquiry is ever undertaken. Most summary proceedings are decided in this manner.

The summary proceeding has existed in New York since 1820. Prior to that time landlords had no recourse other than a common law action of ejectment to remove those unlawfully on their property. This action could be time-consuming since it entitled the parties to use all the procedural options offered by the common law. The landowning class pressured the legislature to establish a summary proceeding, but to protect the rights of tenants the landlord had to comply precisely with the statutory prerequisites. Failure to do this deprived the court of subject matter jurisdiction (authority to hear the case), and the proceeding would have to be dismissed, forcing the landlord to start again from the beginning (see Shaw, 1963: 104–113; *Reich* v. *Cochran*).

The current law governing summary proceedings still requires the landlord to state on the face of the petition all the information governing the landlord–tenant relationship: the name of the tenant, a description of the apartment, the rent, a request for payment of the rent by the landlord, the form of the rental agreement, the name of the registered managing agent, the rent control law applying to the apartment, the rent allegedly due and owing, etc. If any of this information is incorrect or missing, the landlord is not permitted to amend the petition and the court must dismiss it, forcing the landlord to start afresh. It is absolutely irrelevant whether the tenant has paid the rent (*West Realty Corp.* v. *Wood*; *Giannini* v. *Stuart*).

The rationale for such a strict and technical approach is that summary proceedings allow the tenant only a few days to prepare responsive pleadings, deny all rights to pretrial discovery, and terminate in a very brief trial. The only information the tenant receives about the landlord's case is what is stated on the face of the dispossess petition. Thus, a tenant is entitled to a concise statement of the ultimate facts upon which the proceeding is predicated so that he can be prepared to defend himself (*Fisch* v. *Chason*). Motions to amend the pleadings, appropriate in a plenary action, are therefore denied in a summary proceeding. This stringent policy is also intended to discourage landlords from needlessly invoking the power of the court to obtain their rent.

For many experienced tenant attorneys defects on the face of the petition, which are frequent because of the complexity of the law and the incompetence of both landlords and their attorneys, constitute the first line of defense in a summary proceeding. A dismissal of the action means that the tenant is under no obligation to pay the rent until the landlord brings another proceeding and succeeds in obtaining a judgment. Realty interests contend that such a refusal to pay rent can only intensify the deterioration of the housing stock.

When a Legal Services' client in the Bronx refuses to pay the rent, it is usually for one of two reasons: the tenant either does not have the money or is withholding the rent in order to protest illegal conditions in the apartment. In the first instance the client is probably penniless because of a bureaucratic mistake of one of the numerous governmental agencies upon which the poor depend for their livelihood. Delaying the proceeding for a month or two allows the tenant sufficient time to obtain the missing unemployment or veterans check and to pay the rent without being evicted. The latter situation is more common and presents Legal Services lawyers with a difficult question: given the ubiquitous slum housing of the Bronx, what should lawyers seek to gain in court?

One possible goal is to help the client to move. But few Legal Services clients can do so. Inadequate incomes, discrimination against black and Hispanic tenants, and a severe housing shortage in the surrounding communities all conspire to force most residents to remain in their dilapidated homes (Foley, 1975). Therefore, a strategy that seeks to gain the client time to move is rarely appropriate.

Another alternative is to ignore the procedural issues and present the tenant's housing conditions to the judge. Such a decision presupposes that the judge wants to improve housing conditions and has the ability to do so. The first condition is rarely satisfied and the second never is.

Poor tenants and Legal Services lawyers in the Bronx commonly face judicial bias, as they do in other parts of the country (Stumpf and Janowitz, 1969). The normal objective of a Bronx judge in the Landlord–Tenant Court, or of a hearing officer in the Housing Court that replaced it, was to help the landlord and his attorney short-circuit a potentially complex legal proceeding by simply ordering the tenant to pay the rent demanded. If the tenant complained of housing code violations, the judge would tell the landlord to make the repairs once the tenant paid the rent. The outcome was predictable: The landlord received the rent and the tenant continued to live in the same uninhabitable apartment. A few tenants, angered by the injustice of their situation, overcame judicial intimidation and insisted on describing the falling plaster, the rodents, and the days and nights of unbearable cold. But in five minutes the trial would be over, judgment rendered for the landlord, and the tenant ordered to pay the rent in five days or face eviction.[4] One judge, who came from a famous old political club, would often add a few words of solace: "My heart goes out to you but my hands are tied."

At one time such an apologetic response could be defended because few substantive defenses were available to a tenant in a proceeding for nonpayment of rent. But during the last decade important legislative and judicial reforms have considerably eroded the common law obligation of the tenant to pay rent regard-

---

[4]New York summary proceedings mirror those in housing courts around the country. In the Chicago Circuit Court (First Municipal District) the average time allotted to each contested case was approximately two minutes, which included the twenty seconds consumed while the clerk called the case and the parties approached the bench (Fusco, et al., 1979: 105). Even a most positive and glowing account of the Los Angeles Landlord—Tenant Court, written by one of its judges, reports that the average case "generally takes between 10 and 15 minutes to litigate" (Nebron and Ides, 1978: 557; emphasis added). The use of the term litigate to describe cases taking less than fifteen minutes must evoke much mirth from those lawyers who spend days, months, or even years litigating a case in state and federal courts!

less of the condition of the apartment. Since 1971 New York case law has entitled tenants to damages or an abatement of rent for the landlord's failure to provide safe and habitable housing (*Amanuensis Ltd.* v. *Brown*). But most judges and hearing officers have been reluctant to apply it. Indeed, one notorious antitenant judge instructed jurors during a nonpayment trial that in determining the tenant's claim for damages they should consider the effect of reduced rent rolls on New York City's financial crisis!

The failure of the courts to implement this decision was underscored by the New York State legislature in 1975 when it imposed a warranty of habitability on all residential leases (Real Prop. Acts. Law § 235[b], McKinney 1979). In theory, this entitles a tenant to sue for a rent abatement and consequential damages if the warranty of habitability is violated by the landlord. But judicial relief under this statute has also been rare,[5] and judges have undermined its effect by ruling that landlords need not plead compliance with the statute because such a require- ment would "jeopardize the summary nature of summary proceedings" (*Maryano* v. *Peters*). In the words of one Civil Court judge, the law "results in illusory protection of this substantial statutory right to habitability and rent abatement" (Cohen, 1979: 32).

Though the courts have not been amenable to giving tenants monetary dam- ages under warranty of habitability defenses, they are willing to provide other relief. The most common is a stay of the eviction proceeding because of the landlord's failure to make repairs (Real Prop. Acts. Law § 755, McKinney 1979).[6] In this situation the tenant is ordered to pay the rent into court until such time as the landlord corrects the conditions. What frequently happens is that the tenant pays the rent into court for a year or more, no repairs are ever made, and the tenant, weary of living in such an apartment, moves out and stops paying rent. This then permits the landlord to move to vacate the stay and collect all the back rent even though he has never repaired the apartment. Some courts have strengthened the rights of tenants under this section, even granting them a right to a rebate after the stay is vacated (*B.L.H. Realty Corp.* v. *Cruz*). But such decisions are so rare that landlords usually favor this proceeding as an expedient way of assuring eventual payment of rent. Landlords in such cases will admit that

---

[5]Because there are no guidelines for the type of proof necessary to prove dimunition in rental value caused by a breach in the warranty of habitability, tenants have received only nominal "six cents" awards (see *Steinberg* v. *Carreras*; *Kekllas* v. *Saddy*).

[6]A tenant can also defend a nonpayment proceeding if there are rent-impairing violations of record continuing for six months (New York Multiple Dwelling Law § 302-a, McKinney 1974). The tenant is obligated to deposit the rent with the clerk of the court. Since a tenant must first get the building inspector to record the violation and then wait an additional six months before being able to assert his right to a habitable apartment, this statute is all but worthless and rarely invoked by tenants' attorneys. For a judicial critique of the statute, see *Amanuensis Ltd.* v. *Brown*.

violations exist and waive a formal hearing just to speed the order that rents be deposited in court.

The other measure favored by the courts permits the appointment of an administrator to receive rent monies and spend them on housing repairs (Real Prop. Acts. Law, Art. 7–A, McKinney 1979). The essential problem with this statute, apart from its considerable complexity, is that the administrator can use only rent monies, which are usually inadequate to make the major repairs necessary in many of the decaying buildings of the South Bronx. Furthermore, it is only likely to be applicable if there is a rent strike, since at least one-third of the tenants of a building must petition for the remedy. But if the tenants are already sufficiently organized to launch a rent strike, then direct negotiation with the landlord will prove more fruitful than litigation and receivership.

Even if one accepts the argument that the courts are unable or unwilling to resolve the housing crisis, it still does not follow that the correct strategy is to withhold rents from landlords. After all, without rents landlords are unable to make repairs; provide maintenance; pay taxes, mortgage interest, and principal; and make a profit. Tenant interest in having their rent monies used for anything but repairs and maintenance is at best indirect, but a major study of housing deterioration indicates that the inability of landlords to make a "satisfactory" profit on slum housing encourages them to cut back on maintenance and other operating expenses (Nachbaur, 1972: 201).

Undermaintenance is an eminently reasonable response to a declining market (Grigsby, 1967: 239). Reduction in services is the only possible solution in slum housing since all other costs are fixed. Accepting a profit rate inferior to that available elsewhere or operating at a loss defies the laws of capitalism and no rational businessman could pursue such a course for long. Therefore paying a landlord rent will not assure that the apartment is made habitable.

An alternative strategy would be for the tenant to pressure the landlord to make needed repairs by withholding rent, remaining in occupancy, and defeating dispossess petitions through the use of legal technicalities.[7] As overdue rent accumulates, the landlord might become more interested in correcting the violations in return for payment. But this approach will not be feasible if the

---

[7]Landlords claim that a legal strategy that increases the costs and decreases the probabilities of collecting rent will result in a decline in real estate values and cause disinvestment. But even if this is true, disinvestment is not necessarily synonymous with housing deterioration. Indeed, legal procedures that guarantee profits to irresponsible landlords only enhance real estate values by augmenting profits at the expense of building maintenance. The critical factor in assuring quality housing is not the market value of the building to the investor (exchange value) but the social value of the building to its occupants (use value). These are completely different criteria, and their divergence is the primary reason why landlord–tenant relations are antagonistic. For an extended discussion of the causes of housing deterioration, see Harvey (1973) and Tabb and Sawers (1978).

building requires major structural improvements. Rent payments from one, or even several, tenants could not provide sufficient inducement for such a costly undertaking. The only remaining solution is a rent strike, which also tries to defeat the landlord's attempt to use legal leverage and thereby confronts the landlord with the choice of settling the strike by making the repairs or defaulting on the mortgage payments and losing the building. Foreclosure can be very advantageous to tenants because such buildings are usually devalued and sell for below market price,[8] permitting the new owner to restore the building and still recover a profit. Alternatively, the tenants themselves can purchase the building at the deflated price and begin to satisfy their housing needs without the interference of the market (Castells, 1976: 24). Admittedly, this last option is a difficult one in a society committed to housing for profit, and many tenants do not have the skills to manage their own buildings. Still this approach, and the legal strategy that underlies it, is certainly preferable to the present situation in which landlords use the courts to extract their rent, continue to milk the building, and when it has decayed beyond use, torch it for the insurance money (see Blum and Maitland, 1980).

THE STRATEGY OF LEGAL FORMALISM

Procedural defects have always been common in landlord petitions, but it was the practice of most judges in the Landlord–Tenant Court (and later most hearing officers in the Housing Court) to overlook them. After years of such judicial laxity many landlord attorneys had become quite disregardful of the law. Even if a lawyer was aware that the petitions were defective, he hesitated to correct them because he usually had purchased forms by the thousands, each of which would have to be changed by his secretary. For those Bronx lawyers who file several hundred petitions a day this was a time-consuming and expensive task. The judges, and later the Housing Court hearing officers, often allowed landlords a substantial grace period if a new decision required a change in the petitions. In 1974, for instance, a court ruled that unless the recently promulgated Emergency Tenants Protection Act was specifically pleaded, the petition would have to be dismissed (353 *Realty Corp.* v. *Pisla*). But several hearing officers decided not to dismiss petitions for this reason until several months later on the ground that dismissals represented a hardship for the attorneys. A judge responded to one motion to dismiss by reminding me that the attorney had a considerable amount

---

[8]It has been reported that banks in the South Bronx have been selling their mortgages for forty cents on the dollar (Oser, 1972a). After one prolonged rent strike a $30,000 mortgage was offered for $7000 (Oser, 1975). Oser predicted that abandonment would result, but instead a new landlord bought the building and quickly resolved the nine-month rent strike by undertaking the necessary repairs.

of money invested in the old forms. Judges also permitted landlords to amend their petitions even though appellate decisions said jurisdictional defects could not be cured that way. But most of the time defects were not an issue: 90 percent of all tenants defaulted (Cohen, 1979: 79), and only those represented by counsel were capable of presenting a formal legal defense.

Even tenants represented by Legal Services lawyers were denied an adequate hearing. Judges almost invariably overruled almost any evidentiary or procedural objection, no matter how well grounded, and quickly concluded the trial. The opportunity to appeal these cases was very limited for several reasons. Few tenants were represented, and it is next to impossible for an unrepresented tenant to appeal. Tenants with counsel often settled prior to trial or won their trial. Landlords rarely appealed when petitions were dismissed for jurisdictional defects since it is easier to correct the error and start over again. If a tenant represented by Legal Services lost a trial, the tenant often could not appeal because he could not pay or purchase a bond to secure payment of rent allegedly owed or likely to be owed during the pendency of the appeal—a prerequisite for a stay of the trial court eviction order. If the rent owed by the tenant was substantial, it might be wiser for the tenant to vacate the apartment since the landlord could never collect a judgment against a person who was probably indigent and likely to remain so. Furthermore, the rent money saved during the legal conflict might allow the tenant to obtain his or her first habitable apartment. Workload pressures upon Legal Services attorneys also discouraged appeals.

The obstacles to appeal made it necessary to win in the trial court. But most victories depended upon technicalities, and the infrequency of appellate review reduced the pressure to adhere to the law. It also made lawyer objections to judicial error an empty ritual. Thus, most clients were forced to accept the trial judgment as final.

When Ken Schwartz and Richard Fischbein joined the Morrisania office of South Bronx Legal Services in the summer of 1970, they were determined to use the technical defects in dispossess petitions as a source of leverage to pressure landlords to satisfy tenant demands for better housing or else go bankrupt. Prior to their appointment, the Bronx Landlord–Tenant Court operated like an assembly line, a collection agency with the imprimatur of the state. Schwartz and Fischbein believed that the impotence of Legal Services lawyers was largely attributable to the organization of their work. Client representation at the Morrisania office had always focused on resolving individual problems in the narrowest possible manner. There was virtually no effort to develop a political strategy that could improve the legal position of all tenants (see Bellow, 1977). Attorneys had a general caseload, so that they had to appear in forums other than the Landlord–Tenant Court. Several days a week they also had to be in their offices to conduct client intake. Clients usually had the same attorney from intake to final disposition, and though such continuous representation is highly desirable, the limited financial resources meant that few tenants could be represented.[9] This reduced the institutional impact of Legal Services on the daily operation of the Landlord–Tenant Court. Judges habituated to disposing of cases against poor tenants in two minutes were able to continue doing so despite the occasional appearance of an obstinate and aggressive Legal Services attorney.

A strategy focusing on legal technicalities could have an effect only if the Morrisania office greatly increased its court caseload, forcing the judges to recognize that it was critical to the harmonious functioning of the court. A Legal Services lawyer easily could be ignored if he had only one or two cases a day. But if that lawyer had forty or fifty and constantly made the same objections, the court could not disregard him. A large caseload had been successfully used by Manhattan Supreme Court Judge Harold Rothwax when he directed Mobilization for Youth (MFY) Legal Services:

> I realized on a given day that I had eighty cases out of the hundred that were being heard that day. You may criticize the amount of time that I gave to any one case but I will bet you that with eighty cases that was my court. . . . I think the advantage of the caseload, the value of the caseload, the necessity of the caseload is that it provides you with power, and without that caseload you do not have any capacity for achieving law reform [1967: 63–64].

In order to increase the court caseload, the office encouraged tenants who sought advice on housing problems to withhold their rent and force the landlord into court. Community organizers involved in rent strikes and housing improvement efforts were also urged to follow this approach. The office energetically supported rent strikes, which it viewed as both an efficient use of legal resources and a potent method by which tenants could counterbalance the power of landlords. It hoped that landlords who were struck would forgo legal proceedings and settle directly with their tenants, using the money saved from litigation for building improvements. But most landlords had to learn first that the Bronx Landlord–Tenant Court was no longer a captive institution. These diverse strategies swelled the caseload of the Bronx Landlord–Tenant Court, making it the busiest in New York City.

Once the office had achieved a large caseload, it embarked upon aggressive advocacy in obedience to the attorney's obligation to provide "zealous representation of the client's interests within the bounds of the law" (see Bellow and Kettleson, 1978). Attorneys were discouraged from making moral judgments about the substantive merits of the cases, i.e., should the tenant pay the rent? Instead, they were instructed to resist the claims of the landlord, compelling him to prove every element of the case. Staff attorneys had been well trained to conduct highly technical defenses. They began by challenging the personal

---

[9]There is no constitutional right to counsel in civil proceedings because the defendant is not threatened with loss of liberty (*Matter of Smiley*).

jurisdiction of the court by demanding a hearing on service of process. Horror stories of improper service are legion in the Bronx, where "sewer service" is not hyperbole but fact.[10] Major scandals revealed by investigations of process servers and landlord lawyers resulted in several amendments to the statute governing service of dispossess petitions (1965 N.Y. Laws, ch. 910, McKinney; 1971 N.Y. Laws, ch. 83, McKinney). Unfortunately, like most housing law reform, these amendments favored landlords and only simplified service of process on the theory that more complicated procedures would just increase nonservice and fraud. Yet sewer service continued. Revelations by Morrisania Legal Services resulted in the federal prosecution of Arthur Siegel, one of the leading members of the Bronx landlord bar, on fifty-six counts of using false affidavits to obtain default judgments against tenants (*New York Times*, November 7, 1972: 38). Siegel, however, pleaded to a misdemeanor and was able to resume his practice in the South Bronx after a six-month sentence.

Despite the widespread abuse of process in the South Bronx, Legal Services' demands for strict conformity with the law earned them the enmity of many judges. Lawyers were frequently threatened with contempt proceedings and complaints to the bar association when they demanded hearings on service. Judges also accused the Morrisania attorneys of obstructionism. Such a complaint might have been colorable had the judges been genuinely concerned to improve housing and capable of doing so. But to them reaching the merits only meant asking, "Did the tenant pay the rent? If not, when will he do so?"

Service of process could legitimately be challenged in nearly every dispossess proceeding in the South Bronx because process servers rarely complied with the statutory requirements that they first attempt personal service and only if this were not reasonably possible, tape the notice to the door and send a copy by certified mail (Real Prop. Acts. Law § 735, McKinney 1979). One of the largest process servers in the Bronx was so terrified of meeting tenants that he had a reputation for delivering notices at three or four in the morning. He never rang door bells to attempt personal service but instead slipped the notices under the door. On the affidavits he would swear to times of service that were humanly impossible, frequently placing himself at different addresses miles apart within minutes.

The Morrisania Legal Services strategy slowed evictions and encouraged landlords to settle with their tenants outside of court. Every hearing on service of process prolonged the final disposition. It frequently took two or three weeks for a hearing to be scheduled. Even if a landlord successfully proved service, a hearing on the merits of the petition could not be scheduled for another month or more. Meanwhile the tenant remained in the apartment. These challenges also raised

---

[10]"Sewer service" is common in many courts that handle the problems of the poor; See Caplovitz (1967: 161, 189–190), Small Claims Court Study Group (1972: 71), and Novak (1973).

the cost of legal procedures for landlords, who had to pay both the process server and lawyer to attend the jurisdictional hearing. These expenses were especially painful during a rent strike.

Once these maneuvers were exhausted, the next step was the trial. The aim of Legal Services was a settlement, but an acceptable one could be obtained only by demonstrating to the landlord the high cost of securing a favorable judgment. New York law places heavy evidentiary demands on the proof of the elements of a summary dispossess petition. Ownership often requires a property deed. The best evidence rule requires that the original be produced, if available. Landlords rarely have the deed with them and may suffer dismissal. New York law also requires that a foundation be established before the landlord can testify about telephone conversations with tenants and before business records can be introduced. But many landlord lawyers are so incompetent that they do not know how to accomplish this basic task. They also frequently forget to enter the necessary proof into the record. Finally, they almost never prepare their clients to testify. Prior embarrassments on the witness stand painfully remind the experienced landlord of what should be said to win the case. But inexperienced landlords often end up in a screaming contest with their own attorneys outside the courtroom.

Indeed, landlord attorneys greatly contributed to slowing the proceedings. Their improperly phrased questions allowed Legal Services lawyers to object throughout the trial. This gross incompetence irritated most judges; even those who favored landlords quickly tired of trying to instruct their attorneys in the art of asking an unobjectionable question. In the end, the landlord would usually succeed in presenting his prima facie case but only after wasting his own time and that of the court.

On cross-examination Legal Services lawyers probed landlords about every detail, often for two or three hours. Not infrequently landlords expressed their uncontrollable anger, demanding an end to the proceedings and payment of the rent. Memories of these experiences undoubtedly encouraged many landlords to avoid trials and settle their cases.

During direct examination of the tenant the Legal Services attorney would elicit such exhaustive descriptions of the apartment that the stenographic record read like a blueprint of the apartment. In the early phases of the new strategy many trials resulted in judgment for the landlord. But even these proved pyrrhic victories in the battle for control of the court. The time consumed in full-scale trials delayed other dispossess petitions. The Landlord–Tenant Court had only two hearing parts, one of which was preoccupied with the calendar until the afternoon and therefore was unable to hear many cases. Cases calendared but not heard had to be postponed, often for a month or longer. The situation had become so unfavorable to landlords that if a case was assigned a position near the end of the day's calendar, the landlord would voluntarily withdraw the petition, purchase a new case number, and serve a new petition, hoping that the next time the case would be heard when scheduled.

Many of the judges lacked the skill to conduct an orderly trial. Furthermore, frequent lengthy trials were also straining the organizational resources of the Landlord–Tenant Court. The successful tenant defense compelled judges to put pressure on landlords. The strategy of the Legal Services lawyers suggested to the judges a way this might be done. If they responded to defense motions that attacked the pleadings by dismissing the petitions, they avoided lengthy trials. Dismissals warned landlords and their lawyers that defective petitions would be dealt with harshly whatever the "merits" of the case and gave them a real incentive to settle disputes with tenants in the hallways rather than to consume judicial time.

Landlords were forced to reevaluate their position. They could no longer be assured of walking into court at 9:30 in the morning and leaving before lunch with a judgment for eviction. Now it might take several trips to the courthouse before the case was even called for trial. If a Legal Services attorney was representing the tenant, the chances were excellent that the petition would be dismissed and the landlord would have to recommence the entire proceeding, losing precious time and money. In the meantime landlords had to share with tenants the noisy, dingy courtrooms overflowing with angry, abusive people.

Landlords soon recognized that the only reasonable solution was to settle in the hallways of the court building on the day the case was first calendared. If housing conditions were in issue—and they almost always were—the tenant would agree to make partial rent payments as the landlord completed the necessary repairs. In the interim the case would be either withdrawn or adjourned. Because of the weak position of the landlords, tenants obtained rebates of the rent for a month or more because their apartments lacked heat and hot water, had falling plaster, or were overrun by rodents. Rent abatements would otherwise have been difficult to extract from landlords since judges were hostile to such claims and imposed evidentiary barriers that few poor tenants could ever have surmounted.

Landlords often agreed to accept alternative payment schedules when tenants lacked sufficient funds to pay the rent. If the tenant wanted to vacate the premises, his lawyer usually succeeded in gaining an additional month or two in which to move and forgiveness for any past rent owing, in return for giving the landlord judgment of possession. This was of considerable importance to most tenants because a landlord who won at trial would obtain a judgment for both possession and back rent, and the tenant might be hounded by collection agencies. Though tenants receiving public assistance, who were thus judgment proof, might be indifferent, many Legal Services clients worked and others hoped to be off welfare in the future.

Attorneys for landlords frequently encouraged their clients to settle for two reasons. If the case went to trial and was dismissed because of a defective petition, the attorney's reputation would be tarnished. If the case survived the pretrial motions, the attorney would risk becoming embroiled in a prolonged trial that would prevent him from servicing his many other clients. Since most attorneys did not charge their best clients an additional fee for a trial, litigation was extremely costly to the former. The economics of landlord representation thus resembled those of the personal injury plaintiffs' bar (see Rosenthal, 1974).

Landlord attorneys also benefited from the new procedural formalism. First, the number of landlords who attempted to represent themselves diminished sharply when they realized that they lacked the skills to survive the barrage of procedural objections fired by Legal Services lawyers or to conduct a formal trial. In Brooklyn, by contrast, many landlords appeared without an attorney and often were able to overcome objections that would have been fatal in the South Bronx.[11] As a result the number of attorneys with a full-time landlord–tenant practice in the Bronx doubled between 1971 and 1974. Those already in practice enjoyed higher incomes and expanded their offices.

Second, landlord attorneys were able to use judicial hypercriticism of defective petitions to force reluctant landlords to settle their cases and thus avoid a time-consuming trial. Lawyers did this even when the landlords could win—not often with their best clients but with the small landlord who represented little business in the Bronx courts. Third, the Bronx Landlord–Tenant Court developed a body of law unique to that borough. Landlord attorneys from other boroughs, particularly Manhattan, found themselves at a distinct disadvantage when attempting to raid the lucrative Bronx real estate trade. Success in the Bronx depended upon intimate knowledge of that court, which could be obtained only by continuous involvement with it. Many Manhattan attorneys swore never to return to the borough for a landlord–tenant case after becoming embroiled in a one- or two-day trial with an adversary represented by SBLS.

The mutually advantageous relationship between the landlord and tenant bars did not go unrecognized by either side. Legal Services attorneys would often be particularly aggressive toward out-of-county lawyers. Landlord attorneys would often accede to delay evictions or accede to settlements favoring tenants. The interaction resembled criminal plea bargaining, but tenants in the Bronx exerted considerable influence over the outcome, whereas the prosecutor has the upper hand in the criminal courts. In the criminal process the indigent defendant is often incarcerated, and a guilty plea frequently achieves release from confinement long before the trial could be scheduled. In the Landlord–Tenant

[11]At this time corporate landlords were required by law to represent themselves. One of the changes introduced by the Housing Court permitted corporate officers or principal stockholders to represent themselves (City Civ. Ct. Act § 110(1), McKinney 1979). But in the Bronx most corporate landlords continued to be represented by an attorney.

Court indigent tenants can not be evicted until after trial, and the landlord could often obtain possession more quickly through negotiation. Furthermore, the criminal accused is exposed to a risk—the sentence—whose magnitude is extremely uncertain, whereas the tenant faces a risk—eviction—whose only uncertainty is the date.

THE ATTACK ON SOUTH BRONX LEGAL SERVICES

It did not take long for the landlords to counterattack. They enlisted the aid of Alan S. Oser, the real estate correspondent of the *New York Times*. In a series of hard-hitting articles on the front page of the Sunday real estate section, Oser portrayed the Legal Services lawyers and their stranglehold on the Bronx Landlord–Tenant Court as a principal cause of urban blight in the borough. These articles were contemporaneous with the drafting of state legislation to create a new housing court that would seriously erode the gains tenants had made through the use of legal formalism.

Oser argued that this delay in the collection of rent only furthered the trend toward housing abandonment and decay: "Several months may pass before these [eviction] procedures succeed in the heavily clogged landlord–tenant court. If tenants are represented by the Legal Services branches of the Hunts Point or Morrisania antipoverty offices the case is slowed by legal tactics and the shortage of antipoverty lawyers" (1972b: 1). He quoted a Legal Services supervisor as advocating a strategy of "in depth" representation in close cooperation with community organizations representing tenants (1972a: 1). As a result both the number of cases in Landlord–Tenant Court and the number of tenants represented by the Legal Services office had substantially increased. Oser reported that the "entire court procedure is ineffective" because the court could not cope with so many legally represented tenants (*Ibid.*). Oser's interviews with court officials confirmed that the Legal Services offices in the Bronx had successfully halted the flow of landlord–tenant cases.

> The antipoverty legal offices provide only one lawyer to handle 60 or 70 cases a day, according to judicial authorities and as a result court calendars are severely clogged. In addition, the lawyers use all possible legal technicalities to defend tenants. Cases drag on for months. Meanwhile rents may go unpaid, assertedly in some cases for a year and more [*Ibid.*].

One unnamed court official, described as "close to the problem," criticized defense lawyers who adhered to the "letter of the law" because basically "you have a social problem." Oser stated that "the landlords . . . consider themselves the victims of a blatant attack with an ideological motivation made possible by government financed legal services" (1972c: 1). In an interview with Richard Fischbein, then a staff attorney with Morrisania Legal Services and soon to become managing attorney of a borough-wide Legal Services Landlord–Tenant Office, Oser alleged that Fischbein's goal was "to break every landlord in this area and for the tenants to take over" (*Ibid.*). Interviews with tenant organizations revealed that the SBLS strategy had caused a dramatic improvement in the success of rent strikes. Fischbein reported that in the Morrisania office, which represented over 200 rent strikes in a one-and-a-half-year period, there was only one eviction out of 4000 cases.

The attack on Morrisania Legal Services was continued by *Real Estate Weekly*, New York's principal trade newspaper. In a lead editorial, accompanied by a lengthy article, it urged Congress to eliminate funding for Morrisania Legal Services (February 9, 1972: 4). The editors requested a federal investigation of the office because they claimed that rent strikes were leading to massive abandonment in the Bronx. The newspaper also urged support of a campaign by the Bronx Realty Advisory Board to place pressure on elected representatives to halt legal defense of tenants by the Morrisania office. The newspaper stated that public officials "will be shocked to learn that taxpayer money is actually being used to bring about the downfall of the capitalist system" (*Ibid.*).

No formal federal investigation of the office was ever initiated, in part because of opposition by Herman Badillo, then the local congressman and a strong supporter of the office's activities. But a letter was sent to the office by Gerald R. Ford, then also a congressman, warning of serious consequences if its involvement in rent strikes continued.

The Bronx Realty Advisory Board also financed a team of Wall Street lawyers to challenge Legal Services lawyers in the courts. But they proved no more successful in overcoming Morrisania's barrage of procedural objections and left the Bronx court to the regular landlord bar. Another Bronx landlord attorney and former New York City administrator, Edward Rawlins, sued court officials, alleging that it was impossible to have his summary dispossess cases heard in Landlord–Tenant Court and arguing that the New York Supreme Court (a trial court) should exercise its concurrent jurisdiction in summary proceedings and hear his cases. His suit was dismissed (*Rawlins* v. *Thompson; New York Times*, August 25, 1971: 20).

Pressure was also applied against Morrisania through the judiciary. Judge Edward Thompson, the administrative judge of the Civil Court (of which the Bronx Landlord–Tenant Court was a part), held several meetings with various Legal Services officials, including the attorney-in-charge of the citywide program, Community Action for Legal Services. In these meetings Thompson would scream and rant about the activities of Legal Services lawyers in general, but he reserved particular venom for the Morrisania office. He demanded that Morrisania have one attorney at all times in each of the two courtrooms in the Bronx, something the office strongly resisted because of insufficient resources. During one unusually acrimonious meeting Thompson quoted former chief justice Earl Warren in describing the activities of the Morrisania office. "A tiny fragment of irresponsible lawyers seem bent on destroying the system of adminis-tering justice and some are simply ill-mannered and undisciplined noisemakers" (*Tenant*, July 1971: vol. 1, no. 5, p. 1).

The judicial attack on SBLS continued after the passage of the Housing Court, though it did subside in intensity. In the fall of 1973, after the Housing Court opened, Judge Thompson assigned Nat Hentel, then on the Queens Civil Court and now a Supreme Court judge, to the Bronx Housing Court calendar part for two weeks to prepare a report on the activities of SBLS. Judge Hentel, a former Republican district attorney of Queens, had established a reputation for himself as a tough disciplinarian, which may have encouraged Thompson to send him to the Bronx (though a well-respected source reported that he was assigned there because he had once arrived late for a judges' meeting). The Bronx Landlord–Tenant and Housing courts were frequently used to punish judges. Judge Hentel said he did not know why he was sent there but believed it was because he was an outsider with "some fresh ideas."[12]

In the two weeks Hentel spent in the Bronx he clashed repeatedly with the staff of SBLS over its attempt to slow the calendar part by arguing motions in nearly every case. Hentel filed a final report with Judge Thompson that personally excoriated numerous attorneys, charging violations of the canon of ethics and misbehavior. But he made no attempt to initiate contempt proceedings against any of them.

During this period the Bronx Bar Association, controlled by local real estate lawyers contemplated disciplinary proceedings against David Rozenholc, the most highly skilled and aggressive attorney in the office, but then dropped them. The prestigious Association of the Bar of the City of New York, on the other hand, provided support in the form of a team of attorneys who observed the court proceedings and filed a letter praising the legal skills of SBLS attorneys.

ENACTMENT OF THE HOUSING COURT ACT

The New York City Civil Court Act (hereafter, the Housing Court Act) went into effect on October 1, 1973, after a six-month delay because of funding short-ages (see City Civ. Ct. Act § 110, McKinney 1979). The justification for the measure was that it would speed prosecution of housing violations against land-lords by consolidating civil and criminal actions in one forum:

> The legislature finds that the effective enforcement of state and local laws for the establishment and maintenance of proper housing standards is essential to the health, safety, welfare and

[12]This statement was made by Hentel in a telephone conversation with the author on November 15, 1980.

reasonable comfort of the citizens of the state. The legislature further finds that such effective enforcement in the City of New York has been hindered by the dispersion of prosecutions, actions and proceedings to compel compliance with housing standards among a number of criminal and civil courts, so that no single court has been able to deal consistently with all of the factual and legal problems presented by the continuing existence of housing violations in any one building (1972 N.Y. Laws ch. 982, § 1(a), McKinney 1979).

The overwhelming majorities with which it passed both houses of the legislature reflected strong bipartisan support achieved through a series of compromises between tenants, landlords, and the New York City judiciary. The seeds for the Housing Court were sown by a Columbia University proposal for a housing maintenance code. It urged a comprehensive forum whose primary function would be to hear both civil and criminal matters involving code violations (Legislative Drafting Research Fund, 1965). The Columbia report explicitly warned against granting this forum jurisdiction over evictions because these would "unduly burden the court" (Ibid.: 4–5).

Prior to the Housing Court Act, when housing code violations were within the jurisdiction of the criminal court, attempts to obtain convictions against land-lords proved extremely frustrating: Prosecutions were slow, and judges assessed fines that had little or no deterrent effect (Rutzick and Huffman, 1975: 742). The Columbia study sought to change that by charging the proposed Housing and Development Administration (HDA, later renamed Housing Preservation and Development Agency) with responsibility for the swift prosecution of landlords.

The HDA and the Mayor's Office, then occupied by John V. Lindsay, submit-ted a bill to the Albany legislators in 1971 that captured the spirit of the Colum-bia study. It established an administrative tribunal to hear housing violations and impose penalties that could be enforced in court. Its purpose was to provide HDA with an expeditious means of applying rents from delinquent properties to code enforcement projects, such as emergency repairs and rehabilitation loans. Sum-mary dispossess proceedings would remain within the jurisdiction of the Civil Court. The Lindsay proposal fared poorly in the legislature. Landlord interests opposed the agency, fearing that it would dilute their due process rights and impose stiff penalties. Tenant groups had little faith in the HDA, and the judiciary resisted incursions on its jurisdiction.

The defeat of the Lindsay bill set the stage for the passage of a revised Housing Court proposal in the 1972 legislative session, principally drafted by Lorraine E. Miller, then special counsel on housing to the Assembly Democratic Minority Leader (Letter from Miller to Gov. Rockefeller, June 5, 1972).[13] As an attorney in private practice, Miller had been involved in promoting state-financed private housing and had "represented both sides" in landlord and tenant disputes.[14]

[13]This and all of the letters cited herein are reproduced in a legislative memorandum available from the New York State Legislative Service, New York, New York.

[14]This and other statements were made by Miller in a telephone conversation with the author on October 23, 1980.

According to former assemblyman Seymour Posner (a cosponsor of the Housing Court Act, left-wing Democrat, and tenant advocate), Miller acted on her own rather than as a representative of either tenant or landlord interests.[15] Her personal dedication to this cause permitted her to make the necessary compromises with the various interest groups. She received critical support from then assemblywoman Rosemary E. Gunning, a Conservative-Republican from Queens. Gunning's constituents were mostly homeowners, so her principal concern was to protect the interests of landlords with four or fewer rental units. Yet despite Gunning's conservative credentials, both Miller and Posner insisted that she was sincerely interested in protecting tenants, and Posner maintained that she "hated slumlords." She convinced her colleagues in the Republican majority to support the Housing Court. That the new bill eliminated the administrative tribunal also helped it pass, since whatever qualms the landlords might have had were overcome by fear of a worse law (Letter from E. T. Hume, president, Real Estate Board of New York, Inc., to M. Whiteman, Counsel to Gov. Rockefeller May 26, 1972).

The Housing Court Act still reflected the concerns of the Mayor's Office and the HDA to establish a specialized forum with jurisdiction over the various agencies that regulated housing, i.e., the building, fire, and health departments. It empowered the courts to impose civil penalties for code violations, recover money expended by the HDA on emergency repairs, obtain orders correcting code violations, hear applications by the HDA to be appointed receiver of a building, and decide actions by tenants seeking appointment of an administrator to collect rents and repair dangerous conditions in a building.

But in two key respects this law differed from the earlier proposal. The new housing forum was incorporated into the existing New York City Civil Court and given jurisdiction over summary proceedings by landlords to evict tenants and collect back rents. In addition, the Housing Court was staffed not by elected Civil Court judges but by hearing officers appointed to five-year terms by the administrative judge of the Civil Court. Though these hearing officers are not judges under the New York State Constitution, they possess broad equitable powers and are bound to follow the procedural and evidentiary rules of a court of record (*Glass v. Thompson*).

Both landlords and court officials were opposed to the use of hearing officers instead of Civil Court judges. The Real Estate Advisory Board wanted summary proceedings decided by judges, fearing that the hearing officers would lack judicial independence and act like enforcement officers, applying the policies of the city administration (letter from Hume to Whiteman, May 26, 1972). The presiding justices of both the First and Second Appellate Divisions, which together encompass New York City, also expressed their opposition to the use of hearing

---

[15]This and other statements were made by Posner in a telephone conversation with the author on November 15, 1980.

officers (letter from Justices H. Stevens and S. Rabin to Gov. Rockefeller, June 1, 1972). They viewed such a measure as unnecessary, since Civil Court judges were competent to preside over a housing part and any shortage of judges could be alleviated through additional appropriations.

Judge Thompson, who stood to gain through his power to appoint hearing officers, claimed that there were too few Civil Court judges to fill the new positions (letter from R. Gunning to M. Whiteman, May 17, 1972). Thompson probably also realized that budgetary and political considerations made hearing officers the easiest route to expanding the Housing Court. They would be paid less than half the salary of a judge, would not have their own chambers or law clerks, and were not entitled to other costly judicial perquisites. In addition, expansion of the Civil Court judiciary required approval by the Republican-dominated state legislature, a not inconsiderable obstacle because of the patronage it offered to New York City Democrats. Once hearing officers were authorized, more could be appointed without legislative approval.

Some tenant supporters, such as Assemblyman Seymour Posner, also supported the hearing officer concept because they believed that it was necessary "to get rid of the clubhouse hacks."[16]

Because of ambiguity in the language of the act and because of statements in its legislative history, there were also grounds for believing that both judges and hearing officers would decide housing cases (City Civ. Ct. Act § 110(e), McKinney 1979; Memorandum to Gov. Rockefeller from Attorney General L. J. Lefkowitz, June 1, 1972). But when the court opened, a Civil Court judge was assigned only to the calendar part, at which most cases were distributed to hearing officers. The judge ruled only on formal motions. When the calendar was completed the judge usually turned to matters unrelated to housing. SBLS challenged this assignment practice, arguing that the parties had to consent to the designation of a hearing officer. But the appellate courts rejected this claim (*Glass* v. *Thompson*). They ruled that the parties could be guaranteed a judge only by insisting upon a jury trial, but the standard New York City residential lease contains a jury waiver that has been upheld by the courts (*Avenue Associates* v. *Buxbaum*).

Although the final legislation was not entirely to their liking, most landlord organizations favored passage of the bill. The one major exception was the Metropolitan Fair Rent Committee, a real estate group representing owners of rent-controlled property, which recommended a gubernatorial veto (letter from R. S. Fougner, general counsel, Metropolitan Fair Rent Committee, to M. Whiteman, counsel to the governor, May 22, 1972). It contended that the

---

[16]The recent establishment of judicial screening committees in Manhattan and the Bronx, containing representatives of Legal Services and Legal Aid, resulted in the election of several extremely well-qualified and progressive Civil Court judges. They have demonstrated a real determination to protect and expand the procedural rights of tenants in the few housing cases they have heard.

proposed legislation would be too costly, too complex, and difficult to administer. Yet Lorraine Miller maintained that the landlords were "our strongest supporters" and remembered Edward Sulzberger, the leader of the group, as an
important backer of her proposal.

Tenant organizations divided over the Housing Court reform. Metropolitan
Council on Housing, the largest and most active group in the city, strongly
opposed it, though the legislative history indicates that it was not vocal in doing
so. *Tenant News*, Met Council's monthly journal, contained no mention of the
proposed reform throughout the spring of 1972 and only began to propagandize
against the Housing Court after it was in operation. Met Council also organized
protests against the Housing Court on its opening day. Still, Lorraine Miller
remembered Met Council as a consistent critic of the Housing Court: "Met
Council is opposed to everything."

Jane Benedict, the president of Met Council, could not remember if the
organization testified on the Housing Court proposal and attributed the group's
inactivity to its lack of resources.[17] But she said that the organization opposed the
Housing Court because hearing officers would be antagonistic to tenants.

Though Bronx Legal Services was hostile to the legislation, they also avoided
the legislative arena. Richard Fischbein, the former head of the SBLS Landlord–
Tenant Office, said that the "office believed there was nothing that could be
done about it. They [the legislature] didn't like us and the best policy was to
stay away."[18]

Other organizations sympathetic to tenant interests, such as the Legal Aid
Society, the Lenox Hill Neighborhood Association, and the NAACP, supported
the bill in hope that it would produce more effective code enforcement. According to Seymour Posner, these and other protenant groups agreed to accept reduced penalties and weakened enforcement provisions in order to gain passage of
the act.

Rosemary Gunning insisted that the reform measure should not stiffen penalties against landlords because its purpose was "to save the city's present housing
stock and *to avoid, however, such onerous punishment as to scare off investors or
to induce further abandonments*" (letter from R. Gunning to M. Whiteman,
May 17, 1972; emphasis added). Lorraine Miller also wished to encourage private investment. Miller, with the concurrence of Gunning, was successful in her
insistence that landlords not be treated harshly. Together they deprived HDA of
the power to hold landlords personally liable; instead the owner could only be
held liable up to the value of his property (letter from R. Gunning to Gov.
Rockefeller, June 2, 1972). They also insisted on personal service of landlords

[17]This and other statements were made by Benedict in a telephone conversation with the author on
October 20, 1980.

[18]This and other statements were made by Fischbein in a telephone conversation with the author
on October 20, 1980.

because "due process is not to be lightly surrendered or whittled away" and made it difficult for the HDA to levy against rents in order to collect penalties for housing code violations because of the importance of "cash flow" to landlords (letter from L. Miller to Gov. Rockefeller, June 5, 1972). Landlords of older buildings could escape liability if they could show they were unable to obtain financing or to correct the violations that were caused by a third party. As Mayor Lindsay noted, the proposal contained so many loopholes that "many owners will not be liable for any civil penalty regardless of their failure to correct violations after notice" (letter to Gov. Rockefeller, May 24, 1972).

Miller, however, rejected Lindsay's view that it was necessary to "get tough" with the landlords:

> Perhaps the City Administration should change its attitude and if they were more intent on assisting the many owners who are in deep financial trouble instead of seeking to confiscate their property, our housing stock might be in much better shape. Our approach, the logic of which appealed to 195 legislators of every political stripe and belief, is that it is time that we undertook a constructive program of assistance [letter to Gov. Rockefeller, June 5, 1972].

In the end the most vocal opponents of the legislation remained the Association of the Bar of the City of New York and the New York Mayor's Office. Both stressed their preference for an administrative tribunal but also said that the Housing Court Act was defective because of inadequate penalties against landlords and sloppy legal drafting (letters to Gov. Rockefeller from E. J. Morris, chairman, Committee on Housing and Urban Development, Association of the Bar of the City of New York, May 23, 1972, and Mayor Lindsay, May 24, 1972).

The debate over appropriate penalties seems to have diverted attention from the inclusion of summary proceedings in the Housing Court, even though the Columbia University study had specifically warned against doing that. Rosemary Gunning's legislative memorandum did suggest one rationale for inclusion:

> Since tenants frequently allege, for example, in a nonpayment proceeding brought against them, that violations exist as a defense to the claim for rent, and that such violations are then pending in the Criminal Court, it would seem to make good sense to have the issue of rent due, if any, the defenses, etc., all in the same forum. *This, too, would release civil court judges to do other work* [*New York Legislative Annual*, 1972: 218; emphasis added].

Governor Rockefeller's legislative message also indicated that the Housing Court Act had purposes other than those articulated during the hearings. Rockefeller commended the act as promoting the speedier administration of justice: "[It] provides a method for judicially supervised determination of housing violations which would free New York City judges and courts from much of the burden of thousands of housing violation cases, and still assure a fair and judicious forum for resolving owner–tenant disputes" [*Ibid.*: 322]. The New York State Division of the Budget (1972) also approved what it called the "secondary intent" of the act to reduce the demands on judges by using hearing officers to decide housing complaints.

This emphasis on accelerating the pace of summary proceedings and reducing tenant access to judges raises questions about a hidden agenda. Ken Schwartz insisted that the primary provocation for the Housing Court Act was the situation created by Morrisania Legal Services.[19] Lorraine Miller firmly denied this and claimed she was totally unaware of the conflict in the Bronx. This is difficult to believe in light of the articles in *Real Estate Weekly* and the *New York Times*, the *Rawlins* case, and the repeated interventions of Judge Thompson. Miller acknowledged that she had worked closely with Judge Thompson in drafting the act and was familiar with housing issues in New York City. After the reform was passed, Miller visited the Bronx in her new role as chairperson of the Housing Advisory Committee. Richard Fischbein remembered her as being "appalled" by the continued difficulties landlords encountered there. Although Seymour Posner did not recall discussion of the activities of Morrisania Legal Services during the legislative negotiations, he conceded that crowded calendars in the Landlord–Tenant Court, and especially in the Bronx, were a concern at the time.

It is difficult to be certain about the impact of landlord dissatisfaction in the Bronx on passage of the Housing Court Act. Given their vigorous campaign against Morrisania Legal Services, it is hard to believe that the landlords did not use their influence in Albany to help shape a judicial remedy for their problems. Judge Thompson, a key proponent of the Housing Court, never had the Bronx confrontation far from his mind. Whether or not by design, the Housing Court undermined many of the gains won by tenants in the Bronx.

THE CREATION OF THE SOUTH BRONX LEGAL SERVICES LANDLORD–TENANT OFFICE

Although the Morrisania office did not oppose the new law in Albany, it was preparing to continue its aggressive advocacy in the Housing Court by seeking funds to establish an office that would specialize in housing matters and would have additional staff to provide representation in the expanded Housing Court. This application set the office on a collision course with the Bronx civil division of the New York Legal Aid Society, since the funds would be available only if they were diverted from the latter.

The New York Legal Aid Society is a private, nonprofit organization engaged

---

[19]This statement was made by Schwartz in a telephone conversation with the author on October 20, 1980.

principally in criminal defense and supported by the city and state; it resembles public defender offices throughout the United States. The federal Legal Services Program, a branch of the Office of Economic Opportunity (and after 1974, an independent public corporation), has been responsible for most civil representation of indigents in New York City. But the Legal Aid Society also maintains a small civil division that received federal appropriations. SBLS was intent on obtaining these monies.

The funding struggle highlighted critical differences between the two offices, which in part reflected the more conservative attitude and structure of the Legal Aid Society (see Bellow, 1969; Getzels, 1969). Though the Legal Aid Society and Community Action for Legal Services both have boards of directors dominated by elite lawyers, individual Legal Services offices also have community boards that more closely reflect the program's clientele. These local boards participate in policymaking and help keep Legal Services more responsive to the needs of the poor.

These political differences were reflected in the legal strategies of the two offices: The Legal Aid Society refused to represent clients who would not pay rent to their landlords or into the court (Oser, 1972c: 1). Rather than use procedural irregularities to defeat dispossess petitions, Legal Aid Society lawyers were quick to settle cases on terms considerably less favorable to the tenants than those secured by the Morrisania Legal Services office. Attorneys were specifically instructed not to use technical defenses by Howard F. Trussel, the managing attorney, who was soon to be appointed a hearing officer in the new Housing Court. Oser (*Ibid.*) reported that Trussel's approach in landlord–tenant disputes "has gained respect among property managers and banks."

This funding dispute had considerable import for the practice of landlord–tenant law in the Bronx. If the Legal Aid Society received the grant, it would seek payments of rent into court, appointment of an administrator to run the housing units instead of rent strikes, and would accede to the nonadversary approach dictated by the administrative judge and his subordinates. Individual representation would be preferred to a legal strategy that sought to benefit the entire class of indigent tenants. Legal Aid also intended to use a substantial amount of the funding for matrimonial representation, to which Legal Services gave low priority in response to community emphasis on housing problems.

If SBLS were to obtain funding, it would continue to use procedural defense and encourage rent strikes and rent withholding in order to improve housing conditions. Ken G. Schwartz, the director of the Morrisania office, stated: "Legal Aid is not in a position to institute a system of people's control. If the client's goal is to overthrow his exploiter, his goal becomes my goal" (*New York Times*, June 3, 1972: 17). Morrisania was supported by representatives of the indigent community in the Bronx and by Congressman Badillo in obtaining the endorsement of the local community board. But at the last moment the controversy was resolved by additional federal appropriations that funded both the Bronx civil division of the Legal Aid Society and a new SBLS landlord–tenant office.

THE OPERATION OF THE HOUSING COURT

The New York City Housing Court opened on October 1, 1973. An observer would have seen few differences from the Landlord–Tenant Court that first morning. The calendar courtroom was filled to capacity, as usual, with many people leaning against the walls or forced into the smoke-filled corridors for lack of seating. A cacophonous roar, generated by the endless bickering of adversaries, made it difficult to understand the instructions of the court clerk when a reading of the court calendar commenced at 9:30 A.M. As the monotonous drone of the calendar call began, the nervous tenants strained to hear their names in the din, especially those who were Hispanic since their names were often so badly mispronounced as to be virtually incomprehensible.

But once the cases were called and the parties shuffled out of the calendar part to the hearing parts, the differences between past and present became apparent. Instead of one hearing part, there were now five; instead of one black-robed judge elevated upon an imposing oak bench, there were five hearing officers in street clothes sitting behind hastily constructed blond plywood tables. The old courtroom was also no longer in use. In its place were unused rooms whose spatial dimensions and design—cramped, dingy, and poorly lit spaces, often as small as twelve feet square—underscored the high-volume, low-cost virtues of the Housing Court. Perhaps to symbolize its position at the nadir of the judicial hierarchy the Housing Court was located on the ground floor of the court building, with the Civil and Supreme Courts above.

The administrative judge maintained that each hearing officer had been selected according to "training, interest, experience, judicial temperament and knowledge of federal, state and local housing laws and programs" (City Civ. Ct. Act. § 110(f), McKinney 1979). But the backgrounds of the Bronx appointees belied this claim. Only Howard Trussel, former head of the Bronx Civil Division of the Legal Aid Society, had any significant experience in housing law. The others were the life-long law clerk to the administrative judge, a private lawyer with minimal involvement in housing matters, an employee in the office of the New York City Corporation Counsel, and a nightclub operator. None of them lived in the Bronx, although advocates of the Housing Court had argued it would be more sensitive to the needs of the community.

There was also criticism of the procedure by which they were chosen. According to the law the administrative judge selects from a list of eligible appointees prepared by the Housing Advisory Council. The administrative judge also appoints that council so that it represents the interests of tenants, the real estate industry, civic groups, bar associations, and "the public at large" (City Civ. Ct. Act. § 110(g), McKinney 1979). But the two tenant representatives on the council (a distinct minority) did not reflect the viewpoints of tenants: They were the president of the Legal Aid Society (a partner in a large Wall Street law firm) and a consultant to the Mayor's Neighborhood Conservation Program on Relocation and Intergroup Relations. The first landlord representatives, by contrast, were strongly partisan. Fred Trump of the Trump Organization, which owned 21,000 apartments, and Irving Schneider of Helmsley-Spear, the largest commercial realtor in the city. The lawyers, who were supposed to be neutral, specialized in representing landlords (Reisig, 1972: 23). Even the first chairperson of the Advisory Council had once served as counsel to the Rent Stabilization Association, an organization of landlords owning non-rent-controlled properties. The bias of the Advisory Council in favor of real estate interests was reflected in the appointment of Stanley Nason as a hearing officer in Manhattan. In 1971 Nason had been accused of a conflict of interest because his law firm had represented landlords while he simultaneously served as counsel to the New York City Office of Special Improvement, which handled rehabilitation of rent-controlled dwellings in violation of the housing code (*New York Times*, April 13, 1971: 25).

The hearing officers not only were personally unsympathetic to tenants but also lacked the structural independence of judges because they were appointed by the administrative judge. They could not even have their legal opinions (few as they were) published without his approval (Rutzick and Huffman, 1975: 773). Civil Court judges and court personnel treated them with little respect (*Ibid.*). All the hearing officers, but especially the former law clerk, made frequent reference to the administrative judge's emphasis on reducing case backlog whenever Legal Services attorneys insisted on lengthy trials. Judge Thompson's interest in the speedy administration of justice seemed to be directed solely at tenants. Not once did he urge his hearing officers to give low priority to adjudicating poorly prepared petitions.

Hearing officers also receive directives from the administrative judge about how to proceed in each case. One of these required tenants to deposit the rent demanded by the landlord into court if there was any adjournment, even one requested by the court or the landlord.

> It is the firm stated policy of this court that rent shall be deposited into court as a condition precedent to the grant of an adjournment on consent beyond the statutory period, or where successive adjournments postpone the trial date beyond the following rental date due, or whenever the litigation gives indication that it will be more protracted than summary [Goodman, 1979: 59].

This policy had no basis in law and was contrary to the statute prescribing the grounds for adjournments (Real Prop. Acts. Law § 745, McKinney 1979).

Hearing officers tried to compensate for their subordination by seeking the trappings of judicial office. One morning during the second year of the Housing Court they all appeared behind their plywood benches in black robes—compliments of Judge Thompson. But this did not conceal the realities of the Housing Court for long: By afternoon most of the hearing officers had disrobed since the robes' zippers were defective. They also sought to appropriate the title of "judge." Several Legal Services attorneys were threatened with contempt for calling them hearing officers. On one occasion a lawyer was physically ejected from the room for refusing to address the hearing officer as "judge" or "your honor," even though a recent appellate decision had ruled that they were not judges (*Carson* v. *Thompson*). When hearing officers greeted one another in the hallways or courtrooms, it would always be "Hello, Judge." Almost all the hearing officers (except the former Legal Aid attorney) openly aspired to the judiciary, but because none had an independent political base or was particularly enterprising the only route was to please the administrative judge, an influential figure in the Democratic party. Two hearing officers have since become Civil Court judges. For the rest, the legislature provided symbolic elevation. A 1978 amendment to the Housing Court Act retitled hearing officers "housing judges" in the hope of improving the unruly atmosphere in the court, although it still did not make them constitutional judges.

> Many cases [in housing part] involve great animosity and hostility between owners and tenants. The volume of cases and attendant emotions place a tremendous burden upon the 16 hearing officers who preside daily over the court's heavy calendar . . . The title "housing judge" will be more fitting to the position and will lend vitally needed dignity and greater respect to the court proceedings [*New York State Legislative Annual*, 1978: 206–207].

Pretensions of dress and title did little to change the atmosphere of the hearing parts. Shouting matches, fights, even assaults on Legal Services lawyers by landlords continued to disrupt the proceedings. The response of the administrative judge hardly helped to improve the situation. When a Legal Services attorney complained that an influential landlord had harassed him verbally and physically during several trials, Thompson sent an internal memorandum to the hearing officers instructing them to conduct a secret investigation of this attorney's activities!

The lack of judicial decorum was not entirely unintended. The administrative judge ruled at the outset that there would be no stenographic record of the proceedings. Instead, hearing officers had tape recorders that they used to control what was contained in the record. I was personally involved in several cases where the hearing officer turned off the tape recorder whenever the landlord shouted imprecations—and then jumped into the fray himself. Though the Housing Court Act (City Civ. Ct. Act § 110(k), McKinney 1979) stated that any party could request a stenographer upon two days' notice, the administrative judge refused to comply on the ground of lack of funds. A lawsuit challenging this edict briefly produced stenographers in the hearing rooms of the Bronx, but they disappeared for good when the action was dismissed on procedural grounds (*Rivera* v. *Trimarco*).

In some ways taped transcripts proved beneficial to tenants because they were usually so incomprehensible that appellate courts had no choice but to order new trials. But appeals are rare in the Housing Court. Overall, the absence of stenographers further diminished the pressures on hearing officers to behave with judicial impartiality and restraint.

THE FIGHT FOR FORMAL JUSTICE IN THE HOUSING COURT

The SBLS Landlord–Tenant Office intended to pursue the same legal strategy in the Housing Court that Morrisania Legal Services had developed in the Landlord–Tenant Court: to adhere strictly to procedural rules in court and to encourage informal out-of-court settlements. But the structure of the Housing Court made this considerably more difficult. The expansion from two parts to six allowed more cases to be heard and required more Legal Services attorneys for a sustained defense effort. Most of the hearing officers had no judicial experience, were poorly versed in how to conduct a trial, and knew little about the law of summary proceedings. Furthermore, the political and economic assumptions underlying the aggressive litigational strategy adopted by Legal Services were totally inconsistent with the ideology of conciliation and informality that inspired the Housing Court. Judge Thompson's guidelines made this explicit:

> It is a court which seeks to arrange a settlement between tenant and owners as soon as possible. It is a place where humanitarian as well as the legal aspects of a contract of letting premises are sought out. The court seeks informality and rehabilitation. It aims to promote conciliation and compromise rather than confrontation, and verily, removal of violations whether of record or not is the name of the game, not imposing penalties [1974: 2].

The long delay in funding the Housing Court allowed the ten attorneys in the new office, centrally located in the Hunts Point section of the South Bronx, to prepare for the impending struggle. The Landlord–Tenant Office represented only tenants and gave rent strikes special priority. Every day lawyers had to be present both in court to represent clients and in the office to conduct intake and case preparation. To satisfy both demands it was necessary to abandon the policy of vertical representation—in which one attorney represents the client throughout the course of a proceeding. Only an extensive division of labor would ensure sufficient numbers of attorneys both to defend cases before hearing officers and to process the heavy client intake necessary to allow SBLS to dominate the court. Each attorney was assigned two or three days in the office and spent the remainder in court, which made it impossible for an attorney to have his own caseload. The decision to switch to horizontal representation was taken with some reluctance. The quality of individual representation probably declined slightly because no attorney was thoroughly acquainted with any case. Clients often did not know who was representing them until they appeared in court. Perhaps most important, horizontal representation placed a heavy burden on the lawyers, who never felt they had exercised all their professional skills (except in the rare case they represented from beginning to end). In addition, the burden of an extremely heavy caseload was aggravated when the lawyer had to master several new cases on the very morning of the trial. All this seriously demoralized the attorneys, caused high job turnover, and eventually led to the disintegration of the Landlord–Tenant Office. Paradoxically, the most effective and aggressive attorneys were often the first to leave. Their unwillingness to compromise client interests by making peace with their adversaries made the courtroom a cauldron whose emotional and physical demands precluded a long-term commitment (see Bellow, 1977; Katz, 1978).

But the choice of horizontal representation in Landlord–Tenant Court must be differentiated from the sequential defense common in many public defender offices (Gilboy and Schmidt, 1979). In most criminal matters the facts are specific to the case. In addition, personal rapport with the defendant is important both to ascertain what happened and because the character of the accused is relevant for sentencing. Slum housing cases, by contrast, tend to follow a common factual pattern: no heat, no hot water, falling plaster, rodent infestation, etc. These facts can be easily elicited in an intake interview and recorded for the benefit of the trial attorney. Character issues, such as a reputation for veracity or for peacefulness, which do require a more intimate attorney–client relationship rarely arise in a housing case. The critical procedural issues in Housing Court are virtually identical in every case since landlord attorneys use form petitions. A trial attorney who is familiar with the procedural arguments and evidentiary rules in housing matters can be an effective advocate even with horizontal representation.

Computer-instructed typewriters, programmed with form answers, also helped process a larger caseload. Form answers and heavy reliance on paraprofessionals permitted SBLS to represent an average of 40 of the 200 cases on the daily calendar. Still, about half of those seeking legal representation had to be turned away for lack of resources.

Though Legal Services represented a higher proportion of cases in the Housing Court than it had in the Landlord–Tenant Court, this did not have as much of an effect on those who remained unrepresented. Since the Landlord–Tenant Court called and heard cases in their calendar order, unrepresented tenants also benefitted from the delay caused by the enormous backlog. Landlords would also offer them more favorable settlements in the hallways of the court in order to assure a swift and certain outcome. But more important, many landlords chose to resolve tenant grievances without resort to a summary dispossess petition in order to avoid both the courts and the possibility that their tenants would retain Legal Services.

The four hearing parts added by the Housing Court made it much more difficult for lawyers to retard the flow of cases. Unlike the old Landlord–Tenant Court, the Housing Court always completed the calendar call. The hearing officers called the cases of unrepresented tenants first and disposed of each in a few minutes, allowing the landlord to leave with the rent or a judgment in his pocket.

At first the hearing officers strongly resisted the SBLS strategy of insisting on a trial. They attempted to force Legal Services attorneys to engage in settlement discussions inside the courtroom, where the officers could discuss the "merits" of the case, avoid procedural issues that might require dismissal, and speed the disposition of their caseloads. The hearing officers opposed attempts to record these discussions, lashing out at attorneys who persisted in demanding a formal record. Hearing officers and landlord attorneys sought to replace the informal corridor negotiations with discussions inside the hearing room—an environment strongly biased against the tenant. [20] During these discussions the hearing officer sought to discover if the tenant had paid the rent. If not, the officer would propose a settlement in which the tenant paid all the rent claimed and the landlord promised to perform any necessary repairs. The hearing officer rarely granted the tenant's claim to an abatement, even if the apartment had been without heat and hot water for a month or more. After the landlord received the rent he rarely made any repairs. Unless the tenant's attorney was convinced that his or her demands would be satisfied, settlement discussions just served to prejudice the hearing officer against the tenant when the latter rejected the unacceptable settlement and went to trial. In the first few months of my tenure at SBLS I was often threatened with contempt proceedings by hearing officers irritated by my refusal to engage in settlement discussions.

The greatest difference between the hearing officers of the Housing Court and the Civil Court judges of the Landlord–Tenant Court was their attitude toward settlement. Judges usually sat for only a week and rarely more than a month. If they adjourned a case, it would be no longer their problem but that of the next judge. Their principal organizational constraint was to get through the day's caseload; if the parties were unwilling to settle and there was no time for a trial, the judge was glad to adjourn the case. Hearing officers, however, were assigned

[20]The tenant negotiating in the hallway was not under the Damoclean sword of eviction. Furthermore, the poor black or Hispanic tenant was not as verbally disadvantaged there as he was in the courtroom. In the corridor he could express his anger and demand justice in ghetto argot against a landlord who was often psychologically unprepared to confront those he oppressed. In the courtroom, the tenant's inarticulate fury would confirm his powerlessness.

to Housing Court permanently, and cases that were adjourned remained their responsibility. Since the administrative judge measured performance by the size of the backlog, hearing officers had a strong incentive to eliminate it. In addition, the officers viewed the Legal Services strategy of using technical defenses to compel dismissal of petitions as a challenge to the goal of achieving "effective enforcement of proper housing standards in the City of New York" (City Civ. Ct. Act § 110, Legislative Findings (b), McKinney 1979). Dismissal denied the court jurisdiction and prevented it from exercising its remedial powers. The SBLS approach, predicated on the belief that the court was incapable of solving the Bronx housing crisis, directly attacked the legitimacy of both the Housing Court and its officers.

The Civil Court judges of the Landlord–Tenant Court were not as sensitive in this respect since they viewed housing cases as a nuisance and felt no institutional obligation to solve the housing problems of New York. If an attorney wanted to go to trial, a Civil Court judge usually acquiesced. Judges were also likely to be more knowledgeable than hearing officers about courtroom procedures. Although the latter eventually acquired greater expertise about the substantive law of housing, they remained less capable of running a trial.

The expanded number of hearing parts, the greater procedural irregularity, the emphasis upon conciliation, the increased powers of the administrative judge, and the inexperience of the hearing officers all contributed to making the Housing Court inhospitable to the adversary stance of SBLS. Nevertheless, the office persisted in applying its defensive tactics with renewed vigor and creativity. It began to make extensive use of written motions to dismiss petitions because these permitted the moving party to set the date of the hearing and thus extend the first court date from the statutory eight to thirteen days to two to three weeks.[21] Whereas hearing officers invariably rejected similar motions summarily, written motions were heard in the calendar part and thus decided by a Civil Court judge who often would give the legal arguments greater consideration. This difference between judges and hearing officers in their response to formal legal motions reveals the loss suffered by tenants from the growth of informalism. Judges rarely granted the motions, but the time they spent considering them often proved invaluable. In one major rent strike the judge deliberated for almost a month before ruling against the tenants. By this time the landlord had been forced to sell the building to another party with whom a successful compromise was reached (see Oser, 1975). Of course, the increased use of formal motions took a heavy toll on the staff, who were already overburdened.

The most difficult task was to change the procedures within the hearing parts. Hearing officers reacted angrily when Legal Services attorneys demanded formal

[21]It is questionable whether this motion was appropriate in summary proceeding (Civ. Prac. § § 404, 32ll, McKinney 1979), but the mediocrity of the Bronx landlord bar was such that it never challenged SBLS on this point.

trials that adhered to rules of evidence and procedure. They threatened attorneys with contempt, as well as in more subtle ways. I was personally warned by one hearing officer that he would write to the Character and Fitness Committee to prevent me from being admitted to the New York Bar.[22] Hearing officers also denigrated attorneys in front of their clients, warning tenants that SBLS was preventing the court from improving housing conditions.[23] They said that Judge Thompson had warned them against SBLS and promised that we would not be able to do in the Housing Court what we had done in the Landlord–Tenant Court.

At first, motions to dismiss petition for procedural irregularities were met with a wall of resistance. But such inflexibility soon became visibly self-defeating. In the first few months of the Housing Court SBLS considerably slowed the disposition of cases in the hearing parts by means of painstaking trials lasting a day or two. Hearing officers responded by commencing trials when the defense attorneys were occupied in other hearing parts. But this maneuver quickly backfired when SBLS attorneys insisted that the same policies be applied to landlords whose attorneys were not immediately available—and there were more SBLS than landlord lawyers in any one firm.

Legal Services also borrowed a criminal defense technique that dramatically showed hearing officers the prevalence of perjured testimony by landlords. Before commencing a summary proceeding a landlord must make an oral or written demand for rent (Real Prop. Acts. Law § 711(2), McKinney 1979). Landlords usually do not mail such a notice because of the problems involved in proving delivery. Nor do they make the demand by telephone because many tenants either have no telephone or unlisted numbers and lawyers have difficulty developing the necessary foundation for telephone testimony. Thus most landlords or their agents testified that they had personally visited the tenant at the apartment to demand the rent. In a substantial number of cases this was a lie. Such casual perjury may have been encouraged by the facts that both court officials

---

[22]Such committees have frequently delayed, obstructed, or denied the applications of political activists (see Harvard Civil Rights–Civil Liberties Law Review, 1970). Even the bar associations now recognize that they serve no other purpose (see Special Committee, 1978).

[23]Criticism of lawyers who insisted upon technical defenses was common among early-nineteenth-century judges intent on establishing the dominance of capital and commerce.

In 1809 Massachusetts Chief Justice Parson accused a defendant's lawyer of attempting to use his superior knowledge of pleading to evade "the apparent merits of the cases." "All needless refinements," he concluded, "ought to be rejected, and all finese intended to *ensnare* should be avoided." An important result was the increasing frequency with which courts allowed plaintiffs to amend imperfect pleadings instead of throwing them out of court [Horwitz, 1977: 29].

But the attack on technicality was only temporary; once the legal objectives of the dominant class were achieved, formalism regained dominance (*Ibid.*: 253–266).

and landlords viewed summary proceedings as a collection machinery, not as a fact-finding inquiry, and that hearing officers consistently discredited the assertions by poor black or Hispanic tenants that they had never received a rent demand.

Legal Services responded by having someone other than the tenant sit at the defense table. When examined, the landlord invariably pointed to the individual at the defense table as the one upon whom the demand had been made. Once the real tenant was identified in the spectator's section, pandemonium would erupt in the hearing room. This tactic never resulted in a perjury indictment against landlords; landlord criminality was not a major concern of the Bronx district attorney's office. But it did have an effect on the hearing officers. If their tacit assumption that tenants lie and landlords tell the truth was only slightly shaken, it did make them realize that the litigation skills of SBLS could prove an embarrassment to the Housing Court. Once the hearing officers recognized that the full-scale trials demanded by SBLS were as inconsistent with mass-produced "justice" in the Housing Court as they had been with assembly-line procedures in the Landlord–Tenant Court, they exhibited a noticeable change.[24] They displayed greater familiarity with the relevant law and increased willingness to dismiss defective petitions and thus avoid a lengthy trial. Once again the motions made by SBLS gave hearing officers a legitimate means of nipping the burgeoning workload in the bud. After these trials had achieved the goals of educating hearing officers in the technical requirements of a summary dispossess proceeding and demonstrating the ability of the office to reduce caseload dramatically if tenant rights were ignored, they were rarely necessary. Outcomes favorable to tenants could be achieved in informal settlements with landlords and their lawyers in the hallways of the court once the latter understood that litigation was a dubious and costly strategy. The cases that went to trial were usually those in which the tenant's position was so weak that a landlord was assured of a judgment. Still, those cases had to be fought in order to remind both hearing officers and landlords that litigation should be only a last resort.

One hearing officer who had never dismissed a petition changed dramatically; it became almost impossible for a landlord to prove a prima facie case before him. Several months of long trials, most lasting until 5:00 P.M., forced the officer to go home and learn real property law. Once he began granting SBLS motions he was finished with his work by lunchtime almost every day. Ironically, he became the darling of the administrative judge since he had no backlog. Many a naive landlord demanding an immediate trial ended up in his part, only to leave ten minutes later with the case dismissed. And when Judge Thompson transferred a hard-line hearing officer from another borough to the Bronx for a month

---

[24]The tension between justice and court administration is present in almost every civil and criminal urban courtroom; see Heydebrand (1977).

or so, the latter invariably developed an eye for procedural niceties after Legal Services educated him with its litigation strategy.

The distinctiveness of the Bronx Housing Court was revealed in the response of its officers to Judge Thompson's directive that rent monies be deposited in court whenever there was an adjournment. This policy was faithfully followed in every other borough, even when tenants were represented by Legal Services. In the Bronx, hearing officers continually threatened to apply it but never did so when SBLS was counsel. They understood that it would unhinge the delicate balance of forces between landlords and tenants. Ultimately, Mobilization For Youth Legal Services in Manhattan brought an appeal on this issue when one of their clients suffered a default judgment for refusing to make the deposit. The appellate court held that the practice violated due process protection since the rent claimed in the petition was an unproven amount (*Eversman* v. *Collado*). But another attack on the directive failed when the court ruled that it did not bind hearing officers (*Kelley Street Block Association* v. *Thompson*). Housing judges no longer require rent deposits from tenants represented by one of the aggressive Legal Services offices, but they still do so when the tenant is unrepresented or represented by meek or inexperienced counsel.

Although SBLS was strikingly successful in resisting the erosion of tenant procedural rights, the Housing Court still changed the character of corridor negotiation. Settlements were less favorable to tenants, especially the frequent tenant who wanted a rent reduction for the absence of heat and hot water. Since trials were easier to obtain and less time-consuming in the Housing Court, landlords were somewhat more willing to take their chances before a hearing officer and therefore less generous in settling. Even more important, the Housing Court further disadvantaged the unrepresented tenant by reducing the case overload that had encouraged landlords to bargain. Still, the early supporters of the Housing Court remain less than satisfied with its results in the Bronx. Lorraine Miller said that it has had the least impact there. She now favors detaching the Housing Court from the Civil Court altogether, though the former would still be bound by procedural and evidentiary rules. The Real Estate Advisory Board has also criticized events in the Bronx, complaining that summary dispossess petitions are still not processed fast enough and arguing that all tenants should be forced to deposit rent money into court before receiving a hearing (*Real Estate Forum*, February 1976: 1).

Though the Housing Court reform has eased some bottlenecks, the expressed goal of summary proceeding is still not being met: "The object and purpose of Article 7 of the RPAPL [Real Property Actions and Proceedings Law] is to allow one who has a *prima facie* right to possession of real property to acquire possession as quickly as possible" (*Netter* v. *Wilsey*, 575). Randall W. Scott, director of an American Bar Association study of landlord–tenant courts, reported that New

York City's "already severe housing problems are being exacerbated by the operations of the Housing Court. Our clearest finding is that the area of housing is the most serious overload in the area of litigation in the country" (Oser, 1978). Scott pointed to the massive number of housing cases in New York: In 1976 there were 446,000 summary dispossess notices issued by the court, a 17 percent increase over 1975. He argued that three times as many housing officers would be necessary to eliminate the backlog. The study concluded that

> if housing institutions perceive rent collection problems they will be very reluctant to lend even with the best credit of the rehabilitator. In New York . . . housing hopes are buried by litigious delay. Rent losses suffered through slow justice in poor neighborhoods are a prescription for housing abandonment [*Ibid.*].

Scott, however, did not offer any evidence that private financing for low-income housing was available in those jurisdictions that denied tenants any legal protection. The truth is that the private market stopped financing low- and middle-income housing long ago because the return on investment does not justify it (Stone, 1972). In addition, much of the South Bronx has been redlined by banks and insurance companies (*New York Times*, January 1, 1978: 23; January 10, 1978: 37; January 15, 1978: 30). But the argument that case overload causes abandonment and disinvestment is not only an economic fiction but also an ideological attack on the poor at the very moment when they have gained limited access to the levers with which the rich have long manipulated the legal system for their own advantage.

Prior to the advent of an aggressive Legal Services strategy there was never any claim that housing litigation or court overload was a significant factor in urban decay. When the eastern fringe of the South Bronx began to slide toward the precipice of urban blight after World War II, the landlord–tenant courts provided quick and easy "justice"—for the landlords. The oldest and most successful landlord attorney in the Bronx once mused nostalgically to me about how pleasant the Bronx Landlord–Tenant Court was when he first started practicing there in 1940:

> You would get there at 9:00 and be finished by 11:00 in the morning. Contested cases? There weren't any; almost everything ended in a default judgment or maybe you'd talk to some tenants and they'd promise to pay or move out right away. Then I'd go back to my office and work on the next day's petitions. Now I never get out of here and business piles up at the office.

This senior attorney blamed Legal Services for putting an end to the "normal" situation in the Bronx courts.

The efforts of Legal Services to redress the imbalance between tenants and landlords by using procedural forms have not been limited to New York. A study of housing litigation in New Haven revealed that representation by Legal Services lawyers rendered summary proceedings fifty-five days longer than the average, whereas representation by private counsel lengthened them by only twelve days (*Yale Law Journal*, 1973: 1498). The author responded with a proposal to eliminate all formal pleadings, motions, and technical rules of evidence and exclude lawyers (*Ibid.*: 1501). This would severely disadvantage tenants since several major studies have concluded that the tenant does even worse when both parties are unrepresented than when only the landlord is represented (Mosier and Soble, 1973; Court Study Group, 1973).[25]

An extensive study of the Brooklyn Landlord–Tenant Court concluded that the length of trial was directly related to the likelihood of a settlement favorable to the tenant (*Ibid.*). This result is particularly striking since many Brooklyn Legal Services lawyers complained to me that they had little success with the technical defenses that worked in the Bronx; an adversary posture apparently affects outcome even when the judiciary is strongly hostile. An examination of the Detroit Housing Court found that when the tenant was represented the landlord was only half as likely to get a judgment in a contested case and, therefore, seventeen times more likely to settle out of court (Mosier and Soble, 1973: 47, 64).

Because lawyers who assert the procedural rights of tenants are often said to threaten the destruction of the judiciary, it is important to demonstrate that this warning is totally unfounded. Only an infinitesimal proportion of tenants served with dispossess petitions even attempt to contest them, much less retain counsel. In Detroit, landlords obtain default judgments in 74.3 percent of all cases called for trial (*Ibid.*: 26–27). In the 418,000 petitions filed in New York in 1977 (the busiest jurisdiction in the country), tenants failed to answer in 81 percent, 11 percent were settled or discontinued, tenants defaulted at trial in 4 percent, and only 1 percent were tried or dismissed during trial (Cohen, 1979: 29).[26] This theme—that the exercise of procedural rights threatens to undermine the judiciary—echoes the claim of prominent social scientists that disadvantaged strata who invoke civil liberties in support of their egalitarian demands subvert democracy and pave the way for authoritarian measures (Trilateral Commission, 1975).

---

[25]Studies of small claims courts also reveal that *plaintiffs* are not disadvantaged by being denied counsel against unrepresented defendants but that the chances of the *defendant* improve only when he is represented and the plaintiff is not (Yngvesson and Hennessey, 1975: 250–251). This contradicts the arguments by Illich and others that legal deprofessionalization necessarily reduces the disparities of wealth (see Caplan, 1977). In an inegalitarian society the poor often lack the ability to articulate even the facts of nontechnical problems and are likely to be intimidated by all state officials, not just judges.

[26]Another 1 percent received miscellaneous dispositions, such as inquests or mistrials (*Ibid.*) The percentages fail to add to 100 because of rounding error.

Trials are almost as rare in the criminal courts. In New York City, 96 percent of all convictions are the result of guilty pleas (Judicial Conference, 1972: A.77, Table 12).

THE HOUSING COURT AGAINST THE LANDLORDS?

The losses suffered by tenants as a result of the creation of the Housing Court have not been balanced by more effective enforcement of housing codes. Only rarely has the court used its broad impleader powers to take concerted action against slumlords. And even these meager efforts have been obstructed by the rulings of higher courts.[27] There has been particular resistance to tenant attempts to expand the trial beyond a simple dispute about rent. A recently completed study by the Civil Court Advisory Committee on Judicial Education stated that the impleader provision permitting the joinder of "any person or city agency" to improve housing maintenance should be construed narrowly to minimize delay to the landlord. It also warned that participation by additional parties might adversely affect the "other fundamental objectives of summary proceedings" (Cohen, 1979: 42).

The limited funds available for housing rehabilitation and emergency repairs have virtually nullified the authority of the court "to recommend or employ any lawful remedy, program, procedure or sanction, regardless of the type of relief originally sought, to enforce housing standards if it believes such procedure will achieve effective code compliance and promote the public interest" (City Civ. Ct. Act § 110(c). McKinney 1979). And the city comptroller found that the Housing Court has not acted decisively: "It views itself as a traditional judicial forum with narrow responsibility and authority, [and] as a result conditions in a single apartment are argued in court, while scores of violations in the same building are ignored" (Walsh, 1979: 54).

Procedural rules have restricted the capacity of the HDA to use the Housing Court against landlords. The earlier Housing Maintenance Code had permitted service by mail in all enforcement actions (N.Y.C. Charter and Administrative Code D26–50.09, 1970). Ironically, the Housing Court Act imposed more rigid rules for serving landlords in enforcement actions while preserving the very liberal requirements for serving tenants. Indeed, the Association of the Bar of the City of New York opposed the Act on this ground, among others.

> Although the stated object of the law is to provide civil procedures for Code enforcement, instead of criminal, the method of service of a summons, provided in the Bill, is stricter than that provided for in other civil actions by the CPLR [letter from E. J. Morris, chairman of Committee on Housing and Urban Development of the Association of the Bar of the City of New York, to Gov. Rockefeller, May 23, 1972].

This double standard was also visible in the practice of the hearing officers. Though tenants have great difficulty in obtaining adjournments in dispossess

[27]Two major decisions have held that impleader is not permissible when the tenant seeks to compel payment of rent by a third party, such as the Department of Social Services (*Zytelny* v. *Lodge*; *Marcy Realty Co.* v. *Glassey*).

actions, landlords prosecuted by the HDA obtain generous extensions. In one case a tenant appeared in Housing Court twenty times in a fourteen-month period before the court ordered the landlord to correct violations in the tenant's apartment. In another, a landlord received three consecutive adjournments before the tenants were permitted to introduce evidence that they had been without hot water for three months (Rutzick and Huffman, 1975: 770). Needless to say, landlords sued by the HDA invoke the same technicalities as do tenants. In the Bronx, a landlord successfully resisted a motion for a preliminary injunction, citing 180 violations because of a defect in the stamp of the notary public on the process server's affidavit (*Ibid.*: 771).

But landlords have little occasion to invoke procedural formality defensively. Of 425,196 residential housing petitions filed in Housing Court in 1977, 418,236 were summary proceedings for nonpayment of rent brought by landlords (Walsh, 1979: 54). In Manhattan in 1977 only fifty-five cases were initiated by tenants (Goodman, 1979: 59). The virtual absence of tenant actions for repairs partly reflects procedural obstacles: the failure of court officials to prepare the necessary forms, disseminate information, provide support staff, or encourage tenants to exercise their rights (Cohen, 1979: 42). Legal Services attorneys have told me that a 1977 amendment to the Housing Court Act requiring clerks to assist tenants in preparing legal papers has done little to increase the number of tenant-initiated actions (City Civ. Ct. Act § 110(o), McKinney 1979).

In those rare instances when a tenant or the HDA sued a landlord for violating the housing code, the court was reluctant to impose even civil penalties and did so in only 370 cases in 1979 (Cohen, 1979: 29).[28] The primary function of the Housing Court, in the words of two former HDA attorneys, "has become rent collection and the eviction of nonpaying tenants, and the original purpose for the forum—code enforcement—is now little more than a secondary consideration" (Rutzick and Huffman, 1975: 759).[29]

CONCLUSION

The proclaimed goal of the Housing Court was to eliminate the formal legal barriers that have prevented tenants and landlords from reaching agreement on the problems of housing in New York. There is no reason to assume that courts have the power to rehabilitate slums. Though they have not resisted an economic

[28]Courts can impose fines of $10–100 for each violation and $10–25 for each additional day it remains uncorrected and can send the landlord to jail for contempt for up to a year.

[29]This development resembles the transformation of that other "people's court"—the small claims court—from a forum in which individuals could air their grievances to a mechanism for debt collection by major creditors (see Yngvesson and Hennessey, 1975).

system that emphasizes profit above housing quality, neither have they caused the housing crisis. They have simply supported the claims of landlords who seek profit from substandard housing and assigned a much lower priority to tenants seeking decent housing. The Housing Court attempts to institutionalize the Landlord–Tenant Court's cavalier attitude toward tenants under the pretext of creating a "conciliatory instead of an adversary atmosphere" (*New York Times,* October 2, 1973: 1).

A legal system that encourages conciliation between landlords and tenants— two parties with vastly unequal resources—by curtailing the procedural rights of the weaker can only succeed in amplifying that inequality. Procedural formality recognizes inequality and attempts to compensate for it by making both parties conform to the same standards. Once formality is withdrawn the courts are transformed into collection agencies operating with the seal of the state of New York. Selznick is overgeneralizing when he asserts that "rigid adherence to precedent and mechanical application of rules hamper the capacity of the legal system to take account of new interests and circumstances or to adapt to social inequality. Formal justice tends to serve the status quo" (1969: 13). Like much of the propaganda for informal justice, neighborhood justice centers, and media-tion, this expresses an idealist perspective that is not historically or empirically rooted.

Whether formal justice serves the status quo depends very much on the nature of the status quo. If the social structure is not seriously threatened and the ruling classes are firmly in control, the procedural fairness and blind, mechanical application of the rules are the best defenses of the subordinate classes, even if these rules were the instruments by which the dominant classes came to power. It was this contradictory element of Anglo-Saxon law that E. P. Thompson recog-nized in his materialist examination of the Black Act (1975: cf. Trubek, 1977). At other times, when the forces of reaction are on the defensive and a new social movement is contending for power, procedural formalism tends to inhibit change (Tigar and Levy, 1977). An example is the resistance of the Supreme Court to New Deal reforms. Thus an evaluation of formal and informal justice depends on an analysis of the level of political and legal struggle because law, like state power, is a social relation whose center of gravity is in constant flux (Poulantzas, 1978).

Static conceptions of bourgeois legal rights that criticize legal equality as tending "to reinforce systematic inequalities" (Balbus, 1977: 577–578) are simi-larly mistaken. Not only are they overly abstract in failing to recognize the unequal application of the laws to the lower classes but they are also blind to the numerous contradictions that may prevent courts from guaranteeing exchange values. In the Bronx, the organizational need to process caseload began to interfere seriously with the role of the court in assuring the commodity nature of housing by evicting those who did not pay rent.[30] The insistence upon the formal equality guaranteed by bourgeois law therefore became an important element in the class struggle (Young, 1979).

The strategy adopted by the SBLS attorneys sought to change class relationships within the courts. Because the tenants' movement in New York, and especially in the South Bronx, was weak and disorganized, major changes in the substantive law were not feasible. The few substantive gains achieved by tenants have been checked by a hostile judiciary. But the critical position of Legal Services within the courts permitted it to redefine the relationship between landlords and tenants through scrupulous adherence to the rules of evidence and procedure. The strategy recognized that lawyers as "producers of legal values" can exert a real influence at the "point of production" in favor of a particular social class. In this respect SBLS departed from a simple ideology of advocacy (Simon, 1978). Procedural formalism not only made the courts an arena of social conflict but also simultaneously created space for tenant organizations to mobilize rent strikes in favor of a different social order. As E. P. Thompson writes, "Law has not only been imposed upon men from above: it has also been a medium within which other social conflicts have been fought out" (1975: 267).

REFERENCES

Cases

Amanuensis Ltd. v. *Brown,* 318 N.Y.S. 2d 11 (Civ. Ct. N.Y. 1971).
Avenue Associates v. *Buxbaum,* 371 N.Y.S. 2d 736 (Civ. Ct. N.Y. 1975), rev'd, 373 N.Y.S. 2d 814 (App. Term 1975).
B.L.H. Realty Corp. v. *Cruz,* 383 N.Y.S. 2d 781 (Housing Ct. 1975).
Carson v. *Thompson,* 355 N.Y.S. 2d 65 (Sup. Ct. 1974) aff'd, 379 N.Y.S. 2d 94 (App. Div. 1976).
City of New York v. *Betancourt,* 359 N.Y.S. 2d 707 (Civ. Ct. N.Y. 1974) aff'd 362 N.Y.S. 2d 728 (App. Term 1974).
Eversman v. *Collado,* 388 N.Y.S. 2d 5 (App. Term 1976).
Fisch v. *Chason,* 418 N.Y.S. 2d 495 (Civ. Ct. N.Y. 1979).
Giannini v. *Stuart,* 178 N.Y.S. 2d 709 (App. Div. 1958).
Glass v. *Thompson,* 349 N.Y.S. 2d 57 (Sup. Ct. 1973) aff'd, 379 N.Y.S. 2d 427 (App. Div. 1976).
Kekllas v. *Saddy,* 88 Misc. 2d. 1042 (Dist. Ct. 1976).
Kelley Street Block Association v. *Thompson,* 407 N.Y.S. 2d 158 (App. Div. 1978).
Marcy Realty Co. v. *Glassy,* 361 N.Y.S. 2d. 802 (Civ. Ct. N.Y. 1974).

---

[30]The problems encountered by the Bronx Housing Court in seeking to maintain real estate values and preserve housing profits suggest that the courts are less capable of satisfying the reproductive demands of capital, those "demands which if met, tend to reinforce, stabilize and expand the basic social relationships of capitalism" (Andersen *et al.,* 1976: 199–200). Whether this failure will be a catalyst for the emergence of an alternate system that provides minimal shelter for everyone, or whether it will simply accelerate the deterioration of urban life, remains to be answered.

Maryano v. Peters, 409 N.Y.S. 2d 691 (Civ. Ct. N.Y. 1980).
Matter of Smiley, 369 N.Y.S. 2d. 87 (Ct. App. 1975).
Maxwell v. Simons, 353 N.Y.S. 2d 589 (Civ. Ct. N.Y. 1973).
Netter v. Wilsey, 374 N.Y.S. 2d 572 (Albany County Ct. 1975).
Rawlins v. Thompson, 325 N.Y.S. 2d 75 (Sup. Ct. 1971).
Reich v. Cochran, 94 N.E. 1080 (N.Y. Ct. App. 1911).
Rivera v. Trimarco, 368 N.Y.S. 2d 826 (Ct. App. 1975).
Steinberg v. Carreras, 344 N.Y.S. 2d. 136 (Civ. Ct. N.Y. 1973) rev'd. 357 N.Y.S. 2d. 369 (App. Term 1974).
353 Realty Corp. v. Pisla, 364 N.Y.S. 2d 676 (Civ. Ct. N.Y. 1974).
Velazquez v. Thompson, 321 F. Supp. 34 (S.D.N.Y. 1970) aff'd, 451 F. 2d 202 (2d Cir. 1971).
West Realty Corp. v. Wood, 309 N.Y.S. 2d 524 (Civ. Ct. N.Y. 1971), aff'd 330 N.Y.S. 2d 527 (App. Term 1972).
Zytelny v. Lodge, N.Y.L.J., February 5, 1975, at 17 (App. Term 1975).

Other Sources

Abel, R. L. (1979) "Delegalization: A Critical Review of Its Ideology, Manifestations, and Social Consequences," in E. Blankenburg, E. Klausa, and H. Rottleuthner (eds.) *Alternative Rechtsformen und Alternativen zum Recht*. Opladen: Westdeutscher Verlag (*Jahrbuch für Rechtssoziologie und Rechtstheorie*, band 6).
Andersen, G. E., R. Friedland, and E. O. Wright (1976) "Modes of Class Struggle and the Capitalist State," 4–5 *Working Papers on the Kapitalistate* 186.
Auerbach, J. (1976) *Unequal Justice*. New York: Oxford University Press.
Balbus, I. (1977) "Commodity Form and Legal Form: An Essay on the 'Relative Autonomy' of Law," 11 *Law & Society Review* 571.
Bell, G. (1978) "New Directions in the Administration of Justice: Responses to the Pound Conference—Responses of the Justice Department," 64 *American Bar Association Journal* 63.
Bellow, G. (1969) "Reflections on Case-Load Limitations," 27 *NLADA Briefcase* 195.
_____ (1977) "Turning Solutions into Problems: The Legal Aid Experience," 34 *NLADA Briefcase* 106.
Bellow, G. and J. Kettleson (1978) "From Ethics to Politics, Confronting Scarcity and Fairness in Public Interest Practice," 58 *Boston University Law Review* 337.
Blum, H. and L. Maitland (1980) "Suspicious Fires in New York City Are Found to Follow Patterns," *New York Times* (November 12) Sec. 1, p. 24.
Caplan, J. (1977) "Lawyers and Litigants: A Cult Reviewed," in Ivan Illich *et al.* (eds.) *Disabling Professions*. London: Marion Boyars.
Caplovitz, D. (1967) *The Poor Pay More: Consumer Practices of Low Income Families*. New York: Free Press.
Cappelletti, M. and B. Garth (1978) "Access to Justice: The Newest Wave in the Worldwide Movement to Make Rights Effective," 27 *Buffalo Law Review* 181.
Castells, M. (1976) "The Wild City," 4–5 *Working Papers on the Kapitalistate* 2.
Cohen, L. (1979) "The New York City Housing Court—An Evaluation," 17 *Urban Law Annual* 27.
Court Study Group of the Junior League of Brooklyn (1973) *Report on a Study of Brooklyn Landlord–Tenant Court*. Chicago: National Clearinghouse for Legal Services.
Feeley, M. (1979) *The Process is the Punishment: Handling Cases in a Lower Criminal Court*. New York: Russell Sage Foundation.

Foley, D. L. (1975) "Institutional and Contextual Factors Affecting the Housing Choice of Minority Residents," in S. Gale and E. G. Moore (eds.) *The Manipulated City: Perspectives on Spatial Structure and Social Issues in Urban America*. Chicago: Maaroufa Press.

Friedman, L. M. (1967) "Legal Rules and the Process of Social Change," 19 *Stanford Law Review* 786.

Fusco, A. J., Jr. *et al.* (1979) "Chicago's Eviction Court: A Tenants' Court of No Resort!" 17 *Urban Law Annual* 93.

Galanter, M. (1974) "Why the 'Haves' Come Out Ahead: Speculations on the Limits of Legal Change," 9 *Law & Society Review* 95.

Getzels, M. (1969) "Legal Aid Cases Should Not be Limited," 27 *NLADA Briefcase* 302.

Gilboy, J. A. and J. R. Schmidt (1979) "Replacing Lawyers: A Case Study of the Sequential Representation of Criminal Defendants," 70 *Journal of Criminal Law and Criminology* 1.

Goodman, E. S. (1979) "Housing Court: The New York Tenant Experience," 17 *Urban Law Annual* 57.

Grigsby, W. (1967) *Housing Markets and Public Policy*. Philadelphia: University of Pennsylvania Press.

Harvard Civil Rights–Civil Liberties Law Review (1970) "Comment: Controlling Lawyers by Bar Associations and Courts," 35 *Harvard Civil Rights–Civil Liberties Law Review* 301.

Harvey, D. (1973) *Social Justice and the City*. Baltimore: Johns Hopkins Press.

Heydebrand, W. (1977) "Organizational Contradictions in Public Bureaucracies: Toward a Marxian Theory of Organizations," in J. K. Benson (ed.) *Organizational Analysis: Critique and Innovation*. Beverly Hills, Calif.: Sage Publications.

Hofrichter, Richard (1977) "Justice Centers Raise Basic Questions," 2 *New Directions in Legal Services* 168.

Horwitz, M. J. (1977) *The Transformation of American Law*, 1780–1860. Cambridge, Mass.: Harvard University Press.

Johnson, E., Jr. (1978) "Access to Justice in the United States: The Economic Barriers and Some Promising Solutions," in M. Cappelletti (ed.) *Access to Justice*, vol. I: *World Survey*, Milan: Giuffrè; and Alphen aan den Rijn: Sijthoff and Noordhoff.

Judicial Conference of the State of New York (1972) *Seventeenth Annual Report*. New York: Judicial Conference.

Katz, J. (1978) "Lawyers for the Poor in Transition: Involvement, Reform, and the Turnover Problem in the Legal Services Program," 12 *Law & Society Review* 275.

Legislative Drafting Research Fund of Columbia University (1965) *Legal Remedies in Housing Code Enforcement in New York City*. New York: Columbia University.

Mnookin, R. H. and L. Kornhauser (1979) "Bargaining in the Shadow of the Law: The Case of Divorce," 88 *Yale Law Journal* 950.

Mosier, M. and R. Soble (1973) "Modern Legislation, Metropolitan Court, Miniscule Results: A Study of Detroit's Landlord–Tenant Court," 7 *University of Michigan Journal of Law Reform* 8.

Nachbaur, W. T. (1972) "Empty Houses: Abandoned Residential Buildings in the Inner City," in G. Sternlieb (ed.) *Housing 1971–1972*. New York: AMS Press.

Nebron, I. J. and A. Ides (1978) "Landlord Tenant Court in Los Angeles: Restructuring the Justice System." 11 *Loyola of Los Angeles Law Review* 537.

Novak, Edith M. (1973) *Report of the Default Judgment Study*. New York: New York Regional Consumer Protection Counsel.

Oser, A. (1972a) "Housing in Southeast Bronx Under Continuing Pressure," *New York Times* (January 23) sec. 8, p. 1.

———— (1972b) "Bronx Landlord, 32, 'Communicates'," *New York Times* (January 23) sec. 8, p. 1.

———— (1972c) "Rent Strikes Grow Widespread in the South Bronx," *New York Times* (March 19) sec. 8, p. 1.

———— (1975) "Withholding of Rent Clouds Unit's Future," *New York Times* (February 7) sec. 2, p. 46.

———— (1978) "Rent Collection a Problem at Rehabilitation Projects," *New York Times* (December 15) sec. 1, p. 30.

Poulantzas, N. (1978) *State, Power, Socialism*. London: New Left Books.

Reisig, R. (1972) "The Average Fine was $13.49." *Village Voice* (December 7) p. 23.

Rosenthal, D. (1974) *Lawyer and Client: Who's In Charge?* New York: Russell Sage Foundation.

Rothwax, H. (1967) In D. Lowenstein (ed.) *Proceedings of the Harvard Conference on Law and Poverty* March 17, 18, and 19. Cambridge, Mass.: Harvard Law School.

Rutzick, M. C. and R. L. Huffman (1975) "The New York City Housing Court: Trial and Error in Housing Code Enforcement," 50 *New York University Law Review* 738.

Selznick, P. (1969) *Law, Society and Industrial Justice*. New York: Russell Sage Foundation.

Severo, R. (1969) "Hunts Point: Ruled by Addicts," *New York Times* (Sept. 24) sec. 1, pp. 1, 30.

———— (1977) "Bronx a Symbol of America's Woes," *New York Times* (Oct. 6) sec. 1, p. 18.

Shaw, G. (1963) "Practice Commentary: Summary Proceedings under the Real Property Actions and Proceedings Law," in *McKinney's Real Prop. Acts. Law*. St. Paul, Minn.: West Publishing.

Simon, W. (1978) "The Ideology of Advocacy: Procedural Justice and Professional Ethics," 1978 *Wisconsin Law Review* 29.

Small Claims Court Study Group (1972) *Little Injustices: Small Claims Courts and the American Consumer*. Washington, D.C.: The Center for Auto Safety.

Special Committee on Professional Education and Admissions of the Association of the Bar of the City of New York and Committee on Legal Education and Admissions to the Bar of the New York State Bar Association (1978) "The Character and Fitness Committees in New York State," 33 *The Record* 20.

Sternlieb, G. S. and B. P. Indik (1973) *The Ecology of Welfare: Housing and the Welfare Crisis in New York City*. New Brunswick, N.J.: Transaction Books.

Stone, M. (1972) "The Politics of Housing: Mortgage Bankers," July/August *Transaction/Society* 31.

Stumpf, H. P. and R. J. Janowitz (1969) "Judges and the Poor: Bench Responses to Federally Financed Legal Services," 21 *Stanford Law Review* 1058.

Tabb, W. and L. Sawers (1978) *Marxism and the Metropolis*. New York: Oxford University Press.

Thompson, E. (1974) *Civil Justice in a Dynamic City*. New York: New York City Civil Court.

Thompson, E. P. (1975) *Whigs and Hunters*. New York: Pantheon.

Tigar, M. and M. Levy (1977) *Law and the Rise of Capitalism*. New York: Monthly Review Press.

Trilateral Commission Task Report (1975) *The Crisis of Democracy: Report on the Governability of Democracies to the Trilateral Commission*. New York: New York University Press.

Trubek, D. M. (1977) "Complexity and Contradiction in the Legal Order: Balbus and the Challenge of Critical Social Thought About Law," 11 *Law & Society Review* 529.

Walsh, A. A. (1979) "Housing Code Enforcement in New York City—Another Look on an Administrative Tribunal," 17 *Urban Law Annual* 51.

Yale Law Journal (1973) "Note: Legal Services and Landlord–Tenant Litigation: A Critical Analysis," 82 *Yale Law Journal* 1495.

Yngvesson, B. and P. Hennessey (1975) "Small Claims, Complex Disputes: A Review of the Small Claims Literature," 9 *Law & Society Review* 219.

Young, J. (1979) "Left Idealism, Reformism and Beyond: From New Criminology to Marxism," in B. Fine *et al.* (eds.) *Capitalism and the Rule of Law*. London: Hutchinson.

III

Theoretical Perspectives

7

The Dialectics of
Formal and Informal Control*

STEVEN SPITZER

> *We affirm that we can change the historic course of the country while respecting legality, and that within existing legal channels we can alter reality and, consequently, the law itself. No democrat can deny us this possibility.*
>
> (JOSE ANTONIO VIERA-GALLO [1972: 759], subsecretary, Ministry of Justice of the Republic of Chile under Allende)

> *Depend on the rule of man, not the rule of law.*
>
> (MAO TSE-TUNG [1968: 23])

> *Dialectics is not identical with development. Two contradictory moments, the transition to state control and liberation from it, are seized as one in the concept of social revolution.*
>
> (MAX HORKHEIMER [1973: 12])

There seem to be two discrete steps that must be taken whenever we try to imagine the possibilities for humanizing both society and the law. The first is to confront the brute facts of power, domination, and exploitation in social hierarchy and the role of law in preserving and legitimating those hierarchical forms. Here we are concerned with limiting power, demystifying authority, and exposing the connections between the order of law and the disorder of social life. We ask, in other words, how we can remove the coercive, constraining, and dehumanizing features of law to arrive at a less limiting, fragmented, and alienating

*Richard Abel made a valiant effort to improve the readability of my prose and the clarity of my argument. For this effort I am deeply grateful. I would also like to thank a number of readers who made helpful comments and criticisms: John Baumann, Piers Beirne, Ranko Bon, Jim Brady, Stan Cohen, Bob Gordon, Gary Marx, Nicky Rafter, Nancy Reichman, and Gary Young. Some of the ideas contained herein were presented at the annual meeting of the Law and Society Association in June 1980 and discussed with the Boston Area League of Left Study Groups in January 1981.

167

social experience. At this point, the task is one of peeling away the legal integument, exploding the legal myths, and dismantling the legal institutions that stand in the way of human emancipation. This critique, located along the single dimension of constraint and freedom, envisages liberation as part of a process through which "lawlessness"[1] is promoted and law as we know it disappears. Because it identifies law with oppression, exploitation, and false consciousness, the problem becomes one of subverting institutionalized forms of legal authority and exorcizing all mystifying forms of legal reasoning and thought. If law is an expression of class society, then the legal order must be shattered before a truly classless society can come into being. At a minimum, the revolutionary project must therefore give priority to decentralizing decision making and deformalizing legal structures and processes. But if this project is to reach completion, social relationships themselves must be delegalized so that crucial political and economic choices can be made directly by the people who must live with their consequences. It is only when social life can be freed from the stranglehold of legal thought and practice that the possibilities for liberation finally emerge and human association can become more spontaneous and more complete.

But once we have taken this first step in the critique of legal order—identifying delegalization as one of the preconditions and goals for emancipatory politics—it immediately appears inadequate. To nurture the seeds of social progress we must have some concrete conception of the soil in which they are intended to grow. We must determine how to give substance and direction to the energies, visions, and hopes that have been released from the shackles of class society. And we must consider how the conflicts and disorders that inevitably accompany such experiments in human realization should be addressed in the vacuum left by the destruction of prerevolutionary forms of administration and regulation. It is here, at this deeper level of critique, that our visions of community come to the fore. Our image of these forms of association will necessarily depend on the type of social ordering we believe is historically possible and universally desirable. This concept of community must be both practical and visionary. It must be able not only to identify the tensions between what is and what ought to be but also to specify how to conduct the immediate project of reorganizing social, political, economic, and cultural life. The problems of establishing a legal order are not solved by the destruction of class-based society. In fact, it is only as the social order is reinvented that the student of law can fully understand the essential embeddedness of the legal order in everyday life. In this sense the contemporary critique of law requires more than a mere stripping away of ideas and institutions; it also demands the creation of a model of social organization. For this reason my chapter concerns the problems to be faced in remaking the legal order not only

---

[1]See, for example, the editorial "In Praise of Lawlessness," which appeared in the *People's Daily* during the Chinese Cultural Revolution (cited in Leng, 1977: 359).

where socialist revolutions have been absent or failed (e.g., the United States and Chile) but also in their aftermath (e.g., China and Cuba).[2]

The attack on "old" legal form and the search for "new" legal substance represent two sides of the malaise that afflicts contemporary scholarship and practice. At a relatively prosaic level this malaise is translated into a question of the formality or informality of legal arrangements. Even though many who criticize bourgeois law seek to do no more than to render the legal order more "efficient" and "responsive," they share with the most radical critics a concern over the impersonality, rigidity, remoteness, insensitivity, and formality of the law. They express, albeit in a shallow and truncated fashion, a profound and widely felt discontent with the law as an objectification and reification of social relations in capitalist societies (cf. Lukacs, 1971; Gabel, 1980). But even if "the politics of informal justice" is no more than an ideological arena in which larger social struggles are being fought, the very visibility and ubiquity of these politics make them an important subject for investigation. And though the formalization and deformalization of the law cannot be taken as the only "window" on the contemporary legal crisis, or even the clearest, it is one that offers us a chance to see how the dialectical character of the law permeates the very core of social, political, and economic life.

The term *dialectical* can obfuscate as easily as it can enlighten. Because of this, I have tried to use it in a specific and consistent way. Social forms and processes are dialectical when they are (*a*) contradictory; (*b*) deceptive; and (*c*) transformable from within. Contradictory relationships are characterized by nonidentity, disunity, and divergence *within* a larger whole: a unity of opposites. Elements in a dialectical contradiction are integrated, bound together, and interpenetrate one another; they need to be distinguished from elements in contrariety, in real opposition to one another (Colletti, 1975). Contradictory relationships, such as those within capitalist production or law, mediate one another. Relationships of contrariety, such as those of repulsion and attraction in Newtonian physics, are based on genuinely antagonistic forces or tendencies. Efforts to reduce dialectical relationships to entries in an analytical balance sheet and to predict which set of forces or elements will win out confuse contradiction with contrariety. They ignore the internal relations that unify opposites (cf. Ollman, 1971: 65).

The deceptive features of dialectical relationships arise from the fact that their essence is at variance with their appearance. For example, to the extent that the "rule of law" is understood to promote justice, freedom, and reason but actually produces injustice, coercion, and irrationality it is clear that essence is inconsis-

---

[2]The perspective adopted in this introductory section, as well as the general structure of this chapter, was significantly influenced by the ideas developed by Roberto Mangabeira Unger in a course in jurisprudence offered at Harvard Law School in January 1980.

tent with appearance. Understanding the dialectical features of any contradictory social arrangement, symbol, or mode of thought requires that we develop a way of penetrating the surface of social reality. In contrast to positivists who assume that a "scientific description can contain only the structure . . . of objects, not their 'essence'" (Neurath, 1973: 309), Marx (1958: 797) argued that "all science would be superfluous if the outward appearance and the essence of things directly coincided." This lack of coincidence is at the heart of dialectics.

Finally, when speaking of dialectical processes here I will be attending to the ways in which social arrangements and structures are transformed from within. In this context the problem becomes one of explaining change by reference to "contrasts which cannot be solved within the given mode of existence, so that the contrasts break down the current mode of existence and create a new one" (Reich, 1972: 28). When we focus on the interpenetration of contradictory forces we can understand why change does *not* occur in the face of internal strains. Conversely, when we examine the centrifugal pressures within the unity of opposites we can begin to see why stability gives way to change. Whether law serves progressive or regressive purposes in any given instance, its transformation is dialectical insofar as it is produced by internal contradictions.

Several distinctions are important here. First, I am not saying merely that it is useful to interpret legal phenomena and other social orderings dialectically, to apply a dialectical perspective from without. My argument is more ambitious: Dialectical features of these phenomena and changes are *real*, not simply the artifact of "a method slapped on outwardly, at random" (Adorno, 1973: 5). When we see law and legal relationships as dialectical we are not simply dropping legal forms and processes into a dialectical mill to reduce them to a "merely logical form of contradiction" (*Ibid.*); we are asserting that contradictions pervade their very essence and "laws of motion."

Second, it is important to recognize that the paradoxes, ironies, and surprises that come to light when we explore the dialectics of informal and formal control transcend both a nihilist critique (Tushnet, 1980) and a lesson in unanticipated consequences (Merton, 1981). They are, rather, clues to the underlying fabric of contradictions and conflicts upon which the entire symbolic and operational edifice of the law rests.

Finally, it is essential to make clear just how the process of dialectical change described in the preceding discussion is approached in the analysis that follows. The boundaries I prefer to draw around the use of dialectical concepts for understanding legal and social change fall between the two extremes of determinism and indeterminism. The determinist model, frequently associated with the "iron laws" of social change prescribed by evolutionist Marxism, sees the unfolding of contradictions as following a single inexorable path. The problems with this sort of interpretation are quite clear. Once legal change is seen as necessary and inevitable it becomes impossible to understand such persistent anomalies as the genuine protection of freedom in capitalist states through such bourgeois institutions as the jury (Thompson, 1978) or the abuse of emancipatory symbols and structures in a variety of worker states (which is discussed later in this chapter). Horkheimer's (1973: 12) caveat that "dialectics is not identical with development" summarizes at least one line of objections to this model (see Jacoby, 1977–1978).

On the other hand, it is clear that if we assume that all dialectical transformations are open-ended, free-floating, and totally contingent, we must sever the connection between our understanding of history and social change. The crucial issue here, and it is one that can only be sketched in the present context, is related to the embeddedness of any given contradiction in particular sociohistorical formations. The Marxian critique of capitalism begins with the assumption that "capitalism is contradictory not because it is a *reality* and all realities are contradictory, but because it is an *upside-down,* inverted reality (alienation, fetishism)" (Colletti, 1975: 29). In this sense, contradiction is not a universal and unchanging social fact; it is a particular feature of relationships and structures in historically bound class societies. To the extent that the dialectical processes discussed are timeless, abstract, and deracinated it is impossible to preserve the critical standpoint from which an alternative to class societies can be glimpsed. But to the extent that we view this alternative as achievable through an unswerving, unilinear, and historically necessary march toward human liberation, the "arrow of history," we sacrifice the critical power of the dialectic to "a mechanical development of the thesis–antithesis" (Jacoby, 1977–1978: 77). In what follows I have attempted to sketch the most important theoretical problems surrounding the dialectics of formal and informal control without succumbing to either the ahistoricism of contingency or the rigidity of determinism.

THE CONTRADICTIONS OF LAW, JUSTICE, AND POWER IN BOURGEOIS SOCIETY

To decipher the dialectics of formal and informal control we must begin with a focus no less ambitious than the intersection of law, justice, and power. Why we must cast our conceptual net so broadly is suggested in the following observation by Max Weber (1946: 220–221).

The position of all "democratic" currents, in the sense of currents that would minimize "authority," is necessarily ambiguous. "Equality before the law" and the demand for legal guarantees against arbitrariness demand a formal and rational "objectivity" of administration, as opposed to the personally free discretion flowing from the "grace" of the old patrimonial domination. If, however, an "ethos"—not to speak of instincts—takes hold of the masses on some individual question, it postulates *substantive* justice oriented toward some concrete instance and person; and such an "ethos" will unavoidably collide with the formalism and the rule-bound and cool "matter-of-factness" of bureaucratic administration. For this reason, the ethos must emotionally reject what reason demands. The propertyless masses especially are not served by a formal "equality before the law" and a "calculable" ajudication and administration, as demanded by "bourgeois" interests. Naturally in their eyes justice and administration should serve to compensate for their economic and social life-opportunities in the face of the propertied classes. Justice and administration can fulfill this function only if they assume an informal character to a far-reaching extent. It must be informal because it is substantively "ethical" ("Khadi-justice"). Every sort of "popular justice"—which usually does not ask for reasons and norms—as well as every sort of intensive influence on the administration of so-called public opinion, crosses the rational course of justice and administration just as strongly, and under certain conditions far more so, as the "star chamber" proceedings of an "absolute" ruler has been able to do. In this connection, that is, under the conditions of mass democracy, public opinion is communal conduct born of irrational "sentiments." Normally it is staged or directed by party leaders and the press.

The ambiguity that Weber addressed is directly relevant to our topic because it exposes the dialectical crosscurrents embodied in the movements to formalize and deformalize the law. To the extent that law aspires to protect the weak against arbitrary authority, it must introduce formality, rational administration, rule-boundedness, and impersonal handling of cases. Yet when the law is actually invoked to achieve social justice, that is, to compensate, protect, and guarantee the "economic and social life-opportunities of [the masses] in the face of the propertied classes," it typically represents an expression of informal, "ethical," concrete, and personalized varieties of "substantive justice." And these modalities of legal processing can easily be subverted to the advantage of the very groups they are supposed to control. Moreover, as the movement toward greater "equality before the law" progresses and as the champions of formalization (typically the bourgeoisie) gain power, the "matter-of-factness" of bureaucratic administration increasingly transforms the law into an unassailable, abstract, and reified tool of the ruling elite; any attempt to overturn or question legal authority consequently appears increasingly "irrational" and less and less within the reach of those who are most victimized by "equality before the law" and "calculable" adjudication and administration. Put somewhat differently, Weber asserts that though law as form and law as substance may each be equated with social justice, fairness, and equality (if for very different reasons), neither is able to deliver on its claims; both have been, and will continue to be, invoked as ideologies, policies, and procedures that serve to dominate rather than liberate the oppressed.

But for Weber this contradiction is much more than a struggle between "rational" and "irrational" forces in history. It reflects the deeply antagonistic and complex relationship between law as form and substance (cf. Kennedy, 1976; Fraser, 1978; Klare, 1979). And because the relationships between law, justice, and power are dialectical, we must always be sensitive to the ways in which movements toward formalism and informalism contain dynamics that transform them into something very different from what they appear or are proclaimed to be—even the exact opposite.

When this dialectic is examined more closely it is clear that the nexus between law as form and law as substance is not a unity of opposing forces of equal strength. Weber sees the rise of Western capitalism as a movement toward the dominance of form over substance, of formal rationality over substantive rationality. The consequences of this movement are the declining role of spontaneous law and popular justice and the increasing penetration, leveling, and atomization of the masses by faceless legal (bureaucratic) forms.[3] As the "regressive equality" of legal formalism erodes the basis for attacking capitalism on extraformal (substantive) grounds, it prepares the way for bureaucratic centralization and relegates protest against rational–legal authority to an ever more precarious and "irrational" sphere. It is for this reason that Weber (1968: 893) can conclude that any trend toward greater informalism is ultimately doomed and that "it is by no means certain that those classes which are negatively privileged today, especially the working class, may safely expect from an informal administration of justice those results which are claimed for it by the ideology of jurists."

But before we dismiss Weber's theory as thoroughly undialectical—a profound pessimism that describes the history of law as nothing more than the triumph of power over justice—it is important to keep in mind that Weber viewed the rationalization of social life as a tendency, not an immutable law. Jean Cohen (1972: 65) observes:

> For Weber, rationalization, as the extension of formal rationality, is not simply a unilinear, monolithic process immanently unfolding in all areas of modern life. Instead, as formal rationality advances, it evokes counter forces all along the way. It is itself very often an unintended consequence of action oriented to substantive values, and usually results in unintended consequences in turn—in irrationalities from both the formal and substantive point of view. In short, the process of rationalization can be seen as a dynamic between formal and substantive rationality.

Reading Weber in this way, we can recast the problem of our study: to unravel and anchor this dialectical process and discover some of its laws of motion. We can appreciate not only why movements to democratize form and substance give

[3]Weber's all-embracing pessimism prevented him from accepting a concept of substantive reason as a viable alternative to the rationalization process he describes. As Horkheimer (1974: 6) points out, Weber "did not conceive of any rationality—not even a 'substantial' one by which man can discriminate one end from another. If our drives, intentions, and finally our ultimate decisions must *a priori* be irrational, substantial reason becomes an agency merely of correlation and is therefore itself essentially 'functional.'" This form of analysis is, of course, directly at odds with those critical directions in social theory that posit the possibility of transcending subjective reason and creating a society based on truly "objective reason"—on the approximation of goodness, tolerance, justice, and truth. For another critique of Weber's analysis of rationalization see Beirne (1979).

rise to decidedly antidemocratic consequences but also how and why these movements "call forth counter-effects which hamper, retard, and partly paralyze" (Spitzer, 1979a: 188) their developmental tendencies. In the remainder of this chapter I will attempt to expose some of the complexities and nuances of this dynamic relationship and offer historical and contemporary examples.

There are four major elements whose interrelationship we have considered thus far: legal form, legal substance, class domination, and social justice. Each of these phenomena may be seen as bounded within the dialectical unity I have described. Following Weber, I will define formally rational law as relatively abstract, coherent, clear, calculable, rulelike, oriented to observable elements of behavior rather than social relationships and statuses, "value-free," impersonal, and formulated so as to facilitate generalization across cases. Conversely, substantively rational law is relatively concrete, unsystematic, ambiguous, unpredictable, rule-free, oriented to social situations and characteristics rather than abstract components of behavior, "value-directed," personalized, and attentive to differences rather than similarities between cases.[4]

Thus far I have argued law may take on either formal or substantive characteristics in the service of either social justice or class domination. Weber asks why both formally and substantively rational law have functioned as tools of class domination despite their important historical role as counter-ideologies or rhetorics of opposition. When it is presented in this way we are forced to recognize another important distinction between law as an ideology and law as an instrument of class domination, between the way law is presented and apprehended and the reality of law. I will return to this problem later in this chapter.

Legal Form

First, let us consider the legal form. It should be clear by now that the process of legal formalization is equivocal in several important respects. On the one hand, the defeat of precapitalist modes of domination required (a) the limitation of caprice and arbitrariness by traditional elites; (b) the demystification of what variously have been called ideologies (Marx), collective representations (Durkheim), legitimations (Weber), myths (Sorel), derivations (Pareto), and political formulae (Mosca)—systems of belief that concealed the process of social domination and gave moral force to premodern forms of "hypercentralized" power (cf. Spitzer, 1975, 1979b); and (c) the creation of publicly enunciated "legal rights"

---

[4]For far more elaborate attempts at isolating and interpreting these dimensions, see Kennedy's (1976) discussion of a "regime of rules" and a "regime of standards" and Unger's (1976: 192–223) analysis of the "disintegration of the rule of law in postliberal society." For a discussion of legal formalism and the model of rules, see Nonet and Selznick (1978: Ch. 3).

against both the traditional structures and processes of social subjugation (i.e., the church, kinship groups, feudal bonds, etc.) *and* the newly emerging powers of the modern state. But as Weber, Marx, and others have pointed out, the proclamation of "legal equality" hardly guaranteed the restraint of centralized authority and, in fact, permitted a far more streamlined and effective system of class domination. This transformation took place on three levels: the *economic*, where the "laws of the market" replaced the habits, customs, and redistributive policies of precapitalist social formations; the *political*, where "mass democracy makes a clean sweep of the feudal, patrimonial, and—at least in intent— plutocratic privileges of administration" (Weber, 1946: 225); and the *ideological*, where the ethos of "equality before the law," "a government of laws, not men," and "the natural rights of man" supplanted appeals to "the divine right of kings," *lèse majesté, noblesse oblige,* and other ideological props of customary privilege. It was this last process of substitution that led Marx (1975: 46) to remark with characteristic sarcasm:

> It was a definite advance in history when the *Estates* were transformed into social classes so that, just as the Christians are equal in heaven though unequal on earth, the individual members of the people become *equal* in the heaven of their political world, though unequal in their earthly existence in *society.*

Perhaps the best-known contemporary description of the ambiguous character of bourgeois legal form is provided by E. P. Thompson (1975). In this analysis of crime and punishment in eighteenth-century England, Thompson considers the contradictory character of "the rule of law" and the relationship between legal ideology and legal practice. Arguing against a simple equation of law and class power, he notes that

> the rhetoric and the rules of a society are something a great deal more than sham. In the same moment they may modify, in profound ways, the behaviour of the powerful, and mystify the powerless. They may disguise the true realities of power, but, at the same time, they may curb that power and check its intrusions [*Ibid.*: 265].

Even though "the rule of law" can reify, mystify, and objectify social relationships in ways that make them more effective tools of class power, still "the essential precondition for the effectiveness of law, in its function as ideology, is that it shall display an independence from gross manipulation and shall seem to be just" (*Ibid.*: 263). As a result, the law will actually turn out to *be* just in many cases. In this sense, formal law is *both* a guarantor of social justice and a mechanism of class domination. By emphasizing the equivocal character of formal law, Thompson is able to make a case for the preservation of the "forms of rhetoric of law . . . which may, on occasion, inhibit power and afford some protection to the powerless" (*Ibid.*: 266). He prefers the mediated force and masked injustice of the bourgeois legal form to "the exercise of direct unmediated force (arbitrary imprisonment, the employment of troops against the crowd, torture, and those other conveniences of power with which we are all conversant)" (*Ibid.*: 264).

In delineating advantages of a "regime of rules" (Kennedy, 1976), Thompson cautions us against throwing out the protective "baby" of formal and calculable rules along with the repressive "bathwater" of capitalist legal structure. But how far can we go in preserving the legal framework of capitalism without providing sustenance to capitalism itself? Surely, as Karl Klare has pointed out, "socialist law cannot be the mere pouring of new content into the institutional forms of liberal legalism" (1979: 135). Moreover, "once we discard the purely instrumental view of law as sham, the *form* of law is no longer a mere detail but a profound channeling mechanism in part through which legal practice in class society takes on its character as alienation" (*Ibid.*: 134).

A more specific challenge to Thompson's position is found in a discussion of "Crime, Law and the State" by Stuart Hall and others.

> The inscription within the "rule of law" of the key relations of capital—private property, the contract—is no well-kept secret. If the law demarcates illegal forms of appropriation, it makes the legal forms public and visible—the norm—and sanctions them positively. It protects life and limb. But it also preserves public order; and, under this rubric, it frequently secures, in moments of open class confrontation, just that stability and cohesion without which the steady reproduction of capital and the unfolding of capitalist relations would be a far more hazardous and unpredictable affair. It preserves society against its enemies, within and without. It raises existing social relations—for example those stemming from the social and sexual division of labour—to the level of universal norms. By operating strictly within judicial logic, juridical norms of evidence and proof, it constantly brackets out those aspects of class relations which destroy its equilibrium and impartiality in *practice*. It equalises, in the formal eye of the law, things which cannot be equal. . . . The law thus comes to represent all that is most impartial, independent, above the play of party interest, within the state. It is the most formal representation of universal consent. Its "rule" comes to stand for the social order—for "society" itself. Hence a challenge to it is a token of social disintegration. In such conjunctures "law" and "order" become identical and indivisible [1978: 208].

Whether we endorse Thompson's arguments in favor of the preservation of the "rule of law" or those of his critics will ultimately depend on whether we emphasize the hegemonic or the instrumental functions of law in capitalist society. If we adopt the crude view that law is nothing more than an epiphenomenon of the economic infrastructure, "that the juridical relation is like a knee-jerk produced by an economic hammer-tap, or the mechanism of a Pavlovian dog emitting juridical saliva in response to economic stimuli" (Wood, 1972: 252), then the dialectical relationship between form and substance dissolves: The fate of repressive law is identified with that of capitalism, and in a revolutionary situation legal domination is swept away with the relations of production upon which it is based. However, when we join with Thompson and a growing number of others (e.g., Balbus, 1977; Tushnet, 1978; Fraser, 1978; Hirst, 1979; Klare, 1979) in recognizing that law and legal discourse are thoroughly implicated in social and psychological existence under capitalism and that the power of the law may be far greater when it is *not* invoked or invoked only symbolically, then the problem of legal form becomes decisive. Moreover, to the extent that the form and content of law are thoroughly intertwined in complex and contingent ways (an assumption that underlies the entire debate about the "relative autonomy" of law and state), then it is not enough to say either that "with the advent of justice, the law disappears" (Horkheimer, 1978: 71), or that "the rule of law itself [is] an unqualified human good" (Thompson, 1975: 263).

The importance of anchoring this problem within specific historical contexts becomes even clearer when we acknowledge that the political—and therefore legal—forms taken by systems of domination under capitalism do not correspond in any direct or simple way to what is abstractly defined as "capitalist development." As we shall see later, capitalism has not always grown most rapidly in the soil of "the rule of law"; in some cases the most favorable conditions have been created by regimes that emphasize law as substance rather than form. Weber's well-known investigation of "the England Problem" and his comparison of English and Continental legal forms led him to conclude:

> Modern capitalism prospers equally and manifests identical economic traits under legal systems containing rules and institutions which considerably differ from each other at least from the juridical point of view. . . . Indeed we may say that legal systems under which modern capitalism has been prospering differ profoundly from each other even in their ultimate principles of formal structure [1968: 890].

Similarly, in trying to account for the variable relationships between capitalist development and legal form, Gramsci (1971) emphasized the contingent connection between infrastructure and superstructure and made a distinction between normal and exceptional modes of the liberal and postliberal state. As Hall and others note:

> Although the precise nature of the relationship between fascism and capitalism in a degenerate phase is still a matter of considerable controversy, it must now be acknowledged that capitalism is also compatible with—and may be required to be "rescued" by—certain quite *exceptional* forms of the state (e.g., the fascist state), in which many of its normal modes are suspended. Gramsci had cause to understand the significance of these "exceptional" moments, since it was precisely one such state, the state of Mussolini's fascist Italy, which imprisoned him [1978: 209].

Although Weber (1946: 217) focused on "the lawfully autonomous development of the respective structures of domination" and Gramsci (1971: 178) on "the correct relation between what is organic and what is conjunctural" in capitalist formations, both expose the pitfalls in overlooking the dynamic interplay between the political and the economic, the substantive and the formal.

Before addressing substantive rationality more directly, it may be valuable to consider the view of Max Horkheimer. In a fragment entitled "Power, Right, Justice" he begins by observing:

> "Might before right" is a misleading proverb, for power need not compete with the law; the law is its attribute. Power has the law on its side, whereas powerlessness needs it. To the extent that power is unable to grant or refuse a right, it is itself limited though certainly not by the law but by other powers which restrict its scope. This constellation is obscured because as a convention between powers in the bourgeois state, the law seems to live a life of its own, especially when a bureaucracy that is relatively neutral vis-à-vis the various bourgeois parties administers it. But how things really are becomes apparent the moment the ruling elements, or rather groups within the ruling class, are of one mind, i.e., when the proletariat is the enemy. Quite independently of its formulations, the effect of the law then becomes the precise expression of the extent of their power [1978: 71].

Up to this point, Horkheimer's position may be understood as purely instrumentalist: The law is a precipitate of power relations and the "relative autonomy" of the law no more than "a convention between powers in the bourgeois state." Horkheimer then notes, however, that the preceding observation "is true of positive law. But the concept of justice epitomizes the demands of the suppressed at any given moment, and it is therefore as changeable as those demands themselves. Its essence today ultimately calls for the elimination of classes and therefore also the abolition of law as set forth above" (*Ibid.*).

Taken in its entirety, what is perhaps most interesting about this excerpt is its distinction between positive law and justice and its sensitivity to the role of class struggle in shaping the relationship between the two. Taking up a theme that was also of vital interest to Weber and Gramsci, Horkheimer argues that the connection between law as a tool of power and as a symbol of justice will always be mediated by the fluctuating demands of the oppressed, on the one hand, and the shifting configuration of class forces (in Gramsci's terms, the "ensemble of class fractions" or "historical bloc"), on the other. Horkheimer thus differs from Thompson in maintaining that "to the extent that power is unable to grant or refuse a right, it is itself limited *though certainly not by the law* but by other powers which restrict its scope" (*Ibid.*). Horkheimer thereby acknowledges factors *outside* the legal form—political, economic, and ideological considerations that may either make law a weapon of the powerful or erect formal barriers to its arbitrary and class-specific use. I will now consider these "extralegal" factors and their expression in the *substance* of bourgeois law.

Legal Substance

The central question that confronts us here is whether the application of "substantive law" to social arrangements and relationships is consistent or inconsistent with "justice," "freedom," and "equality." Of course, we will have to specify the meaning of these abstract social goals (and may even challenge whether they are inherently "social" at all), but this need not interfere with our attempt to clarify the issues involved. In considering substantively rational law, the decisive contradiction becomes apparent when we recognize that if the law is to reflect and reinforce the processes through which a socialist order is achieved, it must provide a genuine alternative to the alienating, reified, commodified, and bureaucratic legal forms of capitalist society. It must, in other words, incorporate, articulate, and express the sentiments, moral standards, and "collective will" of the masses. Yet it is precisely these social functions and moral aspirations of the law that render it most vulnerable to distortion, subversion, and misapplication. [5] To say that we wish the law to be an instrument of "people's justice" and a crystallization of "collective will" not only is an attack on what the law has been under precapitalist and capitalist forms of domination but may also be an invitation to recapitulate or even strengthen the most dehumanizing and unjust aspects of law, albeit within the framework of what appears to be noncapitalist social arrangements.

But the relative power of formal and substantive mystifications cannot be separated from the concrete process of historical development of which they are a part. The fit between legal ideology (whether based on substantive or formalist rhetoric), structures of domination, and the entire ensemble of social relations will always reflect the level of contradictions characterizing any particular social formation. To suggest that formal and substantive rhetorics are fungible alternatives whose choice depends only on their utility for the "problem at hand" is to forget that appeals to form or substance are most likely to emerge in the context of a "legitimation crisis"—a crisis that is historically specific and embedded in a particular set of structural contradictions. Oliver Cromwell's assertion that "the law as it is now constituted serves only to maintain the lawyers and to encourage the rich to oppress the poor" (cited in Hill, 1975: 270) could have been advanced in a socialist as well as a bourgeois revolution, in the twentieth century as well as the seventeenth, in Cuba as well as England. Yet this expression of antilegalism can be severed from its historical moorings only to the extent that it remains unmediated and abstract. As soon as we begin to specify the content of appeals to substantive justice and the sociohistorical matrix within which those appeals are made, it is quite clear that we must study each episode of antiformalism on its own terms. As we shall see in the following section, the movements toward

---

[5]Nietzsche (1967: 50) put the problem this way:

One is deceived every time one expects 'progress' from an ideal; every time so far the victory of the ideal has meant a retrograde movement. Christianity, the revolution, the abolition of slavery, equal rights, philanthropy, love of peace, justice, truth: all these big words have value only in a fight, as flags: *not* as realities but as *showy words* for something quite different (indeed, opposite!).

formalization and deformalization take on very different meanings depending on their cultural, historical, and political surroundings.

A common feature of many "reforms of substance" is the effort to make political activity and institutions consonant with the priorities and goals of the masses. In this sense, the reform of law represents part of the larger struggle against political alienation (cf. Wolfe, 1977) and toward the discovery of a genuine "social harmony." Whether these reforms are put forward in the rhetoric of "natural law," "God's law," "socialist justice," or "community rights," they look either forward or backward to an alternative to the present world in which the mechanisms of social control and coordination have become estranged from their roots and confront the masses as an impersonal and thoroughly alien force. That it is often difficult to distinguish progressive "reforms" from regressive and virtually impossible to tell whether any specific proposal for deformalization will move society closer to a "refeudalization" or a "socialization" of legal arrangements reflects the historically specific character of the alienation involved.

One stage in the historical progress of this estrangement is associated with the destruction of an organic unity of economy and polity under feudalism and the substitution of a system wherein political forms (exemplified by "the law") could be distinguished from their economic origins and functions (Anderson, 1974: 19). Under feudalism, and indeed under slavery and other modes of personalized domination, there was a fusion of economic exploitation and political–legal coercion within such arenas as the village, manor, plantation, fief, parish, or company town. The defocalization, depersonalization, and nationalization of political control that accompanied capitalist development and the rise of an international market economy not only permitted (and was made possible by) the emergence of the modern state and the triumph of the commodity form but also effectively destroyed the "cellular unity" that characterized precapitalist varieties of social control.[6]

When we look at the announced objectives of various substantive reforms, it is plain why all attempts to (re)create the unity of the precapitalist era, whatever their visions of a just society, must ultimately come to terms with the fact that the new legal order may be nothing more than a repackaged version of the old. This

---

[6]Thus, we may say that the "relative autonomy" of politics and the law, a formulation that has become an almost reflexive escape route from the intellectual lock-step of "mechanical Marxism," is much more a peculiarity of social organization under capitalism than an invariant and transhistorical feature of social existence. The very independence of law and society, polity and economy, must be understood as a discrete historical product, not merely a contrivance of neo-Marxist critics. This product has been fashioned by the actual development of the capitalist social formation and its progressive penetration of everyday life. The problem remains: How can we reintegrate politics and society without recreating the framework of domination and exploitation upon which such integration has been based?

is not to suggest, however, that the "glue" holding precapitalist and postcapitalist social formations together is the same. Before capitalism, the unification of social production and social control was achieved within relatively small, localized, autonomous communities: "The organic unities of pre-capitalist societies organised their metabolism largely in independence of each other" (Lukacs, 1971: 92). During the growth and eventual triumph of capitalism, this organic unity was dissolved through the destruction of all precapitalist production units and relations of dependence and their replacement by the laws of the marketplace and the "phantom objectivity" (*Ibid.*: 83) of the state and its laws. What makes the movement to socialism much more than a return to the "cellular metabolism" of precapitalist life is its goal of establishing a synthetic relationship that integrates society as a whole—a unity that *shares* with capitalism the goal of a universalized rather than a segmented organization of social, political, cultural, and economic life. The difference, of course, is that socialism seeks this universalization through a coalescence of these spheres, whereas capitalism increases massification through the further fragmentation, atomization, and objectification of social structure and processes.

In analyzing these antimonies and the equivocal character of legal reform we must delve much more deeply into the specific historical bonds between capitalist development and legal organization. To determine whether substantive criticism of legal formality will open the way to the realization of a socialist society or simply provide a fresh reservoir of "fixed ideas" (Stirner, 1971) and "showy words" (Nietzsche, 1967: 50) to mystify and befuddle the masses, we must be able to separate what is common to all criticism of positive law and legal institutions from what is peculiar to the movements for deformalization and reformalization that have emerged under particular conditions of social organization and social change.

FORMS OF CAPITALISM AND LEGAL FORMS

One purpose of the foregoing discussion has been to identify some of the contradictions permeating the relationship between legal and social change. Another has been to question both Weber's linear model of formalization and capitalist development and the vulgar materialist view that law is merely an epiphenomenon of economic life. A third has been to suggest how the economic, political, and ideological functions performed by positive laws and the law in general may both advance and inhibit progressive change.

The law has taken different forms and shapes under capitalism because of the inevitable tension between law as an instrument of class power and law as a symbol of equal (i.e., classless) rights (cf. Hay, 1975). Moreover, the law is sometimes at odds with a certain category of capitalist interests insofar as the state must act with some independence from individual capitalists to ensure the survival of capitalism as a whole. But in addition to these sources of discontinuity and slippage between socioeconomic and legal development, the changing nature of capitalism itself must be examined as one possible explanation of the dialectical twists taken by movements toward formal and substantive justice. The Weberian association of capitalism and legal formalism can be sustained only for a limited period. And because capitalism is neither monolithic nor static, we need to explore the historically contingent interplay between capitalism and its laws as part of a process that can be contradictory as well as complex.[7]

There is a considerable body of evidence documenting the role of legal formalism in promoting the rise of modern capitalism (e.g., Polanyi, 1944; Hall, 1952; Neumann, 1957; Weber, 1968; Friedmann, 1972; Kennedy, 1973; 1980; Horwitz, 1977; Spitzer and Scull, 1977a). The argument is well known: In order for a market economy to emerge it was necessary to create a legal (as well as a social and ideological) environment where relationships between independent parties were governed by calculability, uniformity, predictability, stability, abstraction, generality, and inclusiveness.

> Freedom of the commodity market, freedom of the labor market, free selection within the entrepreneurial class, freedom of contract, and above all, calculability of the decisions of the judiciary are the essential characteristics of the liberal competitive system which, through continuous rationalistic, and capitalistic enterprise, produces a steady flow of profits. It is the primary task of the state to create such a legal order as will secure the fulfillment of contracts. A high degree of certainty of the expectation that contracts will be executed is an indispensable part of the enterprise [Neumann, 1957: 40].

So far so good. But what is far less understood is the way in which transformations in fully developed capitalist societies have influenced and been influenced by legal institutions, practices, and ideas. In other words, we need to explore whether or not the trajectory established by the initial fusion of legal formalism and capitalism has been sustained, and whether or not the legal relationships and rhetorics following the triumph of capitalism represent an extension of, or a departure from, the secular trend.

The separation between politics and economics, the state and the market, as well as public and private life, were the great ideological breakthroughs of classical liberal political economy. Once coercion in the public sphere could be defined as the imposition of state control, and coercion in the private sphere, as "contract," it became possible both to justify laissez-faire capitalism and to envi-

---

[7]Marxists who fail to appreciate the variegated and historically specific character of capitalism and other modes of production fall into the idealism of which Weber and others are frequently accused. As Anderson (1974: 403) has suggested: "A colour-blind materialism, incapable of appreciating the real and rich spectrum of diverse social totalities within the same temporal band of history . . . inevitably ends in a perverse idealism."

sion a legal system that balanced and held in check substantive interests. These bifurcations were far less evident in reality than in the conceptions of capitalist ideologues (cf. Polanyi, 1944; Neumann, 1957; Williams, 1961; Samuels, 1979); furthermore, as capitalism began to move toward its modern configuration the watertight separations between these categories became more and more difficult to defend. A capitalism that became far more monopolistic, corporate, and responsive to the dictates of an expanding state arrested and even reversed the legal drift from status to contract (Maine, 1861). Not only have status and organizational affiliation become increasingly important in defining the legal rights of the individual (Fraser, 1978), but the entire distinction between private and public law has been under sttack (cf. Tobriner and Grodin, 1967; Unger, 1976: Ch. 3; Klare, 1979). The rise of administrative law (Nonet, 1969), government by private groups (Jaffe, 1937; Friedmann, 1957), the "death of contract" (Gilmore, 1974), contracts of adhesion (Kessler, 1943), the "security state" (Miller, 1958), and the "therapeutic state" (Kittrie, 1973) are but a few of the politicolegal manifestations of this trend.

But the movement from status to contract to status is in no sense cyclical. The corporate and bureaucratic character of modern capitalist societies creates an "organic unity" profoundly dissimilar from precapitalist bonds of kinship, fealty, community, religion, and ethnicity. Moreover, whereas precapitalist status defined rights and obligations as flowing naturally from social position, the modern forms of status are bestowed by patterns of organizational development and vicissitudes of public law. What *is* similar about the new status and the old is that both are compatible with social regulations that are concrete, fact oriented, and particularistic, and with patterns of decision making that are centralized rather than determined by either reciprocal obligations or the "wisdom" of the market (cf. Polanyi, 1944: Ch. 4).

Several factors seem to be at the heart of the intrusion of substantive rationality into the formalized law of advanced capitalist societies. First, insofar as the market is attenuated as a "transactional mode" (*Ibid.*; North, 1977) and loses its centrality in the allocative system, other (i.e., extraeconomic) methods must be found to extract and redistribute surplus value. Without the "laws of the market" to regulate labor, institutionalize inequality, and support the concentration of wealth, stratified societies must rely to a far greater extent on political and ideological mechanisms (Spitzer, 1975). In precapitalist societies redistribution was legitimated and made possible by the fact that "the 'superstructures' of kinship, religion, law or the state necessarily enter into the constitutive structure of the mode of production" (Anderson, 1974: 403). There was, in other words, a far more substantive and direct involvement of the "legal" structure in the process through which wealth was pumped out of laborers and accumulated by ruling elites. These arrangements had little use for an abstract, general, calculable "rule of law" since conceptions of justice, freedom, obligations, and rights were not placed in a separate realm but were thoroughly embedded in the social order of things. And if that order was violated, it was clearly not a question of "private" individual rights being balanced against "public" interests (cf. Kennedy, 1980) but rather a question of *how* the social standards and hierarchies were to be upheld, reinvigorated, or redefined. Under these circumstances, "man's economy... is submerged in his social relationships. He does not act so as to safeguard his individual interest in the possession of material goods; he acts so as to safeguard his social standing, his social claims, his social assets" (Polanyi, 1944: 46).

In a similar sense, the corporate, bureaucratic, and "planned" capitalisms of the last half century cannot rest upon a structure of social control that is significantly divorced from the hierarchy of vertical loyalties that order the "new industrial state." To the extent that formalism requires strict procedural rules, elimination of discretion, and attention to behavioral events rather than ongoing relationships and crystallized statuses, it sets law outside of the constitutive order of a society that is moving toward greater and greater reliance on nonmarket forms of economic *and* political organization. These new directions in the development of the capitalist economy and state not only signal a decline in the market and a rise of state redistribution as the dominant allocative mechanism in economic affairs but also reflect a growing reliance on legal institutions as substantive, rather than simply formal, foundations for the modern capitalist state. That this intrusive and affirmative role of law flies in the face of classical conceptions of "freedom in the marketplace" and "equality before the law" is yet one more feature of the legitimation crisis associated with the growing discrepancy between legal ideology and legal practice.[8]

From a slightly different perspective, another reason for the decline of formality in advanced capitalism is to be found in the changing relationship between law and economic organization. Rational law, as Neumann (1957: 57) points out, "has not only the function of rendering the process of economic change calculable, but it served at the same time to protect the weaker partner." Under competitive capitalism formal, rulelike law is an indispensable guarantor of the minimum conditions of both commodification and capital accumulation when economic power is either concentrated in the hands of local landowners or monopolized by the precapitalist protectionist state. The most important function of the "rule of law" is thus *negative*: as a solvent of relationships and arrangements standing in the way of the emerging commodity form. But as the

---

[8]This discrepancy cannot be dissolved by arguments that "our legal system is reviving status concepts—not from nostalgia for a bygone society, but to meet the challenges of today" (Tobriner and Grodin, 1967: 1253) or that this moment is nothing more than the discovery of more "responsive law" (Nonet and Selznick, 1978). These accounts represent little more than repackaged versions of the functionalist, evolutionist, "march of progress" approach to interpreting the relationship between a reified "law" and an anthropomorphized "society."

state is transformed from an institutionalization of feudal privilege to a paladin of capitalist development (i.e., state capitalism) and control over national and international capital becomes concentrated in a small number of firms (i.e., oligopoly or monopoly capitalism), there is no longer any need for law to promote the ideal of the self-regulating market. In fact, such protection becomes an obstacle to the expansion and consolidation of economic power and gives way in practice (if not in ideology) in favor of "general principles." Thus, according to Neumann (1957: 58–59):

> In a monopolistic economy "general principles" operate in the interest of the monopolists. The irrational norm is calculable enough for the monopolist since his position is so powerful that he is able to manage without the formal rationality of the law. He can manage not only without rational law; frequently the latter operates even as an impediment to the full development or, if desirable for him, to a restriction of production facilities. . . . Moreover, the monopolist tries to abolish the supplementary guaranties of private property in the means of production—namely, freedom of contract and enterprise—and to have the formal rationality of the law completely terminated. The direct commands of the sovereign state, the administrative acts which directly protect the interests of the monopolists and restrict or abolish the old guaranties, now assume the function of a new auxiliary institution. The apparatus of the authoritarian state realizes the juridical demands of the monopolists.

An instructive, although in many ways anomalous, example of the substitution of "general principles" for formal law can be discovered in the legal transformations accompanying the rise of National Socialism in Germany (cf. Kirchheimer, 1940; 1969; Neumann, 1944). Without assuming that the patterns revealed in the case of the Third Reich provide an accurate foretaste of the path to be followed by legal revolutions in all state capitalist societies, we can nevertheless develop an overview of the most important features revealed in the "derationalization" process within this "degenerate" capitalist state.

A distinctive aspect of National Socialist legal doctrine, and one that is common to most reforms of substantive rationality, is its claim to have "overcome the traditional gulf between private and public law" (Kirchheimer, 1969: 95). By turning the entire legal system into a direct expression of the underlying morality of the people, the liberal distinctions between law and morality, citizen and state, and procedure and substance are obliterated in a single stroke. The philosophical separation of law and morality, begun by Grotius and expanded by Hobbes and Kant (Neumann, 1944: 443), is thus cast aside in favor of a new organicism. In the place of the rule of law there is a fusion of private advantage and public purpose that turns all questions of goals, standards, and procedures into questions of technical rationality.

> Rationality here does not mean that there are universally applicable rules the consequences of which could be calculated by those whom they affect. Rationality here means only that the whole apparatus of law and law-enforcing is made exclusively serviceable to those who rule. Since no

general notions prevail which could be referred to by the ruling and the ruled alike and which thus might restrict the arbitrariness of the administrative practice, the rules are being used to serve the specific purposes of those ruling. The legal system that results is rational for them only [Kirchheimer, 1969: 99].

The outlines of the process through which substance triumphs over form are visible on a number of different levels. Most generally, the law loses its general, abstract character and "every man and each concrete situation must be dealt with by a particular rule... by individual decisions" (Neumann, 1944: 452). This approach is based on the juristic theory of the fascist state: "decisionism." To accomplish these changes the liberal institutions of the separation of powers, an independent judiciary, and legal categories such as "property owner" are overturned. In their place we find that "administrative political decisions take on the form of normal court decisions," "the judge has been reduced to the status of a police official," and "National Socialist legal theory replaces the legal person by the 'concrete personality'" (*Ibid.*: 446–447). On the ideological level "it becomes advisable to replace the concept of the state and its sovereignty by the community and its leader. The state is now characterized as a *Gestalt*, as 'the political *Gestalt*' of the German people" (*Ibid.*: 449). In the criminal law, the principles of *nulla poena sine lege, nullum crimen sine lege* (no punishment without a law, no crime without a law) are abandoned, as are all distinctions between attempting and consummating a criminal act. The law of property in the Third Reich transforms property "from a subjective right belonging to a legal person into an institution, a reified social relation" (*Ibid.*). Property law thus dictates that "what profit an individual is able to draw from his real property, trade, or ownership of means of production depends mainly on his status within his professional group and on the general economic policy of the government" (Kirchheimer, 1969: 90). And finally, in contract law "rights and duties are no longer bound to the will of legally equal persons but to objective facts. The status of man in society becomes decisive. Sir Henry Maine's formula that law develops from status to contract has been reversed" (Neumann, 1944: 449).

Whatever lessons can be drawn from this brief sketch of the National Socialist legal order—and these lessons are undoubtedly limited by many of the cultural, geopolitical, and psychosocial anomalies of this period in German history—one thing is clear: As capitalism becomes less of a market system and is increasingly dominated by administrative criteria and decisions, it is likely to experience a profound transformation in the structure and content of its law. Though the specific changes described above may not represent a condensed version of future capitalist development, they do suggest that the decline of formalism may be both consistent with trends in the contemporary capitalist world system and inconsistent with the realization of the very social goals (i.e., freedom, justice, equality, autonomy, progress, etc.) in whose name formalism continues to be attacked. But even if the relationship between economic concentration, political centralization, legal deformalization, and systematic oppression can be established—as it seems to have been in the Nazi case—do all reforms in the direction of substantive rationality necessarily lead down the same path? Is it not possible that certain "emergent" attacks on bourgeois legality can break through the integument of technical rationality toward a more objectively rational order (Horkheimer, 1974)? Is there no hope for such reforms as procedural informalism, community dispute resolution, neighborhood justice centers, delegalized divorce, and other innovations discussed in this volume—at least as transitional or experimental models in the struggle toward socialism?

To begin to answer these questions we need to explore a different set of changes in the increasingly diversified face of modern social control. We must disentangle the ways in which tendencies in capitalist societies toward centralization and decentralization interact to complicate further the dialectic of formal and informal control.

THE CONCENTRATION OF POWER AND THE DISPERSAL OF CONTROL

Most of the current proposals and projects that can be classified under the rubric "delegalization" (Abel, 1979) are rationalized and promoted as mechanisms for establishing or reviving the strength, autonomy, and self-sufficiency of local social units (i.e., communities, neighborhoods, families, etc.) at the expense of bureaucratically encrusted, impersonal, professionalized, and otherwise "removed" monoliths of control. What advocates of decentralization do not seem to recognize, however, is that the dispersal of control into local and traditional structures is not inconsistent with the *functional* expansion of politically organized and centrally managed forms of social control. It is for this reason that even when these reforms originate in grass roots sentiment they are quite easily "coopted" and absorbed from above (as several chapters in this volume suggest). But what appears to be cooptation and absorption by the more powerful of two antagonistic forces—the destruction of "good" substance by "bad" form—may really be nothing more than the unfolding of a contradictory, yet unitary, process. If we see centralization of power and decentralization of control as part of a dialectical unity, rather than as separate and antithetical tendencies, we may be better able to explain why so much of the scaling down that characterizes modern social control actually serves an increasingly integrated system of making and implementing control decisions.

Starting from the assumptions that (*a*) "the completion of centralization in society and state pushes its driving forces to decentralize" (Horkheimer, 1973: 18); and (*b*) the level of contradictions that have surfaced within capitalism may require a far more intensive and thorough invasion of social activity and consciousness (cf. Hirschhorn, 1978; Spitzer, 1979a; Heydebrand, 1979), we can begin to see how programs that seem to weaken hierarchies of power may actually establish new channels through which those hierarchies can be strengthened, extended, and made more responsive to the complexities of modern social administration. Once we call into question the propositions that control necessarily means impersonality and that capitalism can expand only by bureaucratizing, regimenting, and homogenizing social arrangements, then we need no longer see centralization and decentralization as the ends of a continuum. They become, instead the "two" sides of a mobius strip: processes that coalesce and interpenetrate under historical conditions that have rendered the time-worn premises of capitalist social policy increasingly obsolete.

The administrative revolutions that have accompanied capitalist development—including the political innovations that gave rise to decentralized social control—can be traced, in part, to the contradictions of capitalist economic organization (cf. Pollard, 1965; Braverman, 1974). The problems associated with the realization of surplus value have forced a continuing rationalization of production in particular and social life in general. Rationalization of production has involved the historical movement from Taylorism, to operations research, to organized creativity. As Hirschhorn (1978: 69) has argued, profits are increased no longer by economizing labor time (Taylorism), or by optimizing materials flow (operations research), but by creating and servicing a market. Thus "Taylorist engineers organized *labor* time, systems engineers organized *production time*, whereas researchers and developers organize *social* time. In this sense we can say that the system for creating profits has moved from *human* engineering to *systems* engineering to *social* engineering." Social engineering extends capitalist planning and administration beyond the worker and the factory to the very conditions of social existence. The problem is no longer to adapt the worker to the conditions of production or to invest in social supports to improve his or her performance *qua* worker but rather to shape the entire ensemble of social relations to promote the accumulation of capital, on the one hand, and the legitimation of capitalism, on the other.

The rigid, remote, faceless, uniform structures of the first administrative revolution of industrial capitalism are ill-equipped to carry out the "reinvention" of society that has become the *conditio sine qua non* of capitalist growth. Instead of establishing total institutions (i.e., factories, schools, police departments, prisons, etc.) within a society hostile to capitalist intrusion—the policy of capitalism's golden age—mature capitalism appears to be abandoning exlusionary social organization and control in favor of an inclusionary strategy. Rather than creating enclaves of reason and order within an unreasonable and disordered environment, controls penetrate, suffuse, and transmute the very meaning and rhythms of social life.[9] Of course, the success of all such inclusionary efforts

---

[9]The contrast between exclusionary and inclusionary styles of regulation may be seen most vividly during the period of capitalism's first incursions into the precapitalist social order. An instructive

to create total societies rather than total institutions necessarily hinges upon the relative domestication of the masses and the removal of major threats to the order of capitalist life. And it is here that we see, once again, the central paradox of decentralized and deformalized control: What is represented as a return to the values and traditions of a simpler age, a reaction against and antidote to mass society,[10] is in fact a more complete subversion of those traditions and values. The professed celebration of community, family, and other localized institutions is, at its core, a renunciation of the principles of autonomy and uniqueness upon which such institutions are based. In sum, our eagerness to read "progress" into such transformations allows us to forget that

> whatever raises from within itself a claim to being autonomous, critical and antithetical—while at the same time never being able to assert this claim with total legitimacy—must necessarily come to naught; this is particularly true when its impulses are integrated into something heteronomous to them, which has been worked out previously from above—that is to say, when it is granted the space in which to draw breath immediately by that power against which it rebels [Adorno, 1978: 101–102].

A thorough consideration of the precise mechanisms through which the penetration and reintegration of capitalist society is being attempted lies beyond the scope of this chapter. It *is* possible, however, to sketch the broad outlines of this process in the economic sphere and suggest how such developments reverberate through certain instances of political and legal change.

The general tendency toward decentralizing, deformalizing, and "de-massifying" the relations of production in late capitalism has been described by Alvin Toffler (1980) as part of what he calls the "Third Wave."[11] Pointing to innovations such as flextime, the spread of part-time work and computerized scheduling in the reorganization of work time, geographic dispersal through the creation of autonomous "profit centers," as well as administrative experiments in "multiple-command systems," disaggregated management, the dethroning of experts and the flattening of hierarchies, Toffler catalogues what he believes to be a confirmed movement away from the centralized, synchronized, standardized solution of the industrial revolution (the "Second Wave") toward a new principle: "small within big is beautiful." The touchstones of this economic reorgani-

---

example of one type of "control by exclusion" may be found in the short-lived operation of early company towns and the efforts of industrial entrepreneurs to create an *imperium in imperio* (Spitzer and Scull, 1977a; 1977b).

[10]Movements to delegalize social arrangements experience a rebellious moment, but it is one that resembles the religion of the oppressed. As Marx (1967: 250) pointed out: "*religious* suffering is the *expression* of real suffering and at the same time the *protest* against real suffering."

[11]Toffler's newest effort (1980), like his earlier works, is a paean to technology as the handmaiden of progress. Nevertheless, he does sketch the broad contours of some of the changes that concern us here.

zation are *flexibility* and *responsiveness,* and these desiderata are reflected in the search for

> managers who can operate as well in an open-door, free-flow style as in a hierarchical mode, who can work in an organization structured like an Egyptian Pyramid, as well as in one that looks like a Calder mobile, with a few thin managerial strands holding a complex set of nearly autonomous modules that move in response to the gentlest breeze [Toffler, 1980: 281].

The political and/or legal counterpart of this economic trend may be seen most vividly in what Stanley Cohen (1979) calls the "dispersal of social control." Even though the origins and power of the breezes (sometimes more like "gusts" or "hurricanes") that shake systems of social control may differ from those afflicting the economic order, the structural parallels are unmistakable. Cohen argues that there are major efforts afoot to reduce the scope of state involvement in the organization and application of social controls and that these efforts are expressed in specific movements toward "community" and "diversion." The actual impact of these movements, however, has been "to increase rather than decrease the *amount* of intervention directed at many groups of deviants in the system and, probably, to increase rather than decrease the total *number* who get into the system in the first place" (*Ibid.*: 347). Deformalizing and decentralizing the law has the practical effect of both "thinning the mesh and widening the net." And through this process, discretionary and screening powers get formalized and extended in ways that increase both the intensity and extensiveness of politically organized social controls. In addition to the isolated pockets of coercion reserved for the most recalcitrant in a "free" society we find an ever-widening expansion and diffusion of "hundreds of tiny theatres of punishment" (Foucault, 1977: 113). Centralization and decentralization come face to face, but the results of this new "synthesis" offer little cause for celebration.

SOCIALIST REVOLUTION AND SOCIAL CONTROL: REFLECTIONS ON LAW AND JUSTICE IN THE PEOPLE'S REPUBLIC OF CHINA

Thus far I have examined the dialectical character of informal and formal control in connection with struggles and movements occurring within pre-capitalist and capitalist societies. But since so much of the debate about deformalization is couched in the language of social progress, my analysis would not be complete without a more direct consideration of how the relationship between form and substance is played out in societies that have attempted to move significantly beyond the market.

The paradox surrounding legal transformations under socialism has been well stated by Georg Lukacs (1972: 51–52).

If, on the one hand, the proletariat creates its own labor discipline, if the labor system of the proletarian state is built on a moral basis, then the external compulsion of the law will automatically cease with the abolition of the class structure of society. In other words, the state will wither away. This liquidation of the class structure will of itself create the beginning of true human history: as Marx prophesied and hoped. If, on the other hand, the proletariat adopts a different course, it will be obliged to create for itself a legal order which cannot be abolished automatically through historical progress. In that case, a tendency could evolve that would endanger both the physiognomy and the achievement of the ultimate objective. For if the proletariat is compelled to create a legal order in this way, that legal order must itself be overthrown—and who can tell what convulsions and sufferings will be caused by the transition from the realm of necessity to the realm of freedom via such a circuitous path?

Though the initial vision outlined by Lukacs—the law as part of an emergent moral order and the withering away of the state—is routinely put forward as the aspiration of socialist societies, the dominant reality of these societies has been much closer to his second case. When modern societies define their moral order as revolutionary socialist they typically construct a jerry-built contradictory system of social control, a legal order that is provisional and at least partially imposed and that must "itself be overthrown" if true socialism is to be achieved.

The ramifications of this problem may be seen most clearly in the duality that pervades modern socialist states and compromises all their efforts to deformalize the law in search for "socialist justice." This duality, based on the ubiquitous contrast between present reality and future goals, is expressed in the fluctuation between participation and centralism (Unger, 1976: 233), concretely illustrated in China, Cuba, and other socialist nations in a dialectical movement between bureaucratic commands and self-regulation. Describing the ways in which a revolutionary socialist society may be torn between "the trials of its present and the image of its future," Unger (*Ibid.*) notes:

In the area of the law of bureaucratic commands, concerns with legal generality and autonomy are decisively subordinated to the achievement of the desired political or economic result in each particular situation. The use of open-ended standards, the turn to instrumental rationality, and the emphasis on substantive justice assume more uncompromising forms in revolutionary socialist society than in postliberal society. Side by side with this bureaucratic law, there is an emergent quasi-customary law of communal organization. The chief task of the popular tribunals, councils, or committees is to reconcile these two aspects of law: to educate the people in the law of the bureaucracy while allowing them to begin regulating themselves.

But our recognition of the contradiction between participation and centralism not only is valuable as an insight into the dialectics of control in socialist societies but also offers us yet another chance to see, within a very different context, the same paradoxes of social regulation we explored in the modern capitalist state. Though we must be careful, as Unger (1976: 234) warns, not to conflate revolutionary socialism and state capitalism, their political and legal crises are too similar either to explain away or to ignore. My argument is not that socialist and capitalist societies are converging toward a single social, political, and economic form but rather that the parallelism between their dialectical experiences indicates the presence of major structural contradictions in *both* capitalist and socialist attempts to unify the form and substance of social control.

Any attempt to describe the relationship between formal and informal controls in societies that call themselves socialist must confront the fact that each society has a unique prerevolutionary backdrop of laws and customs against and through which transformations in control arrangements have taken place. The divergent cultural traditions, geopolitical conditions, revolutionary aspirations, economic and demographic constraints, and levels of popular support characterizing each society and its revolutionary experience make any cross-societal comparison extremely risky. It is possible, however, to identify some of the general problems surrounding the interplay between form and substance during periods of rapid and fundamental social change by focusing attention on a particularly interesting case—the People's Republic of China. Without assuming that China is the only or the best model to follow in generalizing about this problem,[12] we can still use the Chinese example to learn a great deal about how deformalization and formalization are related to major structural change.

One of the most valuable opportunities afforded by the study of legal arrangements in postrevolutionary China is the chance to see how and why pressures toward formalism have operated to support, inhibit, or deflect the direction of political and social development in a society with an explicit commitment to "class struggle" and "justice without law." Though our exploration of feudal, capitalist, and neocapitalist societies shed a great deal of light on how legalism and formalism were first the preconditions for and then impediments to capitalist growth, it only illuminated one part of the dialectical process. Another part—the way in which "new" substance has surrendered to "old" form—can be identified most clearly by looking at a number of specific "movements to the right" in the brief history of the People's Republic of China.

Before examining these episodes in detail, it will be useful to sketch some of the background features of the situation in which the struggle between formalism and informalism has emerged in modern China. First, it is important to recognize that decentralized, grass roots mediation of social conflict had a well-established place in prerevolutionary China. As Cohen (1966), Lubman (1967), Unger (1976), and Hipkin (1980) point out, informal, extralegal conciliation was strongly advocated by Confucianism. This orientation to social regulation, embodied in the cultural and political institutions of Imperial China, provided a

---

[12]Other societies that might profitably be examined in these terms are Cuba (Berman, 1969; Loney, 1973; Cantor, 1974), Poland (Podgórecki, 1969; Pomorski, 1975; Kos-Rabcewicz-Zubkowski, 1976; Kurczewski and Frieske, 1978), the German Democratic Republic (Blankenburg *et al.*, 1979; Weiss, 1972), the Soviet Union (Berman and Spindler, 1963; Smith, 1974), and Portugal (Santos, 1982).

familiar and flexible infrastructure upon which the "new informalism" could be built. [13] Framing the historic forms of locally based coercion was *li*—an elaborate moral code drawing on the tenets of Confucianism and divorced in most important respects from the formal inaccessible positive law (*fa*). Informal approaches to social conflict did not, therefore, have to be woven out of whole cloth. Notwithstanding its sweeping and radical rhetoric, the revolutionary regime actually implemented a deformalized system of social control without doing too much violence to the structure, rhythms, and assumptions of prerevolutionary sanctioning patterns.

On the other hand, because the traditional moral code had been thoroughly hierarchical—linking sanctions and solutions to the status of offenders or litigants—the *li* did not provide a congenial medium for the development of the mass line and its policies of social leveling. This fact, combined with the problem that the "*Li* was insufficient to govern the empire" (Lubman, 1967: 1290), meant that legalism retained a central place in Chinese conceptions and methods of social control. The strength of this counter-tradition could not be ignored in efforts to generate people's law insofar as the Chinese continued to look toward "the positive and public rules of bureaucratic law for a way of dealing with the trials of their historical situation" (Unger, 1976: 109). But even when we acknowledge these qualifications, it is clear that there was a cultural foundation upon which the new policy of informal and community-based law could rest. Accordingly, postrevolutionary attempts to deformalize the law clearly struck a responsive, if not entirely harmonious, chord in the moral and social ordering of Chinese life.

An additional feature of the context within which formalist pressures emerged in the postrevolutionary period was the resurrection of what might be called the binary system of normative politics. Although there was clearly an attempt to establish standards of justice that were far more equitable and uniform than the traditional law based on class and status, the theory and practice of Maoist class justice in some ways breathed new life into the same type of moral compartmentalizations that had justified the very tyrannies that people's justice was intended to overcome. The evaluative criteria promoted in the People's Republic of China have been based on distinctions that are political rather than religious, cultural, or proprietary, but the deeply engrained habit of imposing qualitatively different standards on those who fall inside and outside the approved moral universe has remained very much in force. The new programmatic basis of this continuing moral dichotomy was Mao's famous 1957 speech "On the Correct Handling of

---

[13]Comparing patterns of vertical integration in Imperial and postrevolutionary China, Cohen (1977: 349) argues that "the PRC's creation of a semi-official substructure that is closely integrated with the official structure to form a single sanctions system is itself an extrapolation of the traditional imperial process that linked, albeit in a looser way, village, clan, guild and other social groups to the mandarin magistracy."

Contradictions among the People." In this document, Mao (1977: 80) argued that "we are confronted by two types of social contradictions—those between ourselves and the enemy and those among the people themselves." The former were seen as antagonistic, the latter as nonantagonistic. One implication of this distinction was the creation of a two-tiered system of social justice and conflict resolution. Didactic, informal, rehabilitative methods of control and dispute resolution were appropriate for conflict among "the people." Here "the only way to settle questions of an ideological nature or controversial issues among the people is by the democratic method, the method of discussion, of criticism, of persuasion and education, and not by the method of coercion or repression" (*Ibid.*: 86–87). But where contradictions are antagonistic and conflict is created by "enemies of the people," these "counterrevolutionaries and other criminals" must be suppressed whenever discovered.[14]

This speech unleashed an intense and open-ended debate about whether any particular set of contradictions (and contradictors) was antagonistic or not. It also created pervasive inducements to remain "within the fold" and avoid the consequences of being labeled counterrevolutionary. Interestingly, the basis for classifying miscreants as enemies or members of the people was at least partially independent of their behavioral and attitudinal commitment to societal goals, as it had been before the revolution (cf. Hsiao, 1960; Watt, 1972; Metzger, 1973; Wakeman and Grant, 1975). Mao defined the people as workers, peasants, and petty and national bourgeosie and the enemy as the "five black elements" of landlord, rich peasants, counterrevolutionaries, rightists, and other bad elements.[15] The effect of these distinctions has been most pronounced during political campaigns "when members of the 'black elements' often provide convenient targets for class hostility and abuse" and "persons of good class background are reported to have received lenient treatment even in serious cases such as rape" (Leng, 1977: 365). In sum, even though the methods of handling contradictions "among the people" are not always free of coercion (cf. Vogel, 1967) and those reserved for antagonistic elements need not be purely repressive (cf. Brady, 1974), there is an important and familiar bifurcation underpinning both the form and substance of legal processing in postrevolutionary China. And it is this attempt to maintain two sets of standards and practices—one for "the people" and another for their "enemies"—that helps us to understand why the development and transformation of social control in China has been as much a product of political struggle as its cause.

A third aspect of the setting surrounding the dialectical interplay we have been

[14]For a detailed discussion of the treatment of counterrevolutionaires and other "class enemies," see *Amnesty International* (1978).

[15]As Leng (1977: 365) points out, these categories are subject to redefinition. For example, the 1975 constitution identifies the people as workers, peasants, and nonagricultural individual laborers and the enemy as "the landlords, rich peasants, reactionary capitalists, and other bad elements."

discussing is a phenomenon common to all contemporary socialist societies: the contradiction between the hierarchical forms of organization required for political and economic progress on the one hand, and the ideological objectives of a fraternal, egalitarian, self-regulating community on the other. This contradiction has been identified by Brady (1977: 128–129) as the antagonism between the "ethic of social revolution" and the "ethic of bureaucratic centralization"; it is rooted in the fact that "the economy demands social discipline and the politics call for social change."

From a slightly different perspective, we may see this conflict expressed in the competition between two kinds of law: "a law of bureaucratic commands and a law of autonomous self-regulation," each of which "represents one of the two faces of consciousness and organization under revolutionary socialism" (Unger, 1976: 233). The first clear movement toward more formal and bureaucratized legal arrangements in postrevolutionary China occurred between 1954 and 1957. During this period, described by Leng (1977: 358) as the "constitutional experiment," the People's Republic of China was strongly influenced by the Soviet model of political and economic organization. Some of the consequences were

> the adoption of a constitution, organic legislation for the courts and procuracy, and a series of substantive and procedural laws and regulations. Equality before the law, the right of legal defense, protection against arbitrary arrest, and independence of the judiciary were guaranteed by the Constitution and other documents. Efforts were also made to draft civil, criminal, and procedural codes [*Ibid.*].

These measures were supported by Liu Shao-ch'i, one of the earliest and most powerful advocates of formalization, who argued in September 1956 that

> the period of revolutionary storm and stress is past, new relations of production have been set up, and the aim of our struggle is changed into one of safeguarding the successful development of the productive forces of society; a corresponding change in the methods of struggle will consequently have to follow, and a complete legal system becomes an absolute necessity [cited *ibid.*].

One of the most interesting facets of this push toward centralization, professionalization, and regularization of legal controls—which parallels certain stages of capitalist development—was the emphasis on "social predictability" (Cohen, 1969: 982) as a precondition of social stability and economic growth. As part of this push toward rationalization,

1. Judges "were generally free to decide cases on 'legal' issues and the People's Courts did move a long distance toward the stable legal bureaucracy outlined in the Constitution" (Brady, 1974: 181).

2. "The formation of the National Institute of Law of the Chinese Academy of Sciences began in 1956–1957 and law schools across the country were expanded and geared to a more technical curriculum" (*Ibid.*).

3. "There was a rapid growth of professional–legal journals, as the number of publications increased from 11 in 1951 to 21 in 1953; to 46 in 1955 and a peak of 53 in 1957" (*Ibid.*).

4. "By 1957 over 2700 lawyers were organized in local People's Collectives serving defendants without fees" (*Ibid.*: 182).

5. In 1954 "mediation was explicitly limited to minor civil and criminal cases and any individual could bypass mediation and take his case directly to court. Mass organizations would no longer have the authority to impose mediation on their members, as mediation could not be employed without consent of all involved parties" (*Ibid.*: 188).

6. "In 1955 a major shift began with the creation of the Ministry of Control, which was to watch and regulate other government bureaus. . . . The creation of the Control Ministry, like the expansion of the court and Procurate, was designed to stabilize the revolution and channel public energies into support for the regular bureaucracies" (*Ibid.*: 192–193).

The scope and diversity of this first instance of postrevolutionary formalism would seem to suggest that China was indeed entering a new era, that a genuine change in the "methods of struggle" was underway. But from 1957 to 1959 the "One Hundred Flowers Rectification Campaign" (1956–1957), the "Anti-Rightist Movement" (June 1957), and the "Great Leap Forward" (1958) completely subverted or reversed most of the legalist gains made during the first formalization. To a certain extent, these countermovements were the result of an informalization and politicization (cf. Lubman, 1967; Cohen, 1969; Li, 1970) that had been gaining momentum alongside of the process of formalization. In other respects, the ideological conflict between the bureaucratic ethic and the mass line—much like the conflict between the Confucianist *Li* and notions of mass democracy—exposed much more deeply rooted antagonisms in the structure and organization of Chinese social life. As Brady (1974: 195) notes:

> The strategy of conservatism and centralized regulation was costly in political support. The mass line was not so easily coiled and hung on the rack of bureaucratic convenience, and neither the public nor the Party radicals were prepared to accept a freeze-up in the social revolution—even if it bought Soviet aid and socialist "legal respectability."

In addition, it is clear that

> Mao was concerned with the possible rise to power within the party of the "codification" faction led by Liu Shao-ch'i and Teng Hsiao-p'ing. They would, he believed, remove the revolutionary dynamic necessary in the party's use of law as an instrument of socialist reconstruction. He further believed that such codification . . . would stimulate the growth of bureaucracy and drive a wedge between the party, the State and the individual [Hipkin, 1980].

The practical effects of this deformalization on the apparatus of social justice have been summarized by Leng (1977: 358–359):

China's progress toward a stable legal order came to an abrupt end in 1957 when the Communist elites launched an Anti-Rightist campaign as a counter attack against strong criticisms of the Party evoked by the Hundred Flowers Movement. Even more far-reaching was the PRC's decision to abandon the Soviet model in favor of the Maoist developmental strategy (the Great Leap Forward) that stressed mass mobilization and "politics in command." The impact on the legal field was a decisive shift from the jural model to the societal model. On the whole . . . the post 1957 trend continued to show the decline of the judiciary and procuracy in importance and the ever-expanding role of Party committees and public security organs in law enforcement.

Unlike China's initial postrevolutionary experience with formalization, its second and third encounters with "the rule of law" were more like temporary political excursions than full-scale expeditions down "the capitalist [i.e., bureaucratic] road." In each instance formalization was part of a general retreat from the excesses of people's law, class struggle, and decentralized control—a tempering of revolutionary fervor to meet the demands of economic and political life.

The first retrenchment occurred between 1961 and 1966. Its conservative character largely reflected the growing influence of Liu Shao-ch'i, the "apostle of organization" (Schurmann, 1966: 536). Strongly influenced by the Soviet example, Liu maintained a thorough commitment to the cultivation of "correct" thought and practice "through struggle and persuasion within the confines of the Party" (*Ibid.*: 514). Mao, on the other hand, was comfortable with open struggle in the social arena and believed that such struggles would lead to true revolutionary consciousness. He was willing to allow the masses greater freedom and had less confidence in thought and behavior directed by an untouchable and sacred party.

Another element contributing to this retrenchment was China's economic crisis in the early 1960s, which necessitated a decentralization of economic (as opposed to political) control, the return of autonomy to smaller brigades and teams of workers, the development of private plots, and the growing use of work incentives (cf. Harrison, 1972). In consequence, there was at least a minimal endorsement of the market principle of the "exchange of equal values," exemplified by the Teng Hsiao-p'ing policy of "Three Freedoms and One Responsibility" (Collier and Collier, 1973: 52)—an endorsement reflecting the fact that "the party had to loosen its grip on the country in general and the content of bourgeois style legal rights in particular, and allow elements of bourgeois equality, i.e. exchange of equal values, to take place" (Hipkin, 1980).

Although Liu's rise to power and the exigencies of the economic crisis did not restore the courts and procurate to their former prominence, "legal professionalism did . . . make a limited comeback, particularly in the newly strengthened police bureaucracy," and "the Communist Party played an increasingly direct role in justice and other aspects of government" (Brady, 1977: 147). There was considerable evidence of the increase in bureaucratically orchestrated professionalism: "in the early 1960s legal forums were held, and books and articles were written on such subjects as 'philosophy of law,' 'state and legal theories,' 'history of Chinese law,' etc. The 1962 issues of Chen-Fa Yen-Chiu (Political-legal studies) contained many serious articles on legal questions" (Leng, 1977: 358–359). Brady argues that popular justice suffered at the hands of party control:

> After 1961–2 the police and other government officials were answerable only to the Party apparatus. The police became increasingly a conservative force, committed to order and social discipline, but little concerned with social change, educational reform, and mass line politics. The Party conservatives depended upon the police and the law to secure their powers and privileges in the face of inequalities produced by the conservatives' political and economic policies [1974: 280].

All of this changed with the advent of the Cultural Revolution (1966–1969). The influence of Liu Shao-ch'i, the party machine, and the "revisionist" policies and reforms he sponsored were thoroughly condemned and eclipsed by a pervasive ferment from below. Once again, but now with a ferocity unprecedented in the postrevolutionary era, the ethic of social revolution took hold. The events of the Cultural Revolution and their immediate impact on structures of control are far too complex to be examined here (cf. Harrison, 1972; Greenblatt, 1977). It is clear, however, that the level of mass mobilization, open conflict, and iconoclasm percolating throughout Chinese society was so high that one of two courses had to be taken: Either the slogan of "continuous revolution" must have consequences its progenitors had never intended, or the masses had to be restrained in the interests of stability, progress, and the preservation of oligarchic control. By the early 1970s a policy of economic consolidation, political reintegration, and ideological retrenchment had been implemented, and much had been done to restore the regularity and lawfulness that the Cultural Revolution had so badly shaken.

An early expression of this return to hierarchy and consistency in the sphere of legal relationships and thought, which I view as the third formalist episode, was the "Anti-Confucian and Pro-Legalist Campaign" of 1972–1974. Although it remained largely at the level of ideological conflict and exhortation, it broke important ground in relegitimating the "rule of law" and reconciling formalization with socialist development. By transposing the conflict between formalism and informalism to the past, contemporary political dragons could be slain with the sword of long extinct ideas and ideologues. The adversaries in this anachronistic politics, historically located in the Spring and Autumn Period (sixth century B.C.) and the Warring States Period (403–221 B.C.), were Confucianism and Legalism (cf. Unger, 1976: 105–109).

The contours of this ideological struggle, as well as its political and legal implications, are complex. Yet without going into the historical details, it will be useful to consider Leng's (1977: 370) description of the dynamics of the conflict.

The "radicals" initially launched the anti-Confucian campaign in an implicit yet unmistakable attack against Chou En-lai and his bureaucratic associates for their retreat from the Cultural Revolution and the rehabilitation of many purged officials, but the "moderates" subsequently succeeded in transforming the target of the campaign by linking anti-Confucianism with the movement against Lin Piao. Throughout the campaign the two groups manipulated historical figures and events to advance their respective policy lines. The "moderates" expounded the themes of stability, unity, institutionalization, and economic development, while the "radicals" argued for struggle and reform and argued against "the tide" and the Confucian-type "retrogression and restoration." . . . In contrast to the "reactionary" features of Confucianism, Chinese writers in the campaign praised Legalism because of its stand for progress and reform, for law and order, for economic and scientific development, and for unification. . . . Han Fei, for instance, was one of those credited with the development of the theory of "rule by law" on which to establish a centralized feudal state. From his examination of historical experience, Han Fei arrived at the conclusion that only by strengthening the "rule by law" (appointing officers according to ability, bestowing titles according to merits, etc.) could the ruler expect to build a rich and strong country, consolidate a centralized political system, and suppress the "restoration activities" of the slave-owning aristocracy.

Even though it began to ebb in early 1975, the Confucian–Legalist debate accomplished two important things: It demonstrated once again that it was possible to justify the introduction of "good" form despite its association with "bad" (in this case feudal) substance, and it set the stage for important innovations in the legal structure of China. The events of the late 1970s suggest that the death of Mao and the successful purge of the "Gang of Four" may have removed much of the impetus behind the "ethic of social revolution." Indeed, we can begin to see the outlines of a fourth formalization movement. Its internal dynamics and external consequences are still unclear, but they appear to parallel the first "movement to the right" (1954–1957) in several respects. The current episode of "legalism" emphasizes centralization, proportionality, codification, and "equality before the law" but with one important difference—it is much more an indigenous experiment, blending "revolutionary" and "bourgeois" structures and concepts without any clear allegiance to either the Soviet[16] or the capitalist models of legal development. The process of formalization includes the passage (on January 1, 1980) of lengthy criminal and criminal procedure codes, the opening of most criminal trials to the public, assurances by Peng Zhen (director of the legislative affairs commission of the People's Congress) that judges will be independent (Newsweek, 1979), and the reexamination by Peking courts of 13,000 instances of imprisonment of "counterrevolutionaries" between 1966 and 1976 (*Boston Globe*, November 18, 1979: 4). Taken together, these developments seem to represent a tentative step in the direction of "the rule of law."[17]

[16]Cohen (1977: 351) points out that the current movement is very "careful to condemn the 'counter-revolutionary revisionist line' of former President Liu Shao-Ch'i who to Mao's distaste had advocated a Soviet-style legal system in the mid-1950s and who, it is said, had sponsored some irrational rules and regulations that had to be abolished."

[17]The show trials of the "Gang of Four" reveal just how equivocal and contradictory the move-

But before we reach such a conclusion and join those who see China embracing the bourgeois path to modernization, it is valuable to recall the speed with which the political and/or legal winds have changed in the People's Republic of China. It is clear that reports of the death of socialism in China (like those of the death of Mark Twain) are greatly exaggerated. The struggle between competing visions of law and society can be understood only within the context of the ideological confrontation between socialist and capitalist models of development and the political confrontation between socialist, capitalist, and Third World states.

The most obvious lesson to be drawn from our investigation of formalization movements in China and of the problems of socialist legal reconstruction in general is that movements toward formal or informal control are less the decisive swing of a pendulum from one direction to the other than the tentative, fitful, equivocal unraveling of transformational politics. Because pressures toward formalization develop simultaneously with those toward deformalization, official policy decisions and administrative reforms that seem to signal a victory of one of these two "roads to socialism" always turn out to be merely temporary truce lines in an ongoing struggle. In this sense, the fluctuations between formal and informal policies and practices are not a series of alternations between "correct paths" but rather a periodic bubbling over of forces and counterforces that have been held in check, though not destroyed, by either the "regime of rules" or the "regime of standards." And until the structural contradictions generating these conflicts are either resolved or contained more effectively (as they are by the ideological and political continuity in the more stable industrial states of both the East and West), we will find that the "continuous revolution" in China means further vacillation between these two very different routes to the creation of a socialist society.

CONCLUSION

The dilemma presented by the alternatives of popular justice and the rule of law may be compared to that of a person in quicksand who must choose between two methods of escape: grabbing the tail of a passing tiger or improving his or her footing by adding more sand and rock. The first option promises "liberation" but at what threatens to be a terrible cost. The second offers a chance to establish a more "concrete" foundation, but the concrete may congeal so quickly and thoroughly that freedom will be lost entirely.

---

ment toward bourgeois legal rights can be. The new bureaucratic ethos seems consistent with open rather than closed court proceedings, but the scripted character of these confessionals is so blatant that the formal discovery and presentation of the "criminal facts" (*New York Times*, November 21, 1980: sec. 2, p. 1) can hardly be called a step in the direction of the rule of law.

We cannot solve this conundrum simply by embracing what appears, at the moment, to be the lesser of two evils. Instead of oscillating between these polarities we must find a perpendicular path away from both. It has been the intent of this chapter to take a small step in this direction notwithstanding the growing impatience and "sinking feeling" many of us feel. A narrow critique of either form or substance can never succeed. We need a perspective capable of grasping and exposing the contradictions, ironies, and complexities of deformalization and formalization movements, a perspective that enables us to benefit, theoretically and politically, from the paradoxes these social episodes reveal. From such a starting point, we may be able to give substance to Lukacs's (1971: 262) critique of reified conceptions of law and his metaphor for revolutionary theory and praxis.

> Marxist theory is designed to put the proletariat into a very particular frame of mind. The capitalist state must appear to it as a link in a chain of historical development. Hence it by no means constitutes "man's natural environment" but merely a real fact whose actual power must be reckoned with but which has no inherent right to determine our actions. The state and the laws shall be seen as having no more than an empirical validity. In the same way a yachtsman must take exact note of the direction of the wind without letting the wind determine his course; on the contrary, he defies and exploits it in order to hold fast to his original course.

Without a dialectical starting point, we are likely to remain shipwrecked on the reefs of form and substance, seeing existing legal relationships as "man's natural environment" and unable either to discover our navigational errors or to chart a course forward.

REFERENCES

Abel, R. L. (1979) "Delegalization: A Critical Review of Its Ideology, Manifestations, and Social Consequences," in E. Blankenburg, E. Klausa, and H. Rottleuthner (eds.) *Alternative Rechtsformen und Alternativen zum Recht*. Opladen: Westdeutscher Verlag (*Jahrbuch für Rechtssoziologie und Rechtstheorie*, band 6).

Adorno, T. W. (1973) *Negative Dialectics*. New York: Seabury Press.

———— (1978) "Culture and Administration," 37 *Telos* 93.

Amnesty International (1978) *Report on Political Imprisonment in the People's Republic of China*. London: Amnesty International Publications.

Anderson, P. (1974) *Lineages of the Absolutist State*. London: New Left Books.

Balbus, I. (1977) "Commodity Form and Legal Form: An Essay on the 'Relative Autonomy' of the Law," 11 *Law & Society Review* 571.

Beirne, P. (1979) "Ideology and Rationality in Max Weber's Sociology of Law," in S. Spitzer (ed.) *Research in Law and Sociology*, vol. 2. Greenwich, Conn.: J.A.I. Press.

Berman, H. and J. Spindler (1963) "Soviet Comrades' Courts," 38 *George Washington Law Review* 842.

Berman, J. (1969) "Cuban Popular Tribunals," 69 *Columbia Law Review* 1317.

Blankenburg, E., E. Klausa, and H. Rottleuthner (eds.) (1979) *Alternative Rechtsformen und Alter-*

nativen zum Recht. Opladen: Westdeutscher Verlag (Jahrbuch für Rechtssoziologie und Rechtstheories, band 6).

Brady, J. P. (1974) *Popular Justice: Conflict and Community in the Chinese Legal System.* D.Crim. Dissertation, School of Criminology, University of California, Berkeley.

———— (1977) "Political Contradictions and Justice Policy in People's China," 1 *Contemporary Crises* 127.

Braverman, H. (1974) *Labor and Monopoly Capital.* New York: Monthly Review Press.

Cantor, R. (1974) "Law without Lawyers: Tribunals in Cuba," 4 *Juris Doctor* 24.

Cohen, J. (1972) "Max Weber and the Dynamics of Domination," 14 *Telos* 63.

Cohen, J. A. (1966) "Chinese Mediation on the Eve of Modernization," 54 *California Law Review* 1201.

———— (1969) "The Chinese Communist Party and 'Judicial Independence': 1949–1959," 82 *Harvard Law Review* 967.

———— (1977) "Reflections on the Criminal Process in China," 68 *Journal of Criminal Law and Criminology* 323.

Cohen, S. (1979) "The Punitive City: Notes on the Dispersal of Social Control," 3 *Contemporary Crises* 339.

Colletti, L. (1975) "Marxism and the Dialectic," 93 *New Left Review* 3.

Collier, J. and E. Collier (1973) "China's Socialist Revolution," 1 *Stage* 52.

Foucault, M. (1977) *Discipline and Punish: The Birth of the Prison.* New York: Pantheon.

Fraser, A. (1978) "The Legal Theory We Need Now," 40–41 *Socialist Review* 147.

Friedmann, W. G. (1957) "Corporate Power, Government by Private Groups and the Law," 57 *Columbia Law Review* 155.

———— (1972) *Law in a Changing Society.* Baltimore: Penguin Books.

Gabel, P. (1980) "Reification in Legal Reasoning," in S. Spitzer (ed.) *Research in Law and Sociology,* vol. 3. Greenwich, Conn.: J.A.I. Press.

Gilmore, G. (1974) *The Death of Contract.* Columbus: Ohio State University Press.

Gramsci, A. (1971) *Selections from the Prison Notebooks.* New York: International Publishers.

Greenblatt, S. L. (1977) "Campaigns and the Manufacture of Deviance in Chinese Society," in A. A. Wilson, S. L. Greenblatt, and R. W. Wilson (eds.) *Deviance and Social Control in Chinese Society.* Beverly Hills, Calif.: Sage Publications.

Hall, J. (1952) *Theft, Law and Society.* Indianapolis: Bobbs-Merrill.

Hall, S., C. Critcher, T. Jefferson, J. Clarke, and B. Roberts (1978) *Policing the Crisis: Mugging, the State, and Law and Order.* London: Macmillan.

Harrison, J. P. (1972) *The Long March to Power: A History of the Chinese Communist Party, 1921–72.* New York: Holt, Rinehart and Winston.

Hay, D. (1975) "Property, Authority and the Criminal Law," in D. Hay, P. Linebaugh, J. G. Rule, E. P. Thompson, and C. Winslow (eds.) *Albion's Fatal Tree: Crime and Society in Eighteenth Century England.* New York: Pantheon.

Heydebrand, W. (1979) "The Technocratic Administration of Justice," in S. Spitzer (ed.) *Research in Law and Sociology,* vol. 2. Greenwich, Conn.: J.A.I. Press.

Hill, C. (1975) *The World Turned Upside Down.* Middlesex: Penguin.

Hipkin, B. (1980) "State, Law and Politics in China," in S. Spitzer (ed.) *Research in Law and Sociology,* vol. 3. Greenwich, Conn.: J.A.I. Press.

Hirschhorn, L. (1978) "The Political Economy of Social Service Rationalization: A Developmental View," 2 *Contemporary Crises* 63.

Hirst, P. (1979) *On Law and Ideology.* Atlantic Highlands, N.J.: Humanities Press.

Horkheimer, M. (1973). "The Authoritarian State," 15 *Telos* 3.

———— (1974) *Eclipse of Reason.* New York: Seabury Press.

———— (1978) *Dawn and Decline: Notes 1926–31 and 1950–1969.* New York: Seabury Press.

Horwitz, M. J. (1977) *The Transformation of American Law, 1780–1860*. Cambridge, Mass.: Harvard University Press.

Hsiao, K. (1960) *Rural China: Imperial Control in the Nineteenth Century*. Seattle: University of Washington Press.

Jacoby, R. (1977–1978) "The Politics of Objectivity: Notes on the U.S. Left," 34 *Telos* 74.

Jaffe, L. L. (1937) "Law Making by Private Groups," 51 *Harvard Law Review* 201.

Kennedy, D. (1973) "Legal Formality," 2 *Journal of Legal Studies* 351.

_____ (1976) "Form and Substance in Private Law," 89 *Harvard Law Review* 1685.

_____ (1980) "Toward an Historical Understanding of Legal Consciousness: The Case of Classical Legal Thought in America, 1850–1940," in S. Spitzer (ed.) *Research in Law and Sociology*, vol. 3. Greenwich, Conn.: J.A.I. Press.

Kessler, F. (1943) "Contracts of Adhesion," 43 *Columbia Law Review* 629.

Kirchheimer, O. (1940) "Criminal Law in National Socialist Germany" 8 *Studies in Philosophy and Social Science* 444.

_____ (1969) "The Legal Order of National Socialism," in F. S. Burin and K. L. Shell (eds.) *Politics, Law and Social Change: Selected Essays of Otto Kirchheimer*. New York: Columbia University Press.

Kittrie, N. (1973) *The Right To Be Different: Deviance and Enforced Therapy*. Baltimore: Penguin Books.

Klare, K. (1979) "Law-Making as Praxis," 40 *Telos* 123.

Kos-Rabcewicz-Zubkowski, L. (1976) "Conciliation Commissions in Poland," 24 *American Journal of Comparative Law* 319.

Kurczewski, J. and K. Frieske (1978) "The Social Conciliatory Commissions in Poland: A Case Study of Nonauthoritative and Conciliatory Dispute Resolution as an Approach to Access to Justice," in M. Cappelletti and J. Weisner (eds.) *Access to Justice*, vol. 2: *Promising Institutions*. Milan: Giuffrè; and Alphen aan den Rijn: Sijthoff and Noordhoff.

Leng, S-C. (1977) "The Role of Law in the People's Republic of China as Reflecting Mao Tse-Tung's Influence," 68 *Journal of Criminal Law and Criminology* 356.

Li, V. (1970) "The Role of Law in Communist China," 44 *China Quarterly* 66.

Loney, M. (1973) "Social Control in Cuba," in I. Taylor and L. Taylor (eds.) *Politics and Deviance*. Baltimore: Penguin Books.

Lubman, S. (1967) "Mao and Mediation: Politics and Dispute Resolution in Communist China," 55 *California Law Review* 1284.

Lukacs, G. (1971) *History and Class Consciousness*. Cambridge, Mass.: MIT Press.

_____ (1972) "The Role of Morality," in R. Livingston (ed.) *Political Writings, 1919–1929*. London: Macmillan.

Maine, H. (1891) *Ancient Law*. London: J. Murray.

Mao Tse-Tung (1968) "Completely Smash the Feudal Capitalist and Revisionist Legal System," in *Selections from China Mainland Magazine*. Hong Kong: U.S. Consulate-General.

_____ (1977) "On the Correct Handling of Contradictions Among the People," in *Five Essays on Philosophy*. Peking: Foreign Languages Press.

Marx, K. (1958) Capital, vol. 1 (S. Moore and E. Aveling trans.) Moscow: Progress Publishers.

_____ (1967) "Toward the Critique of Hegel's Philosophy of Law: Introduction," in L. D. Easton and K. H. Guddat (eds.) *Writings of the Young Marx on Philosophy and Society*. Garden City, N.Y.: Anchor Books.

_____ (1975) "Critique of Hegel's Doctrine of the State," in L. Colletti (ed.) *Marx's Early Writings*. Middlesex: Penguin Books.

Merton, R. (1981) *Unanticipated Consequences of Social Action: Variations on a Sociological Theme*. New York: Academic Press.

Metzger, T. A. (1973) *The Internal Organization of Ch'ing Bureaucracy: Legal, Normative, and Communication Aspects.* Cambridge, Mass.: Harvard University Press.

Miller, A. S. (1958) "The Constitutional Law of the 'Security State,'" 10 *Stanford Law Review* 620.

Neumann, F. (1944) *Behemoth: The Structure and Practice of National Socialism, 1933–1944.* New York: Harper & Row.

———— (1957) *The Democratic and the Authoritarian State.* New York: Macmillan.

Neurath, O. (1973) "The Scientific Conception of the World: The Vienna Circle," in O. Neurath (ed.) *Empiricism and Sociology.* Holland: Dordrecht.

Newsweek (1979) "China: Back to the Law," *Newsweek* 110 (October 22).

Nietzsche, F. (1967) *The Will to Power* (W. F. Kaufmann, ed.). New York: Vintage Books.

Nonet, P. (1969) *Administrative Justice: Advocacy and Change in a Government Agency.* New York: Russell Sage Foundation.

Nonet, D. and P. Selznick (1978) *Law and Society in Transition: Toward Responsive Law.* New York: Farrar, Straus and Giroux.

North, D. C. (1977) "Markets and Other Allocation Systems in History: The Challenge of Karl Polanyi," 6 *Journal of European Economic History* 703.

Ollman, B. (1971) *Alienation: Marx's Conception of Man in Capitalist Society.* New York: Cambridge University Press.

Podgórecki, A. (1969) "Attitudes to the Workers' Courts," in V. Aubert (ed.) *Sociology of Law.* Baltimore: Penguin Books.

Pollard, S. (1965) *The Genesis of Modern Management.* Middlesex: Penguin Books.

Polanyi, K. (1944) *The Great Transformation.* Boston: Beacon Press.

Pomorski, S. (1975) "Lay Judges in the Polish Criminal Courts: A Legal and Empirical Description," 7 *Case Western Reserve Journal of International Law* 198.

Reich, W. (1972) *Sex-Pol: Essays, 1929–1934,* Lee Baxendall (ed.). New York: Vintage.

Samuels, W. J. (1979) "The State, Law, and Economic Organization," in S. Spitzer (ed.) *Research in Law and Sociology,* vol. 2. Greenwich, Conn.: J.A.I. Press.

Santos, B. S. (1982) "Law and Revolution in Portugal: The Experiences of Popular Justice After the 25th of April 1974," in R. L. Abel (ed.) *The Politics of Informal Justice,* vol. 2: *Comparative Studies.* New York: Academic Press.

Schurmann, F. (1966) *Ideology and Organization in Communist China,* 2d ed. Berkeley: University of California Press.

Smith, G. (1974) "Popular Participation in the Administration of Justice in the Soviet Union: Comrades' Courts and the Brezhnev Regime," 49 *Indiana Law Journal* 238.

Spitzer, S. (1975) "Punishment and Social Organization: A Study of Durkheim's Theory of Penal Evolution," 9 *Law & Society Review* 613.

———— (1979a) "The Rationalization of Crime Control in Capitalist Society," 3 *Contemporary Crises* 187.

———— (1979b) "Notes toward a Theory of Punishment and Social Change," in S. Spitzer (ed.) *Research in Law and Sociology,* vol. 2. Greenwich, Conn.: J.A.I. Press.

Spitzer, S. and A. T. Scull (1977a) "Social Control in Historical Perspective: From Private to Public Responses to Crime," in D. F. Greenberg (ed.) *Corrections and Punishment* Beverly Hills, Calif.: Sage Publications.

———— (1977b) "Privatization and Capitalist Development: The Case of the Private Police," 24 *Social Problems* 18.

Stirner, M. (1971) *Max Stirner: The Ego and His Own,* (G. Steiner, ed.). New York: Harper & Row.

Thompson, E. P. (1975) *Whigs and Hunters: The Origin of the Black Act.* New York: Pantheon.

———— (1978) "The State versus its 'Enemies'," *New Society* 2 (October).

Tobriner, M. O. and J. R. Grodin (1967) "The Individual and the Public Service Enterprise in the New Industrial State," 55 *California Law Review* 1247.

Toffler, A. (1980) *The Third Wave*. New York: Morrow.

Tushnet, M. (1978) "A Marxist Analysis of American Law," 1 *Marxist Perspectives* 96.

———— (1980) "Truth, Justice, and the American Way: An Interpretation of Public Law Scholarship in the Seventies," 57 *Texas Law Review* 1307.

Unger, R. M. (1976) *Law in Modern Society: Toward a Criticism of Social Theory*. New York: Free Press.

Viera-Gallo, J. A. (1972) "The Legal System and Socialism," 1972 *Wisconsin Law Review* 754.

Vogel, E. F. (1967) "Voluntarism and Social Control," in D. W. Treadgold (ed.) *Soviet and Chinese Communisms: Similarities and Differences*. Seattle: University of Washington Press.

Wakeman, F., Jr. and C. Grant (eds.) (1975) *Conflict and Control in Late Imperial China*. Berkeley: University of California Press.

Watt, J. R. (1972) *The District Magistrate in Late Imperial China*. New York: Columbia University Press.

Weber, M. (1946) *From Max Weber: Essays in Sociology*, H. H. Gerth and C. W. Mills (eds.). New York: Oxford University Press.

———— (1968) *Economy and Society*, 2 vols. (G. Roth and C. W. Wittich, eds.). Berkeley: University of California Press.

Weiss, J. (1972) "East German Social Courts: Development and Comparison with China," 20 *American Journal of Comparative Law* 266.

Williams, W. A. (1961) *The Contours of American History*. Chicago: Quadrangle Books.

Wolfe, A. (1977) *The Limits of Legitimacy: Political Contradictions of Contemporary Capitalism*. New York: Free Press.

Wood, A. W. (1972) "The Marxian Critique of Justice," 1 *Philosophy and Public Affairs* 244.

Neighborhood Justice and the Social Control Problems of American Capitalism: A Perspective*

RICHARD HOFRICHTER

INTRODUCTION

The essence of American capitalism is the unending effort by the social class that owns and controls the apparatus of production to increase the rate of capital accumulation. Sustaining capital expansion requires appropriation of labor power and the value produced by labor and simultaneous concealment of the

*This is a revision of a paper originally prepared for the Second National Conference on Critical Legal Studies, Madison, Wisconsin, November 10–12, 1978. I would like to thank the following people for their comments on and criticism of that earlier version: Richard Abel, UCLA Law School; Deborah Baskin, University of Pennsylvania; Mike Brown, City University of New York; Robert Engler, City University of New York; Christine Harrington, Rutgers University; Frank Munger, Antioch Law School; and Boaventura de Sousa Santos, University of Coimbra, Portugal.

207

class basis underlying the social relations of production.[1] Class struggle in which capital defends its control over the surplus produced by labor and labor resists—the most fundamental conflict in capitalist society—is the primary dynamic of social change.

The conditions necessary to harness productive labor, reduce investment risk, and neutralize political opposition to capitalist domination must be recreated with changes in the mode of production and of social relations. Although class struggle remains a constant, its form and content fluctuate, requiring reorganization of those institutions (e.g., schools, mental institutions, criminal justice agencies) that regulate social life, contain class conflict, and mediate class interests by disguising the direct confrontation of classes.

New patterns for regulating and rationalizing social life emerge out of the contradictions of accumulation and class struggle. The judicial system is one important arena for these processes, since it is simultaneously involved in the active regulation of social life, the management of social conflict, and the class struggle. Transformations in judicial institutions may reflect changes in the character of class conflict. The role of judicial institutions in helping to sustain the conditions for capitalist expansion, define order, sanction deviance, and otherwise mediate conflict has been described at length (Neumann, 1957; Horwitz, 1977; Heydebrand, 1978).

A particularly noteworthy trend in the transformation of juridical institutions is the reemergence of "informal," decentralized alternatives to courts for the resolution of a wide range of citizen disputes and grievances, both criminal and civil (McGillis and Mullen, 1977; Johnson et al., 1977; Sander, 1976). Most of the quasi-judicial and nonjudicial institutions and procedures referred to as alternatives to courts—informal justice or, most recently, neighborhood justice centers (NJCs)[2]—have existed for many years. In the United States their roots can be traced to the mid-nineteenth century (Doo, 1973). In 1920 the Jewish Conciliation Board was established in New York City (Fischer, 1975). Current interest in the concept can be traced to Danzig (1973), Fischer (1975), and Sander (1976). Contemporary models include conciliation, mediation, arbitra-

---

[1]The social relations of production under capitalism are those relations that arise within the productive process between the working class, which produces surplus value, and the capitalist class, which appropriates it. They include both the formal relationship of ownership and control over the organization of the labor process.

[2]The term *neighborhood justice center* technically refers to three experimental dispute resolution projects established by LEAA. In this chapter I will use it to refer both to a broad range of nonjudicial, informal, state-funded or organized neighborhood dispute forums, existing or potential, that resolve interpersonal civil or criminal disputes and to the types of dispute resolution, such as mediation or arbitration, that occur within these forums. LEAA now calls its newest projects "Metropolitan Mediation Centers."

tion, ombudsmen, and administrative tribunals, to name but a few, and are used for disputes between individuals—such as family members, neighbors, landlords and tenants, merchants and consumers—and between groups or represented aggregates—such as management and labor and community organizations. The procedures used are less adversarial and less formal than litigation; proponents emphasize the mutually acceptable, voluntary nature of agreements between parties who know one another. Structure and administration vary, depending on the resources and objectives of project planners.

The developments are significant because they may foreshadow a transformation of the legal order, the implications of which transcend the immediate significance of particular mechanisms for dispute resolution. Their revitalization may be related to contradictions within and threats to continued capitalist expansion, particularly the difficulties of coordinating labor power and containing the political threat posed by labor and surplus populations (the underemployed, unemployed, and unemployable).

Current experiments with informal justice differ from historical antecedents in that the federal government now plays a greatly expanded role in planning judicial institutions. Federal planning of criminal justice began in earnest with the Omnibus Crime Control and Safe Streets Act of 1968, which created the Law Enforcement Assistance Administration (LEAA). By means of standards and goals, rules, programs, technologies, and exemplary project models, LEAA has significantly influenced the shape of criminal justice throughout the nation. It has monitored, evaluated, and coordinated informal dispute resolution programs. The combination of federal resources with those of local jurisdictions further suggests that NJCs deal with social order problems that exceed the capability of courts and escape the interest of indigenous populations.

What imperatives guide the emergence of nonjudicial, informal, decentralized forums for dispute resolution? Why do they reappear at this time with state support, given the historical possibility of other options (e.g., expansion of conventional courts to process more cases, creation of more specialized courts, expansion of other social service, political, or private agencies to handle dispute settlement functions)? What has this to do with class struggle?

This chapter presents an interpretation of the revitalization of community-based alternatives to courts, most of which are funded and planned by the state. My intention is to demonstrate the relevance of certain categories of analysis and the utility of particular theoretical structures rather than to document or prove a hypothesis. My central thesis is that the reemergence of NJCs is associated with transformations in the character of class struggle, requirements for the reproduction of labor, and systemic tendencies that propel advanced capitalism in the United States. Before introducing my analytic structure, I will summarize the characteristics of neighborhood justice, present evidence suggesting that important changes in adjudication are occurring, and offer a brief critique of the liberal legal reformist perspective that dominates discussion of the subject.

Trends in State-Organized Dispute Resolution

The development of informal, nonjudicial forums for dispute resolution in the United States is neither linear nor uniform. Similar experiments were tried as early as the 1920s (Danzig, 1973; Fischer, 1975). But the scope, intensity, and pace of government activity concerned with alternatives to courts increased dramatically during the mid-1970s (Aaronson *et al.*, 1977). LEAA funded numerous diverse "alternative" community justice pilot projects in the early 1970s (Hoff, 1974; McGillis and Mullen, 1977). Nationwide, at least 100 programs are operational today, many sponsored by local courts, local government, business, and criminal justice agencies (McGillis, 1980a).[3]

In 1978 the Office of Testing and Dissemination within LEAA provided funds for three eighteen-month experiments with neighborhood justice centers in Atlanta, Los Angeles, and Kansas City. Sponsored by, respectively, a nonprofit agency with links to the courts, the local bar association, and the Community Services Department of the city government, each operated in accordance with guidelines promulgated by LEAA (Lively, 1977). As LEAA terminated its contributions to these projects (which still seek local support) it continued to fund other programs. In 1980 the adjudication division established projects in Honolulu, Houston, and Washington, D.C. for another eighteen-month period.[4] These programs are all located within the criminal justice system and are now referred to as Metropolitan Mediation Centers because their jurisdictions are citywide. The Office of Community Anti-Crime Programs, in conjunction with another federal agency, plans to support approximately ten additional experiments under the President's Urban Crime Prevention Program. Each grantee can choose among four models of service, including dispute settlement, in allocating its funds. The majority of grantees will probably include dispute settlement as one model (Law Enforcement Assistance Administration/Action, 1980).

Although dispute resolution projects do not conform to a single organization, they do share some common characteristics. Most operate within the courts or

---

[3]Some of the more notable and well-researched dispute resolution forums include the 4–A arbitration projects established by the American Arbitration Association, the Dorchester Mediation Project in Boston, the San Francisco Community Board Program, and the dispute settlement programs sponsored by the Office of the State Court Administrator in Florida.

[4]Telephone interview with Frank Herner, adjudication division, LEAA, Washington, D.C.

agencies connected with the courts, although some are independent. They accept cases referred by the police, courts, and prosecutors. A small proportion of cases come from social service agencies or are "walk-ins," and these may be more numerous in programs located outside the courts. Cases referred by the criminal justice system usually involve misdemeanors. But many programs handle noncriminal disputes; some even specialize in consumer matters. Once the case has been screened and accepted and the parties have agreed to submit their dispute, an intake counselor or coordinator contacts the parties, prepares them for the mediation session, and collects background data. A hearing is then held before trained, volunteer, nonlawyer mediators who reside in the community or professional mediators with backgrounds in law, psychology, or counseling. The dispute is usually resolved by some form of third-party mediation or arbitration that produces an agreement signed by each party. The dispositions may involve referral of one or both parties to social services. Noncompliance may result in return of the case to court for the resumption of the prosecution. The communities served by most programs tend to be lower middle class or poor, and disputants generally fall within lower income brackets and lack a college education (McGillis and Mullen, 1977; Snyder, 1978; Sheppard, 1979).

The Dispute Resolution Act of 1980 (PL 96–190) seeks "to assist the States and other interested parties in providing to all persons convenient access to dispute resolution mechanisms which are effective, fair, inexpensive, and expeditious."[5] It establishes a Dispute Resolution Resource Center within the Office for Improvement in the Administration of Justice in the Department of Justice. By surveying and evaluating experimental programs, the resource center, in its first year of activity, will function as a clearinghouse for the exchange of information and provide technical assistance to those who wish to improve or create dispute resolution mechanisms. Its research will be used to establish national priorities and guidelines. In each of its second through fifth years the Resource Center has an authorization of ten million dollars, out of which it may take grants to any nonprofit organization, business, bar association, or municipal agency for the purpose of improving or creating dispute resolution mechanisms.

A variety of private organizations now also promote alternative systems of dispute resolution, particularly community-sponsored dispute centers. They include the Grassroots Citizen Dispute Resolution Clearinghouse,[6] the National Association of Dispute Resolution, and the Western Association of Mediation Organizations.

Influential professional organizations, such as the American Bar Association,

---

[5]As of this writing (1980), funds have not been appropriated because of the President's budget-cutting policies for fiscal 1981.

[6]The American Friends Service Committee terminated its support of the Clearinghouse in the summer of 1980, and the latter is presently seeking alternative funding.

the National Center for State Courts, the Judicial Conference of the United States, the Conference of Chief Justices, and the American Arbitration Association, have advocated and encouraged alternative forms of justice, as have newer organizations such as the National Peace Academy Campaign in Washington, D.C., established to develop support for congressional funding of a National Peace Academy that would "teach, conduct and coordinate research in the methods of peacemaking, including conflict resolution" (Conner and Mapes, 1979).

Major foundations are becoming increasingly involved in the field, including the Edna M. Clark, Rockefeller, Robert Wood Johnson, and Ford foundations, the Lilly Endowment, and the Carnegie Corporation (Ford Foundation, 1978a). The Ford Foundation has produced two reports on the subject and, in 1979, awarded nearly $500,000 in grants to research or demonstration projects on alternative forms of resolving conflict (Ford Foundation, 1978a; 1978b).

The phenomena of decarceration, deinstitutionalization, and decriminalization offer many parallels with aspects of the NJC. All are community-based institutions that regulate human behavior. Decarceration refers to community-based alternatives to prison that usually require involvement in some form of employment, counseling, education, or other social service as a condition of release. Adult and juvenile offenders are diverted either before trial or at the dispositional phase of the criminal prosecution. Deinstitutionalization describes the removal of patients from mental hospitals to community-based care in half-way houses or board-and-care facilities that claim to provide the services such people need to function normally in the community. Decriminalization substitutes a civil sanction for a penalty in responding to conduct formerly defined as criminal, such as public drunkenness.

All these phenomena, as well as the NJCs, may be seen as steps to decentralize state management of problem populations and to replace a policy of containing such populations with one of actively penetrating into the lives of everyone. But NJCs are the most radical of these developments: They have the potential to manage virtually the entire population and to control behavior that bears no relation to legal or even moral definitions of deviance or misconduct. The similarities in the form of these institutional solutions to the problem of managing populations within communities suggest that NJCs are related to contradictions in society that extend beyond both disputes or the organizational inadequacies of courts.

The Perspective of Liberal Legal Reformism

Most recent writing on alternatives to courts and conventional legal processes shares a number of assumptions about the nature of social conflict, the role of the state, and the definition of legal crisis (Danzig, 1973; Sander, 1976; Johnson *et al.*, 1977; Ford Foundation, 1978a; Cook *et al.*, 1980). These assumptions derive from a tradition I call liberal legal reformism that accepts the existing social order of power as a given and seeks limited, short-term solutions to practical problems. It aspires to solve the problem of social order through cooperation, administrative management of irrational political conflict, and impartial mediation between opposing classes. It views conflict as an evil to be avoided, absorbed, or resolved—all within the prevailing order. Only certain types of conflicts are acknowledged as legitimate (e.g., conflict between individuals, or interest groups, that does not challenge the fundamental right of capital to own and control the means of production). All other conflict must be managed by being translated into technical issues devoid of political content and isolated from more profound struggles or antagonisms that transcend the individual or limited group. This tradition denies the possibility that conflict might be associated with property rights, the extraction of value from labor, or competition for economic resources.

One major objective of conflict resolution, in this perspective, is order maintenance. Formal legal procedures and authoritative judicial decision making obstruct the capacity to resolve a dispute; they merely impose a solution (Ford Foundation, 1978a; 1978b; Greason, 1980).

The crisis of the judicial system is defined in managerial terms. Imperfections and inequalities in the social order are remedied by rules, due process, fairness, and social engineering techniques that ameliorate the consequences of conflict, guarantee equality of opportunity, and reduce the arbitrariness of law. LEAA officials, for example, concerned to increase the organizational efficiency of the judicial system, emphasize case overload, understaffing, delay, waste, and cumbersome procedures (McGillis and Mullen, 1977; Cook *et al.*, 1980). They reject a more substantive conception of justice. At the same time, however, they stress the threat to the legitimacy of the judicial system created by unresponsive, costly, ineffective courts (Downie, 1971; Johnson *et al.*, 1977).

Undoubtedly citizens are dissatisfied with the quality of justice. Few would dispute the value of flexibility, informality, and responsiveness in dispute processes. Yet the instrumental and apolitical approach of the reforming liberal denies the objective interests that generate social conflict by obscuring those struggles that express class interests. Reformist analysis stresses the benefits of NJCs to individuals and measures the success of these institutions in terms of the number of disputants who reached agreements and were satisfied (Florida Supreme Court, 1978; Cook *et al.*, 1980). This interpersonal view of disputes ignores the ways in which individuals may benefit qua individuals but lose as members of a larger social class whose interests cannot be fully satisfied through law or private case-by-case resolution of personal grievances because the issues involve questions of political power that extend beyond legality. Reformist analysis thus prevents us from understanding NJCs as institutions of social control by refusing to consider how conflict resolution may relate to the underlying values, political structure, and social order of capitalist domination (Hay *et al.*, 1975; Thompson, 1975).

What is needed, therefore, is an analytical framework that can explain contemporary transformations in the regulation of social life—specifically, the management of social conflict by means of nonjudicial, informal administrative mechanisms.

A Marxist Perspective

In the preface to *A Contribution to the Critique of Political Economy*, Marx states:

> Neither legal relations nor political forms could be comprehended . . . by themselves or on the basis of a so-called general development of the human mind . . . on the contrary they originate in the material conditions of life. . . . In the social production of their existence, men invariably enter into definite relations, which are independent of their will, namely relations of production appropriate to a given stage in the development of their material forces of production [1970b: 20].

An alternative framework for interpreting the origin and significance of neighborhood justice emerges out of this Marxist tradition and offers a more adequate explanation than that provided by liberal legal reformism. It relates judicial institutions to the foundation of political power in American capitalism—the organization of labor and capital. Transformations in the work force, work processes, the social environment, and the composition of capital constitute central components in such an analysis. "Rights and the transformation they undergo depend on the mode of production, not on advances in the intellectual or moral spheres" (Lefebvre, 1969: 115). In this perspective, class conflict is central. Whereas liberal legal reformism takes conflict between interest groups or even individuals as its basic analytic category, the Marxist perspective identifies the struggle between antagonistic classes, specifically capital and labor, as the most basic form of conflict—and one that cannot be resolved within capitalism.

The analysis proceeds as follows: The first section outlines contemporary American capitalism, focusing on impediments to capital accumulation in the workplace and the community, the limitations of conventional forms of social control (including the judicial system), and the responses of capital to the problems of social control. The succeeding section speculates about how neighborhood justice forums parallel the emerging forms of social control that regulate social life and depoliticize the class conflict generated by developments in capitalist social relations in the workplace and the community.

CLASS STRUGGLE AND SOCIAL CONTROL

Introduction

THE INTERESTS OF CAPITAL AND LABOR

The central goal of a capitalist society is the continuous, unrestricted accumulation of capital. Within each historical period, however, impediments arise, the most important of which is the resistance of labor. Class struggle is based on the unresolvable conflict between those who own and control the nation's wealth and the means of production and those who do not. Each class, as a class, has objective interests, whether or not its members consciously act on them.

The interests of capital are to ensure an ever-expanding rate of capital accumulation while defending the right to own the means of production and organize the productive process. In order to accomplish this, capital must control workers—direct, evaluate, and discipline them—and expropriate the value workers produce while obscuring the source of control. Increase in relative surplus value is achieved by increasing worker productivity and reducing the cost of reproducing labor. Without an increase in productivity, capital expansion becomes impossible.

> Monopoly capital dreams of a particular kind of specialized technician, recognizable by the coexistence in one and same person of zest for his job and indifference about its purpose, professional and social submission, power and responsibility over technical questions and impotence and irresponsibility over questions of economic and social management [Gorz, 1972: 489].

Sustaining capital accumulation also requires domination of workers in their capacity as citizens and consumers. Capital must be able to organize the means of production without interference, invest freely in new means of production, create and dispose of property, and obtain access to raw materials.

Labor's interests and priorities, as a class diametrically opposed to capital, are to maintain control over its own productive labor, the surplus value it produces, and the social conditions of existence, both in the workplace and outside. Labor seeks to produce for need rather than market exchange and to expand the range of commodities and services available for collective consumption—e.g., health care, public mass transportation, social services, utilities, housing, education, and clean air and water. Increased wage rates, reduction in the cost of living, and an increase in the collective living space constitute its central interests. In the workplace, labor seeks to control the work process: work rules; the definition of rates, jobs, and skills; and decision making. In the community, labor wants control over the essentials of daily life and access to basic social services. These interests are mediated by a variety of organizations, such as trade unions, political parties, and community groups.

CONTRADICTIONS OF CAPITALISM AND CLASS STRUGGLE

These interests clash within a context beset by contradictions: Some are built into the structure of a capitalist economy; others emerge from class struggle.[7] These contradictions create crises that place absolute limits on capital expansion and the ability of capital to dominate labor. One contradiction is that the success of the system leads to periodic breakdowns (recessions), which are disruptive but necessary to restore accumulation.[8]

A capitalist system cannot succeed too well or expand continuously without limiting profits, for a variety of reasons. First, overinvestment and overproduction reduce the capacity of markets to absorb the goods and services produced, so that the capitalist cannot realize the surplus value. Second, high levels of investment brings about low levels of unemployment, thereby weakening capital's grip upon workers and the amenability of labor to capitalist discipline. Third, success increases the rate of inflation. Fourth, resources may be exhausted. These combine to slow down growth by means of a recession that, in turn, reduces the rate of accumulation.

Such a recession limits investment. But expansion cannot occur without perpetual investment. Because of uneven economic development, the anarchic, unplanned character of capitalist production, and competition between capitalists for larger shares of profits, capital often cannot generate sufficient investment to sustain profits. The desire to realize profits is an additional hindrance to maintaining investment at the level necessary for sustained expansion.

A second contradiction is that capitalism depends on constant innovation in

[7]Claus Offe defines contradiction as

the tendency inherent to a specific mode of production to destroy those very preconditions on which its survival depends. Contradictions become manifest... where a collision occurs between the preconditions and the results of a specific mode of production or where the necessary becomes impossible and the impossible necessary [1975: 246].

[8]Overproduction during successful periods expands the power of labor, thereby endangering the portion of surplus value received by capital.

the instruments and organization of production (Hirschhorn, 1978), but such change undermines the established political institutions and ideologies that maintain legitimacy, as well as the control systems in the workplace. Technological innovation thus subverts the social stability necessary for predictable capital accumulation because, in part, the institutions that legitimate capitalist domination develop with a historical momentum of their own. The forces of production are always in contradiction with the social relations of production that sustain them.

A third contradiction is that between the increasingly public, social character and consequences of production and the ever more concentrated, centralized private ownership. The social consequences expose the capitalist to unwanted interventions by the state at the insistence of the public. In response to these interventions the capitalist is forced to make expenditures that reduce the available surplus and therefore the rate of capital accumulation.

CONTEMPORARY LIMITS TO CAPITAL ACCUMULATION

Several features of contemporary capitalism impede the necessary conditions for capital expansion and dramatically transform the character of class struggle by influencing the ways in which social populations are managed.

First, the centralization and concentration of capital means that a crisis in one sector of the economy affects the entire economy—witness the response to threatened plant shutdowns by large corporations such as Chrysler, Lockheed, and United States Steel. Given the interdependence of the stages of production in the primary (or monopoly) sector, production stoppages cannot be tolerated. This means that the ways in which labor power is appropriated must change in order to achieve the necessary coordination of the labor process.

Second, the interdependence of the world political economy and the inability of the United States politically to dominate other capitalist and developing nations diminish the access of capital to cheap labor, raw materials, and new markets. Our balance of payments problems have devalued American currency.

Third, increased corporate debt and rising interest costs have increased the rate of inflation and limited expansion. Corporations cannot generate enough capital for investment without excessive borrowing. The economy cannot easily absorb the expanded credit. The extraordinary increase in debt makes corporations vulnerable to even minor shifts in the level of economic growth.

Fourth, capital's ability to move freely, to seize the most profitable investment opportunities, has been restricted. New markets cannot easily be found or generated for all of the surplus produced in the United States. Government efforts to manage the consequences of unchecked expansion restrain capitalist power, as does the political system of liberal democracy, which tolerates demands for political participation, civil rights, and control over basic investment decisions (Wolfe, 1977; Gintis, 1980).

Finally, high inflation and unemployment disrupt planning and trade and create discontent. The cycles of boom and bust occur more frequently now than they did in the past, and the recovery periods are shorter. Under these conditions, the maintenance of public order and the control of capital over production and the social environment supporting production must be transformed. This brings us to the role of the state in managing capital expansion.

The Role of the Capitalist State

Without presenting a theory of the capitalist state in the United States, let me summarize some of its basic characteristics and the ways in which its institutional forms constrain its capacity to manage labor and surplus populations (see generally, Miliband, 1973; O'Connor, 1973; Poulantzas, 1975; Gold et al., 1975; Offe, 1975; Wolfe, 1977; Wright, 1978). According to one dominant theory in Marxist analysis, the state serves to create and guarantee the conditions for capital accumulation by socializing the costs of production, creating effective demand, providing infrastructure, and otherwise supporting a stable social order (Offe, 1975). But the state arises out of class struggle and cannot be fully dominated by capitalist interests. In order to direct the economy and sustain production, the state does not merely respond to crisis; it interacts with capital and labor in contradictory ways and generates its own crises (*Ibid.*; Wolfe, 1977; Wright, 1978).[9]

Under contemporary American capitalism, the state becomes increasingly and permanently involved in civil society not only when it deals with economic dislocation through regulation, a traditional state activity, but also when it organizes and subsidizes production directly through its taxing, spending, and social policies. This increased activity enhances capital accumulation by socializing costs. However, it also sets limits on capital expansion by creating more unproductive social expenses that decrease accumulation (O'Connor, 1973). Moreover, social welfare policies generated in response to crises quickly become institutionalized legal rights. It is difficult for the state to eliminate such programs or reduce expenditures without loss of legitimacy.

The involvement of the state in the accumulation process politicizes that process and repoliticizes relationships formerly disguised by capitalist ideology (Wolfe, 1977; O'Connor, 1978; Wright, 1978). For example, state socialization of production (such as direct subsidies to corporations or tax breaks for the large

[9]The state expresses class struggle and must be understood primarily as a relation rather than as an entity, even though one can speak of the state as embodied in particular institutional forms.

oil companies) may reveal the class bias of the state. State planning of energy, farm policy, education, and now justice creates the possibility of struggle in the public arena over issues that once were said to be relegated to market rationality. Planning is more comprehensive in almost all aspects of production as capital becomes more concentrated and centralized. The expanded role of the state in planning the production process has important implications for the character of judicial institutions of social control.

Because the state insists on preserving its monopoly over judicial institutions, it necessarily plays a significant role in planning NJCs. These are part of the state apparatus and absorb some of the functions of other state institutions (such as the judiciary and police) as well as perform new functions of social control.

The Meaning of Social Control in Contemporary Capitalism

I use the concept of social control to refer to the material and ideological means by which the economic and political order is reproduced in a capitalist society. Capital seeks to reproduce labor and surplus populations in the workplace and the community in two ways: through active regulation of social life and through depoliticization.

The regulation of social life includes investment in human capital to sustain labor by ensuring that workers remain healthy and otherwise capable of satisfying the technical demands of the labor process. It also includes supporting the surplus population from which is drawn the reserve army of the unemployed that helps capital to discipline labor by threatening to replace it. Finally, regulation involves the direction and monitoring of the labor process and the supervision of "deviant" or problem populations in the community.

Depoliticization refers to the means by which labor is made to accept the social organization dictated by capital—the unquestioned right of capital to extract the value produced by labor and to determine the conditions of the labor process. It also refers to the specific ways in which capital contains and defuses organized political challenges by labor. This also means depriving labor of the authority to regulate its own production. For example, the more workers accept the terms of the wage bargain and their role as instruments of production, the more they are inhibited from identifying their grievances as collective problems.

Why is control necessary? Although capitalism today appears more sensitive to social disorder (Polanyi, 1944) and labor more unpredictable, social control is essential at every phase of capitalist development.

David Gartman (1978), David Gordon (1976), and Richard Edwards (1979) all distinguish between the necessity for *some* type of authority and coordination in *any* system of production and the control mechanisms under capitalism. Each recognizes that the worker–capitalist relation is not the automatic result of market forces or the natural attribute of human beings. Because labor seeks to limit the extent of its exploitation by capital, the latter must use what Gartman calls "surplus control" to compel labor to work under conditions that it would not ordinarily accept if it were organizing the work process. "Surplus control [in contrast with basic control] increases the rate of surplus value solely because it represses the resistance of an exploited class" (Gartman, 1978: 103).

Gordon distinguishes quantitative and qualitative efficiency in a capitalist economy. The former refers to the fact that producers in any social system seek to generate the greatest output for the least input (the object of Gartman's "basic control"). But qualitative efficiency (the goal of Gartman's "surplus control") refers to a productive process "that best reproduces the class relations of a mode of production... maximizes the ability of the ruling class to reproduce its domination... and minimizes producers' resistance to such domination" (Gordon, 1976: 22).

Edwards also examines the issue from the perspective of labor resistance but reminds us that labor is not a commodity like any other. Capital purchases *labor power*—the capacity to perform labor. But capital must find special mechanisms to extract *labor*. "Control is rendered problematic because, unlike other commodities... labor power is always embodied in people, who have their own interests and needs and who retain their power to resist" (Edwards, 1979: 12). The mechanisms of social control are transformed by the resistance of labor and the attempt by capitalists to overcome impediments to capital expansion. What kinds of crises in the workplace and the community have threatened that expansion?

Class Struggle and Problems of Social Control in the Workplace

MANAGING THE LABOR PROCESS

Changes in the composition of the work force and the social organization of the work process present management in the monopoly sector with new obstacles to capital accumulation. The work force is less homogeneous than in earlier historical periods: Workers possess diverse skills. The interdependent character of production and the increased size of the wage and salaried labor class reduce the ability of capital to manage the labor force. The expanded labor force produces more individuals with common economic interests and thus a greater potential to oppose capital.

An increasing proportion of the labor force is employed in the service sector and by the state. Many of these workers are either nonproductive or only produce surplus value indirectly. They include workers involved in administration, finance, sales, maintenance, and inspection. Their productivity cannot be evaluated by the same means as that of workers who are directly involved in production. State workers are organizing more rapidly than those in other sectors, and their unions tend to be especially militant. They have not established fixed bargaining patterns, and the demand for their labor is more a function of political considerations than of market conditions.

Struggles with labor, competition among capitalists, advances in technology, and the drive to expand production require constant innovations in the social organization of work. Because of the sophisticated technological base and large scale of the more centralized industries, the retooling required by technological innovation cannot be accomplished quickly. Enterprises cannot switch easily between labor-intensive and capital-intensive production. Job training takes longer. "The quality of labor power must necessarily be raised in all capitalist economies to match the increased sophistication of production and its attendant social processes" (Gough, 1972: 53).

The continuous transformation of labor poses problems. The comprehensive character of the labor process requires workers to understand more about the entire process in order to perform their jobs, thus reducing their dependence on the capitalist to control production. The more knowledge workers have, the more capable they become to make decisions about the organization of work, particularly its pace and content. This generates a contradiction. Capitalists want to wrest control over production away from workers and to deskill them in order to manage them more effectively. But capital expansion depends on increasing the skills of workers.

> The necessity of developing human capabilities imposed by modern processes of production is in contradiction with the political necessity of ensuring that this kind of development of human capabilities does not bring in its wake any augmentation of the independence of the individual, provoking him to challenge the present division of social labor and the distribution of power [Gorz, 1972: 479].

Capital attempts to replace workers with technology, but only labor can produce value. A point is reached when substituting machines for labor restricts productivity, and therefore the rate of production of surplus value. Labor-saving devices require large capital investments and entail additional operating costs for energy and maintenance.

Industries are interdependent, both internally and externally. For example, in the automotive industry each stage of production requires continuous product flow. Each firm is highly dependent on the firms that supply it, as well as on those industries that service it. The communities in which plants are located depend on them for revenue. Thus small disruptions have enormous consequences that sharply affect the rate of accumulation.

By bringing under one corporate roof what were formerly small independent groups linked through the market, the corporation more than proportionately raised the degree of coordination needed. . . . In a large integrated manufacturing operation, such as auto production, a small group of disciplined unionists could cripple an entire system by shutting down part of the line [Edwards, 1979: 19, 128].

But as labor struggles to control the work process on the shop floor, capital seeks to undermine the capacity of workers to mobilize collectively.

THE PROBLEM OF DEPOLITICIZING CLASS STRUGGLE IN THE WORKPLACE

There are several potential challenges to capitalist domination. First, workers resist controls over the pace of production, work rules, job classifications, and layoffs; they seek open corporate ledgers; they assert their rights on the shop floor and challenge management's investment decisions and prerogative to introduce new technology. They also demand greater job security and protective benefits as the economy becomes more unstable and inflation and unemployment rise simultaneously. Recently, workers have begun to consider ways of controlling the investment of their pension funds and of taking over plants that capital wishes to shut down. Second, workers demand better health and safety conditions, especially as more and more disease is traced to the workplace. Third, labor actively resists capitalist control through strikes, slowdowns, and sabotage. Absenteeism and working to rule may also be considered forms of resistance at the individual level.

Finally, in the evolving world political economy, labor recognizes the need to become more involved in decisions affecting the nation as a whole—decisions that concern not only wages and benefits but also issues that are far more fundamental to the capitalist class, such as the distribution of national income and the allocation of capital (Hymer, 1978). Thus, labor organizes collectively around issues such as foreign trade, tax reform, full employment, and energy policy, thereby expanding the scope of debate and escalating the scale of conflict.

Class Struggle and Problems of Social Control in an Urban Environment

CHANGE AND DISRUPTION

Most NJCs, particularly those funded or organized by the state, are established in urban environments because even though some production has shifted to suburban and rural areas, urban environments still remain central production sites, markets, investment sites, and administrative control centers for capital (Castells, 1976; Harvey, 1976; Hill, 1976; Gordon, 1977). These urban centers—and their labor power, roads, schools, services, communications, etc.—must be organized as an element of the productive process so as to create the preconditions for investment.

Since the 1960s the role of the urban environment as a "support center" for capital has changed dramatically. Production in the monopoly sector has moved out of the central city to areas where taxes are lower, land is cheaper, and workers are less organized—leaving behind smaller, competitive industries that lack the resources to move and depend on the local client population for revenue. The sporadic labor needs of the latter lead to an increase in the numbers of unemployed, underemployed, and poorly paid (Hill, 1976; Gordon, 1977).

Urban decay threatens overall capital accumulation. Growing, volatile, surplus populations produce social unrest and create the potential for collective action that disrupts production and challenges capitalist control. These populations have always posed a political threat, but the social transformations we have been describing change the magnitude and nature of that threat: Surplus populations become larger and more permanent. The fiscal crisis of the state precludes substantial increases in social services, which have usually expanded in response to previous economic crises (Piven and Cloward, 1971; O'Connor, 1973).

Minor disruptions in the community (like those in the workplace) can have effects on capital expansion. Mental and physical illness, family fights, alcoholism, drug addiction, neighborhood conflicts, and other "social problems" of urban society cannot be ignored by capitalists precisely because the social environment where disruption occurs has itself become a form of capital (Hirschhorn, 1978). These problems can result in absenteeism and tension at work and thereby reduce productivity. The quality of human capital declines. They also require increased social expenditures and thereby diminish the surplus available for capital.

The "tightly woven political and market ecologies" of contemporary democracy intensify the demand for public order (Silver, 1974). That is, the democratic political system within which capital accumulation functions provides opportunities and obstacles for capital. Many laws and regulations concerning labor, licensing, zoning, and pollution cannot be changed without referenda or bureaucratic action.

DEPOLITICIZING CLASS STRUGGLE IN THE COMMUNITY: PROBLEMS

Class struggle in the community takes two principal forms. First, in place of individuals seeking to consume more goods and services we find collectivities demanding improvements in the environment, the quality of housing, mass transportation, etc. Second, groups seek to expand control over a wide variety of subjects—energy, schools, city planning, community services, bank policies, land use, food distribution, urban renewal, plant closings—thereby breaking down the artificial distinction between public and private interests. They also reject the distinction between workplace and community. The worker and the "citizen" are the same person. These challenges clarify the opposition between the interests of capital and labor and heighten worker consciousness of collective needs.

The neighborhood, consumer, welfare rights, and environmental movements that arose in the 1970s generate new confrontations with capital, contributing to a "class-defined polarization" that parallels labor organizing and "seeks to form broader alliances of the powerless across lines of division like income and racial differences" (Boyte, 1979: 10). These forms of opposition by the working class and surplus populations are a response to the decay of the urban infrastructure contained in "threats to living standards, urban services . . . housing and other essentials of daily life" (*Ibid.*). Perhaps most important, many community organizations "have started to address themselves to the relationship between urban neighborhood deterioration and the flow of capital between urban centers and regions" (Drier, 1979: 12).

Organized protests involve the use of hearings, referenda, administrative review, lawsuits, etc., and express the collective needs of communities at many bureaucratic levels. The fragmentation of local government sometimes restricts the capacity of capital to dominate the city because capital cannot identify a single decision maker from which it can extract the policies it needs at a macrolevel. The NJCs may serve to disorganize community challenges by demobilizing and absorbing demands at the individual level.

CONVENTIONAL FORMS OF SOCIAL CONTROL:
THE LIMITS OF MEDIATING INSTITUTIONS

Traditional state institutions that mediate class conflict, preventing its emergence or escalation and otherwise channeling and absorbing discontent, have become obsolete and ineffective for *capital*. These institutions, some of which are still oppressive and powerful, may not adequately reproduce a politically docile, adaptable, finely honed, productive labor force for a variety of reasons.

Police. Police forces were established in the United States in the mid-nineteenth century in response to class conflict: Capital needed a mechanism to "control . . . strikes, working class organizations . . . working class communities . . . and [to] control and resocializ[e] migrants imported to serve the demands of industry" (Harring and McMullin, 1975). In the twentieth century, as the proportion of the population engaged in industrial production declined, production was decentralized, individual capitalists could no longer pay for policing, and the police became a professional class organized by the state, severed from direct political ties to business interests. Regulating community life is now an important aspect of the police function. Peacekeeping and order maintenance typically emphasize so-called deviant public behavior, such as vagrancy, disorderly conduct, public drunkenness, etc.

Today, capital is threatened by private as well as public disorder: Family fights disrupt the worker qua worker and the community peace. Many police departments have intensified their concern for the private lives of individuals through specialized units, programs, and practices, e.g., family crisis intervention and dispute settlement. But the capacity of the police to respond to disruption with precise and intensive regulation (and thus their effectiveness for capital) is limited by legal procedure, police organization, and police distaste for order-maintenance functions. The police may handle the most visible and violent moments of conflict, but they cannot resolve conflict, prevent it, or regulate the social environment in accordance with the requirements of capitalist control.

The Criminal Justice System.   Few people believe that American criminal processes are fair or equitable, or capable of rehabilitating offenders or helping individuals resolve disputes. Justice system officials hesitate to become involved in neighborhood disputes, family fights, or controversies between parties engaged in an ongoing relationship (Vera Institute of Justice, 1977). The emphasis on adversarial conflict and the constraints imposed by law, combined with limited sanctioning options, further limit the possibilities for effective dispositions. Although judicial authority and judicial roles appear to offer numerous options, the form and content of regulation is too narrow to meet the needs of *capital*. It cannot penetrate to the underlying tensions between disputants or the deeper motivation of defendants.

Mental Institutions and Prisons.   Mental institutions and prisons warehouse people. As such, they neither develop a reserve army of unemployed that can help to depress wages nor invest in the valuable human capital now demanded by the labor market. The control exercised within those institutions is intensive and brutal but without clear direction, expensive for the state and wasteful for capital (Scull, 1977). Moreover, mental patients and prisoners are now seeking new rights—to quality treatment and more autonomy in the mental institution and proper services and facilities in the prison. The former can no longer incarcerate surplus populations without satisfying due process requirements.

Political Machines.   Political machines once provided social services, gave the community a voice, and contained protest. By carefully cultivating ties with constituents, imposing a high level of organizational discipline, and trading services for votes, they were able to temper political demands and handle community conflicts. Today, these machines have all but disappeared. No comparable institution has arisen to absorb and channel discontent, or to identify community problems that could lead to disruption. Machines have been supplanted by fragmented and impersonal social service bureaucracies that no political leader can control and that publicly dramatize the failure of the social system when they cannot handle client demands.

The Legal Crisis of the State

Law is an ideological form of class domination and an expression of state power that protects property and often conceals the way in which the social relations of production and exchange determine entitlements. Law usually regulates social and economic relations in the interests of capital. This assertion of class power is accomplished, in part, by control over what is adjudicated and by differentiation between civil or citizen rights and human rights associated with need (Fraser, 1978). Law transforms economic power into a legal relation and class conflict into legal conflict. Both capital and labor pursue their interests through law, but capital possesses a distinct advantage. Domination is not total; law must be partially autonomous from ruling-class interests or else there would be no struggle over it. Law and legal processes assure formal equality, thereby placing some limits on economic domination and on the productive relations between labor and capital. Law imposes a common code or language that defines rights of ownership and control.

To the extent that this code of legal principles is undermined or separated from universal ideals of justice, the legitimacy of legal principles, and of the property entitlements they support, is placed in question. Yet capital itself is now forced to undermine legality. Although it requires predictability, it must also be able to disorganize and reorganize economic relations in order to meet the demands for innovation in the social relations of production necessary for capital expansion. Such innovation is impeded by fixed legal rules and procedures. For example, efforts to manage inflation and recession, shift from nuclear energy to coal, prevent strikes, or conclude mergers are impeded by health and safety regulations, antipollution laws, antitrust laws, or the requirements of due process. Thus, the strains that develop in legal institutions parallel the inadequacies in other mediating institutions, described earlier in the chapter.

But capital is not alone in using law to pursue substantive ends. Workers do so too, and their efforts undermine the foundations of judicial authority and generate movement toward administrative forms of justice.

The assertion by labor of legal rights to employment or to a safe and healthy workplace threaten capital's rights of property and contract (Gintis, 1980). Capital can no longer invest and move freely; it cannot construct or locate productive facilities (e.g., nuclear power plants or factories producing dangerous chemicals), advertise certain products (e.g., children's breakfast cereals), or produce given products (e.g., large, dangerous, or polluting automobiles). Legal demands for the satisfaction of human needs—nutrition, health care, housing, clean air, and energy—may also reduce the control of capital over labor and its share of the surplus value produced by labor. Conflict centers upon material resources, public policy, market relations, and control of everyday life rather than mere formal equality. The danger for capital is not that property rights will necessarily be undermined—such a fundamental reordering of power cannot occur through legal change alone. It is rather that extending the rights of the laboring class obstructs capital expansion and hinders control over property solely through appeal to legal principle.

Legal rationality obstructs the ability of courts to manage new forms of class conflict and economic dislocation arising from the irrationalities of capitalist production. The problems posed by nuclear waste or genetic engineering cannot be resolved within the narrow framework of technical legal rulings. Limiting what is justiciable proves difficult, not only because courts *must* respond to grievances (e.g., affirmative action) but also because capital requires innovative judicial policies that regulate more aspects of the social environment—both personal and political.

As capital concentrates and centralizes its power, other interests also organize, attempting to achieve some of their goals through judicial action. However limited such collective action may be, this type of challenge reveals the class interests behind the law. These struggles reshape the form and content of legal conflict—usually in ways that highlight the political content of issues.

Labor and marginal populations also demand state benefits, which may come to be viewed as rights. State expansion into more areas of private social life sparks new battles over the distribution of public resources. At the same time, the formal procedures necessary to legitimate state action contain the potential to justify the further expansion of those rights.

Dislocation, actual or threatened (plant shutdowns, dangerous products, unemployment), also stimulates demands for better protection from the unplanned character and irrationality of the capitalist economy through complex regulations of products and liability for damages to those who suffer capitalist "mistakes," as in the recall of automobiles, the shutting of Kepone factories and nuclear plants, and restitution for overcharges. The number and scope of such demands have been growing. They threaten capitalist interests because they challenge the prerogatives of capitalists to produce and invest as they please. The result is new forms of control that share many of the characteristics found in neighborhood justice centers.

Emerging Forms of Social Control in the Workplace and the Community

Contemporary social control is characterized by three central features: planning, the regulation of the totality of social existence, and administrative–technocratic rationality.

PLANNING

Planning has been a major element of capitalist social control since the New Deal, launched in response to the centralization and concentration of capital and the failure of markets to marshal and allocate resources. Now, as then, planning aims to reduce uncertainty about the supply of labor, resources, and financing; to create investment opportunities; to control prices, costs, and demand; and otherwise to limit impediments to accumulation. Contemporary planning is distinguished by two features: first, it supports the interests of capital as a whole, rather than individual industries or some fraction of capital; second, it increases the centralization of decision-making authority and deprives workers and democratically elected officials of control over basic aspects of economic and social life.

During the 1970s corporate executives and former public officials created the Trilateral Commission and the Business Roundtable, along with other political action committees, to generate capital and extend capitalist control by garnering state subsidies, reorienting educational institutions toward specific policy goals, increasing the power of the executive branch of government, and reducing popular challenges to established authority by limiting the growth of democratic institutions and any expansion in the entitlements of the working class.

In the workplace, planning takes the form of comprehensive research into, and coordination of, long-range production needs. Control is centralized to enhance managerial authority and remove decision-making authority from workers. Limiting the autonomy of workers to plan and execute work is necessary for capitalist innovation.

One response by capital to struggles over the control of resources in urban environments has been

> to gain more centralized and efficient executive control over government through devices like . . . national economic planning which would . . . suppress the irrational political character of current programming, and would eliminate both excess service to clients and the excess influence of special interests [Mollenkopf, 1977: 125, 129].

Such planning, as a means of managing politics and limiting access to decision making, is essentially antidemocratic. Prime examples are the creation of regional planning bodies, run by expert administrators, who design urban renewal projects and whole cities in conjunction with real estate interests and banks. Perhaps the most extraordinary instance of planning in recent years occurred in 1975, when New York City created the Emergency Financial Control Board, which effectively undermined the authority of elected city officials by giving finance capital the power "to review revenue and expenditure estimates and to monitor the budget, and... overrule municipal union contracts freely negotiated." (Newfield and Dubrul, 1977: 179). Metropolitan governments encompassing parts of several states are another response to problems posed by fragmented local governments that restrict the capacity of capital to dominate a city because no single authority can develop a comprehensive policy to encourage capital investment and restrict the claims of labor and surplus populations.

REGULATING THE TOTALITY OF SOCIAL EXISTENCE

Another central characteristic of contemporary capitalist social control is its scope and depth. All of society's physical structures, instruments of production, services, and labor are viewed as resources that must be actively organized to foster capital expansion and manage accumulation on a national basis (Harvey, 1976; Hirschhorn, 1978; Spitzer, 1979).

> Thus the logic of subsumption, in which capital presses all social institutions into its service either as ideological or economic apparatuses, forms the core of what may be termed managed capitalism, which extends from the labor process to society as a whole [Aronowitz, 1978: 139].

Fraser elaborates this point in relation to the legal order:

> More and more formerly "private" aspects of the individual's identity and experience become legally relevant. . . . Since all standards of rationality and value within the corporate state stem from the universalizing power of capital, the legal process, if it is to be effective, must ensure that any parochial particularities that cannot be dissolved and reconstituted as an element within the global hegemony of capitalist social relations are not permitted to impede the free flow of the rational forces of technology, capital, and labor, upon which social progress depends [1978: 172–173]

People become targets for intervention not because they engage in legally or morally culpable behavior but because of the relationship of their behavior and attitudes to the labor force and the labor process. The private lives of individuals become of interest to capital. Intervention must be organized on a permanent and ubiquitous basis because everyone and everything represents social capital. The goal of regulation is to direct and prescribe human labor power rather than exclude and confine it (Spitzer, 1982). What we need to consider is why the detailed management of populations takes the form of informal and decentralized control.

In the workplace, the needs of monopoly capital to expand productivity and to minimize the disruption of output make everyone "the subject of management interference" (Braverman, 1974: 309). Innovations in technology (see Noble, 1978) extend management authority over the work process by giving managers "the capability to time study production and skilled workers 24 hours a day. . . . Every minute of the worker's time can be accounted for. . . . The foreman no longer decides to discipline the workers. He merely carries out "the automatic decisions of the system" [Shaiken, 1979: 13]. Monitoring is characterized not merely by detailed observation but also by extensive probing and evaluation. Employers seek simultaneously to limit the discretion of workers, expand productivity, and limit challenges to capitalist prerogatives. To achieve these objectives, capitalists intrude on the privacy of workers by identifying those personality traits and attitudes that render workers amenable to control, regardless of their ability to perform the job function adequately (Edwards, 1979). An increasing number of jobs require applicants to submit to psychological tests (e.g., the Minnesota Multi-Phasic Personality Inventory). Workers in some industries have been genetically screened to determine their susceptibility to certain diseases known to be associated with the tasks performed. Rather than reform the workplace, the capitalist transforms and invests in the worker, using a variety of social engineering techniques: training, job enrichment, and worker satisfaction programs designed to involve workers in their own regulation.

Intervention at the community level is also characterized by extensive scrutiny of private lives by means of informal, decentralized mechanisms, located outside institutional settings, and heavy reliance on professionals in psychology and education (Szasz, 1965; Kittrie, 1971). Methods of punishment, deviance management, social service delivery, and intervention in family life generally appear to be more closely related to labor market and labor force conditions than to conceptions of morality (Platt, 1969; Rothman, 1971; Jankovic, 1977; Foucault, 1977; Scull, 1977; Donzelot, 1979).

Four new modes of intervention can be identified: decriminalization, diversion of juvenile defendants, deinstitutionalization of the mentally handicapped, and public welfare.

A majority of states have decriminalized public drunkenness, in order to "treat" the inebriate as a health problem rather than as a criminal. Inebriates are swept off the streets (often by the police) but not arrested and therefore not protected by principles of due process. They are taken to detoxification centers (in protective custody) and often must submit to extensive supervision by medical professionals and demonstrate their fitness to be returned to the community before they will be released.

Alternatives to conventional adjudication in the criminal justice system, such as expanded use of probation and diversion from prosecution and incarceration, allow judicial authorities to monitor offenders in a community setting. Participation in alternative programs requires cooperation with officials for periods longer than the sentences offenders would have received had they been prosecuted. Many jurisdictions use indeterminate sentences for juveniles; defendants must meet certain criteria for successful completion of the disposition. Control involves structured, detailed diagnosis, screening, supervision, reporting, and classification (Scull, 1977; Cohen, 1979; Feeley, 1980).

A crucial aspect of monitoring is that officials emphasize attitudes and habit more than facts or behavior in an attempt to prevent future deviance or conflict. "Juvenile court does not really pronounce judgment on crime; it examines individuals" (Donzelot, 1979: 110). The goal is to identify

potential pre-delinquents or high risk populations, [but] there is a deliberate attempt to evade the question of whether a rule has actually been broken.... [In the future] it will be impossible to determine who exactly is enmeshed in the social control system—and hence subject to its jurisdiction and surveillance.... The major results of the new movements towards community diversion have been to increase rather than decrease the *amount* of intervention directed at many groups of deviants in the system and, probably, to increase rather than decrease the total number who get into the system in the first place [Cohen, 1979: 346, 347].

Large segments of the mentally handicapped population are being deinstitutionalized, ostensibly in order to enhance their autonomy and enable them to lead natural lives. Many are actively supervised (if not adequately served otherwise) by professionals who monitor their adjustment to community norms rather than minister to their medical or psychological needs (Chu and Trotter, 1974). Portions of these populations are subsidized by the state to generate cheap labor for the competitive sector of the economy at a cost lower than their upkeep in an institutional setting (Scull, 1977).

Perhaps the most common form of monitoring is directed toward the poor and other surplus populations who receive monetary and service benefits from the state in return for allowing officials to scrutinize them (Donzelot, 1979). Recipients must expose the details of their daily lives for examination by social workers, psychologists, and bureaucrats and endure harassment, e.g., house inspections and family interviews by public officials seeking to uncover moral or psychological defects. Many of the requirements and judgments that form the rationale for monitoring derive from concern over the alleged erosion of the work ethic and of labor markets (Piven and Cloward, 1971). The welfare system, however,

is no longer just a system of social control tied to immediate labor market conditions. Rather, the displacement and integration of people in the work system ... is increasingly controlled by the welfare system.... Welfare services ... regulate the growth, structure, and development of the displaced population [Hirschhorn, 1978: 72].

How do informality and decentralization extend control? Informality facilitates early intervention and prevention of social disruption. Control need not be contingent on legal violations. The "helping professional" can engage in detailed inquiry into and surveillance over private lives under the guise of assistance. Discretion is expanded. By blurring formal distinctions about what constitutes deviance, the state expands its authority to regulate (Cohen, 1979).

Community-based institutions disperse social control (Cohen, 1979; Spitzer, 1982). What this means is that deviance management and other control functions can be integrated into patterns of everyday social life, utilizing not only social service agencies but also neighborhood groups, family members, and peers. Control operates within the plant, the office, and the community, whereas planning and decision making are centralized in the state. Problem populations need not be segregated in institutions since the whole social environment can be organized for regulation. State authority thus widens its orbit of control while disguising the explicit coercion that might generate resistance.

ADMINISTRATIVE—TECHNOCRATIC RATIONALITY

Administrative–technocratic rationality is a form of social interaction that mediates class conflict by transforming the organization and language of political challenge so as to conceal class interests and fragment the collective power of labor. This depoliticization of conflict is partially realized by replacing explicitly political democratic decision-making structures with administrative institutions and procedures dominated by experts unaccountable to the public (see Habermas, 1973; Wolfe, 1977). The collective power of labor is disorganized and fragmented, artificially separating public and private interests (citizen versus person), regulating people by relegating them to limited roles (workers, patients, clients, disputants, etc.), and, more generally, transforming class relations into relations between and among individuals, groups, or abstract entities.

The administrative form is not new, but its manifestations in the workplace and community have been expanded in two important ways. First, it inhibits class consciousness, fragments collective action, and reduces political participation and control over work and social life. Second, it handles conflict by emphasizing accommodation, thereby limiting the development of entitlements and political power.

Inhibiting the Development of Working-Class Consciousness and Collective Action.   In the workplace, bureaucratic authority in the form of rules replaces individual discretion in the supervision of work, concealing employer control. Workers thus struggle over compliance with rules but not over their content or source.

> Work activities become defined and directed by a set of work criteria . . . rules, procedures, and expectations . . . [and] formalized job descriptions . . . [rather] than by specific orders, directions,

and whims of the supervisor. . . . From these criteria derive the "customary law" notions of "equity" or "just cause" in firing, promotion, and job assignment. . . . Top echelon management . . . set the criteria, establish the structure, and enforce compliance. . . . Power thus becomes institutionalized by vesting it in official positions or roles and permitting its exercise only according to prescribed rules, procedures, and expectations [Edwards, 1978: 119, 120].

By structuring every detail of the work process through the classification of each job title, task, or procedure and establishing incentives for meeting specifically defined criteria, management encourages workers to

pursue their self-interest in a narrow way as individuals, and [stifles their] impulse to struggle collectively for those same self-interests. . . . The ability to establish rules provided the capitalists with the power . . . to set the basic conditions around which the struggle was to be fought. . . . As workers were isolated from each other, and as the system was made distinct from the bosses who supervise it, the basic capitalist–worker relation tended to shrink from sight [Edwards, 1979: 143, 146].

Workers lose control over grievances when professional experts such as third-party mediators or arbitrators decide the outcomes. Workers rely on the union, management, and even government to translate conflicts into acceptable terms. Agreements rarely deal with daily grievances or the changing conditions in the workplace that accompany the constant reorganization of the work process. Workers usually lack a grievance mechanism that is free of management control.

In handling specific grievances on and off the shop floor, as well as major eruptions such as strikes, conflict resolution procedures are usually established in advance by the capitalist. The process adheres to fixed criteria in a regular, complex, and codified system with limited appeals. Many labor contracts, for example, specify arbitration as the primary tool of dispute resolution in order to guarantee labor peace and reduce labor costs. But arbitration accepts the basic discrepancy in power between capital and labor and reduces struggle to routine administrative formulas. Although negotiation and arbitration are not new, they have now been applied more thoroughly to all realms of industrial conflict, including shop floor grievances.

Administrative criteria also transform the worker and the workers' needs into abstract categories measured according to scientific methods and cost–benefit theory. The capitalist desires to

translate the emotional language of life and limb into the more dispassionate and measurable idiom of cost accounting. . . . What exactly is health "worth"? How does one reasonably trade off profit against safety? Even the most sophisticated methods produce logical absurdities that violate commonsense ideas of justice and equity [Green and Waitzman, 1980: 42].

The application of administrative criteria to the organization of work parallels developments in community politics and in struggles over the distribution of resources, investment, and public policy. The roots of these efforts at depoliticization can be traced to Progressive Era reforms, such as city manager government and nonpartisan elections, which were designed to limit the threat that democratic rule posed to the authority of capital (Hofstadter, 1955; Weinstein, 1968).

Democratic decision making is removed from the community, first, by limiting public participation to attendance at hearings or membership on boards with little authority. Second, officials make many decisions—about services and budgets, for example—according to administrative criteria and managerial efficiency, in processes that are insulated from politics.

What is relatively new in all this is the application of rules, regulations, means tests, and scientific criteria to more and more matters of public policy and entitlement, for example, deterring applications for food stamps by adding a work requirement, or even eliminating social programs and facilities on the basis of fiscal evaluation rather than need. To an increasing degree, the success of clients in diversion and alcohol rehabilitation programs (and therefore their right to be free from further intervention) is measured by administrative criteria (did they attend counseling sessions, cooperate with the probation officer) that are unrelated to questions of equity, justice, or need. The discretionary power of state functionaries is thereby enhanced.

Administrative–technocratic rationality also serves to fragment the organizational capacity of the working class. Industrial psychologists, using the administrative sciences, have developed tangible and intangible incentive schemes— e.g., bonuses, job statuses, or recognition—and attempt to elicit worker cooperation by offering limited, pro forma participation in making decisions about the work process.

These same psychologists and management experts treat each worker as an individual whose problems derive from sources outside the workplace; they do not entertain the possibility of changing the workplace or exploring how oversupervision, an unhealthy work environment, or the pace of work affects the collective experience of workers. Thus "stress management" and other psychological and medical techniques typify the employer response.

Whenever possible, grievances and demands are also handled on a case-by-case basis that stresses their unique qualities but subordinates outcome to a predetermined policy or rule. Potentially explosive issues can thereby be absorbed and hidden from scrutiny.

In the community, the distribution of social welfare benefits helps to keep the working class fragmented.

> Benefits are formed and distributed in ways which inhibit the development of client groups capable of collective action. . . . Benefits . . . isolate low-income people from major social roles, particularly occupational roles. . . . Benefits are designed as individual benefits which discourage the aggregation of clients [Cloward and Piven, 1972: 15–17].

Since bureaucratic rule tends to be less visible and accountable than formal law, benefits can be proferred or withdrawn if organized dissent challenges bureaucratic authority. Those who monitor services—e.g., social workers—are guided by rules that encourage them to control costs and minimize service rather than to mobilize clients or act as their advocates. These state workers are themselves evaluated by criteria that alienate them from those they serve.

The Politics of Accommodation.   In the workplace, negotiation and arbitration legitimate compromise and accommodation—part of the larger strategy of capital to convince labor to cooperate by denying that their interests are really divergent. The capitalist is able to set the agenda by dealing with worker demands through negotiation. Workers can achieve only concessions, at best, not fundamental changes in the social relations of production or what is produced, or a voice in plant closings, plant locations, production schedules, layoffs, and mergers. More importantly, workers relinquish rights as part of their agreements— the steelworkers union has surrendered the right to strike—and accept obligations—some union contracts now specify workloads, work rules, and job classifications and tie wages directly to productivity.

Arbitration, mediation, and other administrative techniques used to resolve conflict in the workplace proliferate in the community. Disputes on major issues involving the environment, education, housing, race relations, age discrimination, police brutality, and energy—especially those between organized community groups and either government or corporations—are attracting greater attention from those promoting administrative techniques designed to forestall the escalation of conflict into the political arena (Institute for Mediation and Conflict Resolution, 1974; United States Department of Justice, Community Relations Service, 1975; Ford Foundation, 1978a).

Neighborhood mediation centers share important similarities with the emerging forms of control described in the preceding discussion; both neutralize demands and resolve new contradictions within the social order through various quasi-legal and administrative dispute resolution mechanisms. The following section speculates about these characteristics, their connection to capitalist social control, and their implications for class conflict.

NEIGHBORHOOD JUSTICE: SPECULATIONS

The neighborhood mediation program, as a state institution, displays in microcosm the reproductive system of capital. The planning, practices, and rules of NJCs parallel many characteristics of social control in the workplace and the community.

The Planning of Neighborhood Justice

Neighborhood mediation forums do not arise out of the deliberations or demands of indigenous populations, although the poor, the unemployed, and minorities constitute a large proportion of the disputants in some programs (see Cook *et al.*, 1980). The impetus for and design of NJCs derives from government administrators and judicial authorities (often national) acting in cooperation with business organizations, large foundations, criminal justice planning agencies, and professional organizations such as the American Bar Association, the American Arbitration Association, and associations of state and local governments.

Many of those who testified in the Congressional Hearings on Minor Dispute Resolution in 1978 and 1979 can hardly be identified with the interests of disputants—e.g., the U.S. Chamber of Commerce, the National Association of Counties, National Center for State Courts, the Motor Vehicle Manufacturers Association, National Manufactured Housing Federation, Sears Roebuck and Company, and the Better Business Bureau (U.S. House, 1978; 1979). Community members are represented on the boards of directors of many NJCs, but overall authority for planning and policy remains in the hands of traditionally powerful organizations and public officials. The Atlanta NJC, for example, "operated under the guidance of a Board of Directors composed of court officials, attorneys and a few representatives from the police and community agencies" (Cook *et al.*, 1980: 12).

Community residents may participate in state-controlled neighborhood justice, but it is not planned or designed with their interests in mind. Rather, the interests served are those of corporate planners and public officials, fearful of excessive democracy and disruption of the established order. The language of a Ford Foundation report reveals these concerns.

Our capacity as a people to resolve conflicts is under severe strain. . . . There is strong evidence that the number and complexity of disputes will continue to increase. . . . What is needed is a systematic approach that expands our understanding of the larger issues in conflict resolution . . . [and helps to] de-escalate conflicts. . . . The changing nature of legal rights and entitlements might also be examined—how these changes affect the adversary system [1978a: 64].

Public officials concerned with maintaining order, avoiding "time-consuming" public debate, and assuring the uninterrupted management of growth may find that NJCs have something to offer. "One selling point is that a properly developed center could be a buffer for elected officials in such diverse areas as housing, welfare, code and zoning violations, and animal control" (American Bar Association, 1979: 2).

If NJCs were truly informal and responsive to community need, there ought to be some evidence of popular demand or some data on community conflict that would justify their formation and structure. Instead we find that once mediation programs begin, they must engage in extensive public relations activities to attract a sizable caseload, unless they resort to court referrals. If NJCs were democratically established, disputants could organize mediation themselves; it is not a scientific or complex process. Instead we find bureaucratic managers, sometimes drawn from the federal government, imposing principles of conflict management and mediator training and detailed blueprints for dispute resolution systems.

The centralization of authority and decentralization of function characteristic of NJC planning follow the logic of corporate planning. Nancy DiTomaso, in a study of the Department of Labor, explains how the combination of decentralization of function and centralized authority obscure the basis of power.

> Precisely because hierarchy concentrates power, it also makes it more "visible." In hierarchical organizational structures, the locus of power is more easily identified than in dispersed organizational structures. When the locus of power is more visible, then the "point of change" is also more easily identified. Therefore, under conditions of resistance from subordinate classes, a diffusion of power or decentralization may be the "best" means to maintain the existing relationships of domination—all other things being equal—because decentralization scatters the point of change [1978: 84].

This analysis may be applied to courts and NJCs. Although each court appears decentralized, the hierarchical judicial systems of every state are connected to the local political system and the federal government. Although most judicial decisions are not highly visible to the general public, a few have received considerable attention in the last decade, as courts have become increasingly involved in major social issues such as nuclear power, the quality of the physical environment, affirmative action, product safety, and abortion. Moreover, the media report judicial activities in more detail than they once did. The activities of dispersed organizational structures such as NJCs, on the other hand, have much less visibility. Their locus of power is not as easily identified, even though most state-funded NJCs either are directly regulated by judicial authorities or are dependent upon them for cases. The state thus retains its monopoly over justice and expands its capacity to regulate diverse populations.

Regulating the Totality of Social Existence

The expansion of state power—the regulation of the totality of social existence—is manifested in the subject matter deemed appropriate for resolution in NJCs. Because they handle cases concerned not only with violations of law but also with behavior identified as a social problem or a threat to community stability, the range of control is greatly extended. The accessibility of NJCs and their informal procedures permit a wide variety of noncriminal but disapproved conduct to be subjected to scrutiny and even to sanctions. In some court-based programs

> there appear to be no formal limitations on the discretion of court clerks, prosecutors, judges, and others in determining which cases are suitable for referral to mediation, no formal limitations on whatever discretion the mediation staff has in accepting referrals, and no formal limitations on the discretion of community mediators in conducting their sessions [Snyder, 1978: 788].

Without the protections of due process—e.g., open hearings and rules of evidence—disputants may be examined by an NJC when they would never be processed by the courts, or even by the police (Harrington, 1980). The sphere of private action immune from state interference will shrink because of the threat of interruptions to capital expansion and the fact that NJC are evaluated by measuring their caseloads (Cook *et al.*, 1980) rather than by judging whether they serve disputant needs.[10]

The range of subject matter handled within NJCs is extensive (Florida Supreme Court, 1978). Preliminary data from some programs indicate that a substantial proportion of cases represent new disputes rather than merely the diversion of controversies already in the courts (Singer, 1979). Moreover, the location of many NJCs in the inner city suggests that disputants tend to have low to moderate incomes, with most on the low side (Snyder, 1978; Cook *et al.*, 1980). The state's concern with seemingly minor intraclass disputes reveals the potential scope of NJC regulation.

The range of control of the NJCs, like that of other modern mediating institutions, is limited by the growing fiscal crisis of the state. But NJCs do not require large expenditures or extensive planning. They may be established fairly quickly and inexpensively because their implementation does not depend on a legislative act or a judicial rule, which are needed to restructure the courts or create new social programs.

In addition, many categories of cases are now processed by other conflict resolution programs that use mediation as a principal technique. The Federal Mediation and Conciliation Service, for example, which formerly handled only contract disputes between labor and management, is now authorized to mediate health care disputes in the private sector and the age discrimination complaints of recipients of federal services (Office of Dispute Settlement, 1979). Mediation is now regularly applied to community disputes involving housing, education, race relations, hospitals, the environment, and corrections (Institute for Mediation and Conflict Resolution, 1974; Ford Foundation, 1978b).

---

[10]The latter criterion cannot be operationalized by asking disputants whether they were satisfied with the outcome. Satisfaction is a subjective concept distinct from the objective fact that disputants would have received a better or worse outcome using some other method.

In the mediation process itself few limits are imposed on the issues investigated if discussion helps disputants reach agreement. Intake counselors usually solicit much diagnostic information from participants before the hearing. Within the mediation session, many programs encourage disputants to "tell their stories," ventilate their feelings, and otherwise reveal details about their personal lives. The purpose is not to punish or reprimand but rather to understand the roots of the conflict. But this sort of therapeutic openness magnifies the extent to which the state penetrates the lives of disputants: Their deepest emotions and most personal problems become part of the process of conflict resolution. This intervention itself is regulation, regardless of its effect on the outcome (Feeley, 1980). Equally important, the mediator, in seeking a successful outcome, may subtly pressure disputants by hinting at the possible negative consequences of failure or channeling them toward an agreement.

The resolution sought by the mediator may require disputants to contact a network of social service agencies that diagnose and monitor them over an extended period of time. In some forums that accept quasi-criminal or even noncriminal disputes, disputants sign a legally binding document in which they agree to work with social service professionals in employment, counseling, and educational settings. Violation of the agreement can result in the initiation or renewal of prosecution. In noncriminal cases, the NJC may assist the complainant in filing an action in civil court.

Thus, just as workers are monitored in the workplace (Edwards, 1979), offenders are supervised by probation officers (Cohen, 1979) and welfare recipients investigated by social workers (Piven and Cloward, 1971), so disputants in the NJC may find their lives exposed to continuing scrutiny. The form of regulation may be less overt and obtrusive than in other institutions, but it still reflects the transformation of control from a focus on limited behavior that violates specific norms to a concern with habits and attitudes and the defiance of bureaucratic authority.

Indeed, it is no longer necessary to house people in large institutions in order to watch them closely (Jankovic, 1977). Modern technology available to the NJC and to social service professionals (computers, information systems, surveillance equipment) permits monitoring by community-based facilities. The state is relieved of the burden of a recalcitrant, intransigent group of patients or inmates who might organize and demand legal rights.

Furthermore, the NJC may achieve more effective control than is possible within total institutions such as prisons or mental hospitals or through the authoritative but limited interventions of the police. The NJC can modify behavior to suit immediate social conditions and labor market demands. The law restricts judicial options in processing cases and makes it difficult to tailor responses to community circumstances. Informality allows the disposition to be adapted to a specific social purpose.

Informality is more flexible because it rejects principles that apply to all in order to realize some abstract public good. Supplementing law with informality thus expands social control.

> The development of state-regulated, monopoly capitalism has also witnessed the erosion of the rule of law and the emergence of less formalistic, more instrumentalist and technocratic modes of social and political control; the law as universal political equivalent gradually gives way to a series of relatively *ad hoc techniques* which, by their very nature, recognize specific interests and specific social origins.... Technocratic modes of social control imply a certain re-emergence of the content and quality from which the legal form abstracts [Balbus, 1977: 586].

Administrative–Technocratic Rationality

INHIBITING AND FRAGMENTING COLLECTIVE ACTION

The neighborhood mediation forum, despite its rhetoric of personal, disputant-controlled justice, is essentially an administrative system of dispute resolution. The administrative form possesses certain special characteristics.

> [The administrative form of legalization] denies all class antagonism, appeals to general standards of harmony and public welfare, pretends to focus on equity emphasizing the unique conditions of every case.... Defining some general goals about public and individual welfare, it legitimizes virtually any administrative activity or non-activity.... [It represents] a return to unrestricted political power. ... It delegalizes social relations by liberating direct power which law tries to formalize [Reifner, 1982].

The NJC dampens class conflict in a number of ways. First, it individualizes conflict by creating a forum that offers an alternative to the neighborhood or union meetings in which collective action might be taken. Jerold Auerbach, a legal historian, asks:

> Are these forums likely to deflect energy from political organization by groups of people with grievances in common (e.g. tenants in slums or neighborhoods slated for development) or even discourage them from developing a litigation strategy that might offer more effective leverage for social and economic change? [1980: 400].

Second, the NJC ignores the social basis of conflict by handling problems on a case-by-case basis without generating a public record. And although disputants can technically raise any question or issue, the content of conflict is divorced from collective interests, segregated from similar cases, and limited to the immediate relationship between the disputants (see Reifner, 1982). Consumers may "win" cases as individuals by getting their money back or obtaining the repair of a product, but they lose as members of a wider social class interested in preventing a recurrence of the incident or effecting a change of policy.

For example, a dispute about the safety of a product purchased in a supermarket would be transformed into an issue between a dissatisfied customer and a local merchant rather than be interpreted as a more fundamental conflict of interest between producers and consumers, with implications that may affect the whole community. This type of transformation in the nature of conflict parallels the use of the administrative form in the workplace, where the refusal of a corporation to install necessary safety equipment is translated from a question of safety or owner responsibility into an issue of compliance with work rules, a dispute between a worker and a plant manager, or a claim for compensation (Edwards, 1979).

In the NJC those issues that cannot be reduced to individual cases are rejected as inappropriate—e.g., challenges to the practices of nursing home operators, the marketing and investment policies of corporations, or redlining by banks.

There are similarities between the fragmented character of justice in the NJC and the nature of the work process. Braverman (1974) describes the rationalization of work and its reduction to abstract labor. The division of labor within the work experience is comparable to the dissection of social conflict into disputes between individuals, torn from the holistic nature of social life and divorced from the discontent generated by poverty or work conditions.

The authority of the state, and the political content of the control exercised (as well as the power differential between disputing parties), is partially obscured by the informal elements of the NJC and the rhetoric of a personal justice. The seemingly voluntary quality of informal negotiated settlements, the absence of an adversarial atmosphere, the presence of an "impartial" mediator who merely wishes to help parties reach a solution, the encouragement given disputants to ventilate their feelings—all contribute to concealing the operation of bureaucratic authority. Just as workers become more dependent on capitalist organization of the work process, so the NJC deprives community members of political competence by transferring power to nondemocratic bureaucracies and experts.

Although mediators define their roles differently—some as catalysts, some as facilitators, some as authority figures—their success is usually measured by the number of disputes they resolve. Sally Merry comments on the evaluation of the three Justice Department NJCs:

> There is no clear evidence in the whole NJC study about the impact on the community. The goal of community development was not seen as a priority. . . . [They could have considered] a greater sense of control and sense of resources available to community residents . . . [or] collective action on community wide problems and people beginning to perceive their problems as community-wide and not individual . . . [or] translation of individual grievances to social action [1980: 56].

Thus, disputants may be led to accept a resolution, but it will not necessarily be one they want or that is in their or the community's interests.

The mediator's pretense of neutrality deflects attention from the underlying interests. Neutrality is not equivalent to refraining from explicitly taking sides, and values may be manifested in ways other than direct advocacy. Mediators bring with them their social class, ethnic heritage, and professional and political ideologies (Starr, 1981). Informal justice does not dispense with norms; they are only articulated less clearly. The unstated assumptions of a professionally trained cadre of middle-class mediators about what constitutes a reasonable claim, the proper use of force, or the content of justice may have a significant bearing on the outcome, particularly when disputants are predominantly poor, inner-city residents.

THE POLITICS OF ACCOMMODATION AND THE NJC

Political conflict deals with the social ends of human activity. The regulation of such conflict by means of accommodation assumes consensus about the values underlying the social order. The legal form is not wholly conducive to accommodation. Adversarial confrontations may raise issues of substantive policy. The capacity of legal conflict to undermine prevailing property rights is limited, but the increasing number of challenges affecting large constituencies—e.g., disposal of toxic wastes, plant shutdowns—constitutes a potential threat to capitalist interests. Legal rules cannot easily be changed, both because they are closely associated with ideals of justice and because constant rule change destroys predictability as well as legitimacy.

The NJC establishes an alternative language for handling conflict by striving for an accommodation between disputants. Adversaries are encouraged to settle the dispute without regard to the issues involved, clearly articulated principles, or even a full airing of ethical questions.

> As rights expand into opaque and technical areas such as the disclosure of finance charges in the consumer credit system and statutory prerequisites to a rent increase when rent control is in effect, the individual has a strong interest in enforcing the letter of the law. In an informal setting, such "technical" rules, which are designed with a larger regulatory purpose in mind, would probably be overlooked as irrelevant to the substance of a particular dispute [Rubinstein, 1976: 81].

The conception of justice lacks social content or ideals. It becomes a bureaucratic procedure for redressing grievances or compensating injuries. Disputants settle their controversies but do not justify their actions according to legal or ethical norms.

Settlement through bargaining restricts the scope of inquiry and thereby reproduces the inequalities of power that enable a local business, for example, to engage in overcharging or otherwise to defraud the consumer without risking a sanction more serious than repayment. Settlement, moreover, is not likely to result in the articulation of general criteria applicable to injurious conduct in the future. The ideology of accommodation conceals patterns of activity that extend beyond the immediate case.

In community disputes accommodation eliminates the language of politics and obscures the clash of real interests. Donald B. Strauss, former president of the American Arbitration Association, is unwittingly revealing on this point.

> With social disputes, there's usually no contractual relationship between the parties. . . . In business you know who the parties in the dispute are and what the basic issues are. Often that's unclear in community conflicts. . . . Perhaps the hardest problem is that you're not dealing with a battery of high-powered lawyers and negotiators; you're dealing with activists who are not coldly logical [Ford Foundation, 1978b: 5].

Like corporate and urban planners, Strauss wishes to rationalize conflict and make it predictable.

Contradictions and Prospects

The NJC, like other forms of social control, exhibits numerous contradictions and therefore cannot permanently contain or reduce class conflict or monitor the working class. Neither law nor decision-making formulas that reify social relations can resolve problems of power. Class antagonisms remain, though they may temporarily be regulated. The contradictions within NJCs will generate further changes in the way in which class conflict is managed.

The first such contradiction concerns the politicization of justice. To the extent that the scope, procedures, and personnel of community justice can be the object of struggle, then people can hope to reappropriate justice from federal planners and professional organizations.

Second, because NJCs are novel institutions, the process of planning them may offer a public forum for questioning the foundations of the legal system and debating the interests behind and consequences of selecting a particular procedure or policy. The NJC must strike a delicate balance between (a) providing a responsive justice that does not generate a demand for democratic control; and (b) managing a complex variety of social populations while retaining their support. It is therefore highly vulnerable to transformation from below that may lead to expansion of extralegal methods of protest and organization of the community around collective interests. At the same time, community residents can learn skills in negotiation, mediation, and advocacy that enhance their legal and political competence.

The outcome of these contradictions is unpredictable; it depends on struggle. Contradictions demonstrate the instability of the system and its susceptibility to challenge. The recapture of justice will require a transformation of the social relations of production and a democratization of economic and social life. But struggle against capitalist power occurs wherever its forms emerge. Neighborhood justice forums represent one important arena.

REFERENCES

Aaronson, David, *et al.* (1977) *The New Justice: Alternatives to Conventional Adjudication.* Washington, D.C.: National Institute of Law Enforcement and Criminal Justice, Law Enforcement Assistance Administration.

Alcaly, Roger (1975) "The Relevance of Marxian Crisis Theory," in David Mermelstein (ed.) *The Economic Crisis Reader.* New York: Vintage.

American Bar Association (1979) "National Conference Examines Mediation and Arbitration Alternatives," 3 *Dispute Resolution* 2.

American Labor and Education Center (1980) "Their Business Is Your Business," 7 *American Labor* 1.

Aronowitz, Stanley (1971) "Law: The Breakdown of Order and Revolution," in Robert Lefcourt (ed.) *Law Against the People.* New York: Vintage.

——— (1973) *False Promises.* New York: McGraw-Hill.

——— (1978) "Marx, Braverman, and the Logic of Capital," 8 *The Insurgent Sociologist* 126.

Auerbach, Jerold S. (1980) "The Two-Track Justice System," *The Nation* (April 5).

Balbus, Isaac (1977) "Commodity Form and Legal Form: An Essay on the 'Relative Autonomy' of the Law," 11 *Law & Society Review* 571.

Bowles, Samuel and Herbert Gintis (1976) *Schooling in Capitalist America.* New York: Basic Books.

Boyte, Harry (1979) "A Democratic Awakening," 10 *Social Policy* 8.

Braverman, Harry (1974) *Labor and Monopoly Capital.* New York: Monthly Review Press.

Budnitz, Mark (1977) "Consumer Dispute Resolution Forums," 13(12) *Trial* 45 (December).

Castells, Manuel (1976) "The Wild City," 4–5 *Kapitalistate* 2.

Chu, Franklin and Sharland Trotter (1974) *The Madness Establishment.* New York: Grossman.

Cloward, Richard and Frances Fox Piven (1972) "The Professional Bureaucracies: Benefit Systems as Influence Systems," in R. Cloward and F. F. Piven (eds.) *The Politics of Turmoil.* New York: Vintage.

Cohen, Stanley (1979) "The Punitive City: Notes On the Dispersal of Social Control," 3 *Contemporary Crises* 339.

Conner, John T. and Milton Mapes, Jr. (1979) "Campaign Underway for National Peace Academy," *Newscope* (Washington, D.C.: National Peace Academy Campaign).

Cook, Royer F., Janice A. Roehl, and David I. Sheppard (1980) *Neighborhood Justice Centers Field Test: Final Evaluation Report.* Washington, D.C.: U.S. Department of Justice, Office of Program Evaluation.

Danzig, Richard (1973) "Toward the Creation of a Complementary Decentralized System of Justice," 26 *Stanford Law Review* 1.

D' Errico, Peter (1978) "A Critique of 'Critical Social Thought about Law' and Some Comments on Decoding Capitalist Culture." Presented at the Second National Conference on Critical Legal Studies, Madison, Wisconsin (November 10–12).

Ditomaso, Nancy (1978) "The Expropriation of the Means of Administration: Class Struggle Over the U.S. Department of Labor," 7 *Kapitalistate* 81.

Donzelot, Jacques (1979) *The Policing of Families.* New York: Pantheon.

Doo, Leigh-Wei (1973) "Dispute Settlement in Chinese-American Communities," 21 *American Journal of Comparative Law* 627.

Downie, Leonard (1971) *Justice Denied: The Case for Reform of the Courts.* New York: Praeger.

Drier, Peter (1979) "The Case for Transitional Reform," 9, no. 4 *Social Policy* 5.

Eaton, John (1966) *Political Economy.* New York: International Publishers.

Edwards, Richard (1978) "Social Relations of Production at the Point of Production," 8 *Insurgent Sociologist* 109.

———— (1979) *Contested Terrain: The Transformation of the Workplace in the Twentieth Century.* New York: Basic Books.

Feeley, Malcolm (1980) *The Process Is the Punishment.* New York: Russell Sage Foundation.

Fisher, Eric (1975) "Community Courts: An Alternative to Conventional Criminal Adjudication," 24 *American University Law Review* 1253.

Florida Supreme Court, Office of the State Courts Administrator (1978) *Citizen Dispute Settlement Guideline Manual.* Tallahassee, Fla.: Office of the State Courts Administrator.

Ford Foundation (1978a) *New Approaches to Conflict Resolution.* New York: Ford Foundation.

———— (1978b) *Mediating Social Conflict.* New York: Ford Foundation.

Foucault, Michel (1977) *Discipline and Punish: The Birth of the Prison.* New York: Pantheon.

Fraser, Andrew (1978) "The Legal Theory We Need Now," 40–41 *Socialist Review* 147.

Galanter, Marc (1974) "Why the 'Haves' Come Out Ahead: Speculations on the Limits of Social Change," 9 *Law & Society Review* 95.

Gartman, David (1978) "Marx and the Labor Process: An Interpretation," 8 *Insurgent Sociologist* 97.

Gintis, Herbert (1980) "Communication and Politics: Marxism and the 'Problem' of Liberal Democracy," 50–51 *Socialist Review* 189.

Gold, David A., Clarence Y. H. Lo, and Erik Olin Wright (1975) "Recent Developments in Marxist Theories of the Capitalist State," 27(5) *Monthly Review* 29 (October), 27(6) *Monthly Review* 36 (November).

Gordon, David (1976) "Capitalist Efficiency and Socialist Efficiency," 28(3) *Monthly Review* 19.

Gordon, David (1977) "Capitalism and the Roots of Urban Crisis," in R. E. Alcaly and D. Mermelstein (eds.) *The Fiscal Crisis of American Cities.* New York: Vintage.

Gorz, Andre (1967) *Strategy for Labor.* Boston: Beacon Press.

———— (1972) "Domestic Contradictions of Advanced Capitalism," in R. Edwards *et al.* (eds.) *The Capitalist System.* Englewood Cliffs, N.J.: Prentice-Hall.

Gough, Ian (1972) "Marx's Theory of Productive and Unproductive Labor," 76 *New Left Review* 47.

Greason, A. L. (1980) "Humanists as Mediators: An Experiment in the Courts of Maine," 66 *American Bar Association Journal* 576.

Green, Mark and Norman Waitzman (1980) "Cost, Benefit, and Class," 7 *Working Papers for a New Society* 39.

Habermas, Jurgen (1973) *Legitimation Crisis.* Boston: Beacon Press.

Harring, Sidney and Lorraine McMullin (1975) "The Buffalo Police 1872–1900: Labor Unrest, Political Power, and the Creation of the Police Institution," 4 *Crime and Social Justice* 5.

Harrington, Christine (1980) "Voluntariness, Consent and Coercion in Adjudicating Minor Disputes: The Neighborhood Justice Center," in J. Brigham and D. Brown (eds.) *Policy Implementation: Choosing between Penalties and Incentives.* Beverly Hills, Calif.: Sage Publications.

Harvey, David (1976) "Labor, Capital, and Class Struggle around the Built Environment in Advanced Capitalist Societies," 6 *Politics and Society* 265.

Hay, Douglas, Peter Linebaugh, John G. Rule, E. P. Thompson, and Cal Winslow (1975) *Albion's Fatal Tree: Crime and Society in Eighteenth-Century England.* New York: Pantheon.

Heydebrand, Wolf (1977) "Organizational Contradictions in Public Bureaucracies: Toward a Marxian Theory of Organizatons," 18 *Sociological Quarterly* 83.

———— (1978) "The Context of Public Bureaucracies: An Organizational Analysis of Federal District Courts," 11 *Law & Society Review* 759.

Hill, Richard Child (1976) "Fiscal Crisis and Political Struggle in the Decaying Central City," 4–5 *Kapitalistate* 31.

Hirschhorn, Larry (1978) "The Political Economy of Social Service Rationalization: A Developmental View," 2 *Contemporary Crises* 63.

Hoff, Bert H. (1974) *Final Evaluation Report: Philadelphia's Arbitration as an Alternative Project.* Washington, D.C.: Blackstone Associates.

Hofrichter, Richard (1977) "Justice Centers Raise Basic Questions," 2 *New Directions in Legal Services* 168.

Hofstadter, Richard (1955) *The Age of Reform*. New York: Vintage.

Horwitz, Morton (1977) *The Transformation of American Law: 1780–1860*. Cambridge, Mass.: Harvard University Press.

Hymer, Stephen (1978) "International Politics/International Economics," 29(10) *Monthly Review* 15.

Institute for Mediation and Conflict Resolution (1974) 1–2 *Conflict*. New York: IMCR.

Jankovic, Ivan (1977) "Labor Market and Imprisonment," 8 *Crime and Social Justice* 17.

Johnson, Earl, Jr., Valerie Kantor, and Elizabeth Schwartz (1977) *Outside the Courts: A Survey of Diversion Alternatives in Civil Cases*. Denver: National Center for State Courts.

Kittrie, Nicholas (1971) *The Right to Be Different*. Baltimore: Penguin.

Law Enforcement Assistance Administration/Action (1980) *Urban Crime Prevention Program: A Guideline Manual*. Washington, D.C.: LEAA/Action.

Lefebvre, Henri (1969) *The Sociology of Marx*. New York: Vintage.

Lively, Martin (1977) *Memorandum to Proposed Neighborhood Justice Center Program Grantees, Grant Application Guidelines and Procedures*. Washington, D.C.: Training and Testing Division, Office of Technology Transfer, Law Enforcement Assistance Administration.

McGillis, Dan (1980a) *Dispute Processing Projects: A Preliminary Directory*. Cambridge, Mass.: Harvard Center for Criminal Justice.

―――― (1980b) "Recent Development in Minor Dispute Processing," 3–4 *Dispute Resolution* 5.

McGillis, Dan and Joan Mullen (1977) *Neighborhood Justice Centers: An Analysis of Potential Models*. Washington, D.C.: Government Printing Office.

McLauchlan, Gregory (1975) "LEAA: A Case Study in the Development of the Social Industrial Complex," 4 *Crime and Social Justice* 15.

Marx, Karl (1970a) *The German Ideology*. New York: International Publishers.

―――― (1970b) *A Contribution to the Critique of Political Economy*. New York: International Publishers.

Merry, Sally E. (1980) "Community Based Evaluation," 3(4) *The Mooter* 53.

Miliband, Ralph (1973) *The State in Capitalist Society*. London: Quartet Books.

Mollenkopf, John (1977) "The Crisis of the Public Sector in American Cities," in R. E. Alcaly and D. Mermelstein (eds.) *The Fiscal Crisis of American Cities*. New York: Vintage.

Neumann, Franz (1957) "The Change in the Function of Law in Modern Society," in *The Democratic and the Authoritarian State*. New York: Free Press.

Newfield, Jack and Paul Dubrul (1977) *The Abuse of Power*. New York: Penguin.

Noble, David (1978) "Social Choice in Machine Design: The Case of Automatically Controlled Machine Tools, and a Challenge for Labor," 8 *Politics and Society* 313.

O'Connor, James (1973) *The Fiscal Crisis of the State*. New York: St. Martin's.

―――― (1978) "The Democratic Movement in the United States," 7 *Kapitalistate* 15.

Offe, Claus (1975) "The Theory of the Capitalist State and the Problem of Policy Formation," in L. Lindberg *et al.* (eds.) *Stress and Contradiction in Modern Capitalism*. Lexington, Mass.: D. C. Heath.

Office of Dispute Settlement, Department of the Public Advocate, State of New Jersey (1979) *Community Dispute Resolution Conference: Summaries*. Trenton, N.J.: Office of Dispute Settlement.

Piven, Frances Fox and Richard Cloward (1971) *Regulating the Poor*. New York: Vintage.

Platt, Anthony (1969) *The Child Savers: The Invention of Delinquency*. Chicago: University of Chicago Press.

Polanyi, Karl (1944) *The Great Transformation*. Boston: Beacon Press.

Poulantzas, Nicos (1975) *Political Power and Social Classes*. London: New Left Books.

Reifner, Udo (1982) "Individualistic and Collective Legalization: Theory and Practice of Legal Advice for Workers in Prefascist Germany," in R. L. Abel (ed.) *The Politics of Informal Justice*, vol. 2: *Comparative Studies*. New York: Academic Press.

Rothman, David J. (1971) *The Discovery of the Asylum: Social Disorder in the New Republic*. Boston: Little, Brown.

Rubinstein, Leonard (1976) "Procedural Due Process and the Limits of the Adversary System," 11 *Harvard Civil Liberties—Civil Rights Law Review* 48.

Sander, Frank E. A. (1976) "Varieties of Dispute Processing," 70 *Federal Rules Decisions* 79.

———— (1977) *Report On the National Conference On Minor Dispute Resolution*. Chicago: American Bar Association.

Santos, Boaventura de Sousa (1977) "The Law of the Oppressed: The Construction and Reproduction of Legality in Parsargada," 12 *Law & Society Review* 3.

Sarat, Austin and Joel Grossman (1975) "Courts and Conflict Resolution," 60 *American Political Science Review* 1200.

Scull, Andrew T. (1977) *Decarceration: Community Treatment and the Deviant—A Radical View*. Englewood Cliffs, N.J.: Prentice-Hall.

Shaiken, Harley (1979) "The Brave New World of Work in Auto," *In These Times* 12 (September 19).

Sheppard, David I., Janice A. Roehl, and Royer F. Cook (1979) *Neighborhood Justice Centers Field Test—Interim Report*. Washington, D.C.: National Institute of Law Enforcement and Criminal Justice, Law Enforcement Assistance Administration.

Shonholtz, Raymond (1977) *Review of Alternative Dispute Mechanisms and a Government Proposal for Neighborhood Justice Centers*. San Francisco: San Francisco Community Board Program.

Silver, Allan (1974) "The Demand for Order in Civil Society: A Review of Some Themes in the History of Urban Crime, Police, and Riot," in R. Quinney (ed.) *Criminal Justice in America: A Critical Understanding*. Boston: Little, Brown.

Singer, Linda R. (1980) "Non-Judicial Dispute Resolution Mechanisms: The Effects on Justice for the Poor," 13 *Clearinghouse Review* 569.

Snyder, Frederick E. (1978) "Crime and Community Mediation—The Boston Experience: A Preliminary Report on the Dorchester Urban Court Program," 1978 *Wisconsin Law Review* 737.

Spitzer, Steven (1975) "Toward a Marxian Theory of Deviance," 22 *Social Problems* 638.

———— (1979) "The Rationalization of Crime Control in Capitalist Society," 3 *Contemporary Crises* 187.

———— (1982) "The Dialectics of Formal and Informal Control," in R. L. Abel (ed.) *The Politics of Informal Justice*, vol. 1: *The American Experience* New York: Academic Press.

Starr, June (1981) "Mediation: Anthropological Perspectives," *American Legal Studies Association Forum* (forthcoming).

Szasz, Thomas S. (1965) *Psychiatric Justice*. New York: Macmillan.

Thompson, E. P. (1975) *Whigs and Hunters*. New York: Pantheon.

Unger, Roberto (1975) *Law in Modern Society*. New York: Free Press.

United States Department of Justice, Community Relations Service (1975) *Annual Report*. Washington, D.C.: Government Printing Office.

United States House of Representatives (1978) Committee on the Judiciary. Subcommittee on Courts, Civil Liberties, and the Administration of Justice. "Dispute Resolution Act." *Hearings*. 95th Congress, 2d Session, July 27 and August 2. Washington, D.C.: Government Printing Office.

———— (1979) Committee on the Judiciary. Subcommittee on Courts, Civil Liberties, and the Administration of Justice and Committee on Interstate and Foreign Commerce. Subcommittee on Consumer Protection and Finance. "Resolution of Minor Disputes." *Joint Hearings*. 96th Congress, 1st session, June 6, 7, 14, and 18. Washington, D.C.: Government Printing Office.

Vera Institute of Justice (1977) *Felony Arrests*. New York: Vera Institute of Justice.

Weinstein, James (1968) *The Corporate Ideal in the Liberal State*. Boston: Beacon Press.

Wolfe, Alan (1977) *The Limits of Legitimacy: Political Contradictions of American Capitalism*. New York: Free Press.

Wright, Erik Olin (1975) "Alternative Perspectives in the Marxist Theory of Accumulation and Crisis," 6 *Insurgent Sociologist* 5.

———— (1978) *Class, Crisis, and the State*. New York: Schocken Books.

Law and Community: The Changing Nature of State Power in Late Capitalism*

BOAVENTURA DE SOUSA SANTOS

The administration of justice in the advanced capitalist countries enters the 1980s with a growing concern for the development of alternatives to the traditional, official court system and formal judicial procedures. Such concern is being translated into reforms and reform proposals that have variously been called informal justice, community justice, delegalization, informalization, conflict resolution, and dispute processing (Felstiner, 1975; Nader and Singer, 1976; Sarat, 1976; Blankenburg and Reifner, 1978; Felstiner and Williams, 1978; Reifner, 1978; Abel, 1979; Galanter, 1979; Merry, 1979; Nader, 1979; Harrington, 1980; Singer, 1980; Felstiner *et al.*, 1981; Garth, 1982; Hofrichter, 1982).

In the following I will offer a theoretical analysis of these trends. I will start by presenting in brief outline a theoretical model of legal domination in the

*This is a revision of a paper presented in Norway at the Scandinavian–American Exchange on Conflict Resolution, sponsored by the Scandinavian Research Council for Criminology, June 1980. Another version was published in 8 *International Journal of the Sociology of Law* 379 (1980). Copyright by Academic Press, Inc. (London) Ltd. I would like to thank Maureen Cain and Richard Abel for their comments on the earlier draft.

249

capitalist state in order to provide the background for analysis. At the end of this chapter I will try to measure the impact of current reforms and reform proposals on the nature of state power and legal domination.

THE LAW OF THE CAPITALIST STATE

In historical terms the capitalist state and its legality owe much to the precapitalist state forms, if only because the establishment of capitalist social relations often took place under the rule of noncapitalist states and noncapitalist legality. But this does not preclude the possibility of establishing structural relations and homologies between the capitalist state (the "political" realm) and the capitalist nonstate (the "social" and "economic" realms), which together constitute bourgeois society. Furthermore, these structural relations—which on the "surface of bourgeois society" (the realm of "Freedom, Equality, Property and Bentham") (Marx, 1976: 280) appear as disparities and contradictions—find their theoretical coherence in a logical derivation of the state form from capitalist social relations.[1] Thus the capitalist state form and capitalist social relations are united in specific structural relations that develop and change in concrete historical situations and processes.

As an entity peculiar to bourgeois society the capitalist state is the political form of capitalist social relations. Its basic characteristic is its *externality* to these relations that, on the surface, are defined as "economic."[2] However, the externality of the political is the condition of its *immanence* within capitalist social relations. This occurs by reason of a double contradiction in the process of capital accumulation and capital valorization; the *real presence* of noncapitalist elements in the reproduction of capitalist relations (aspects of social reproduction within bourgeois society that are not subjected to the law of value) and the *fictive absence* on the surface of bourgeois society of the logic of capital (exploitation as extraction of surplus value through the use of labor power appropriated in the market by means of a contract between free proprietors).

This double contradiction develops historically in the context of two struggles, both inherent in the capitalist mode of production: those between capital and labor and those among individual capitals. These contradictions and struggles reproduce themselves inside the state. The major function of the capitalist state is

---

[1] The fertility of this three-step analysis (historical, structural, and morphological) depends on a careful articulation of the different partial analytical perspectives if it is not to fall prey to the distortions of empiricist historicism, ahistorical structuralism, or abstract theoreticism.

[2] This analysis starts from Marx's work, particularly from *Das Kapital* (1976) and *Grundrisse* (1973). E. B. Pashukanis (1978) developed it in his theory of capitalist legality, and it has dominated the German Marxist debate on the state in recent years (see Brandes *et al.*, 1977; Holloway and Picciotto, 1978).

precisely to "disperse" such contradictions and struggles into an apparently chaotic sequence of administrative failures and successes, honored and violated
political compromises, and acts of facilitation and repression (whether enforced
or merely announced). It performs this function through a conglomeration of its
apparatuses and quasi-apparatuses, measures and nonmeasures, and positive and
negative selections.

The dispersal of contradictions is a complex phenomenon that operates
through a set of mechanisms involving integration, trivialization, neutralization,
and exclusion, according to the historical conditions and specific forms of class
struggle. Since state action is subordinated to the logic of capital (though this
subordination is never homogeneous, stable, or without tension), the contradictions can never be resolved but are at most kept latent, and even such latency is
neither general nor permanent. On the contrary, at each moment the state has to
concentrate itself in those areas of social life where the intensification of class
struggles has become disruptive and where, accordingly, a more intense activa-
tion of dispersal mechanisms has become an urgent political task. This sectoral
concentration implies that other areas of social life will consequently experience
a more diffuse state "intervention." Depending on the specific historical conditions, this fact may in itself contribute to the intensification of class struggle in
the latter areas with the result that, sooner or later, the state will be forced to
concentrate its dispersal mechanisms there. The capitalist state is thus compelled
to engage in constant shifts without ever achieving global pacification. This
process, though chaotic on the surface of social life, develops according to an
internal logic that I call *the negative dialectics of the state* (Santos, 1973: 74).

The form of the capitalist state as external is the logical condition for its
performance of the function of dispersing contradictions. But just because the
form manifests itself only through the functions and structures it preconditions, it
should not be misperceived as a static entity; for these very structures and
functions are performed and developed in history. The capitalist state is thus a
flexible form that allows for structural and historical specification and, as such, is
an object of struggle. At the structural level, the historicity of the state form
means that the capitalist state is not monolithic but rather is a fragmented and
asymmetrical structure (or set of structures). This fragmentation and asymmetry
is reproduced throughout the state apparatus and in its internal relations.

The structural analysis of law and the legal "system" must start from the fact
that the capitalist legal form is external to *both* capitalist social relations (the
"economic" realm) *and* the state (the "political" realm). In each case externality
is the condition of immanence and therefore not inconsistent with the state
monopoly of the production of legality. This monopoly is both fragmented and
asymmetrical, as is the legality it produces.[3] Those characteristics are revealed in

[3]Liberal theorists have always criticized the idea that the state has, or should have, a monopoly

the articulations among the basic structural components of capitalist legality: rhetoric, bureaucracy, and violence. Each is a form of communication and a strategy of decision making. *Rhetoric* is based on persuasion and the production of voluntary compliance through mobilization of the argumentative potential of socially accepted verbal and nonverbal sequences and artifacts. *Bureaucracy* is based on authoritative imposition through the production and mobilization of the demonstrative potential of professional knowledge, general formal rules, and hierarchically organized procedures. *Violence* is based on the use or threat of physical force.

Taken separately, none of these elements is specific to capitalist state legality since all of them existed in one form or another in the precapitalist state. What is new is the complex structural articulation among them. Each element has its own structure and discourse. Every structure and discourse has its own internal logic and organizational principle. But they are interrelated in multiple ways. Indeed, what we call "law" and "legal system" in capitalist societies is a terminal concept that both expresses and hides the complex articulations among the partial structures and their discourses. These articulations are both fragmented and asymmetrical as well as complex and dynamic, and these characteristics account for what is frequently referred to, without adequate specification, as the *ambiguity* of the law in capitalist societies. I will distinguish three major types of structural articulation: quantitative covariation, geopolitical combination, and qualitative interpenetration.

Quantitative Covariation

Based on the rich tradition of legal anthropological and legal historical research and on a systematic comparison between the totality of informal and unofficial juridical and judicial processes inside a squatter settlement in Rio de Janeiro on one side, and the official legal system of the Brazilian capitalist state on the other (Santos, 1974; 1977), I postulate the following relationships: (a) The higher the level of bureaucratic institutionalization of juridical production, the

---

over the production of legality (see Galanter, 1981), but both supporters and critics of the idea have started from a wrong formulation of the problem. Firstly, the state monopoly of legality is a question not of logic but of structure and history. This is crucial to an understanding of the early period of the establishment and reproduction of capitalist social relations. Second, the monopoly is not equally distributed across legal fields. The recognition of an "indigenous law" does not contradict the idea of the state monopoly if it can be demonstrated that the logic of state legality dominates the operation of the "indigenous law." In this sense, the existence of a state monopoly of legality in capitalist societies does not preclude the existence of legal pluralism. In my own research I have been trying to draw attention to situations of legal pluralism in capitalist societies in which the unofficial legality is subjected to the political and legal domination of the capitalist state (Santos, 1974; 1977; 1979).

smaller the rhetorical space of the legal structure and discourse (and vice versa); and (*b*) the more powerful the instruments of violence in the service of juridical production, the smaller the rhetorical space of the legal structure and discourse (and vice versa) (Santos, 1980: 59).[4] If we look at the development of capitalist legality in the light of this correlation it seems clear that legal development has involved a gradual retraction of the rhetorical element of the law and a gradual expansion of its bureaucratic and violent elements (Santos, 1980).[5]

Geopolitical Combination[6]

The fragmentation and asymmetry of the state structure and the constraints under which the dispersal of contradictions is performed account for the fact that political domination is not equally distributed across the universe of social relations. In some areas (which I call the core) the state concentrates its investment in dispersal mechanisms, preferring neutralization and exclusion; there state and nonstate are sharply distinct. In others (the periphery)[7] the state diffuses its investment in political domination, preferring to use the mechanisms of trivialization and integration; there state and nonstate may hardly be distinguishable at times.[8]

[4]The use of methodological tools developed by positivist (structural functionalist) social science in a Marxist analysis represents an attempt to create a new working relationship between the two analytic traditions. Without abandoning the logic of Marxist theory scholars seek to open new analytic fields that are more rigorously mapped out by employing the methodological contributions of positivist social science. The objective is to jolt Marxist thinking out of stagnation that resulted from naive theoretical purism and anachronistic conceptions of political strategy (see Keat and Urry, 1975; Wright, 1978: 9).

[5]Though the relations between bureaucracy and violence in capitalist legality are still to be determined in detail, it is important to recognize that they have developed in the same direction. This accounts for the illusion that the capitalist state is less violent than previous state formations (an illusion that is one of the foundations of liberal political theory).

[6]This expression is meant as a suggestive metaphor justified by the (also metaphorical) underdevelopment of theory on this topic.

[7]The distinction between core and periphery is not meant to imply that the former is more important for global political domination. The overdevelopment of the state at the core probably cannot be understood without its underdevelopment at the periphery. Nevertheless, the distinction remains essential to an understanding of the bond between the capitalist state and the working classes and the relationship between repression and legitimation in its synchronic and historical variation. This is not inconsistent with the fact that, from a strategic point of view, the core defines the periphery and not vice versa. Since the state invests most of its institutional resources in the core, it finds there a kind of reserve repressive armory to be activated in particular crisis situations.

[8]Here, again, the historicity of the state form is revealed. Though that form is always anchored in the contradictory logic of capitalist social relations, it undergoes constant historical transformation and can experience considerable internal differentiation. Thus, in some areas it may appear as a kind of superstate, whereas in others it resembles a watered-down state.

The allocation of political domination reproduces itself in the legal "system," which is also unequally distributed across the universe of social relations. My contention is that until now rhetoric has tended to dominate in the legal periphery, whereas bureaucracy and violence have tended to dominate in the core.

Structural Interpenetration

In its broadest definition, structural interpenetration consists of the presence of a given (dominant) structure inside another (dominated) structure. Although in the preceding types of structural articulation each of the three components of the legal system is conceived as being autonomous with respect to the others, now autonomy becomes susceptible to variation—the degree to which a given structure or discourse reproduces itself in (and in the terms of) another structure or discourse. This type of structural articulation is both richer and less studied than the others, not only because it refers to a structural movement that can be detected only across a long .historical period but also because it involves the analysis of complex qualitative processes.

The relations between oral and written culture provide an illustration. These two forms of cultural production have different structural characteristics (Ong, 1971; 1977; Santos, 1980). For instance, oral culture is concerned with the conservation of knowledge, whereas written culture emphasizes innovation. Oral culture is fully collectivized, whereas written culture allows for individualization. The basic unit of oral culture is the formula, whereas the basic unit of written culture is the word. If we look at modern cultural history in the light of these distinctions it becomes clear that until the fifteenth century European culture, and hence European legal culture, was predominantly oral. From then on written culture gradually expanded, and oral culture declined. But until the eighteenth century the structure of written culture was still being consolidated and remained permeated by the internal logic of the oral culture. In other words, we wrote as we talked. (I think this can be detected in the legal writing of the time.) From the eighteenth century until the first decades of our present century the written word dominated our culture. But then the radio and the audiovisual mass media rediscovered the word's sound, and we entered a period that Ong has called "secondary orality." But this reoralization of culture is different from the previous oral culture in that the structures of the written culture permeate, penetrate, and contaminate the new orality. In other words, we talk as we write.

Based on my research on the sociology of legal rhetoric, I have come to the conclusion that in the development of capitalist legality thus far, rhetoric has been not only quantitatively reduced and peripheralized but also internally and qualitatively "contaminated" by the dominant structures of bureaucracy and violence (Santos, 1980: 101).[9]

I believe that the history of the capitalist state legal system in the last 200 years has been characterized by the displacement and domination of rhetoric by bureaucracy and violence in each of the three types of structural articulation I have identified.[10]

Law, Informality, and Community

Using this theoretical model I will now try to analyze the current legal and judicial reforms that fall under the heading of informalization and community justice. These reforms, though diverse, tend to focus on dispute processing and conflict resolution and to share the following characteristics:

1. Emphasis on mutually agreed outcomes rather than on strict normative correctness
2. Preference for decision through mediation or conciliation rather than adjudication
3. Recognition of the competence of the parties to protect their own interests and to conduct their own defense in a setting that is deprofessionalized and a process that is conducted in ordinary language
4. Choice of a nonjurist as the third party (though one with some legal training) whether or not elected by the community or group to be served by the conflict resolution institution
5. Little if any coercion that the institution can mobilize in its own name

Once in operation these reforms may involve a more or less extensive change in the legal structure.

Let me start my analysis with the first type of articulation, quantitative covariation. The reforms (both those that have been implemented and those that are merely proposed) appear to employ a mode of juridical production dominated by rhetoric. Indeed, widespread legal knowledge and language competence allows the dispute institution to use an argumentative, persuasive discourse in order to

---

[9]"Contamination" or "infiltration" is detected through a close analysis of the types of arguments that become more persuasive and thus more capable of eliciting voluntary compliance. Such "contamination" will exist if it is shown that arguments subsidiary to the logic of bureaucracy or violence tend to dominate the rhetorical discourse. An earlier attempt to offer sociological and psychological explanations for variation in the persuasive power of different rhetorical arguments is Apostel (1963).

[10]This development is neither linear nor is it identical in different capitalist states. It represents a general trend.

gain acceptance of the outcome by both sides. Conversely, both bureaucracy and violence appear as recessive or retracted structures. Because they seem to be withdrawing from the foreground of legal domination they have occupied so prominently for the last 200 years, this may mistakenly be conceived as delegalization, but only by forgetting that rhetoric is as inherent in legal domination as bureaucracy or violence. Reading these reforms in the light of the first structural articulation, I am led to the conclusion that legal rhetoric is reemerging from two centuries of lethargy. But the importance of such reemergence depends upon the range of the reforms and whether they are carried out without major distortions. It is still too early to answer these questions.

Because the impact of these reforms cannot be determined exclusively at the level of quantitative covariation, it is necessary to look to the second type of structural articulation, geopolitical combination. If the rhetorical space of the legal structure is expanding, is this occurring in the core or the periphery? And what is happening in those legal fields and areas of political domination where legal rhetoric is not widening?

The answer to these questions involves complex comparisons across legal fields and corresponding areas of political domination. Here I will restrict myself to contrasting reforms in the areas of informalization, community involvement, and delegalization on the one hand and those in the field of criminal justice and penal policy on the other. The first striking contrast (which, amazingly, has hardly been noticed) is that these two fields are undergoing opposite or contradictory transformations. The former, as I have mentioned, is dominated by a therapeutic model and a treatment ethic that emphasizes consensus and persuasion, integration rather than exclusion, the regulation and normalization of behavior instead of punishment, mutually satisfying outcomes rather than strict observation of legal rules. In the latter we are witnessing the reemergence of what has been called the justice or the neoclassical model (Clarke, 1978; Mathiesen, 1980; Christie, forthcoming),[11] which is grounded upon a radical opposition to the treatment ethic. The latter is seen as "a logical result of the individual responsibility ethic in an age of scientism, the welfare state, consensus politics and reformism." In opposition to all this, the justice model calls for: "a return of power to the judiciary; an end to treatment and its substitution by punishment as desert; increased concern for certainty and for legal rights; greater emphasis on the criminal act rather than on the actor" (Clarke, 1978: 28).

This makes clear the opposition between current developments in the two fields. But even more striking is that both tendencies are ideologically heterogeneous—sponsored by groups with mutually hostile ideologies and sociopolitical objectives. In the informalization field Richard Abel has shown

---

[11]The designation "neoclassicism" derives from the emphasis on a return to classical principles of imprisonment.

how conservatives, liberals, and even radicals may support the same reforms (Abel, 1979: 29–31). In the field of criminal justice we find considerable agreement between the *Struggle for Justice* and the Schwendingers on one side and A. Von Hirsch, Fogel, and R. Hood on the other (Clarke, 1978: 28).

But it is not sufficient merely to acknowledge this opposition. It is also necessary to analyze how the two developments are structurally combined. My hypothesis is that bureaucracy and violence are being concentrated in those legal fields that correspond to the core areas of political domination, where their major function is to define the enemy (not necessarily a class enemy) *as* an enemy and to disperse that enemy through mechanisms of neutralization and exclusion; whereas rhetoric is being expanded in legal fields that correspond to the periphery of political domination, where their major function is to define the enemy *as* nonenemy and to disperse that nonenemy through mechanisms of trivialization and integration.[12]

If this hypothesis holds true, the different developments in the legal "system" are both unequal and combined into a larger whole that cannot be explained by either the ideologies that justify them or the policy orientations that guide them. The geopolitical distribution across legal fields of the three elementary components of the legal structure—rhetoric, bureaucracy, and violence—will enable us to develop a cognitive map of their appropriateness to the areas of political domination—a zoning system as it were.

The geopolitical distribution of legal structures will also enable us to see the question of access to law in a different light. This question cannot be dealt with in monolithic terms because access to law varies with combinations among the three structures. For instance, improved access in a legal field dominated by rhetoric may be accompanied (or compensated) by diminished access in a field dominated by bureaucracy or violence. If the latter corresponds to a core area of

---

[12]This does not mean that the entire legal field of criminal justice and penal policy, and it alone, corresponds to the core of political domination. On the contrary, all traditional legal fields (labor law, contracts, torts, criminal justice, etc.) are heterogeneous in that they cut across the two poles of political domination, and such heterogeneity is reflected in the unequal distribution of rhetoric, bureaucracy, and violence inside each of them. The distinctions among legal fields lie rather in their unequal degree of correspondence to the two areas of political domination, so that some are situated more in the core and others more in the periphery.

The reasons for such differences can be obtained only through detailed historical analysis, which cannot be restricted to capitalist development. Under present conditions, the field of criminal justice and penal policy in the capitalist states tends to be located predominantly in the core of political domination. But this does not mean that the field "belongs" exclusively to this area of political domination, as shown by the fact that some of the informalization and delegalization reforms are also taking place within it. Moreover, it is not impossible that noncriminal legal fields may be located in the core of political domination in the future.

This analytic strategy may also be useful in comparing different states at a given historical moment. It might be hypothesized, for instance, that labor law occupies the core of political domination in one state but the periphery in another.

political domination, the example will show how an expansion of access may actually be a restriction—a grant of access that forecloses it.

The geopolitical distribution of legal structures is still of importance in determining the diversified nature of, and differential accessibility to, legal discourse because the latter varies with those structural combinations. In a combination dominated by rhetoric, legal discourse tends to be based on commonsense knowledge and to be framed in ordinary language; if bureaucracy and violence dominate, that discourse tends to be based on legal scientific knowledge and to be couched in technical language. As a result, some areas of legal discourse are more accessible or penetrable than others, characterized by shared rather than secret knowledge.

The analysis of current experiments with informal or community justice in the light of the two types of articulation already mentioned leads to the following hypotheses: First, such reforms involve an expansion of legal rhetoric. The more a legal field corresponds to a peripheral area of political domination, the greater the tendency for the expansion of rhetoric to concentrate there. Second, this expansion of legal rhetoric is combined with an expansion of bureaucracy and violence. The more a legal field corresponds to a core area of political domination, the greater the tendency for the expansion of bureaucracy and violence to concentrate there.

But these hypotheses still fail to capture the full significance of current developments. It is therefore necessary to take into consideration the third type of structural articulation, interpenetration. The question to be asked is this: Once the space of a given structure is defined, is it possible to detect the presence of other (dominant) structures inside that space? Is there structural "infiltration" or "contamination"? This is important because a given "contaminated" structure may be used to secure the expansion of another "contaminating" structure even while the latter seems to be retracting. More concretely: Is it possible to see signs in current informalization reforms that bureaucracy and violence are expanding within the form of legal rhetoric? With respect to bureaucracy, this type of structural articulation would lead us to analyze the types of arguments that tend to be persuasive in informal settings in order to see if reasoning that depends on bureaucratic logic and discourse is being advanced in the nonbureaucratic setting. For instance, one characteristic of informal dispute processing is that the third party (judge, mediator, or arbitrator) is not a jurist or legal professional. We therefore refer to such a third party as a "layperson." But he or she may still be a professional and be employed in some other state bureaucracy. And since all state bureaucracies are structurally homologous and have the same operational logic, the latter may filter down into the argumentative discourse in the informal setting.

With respect to violence, some reformers have claimed that disputes arising out of "ongoing relationships" are more suitable for processing in an informal setting, which may draw upon the sanctioning power inherent in such relationships (Harrington, 1980: 134). One way of interpreting this phenomenon is that the state is mobilizing "native" coercive power, integrating it in the overall structure of state political and legal domination. Once integrated, this "native" power loses its autonomy and is put to work in a peripheral area of political domination. In this capacity it functions as a kind of state-produced nonstate power, penetrating the argumentative discourse and mutually agreed decisions in the informal setting.

Another symptom of violence infiltrating or contaminating legal rhetoric may be seen in the way in which cases are referred to community justice. Christine Harrington conducted an empirical study of the Kansas City Neighborhood Justice Center and concluded:

> an examination of the sanctions and incentives to participate in NJC suggests that disputants are more likely to participate in mediation when there are strong ties with the official remedy system [Ibid.: 153].

If these interpretations are correct, I would conclude that legal rhetoric tends to expand only in the peripheral areas of political domination and, even there, is a recessive structure infiltrated by the logic of bureaucracy and violence.

These very tentative ideas on the three modes of structural articulation have the merit of leading us: (*a*) to analyze partial or sectoral developments and reforms in the light of the global legal structure; (*b*) to conceive this global structure as highly contradictory and unstable and internally asymmetrical in its correspondence with the different areas of political domination; and (*c*) to recognize that resistance to such domination must also be highly diversified, especially if it is to be a global resistance.

Since, in this conception, any reform, however partial, always involves changes in the overall structure of domination, the next question is this: If informalization and community reforms proceed, what will be their impact on legal and political domination and thus on the nature of capitalist state power?

THE CHANGING NATURE OF STATE POWER

It has been argued that the reforms under analysis serve a triple objective: They help reduce the fiscal crisis; they cushion the impact of a possible loss in the legitimacy of the capitalist state resulting from cuts in state expenditure; and they stabilize power relations in society.

The fiscal crisis argument is well known. The advanced capitalist countries in the 1960s witnessed the emergence of new and more advanced forms of class struggle. Highly mobilized grass roots movements brought new pressures upon the state, which invariably responded with an expansion of social rights and a consequent increase in state expenditures. Though obtained through struggle, the state expansion was made possible (and probably necessitated) by the conditions of capital valorization in this period (which called for an increase in unproductive spending). As a result of this state expansion, the relations of repression and legitimation between the capitalist state and the working class changed significantly. In the early 1970s the conditions of capital valorization started changing. Since state intervention is subordinated to the logic of capital, the state expansion carried over from the previous decade was soon redefined as overexpansion, and the bourgeoisie insistently demanded that it be reduced to a "functional" level. In the realm of law and justice, legalization was reinterpreted as overlegalization, accessibility as overaccessibility. The court system was said to be a costly bureaucratic apparatus; informalization–delegalization reforms would make spending cuts possible in this area by relieving the judiciary of conflicts that could be processed in informal settings at a lower cost.

Two objections can be raised to the fiscal crisis argument. First, it assumes that informal justice is less expensive than formal justice, which is debatable. Second, it explains adopted solutions by their external necessity and not by their internal logic; in other words, it fails to explain why a specific spending cut is chosen instead of any other.

However, the fiscal crisis analysis becomes much more persuasive when coupled with the second argument. Since the state expansion generally took the form of new legal rights, any spending cuts will produce changes in the relations of repression and legitimation between the capitalist state and the working classes. Faced with a legitimacy crisis the state resorts to informalization reforms (and to the spending cuts they permit) because they appeal to popular participation, self-government, a renaissance of real communities, consensual social life, and the struggle against bureaucracy and therefore have the potential to compensate for the loss of legitimacy resulting from spending cuts.

But this argument proves too much: The capacity of these reforms to legitimate the state by appeal to transcendental values is checked by the logic of the reproduction of political domination in the capitalist state. This leads to the third argument—that these reforms stabilize power relations in society. Abel has reminded us that in the liberal state powerful institutions have to be formal institutions (Abel, 1979: 38). Indeed, the so-called absolutist state ceased to be absolutist (and became liberal) when formal law became absolute. In the formulation advanced earlier in the chapter, bureaucracy and violence have been developing hand in hand ever since. Informalization thus means powerlessness. It will help to stabilize social relations since no dramatic changes can be expected from institutions or settings that must be oriented to consensus and harmony because of the limits on their coercive powers.

Many disputes that are intended to be processed by the new informal settings share two characteristics: There are structural differences in social power of the parties, and they occur repeatedly. Landlord–tenant and merchant–consumer disputes are examples. In such cases mediation or arbitration becomes repressive because the setting lacks coercive power to neutralize the power differences between the parties. Repressive mediation leads to repressive consensus, which, I submit, will more and more characterize the exercise of capitalist state power.

In this sense informalization means disarming and neutralizing. Poulantzas (1973) has emphasized that the major function of the capitalist state is to disorganize the working classes through the legal form.

What is new in the current informalization and community justice programs is that whereas the oppressed classes have hitherto been disorganized at the individual level, as citizens, voters, or welfare recipients, in the future they will be disorganized at the community level. I suggest that state-sponsored community organization will be the specific form of disorganization in late capitalism.

Community production of services, whether these involve justice, legality, social control, or regulation, is a nonautonomous mode of production. At most it has a merely negative autonomy—the freedom not to depend on the state for the performance of certain services. There is no positive autonomy—the capacity to struggle for measures and services that, though structurally possible, are functionally incompatible with the corporate interests of the dominant class.

The preceding analysis does not go deep enough in identifying the basic mechanism through which the nature of state power may be changing before our eyes. Bourgeois society is based on a dualistic power conception—two basic modes or forms of power that, though complementary, have been kept separate and even treated as mutually exclusive. I call them cosmic and chaosmic power. The first is centralized, "physically" located in formal institutions, and hierarchically organized. This is the traditional conception of juridical power. It is a macropower that, since the seventeenth century, has found its most complete embodiment in state power. The second is the power emerging wherever social relations and interactions are unequal, in the family, at school, on the street, etc. It is a micropower. It is eccentric, atomized, multiple, without specific location, mobile—in sum, chaotic.[13]

Liberal political theory is based on a militant refusal to recognize this dualistic power structure by reducing it to a unity, namely, state or juridical power. And

[13]What I call chaosmic power echoes Foucault (1971; 1976). But whereas he identifies it as the general form of power and denies the existence of the centralized top-down power (what I call cosmic), in my conception the coexistence of these two forms of power, and the dialectical relations between them are what constitute the "deep structure" of social domination in modern societies. Foucault merely inverts liberal political theory (which identifies cosmic power as the general form) and therefore remains inside its intellectual universe, no matter how radical his formulation.

this, of course, is the source of the distinction between state and civil society. The state is the realm of power and violence, whereas civil society is the realm of freedom and equality.

The present, deep crisis of this theory is the result of two changed perceptions that have been stimulated by transformations in the accumulation process. First, there are two forms of power corresponding to the two basic forms of inequality: macro (or class) and micro (or interactional). Second, these forms of power, though structurally very different, are complementary—each is made tolerable (and is reproduced) by the other.

The proliferation of informalization and community justice reforms (which have counterparts in many other areas of social life)[14] may signify changes in the nature of state (cosmic) power and its relation to the chaosmic power inherent in the social relations of civil society. To the extent that the state tries to coopt the sanctioning power inherent in ongoing social relationships, it is explicitly connecting its cosmic power to the chaosmic power, which until now had been outside its reach. Insofar as the state thereby manages to control actions and social relations that cannot be directly regulated by formal law, and insofar as the entire social environment of the dispute is integrated in its processing, to that extent the state is indeed expanding. *And it is expanding through a process that, on the surface, appears to be a process of retraction.* What appears as *delegalization* is actually *relegalization.* In other words, the state is expanding *in the form of civil society,* and that is why the dichotomy of state and civil society is no longer theoretically useful, if ever it was.[15] And because the state expands in the form of civil society, social control may be exercised in the form of social participation, violence in the form of consensus, class domination in the form of community action. In other words, state power expands through a kind of indirect rule.[16]

[14]It seems to me that in many other areas of social interaction—such as education, health, science, and culture—a parallel development of structural fragmentation and asymmetry can be detected, together with the emergence of a core and a periphery. In the core there is a high level of investment in technological and institutional resources, whose sophistication becomes the condition of elitism and exclusion; in the periphery low levels of investment become the condition of participation and accessibility.

[15]As Marx showed, the distinction between state and civil society is the ultimate mystification of capitalist social relations. It seems to me, however, that in the early stages of capitalism this distinction corresponded, even if only marginally, to contemporary conditions of the establishment and reproduction of capitalist social relations. Civil society *created* the state as its own *opposition,* the mystification lying not in the creation itself but in the *opposition.* Today, I am arguing, the mystification is doubled. The capitalist state is somehow creating civil society as its opposition, and now the mystification lies in both the *creation* and the *opposition.* We are probably witnessing the development of a secondary civil society (state-produced nonstate areas of social life).

[16]Even if they are used only as analogical starting points, the reasons and conditions that led the colonial state to adopt indirect rule deserve close attention since they may help to ellucidate current changes in political domination.

"Native" processes, interactions, atmospheres, and environments are overintegrated in the global strategy of capitalist political domination. On the surface such *overintegration* is negated (hidden) by the *undercodification* made possible by the extensive use of legal rhetoric (which mobilizes commonsense knowledge and ordinary language). This transformation of political domination is also relevant for an understanding of the significance of the fiscal crisis and the crisis of legitimacy. As already mentioned, under conditions of stagnating accumulation the bond between the capitalist state and the working classes runs the risk of collapsing. But the state may repair its legitimacy not only through material expansion (by delivering goods and services) but also through the production of symbols and ideals that make a radically different social life appear either impossible or irrelevant. By appealing to transcendental values, the reforms under analysis will contribute to this shift in the strategy of legitimation. If these reforms signal a general trend, the state under the late capitalism of the 1980s and 1990s will probably survive and expand more through the production of symbols than through the production of goods and services.

The state is therefore reaching far beyond its present formal apparatus; in the process it may become more informal and less organized. State and nonstate may look more and more alike. Indeed, it is not absurd to predict the development of a face-to-face state. The formal institutions that, as Foucault has shown, have always been the "physical" *locus* of state power recently have been criticized and even undermined (Foucault, 1975; Illich, 1973). This movement has its material base in state participation in reproduction of labor power (a process that has become more prolonged and costly and has led to unprecedented institutional growth) under conditions of increasing structural unemployment. The resultant antiinstitutional movements may indeed help to relieve the fiscal crisis, provided that the state develops alternative methods for the production and reproduction of power. I would even speculate that the relations between cosmic and chaosmic power will change in the future, as the latter progressively displaces the former, with a resultant transformation in the relations between core and periphery areas, leading to an acentric domination that has no periphery. In this case there will be a transfer of power from formal institutions to informal networks. Social networks will then become the dominant unit for the production and reproduction of power—a source of power that is diffuse and interstitial, and therefore is as familiar as it is remote.

A CONCLUDING NOTE ON POWER, KNOWLEDGE, AND UTOPIA

Regardless of the accuracy of such long-range speculations, I have tried to show in this chapter that reforms in the field of law and justice may be manifestations of power dislocations occurring inside the capitalist state and that these dislocations result in increasing asymmetry in the structure of capitalist political domination: a high investment of formal institutional resources in the core and an expansion of informal, network-based resources in the periphery. This increasing asymmetry reproduces itself inside the legal system through the dynamics of the multiple structural articulations among rhetoric, bureaucracy, and violence.

Since power structures are always connected with structures of knowledge, we can predict that changes will occur in legal knowledge as a result of power dislocations inside the capitalist state. As state power becomes more heterogeneous, so does the knowledge through which it operates. A new form of lay, commonsensical knowledge will emerge alongside scientific, professional, disciplinary knowledge (Foucault, 1975, has pointedly noted the double connotation of "discipline" as both science and social control). As the increasing asymmetry of political domination reproduces itself in the increasing asymmetry of cognitive domination, a tendency will develop for a high investment of professional disciplinary knowledge in the core areas of political domination (which, for that reason, will become less and less accessible) and an expansion of nonprofessional, "trivial" knowledge in the peripheral areas of political domination.

In light of such tendencies there is no reason to think that capitalist domination can be effectuated only through professional scientific knowledge. On the contrary, if power is displaced from institutions to networks, there will be a parallel shift from scientific to nonscientific knowledge and thus from scientific legal knowledge to nonscientific legal knowledge. The new nonscientific, nondisciplinary knowledge will not be captured by the polarity of truth and falsity, which has been the basic matrix of the scientific paradigm, but will rather point (like utopia) toward a polarity of liberation and oppression. This would be the ultimate crisis for the scientific paradigm and the theory of knowledge upon which bourgeois society has based the permanent technological revolutionization of production and the concomitant degradation of the labor process.

It would be a gross mistake, however, to analyze current reforms as sheer manipulation and state conspiracy. In the particular case I have dealt with—informalization and community justice—the central contradiction is that the reform movement is associated with the powerful symbols of participation, self-government, and real community. This is its utopian transcendental element. It is true that these symbols are imprisoned within an overall strategy of social control. But though their form is distorted, the value of these symbols is nevertheless confirmed since even state-controlled community justice requires a certain amount of popular participation. It thus contains a potentially liberating element, if one that can be unleashed and made effective only through an autonomous political movement of the dominated classes.[17]

[17]In order to inspire a collective movement, the broadest political objectives must be translatable

Let me illustrate this with an example from another field. I believe there is a structural homology between contemporary experiments with informal and community justice and mass or popular culture. One could say of informal and community justice what Fredric Jameson says about the Frankfurt School's critique of mass culture. Mass culture is not to be grasped as an "empty distraction or false consciousness but rather as a transformational work on social and political anxieties and fantasies which must then have some effective presence in the mass cultural text in order subsequently to be managed or repressed" (Jameson, 1979: 141). Similarly, we cannot do justice to informalization or community reforms "unless we are willing to concede the presence within them of a more positive function as well, that is, an utopian or transcendental potential" (*Ibid.*: 144).

Community justice cannot be ideological without at some time being implicitly utopian. It cannot manipulate unless it offers some "genuine shred of content as a fantasy bribe to the community members about to be manipulated" (*Ibid.*). Resistance against manipulation must start from that genuine shred of content.

REFERENCES

Abel, R. (1979) "Delegalization: A Critical Review of Its Ideology, Manifestations, and Social Consequences," in E. Blankenburg, E. Klausa, and H. Rottleuthner (eds.) *Alternative Rechtsformen und Alternativen zum Recht.* Opladen: Westdeutscher Verlag (*Jahrbuch für Rechtssoziologie und Rechtstheorie,* band 6).

Apostel, L. (1963) "Rhétorique, psycho-sociologie et logique," in Centre National Belge de Recherches de Logique, *La théorie de l'argumentation.* Louvain: Nauwelaerts.

Blankenburg, E. and U. Reifner (1978) "Rechtshilfe als Teil eines Beratungssystems." Discussion paper, Internationales Institut für Management und Verwaltung, Berlin.

Brandes, V., J. Hoffman, *et al.* (eds.) (1977) *Handbuch 5 Staat.* Frankfurt: Europäische Verlaganstalt.

Christie, N. (forthcoming) "Limits to Pain." Unpublished manuscript.

Clarke, D. (1978) "Marxism, Justice, and the Justice Model," 2 *Contemporary Crises* 27.

Felstiner, W. (1975) "Avoidance as Dispute Processing: An Elaboration," 9 *Law & Society Review* 695.

Felstiner, W., R. Abel, and A. Sarat (1981) "The Emergence and Transformation of Disputes: Naming, Blaming, Claiming... ," 15 (3) *Law & Society Review* (forthcoming).

Felstiner, W. and L. Williams (1978) "Mediation as an Alternative to Criminal Prosecution," 2 *Law and Human Behavior* 223.

Foucault, M. (1971) *L' ordre du discours.* Paris: Gallimard.

_____ (1975) *Surveiller et punir.* Paris: Gallimard.

_____ (1976) *La volonté de savoir.* Paris: Gallimard.

Galanter, M. (1979) "Legality and Its Discontents: A Preliminary Assessment of Current Theories of

---

into individual grievances. This individualization is what the legal form provides in a mystified way since, within it, individualization means insulation and atomization. It is up to the autonomous political movement to establish the missing link between the individual and the collective.

Legalization and Delegalization," in E. Blankenburg, E. Klausa, and H. Rottleuthner (eds.) *Alternative Rechtsformen und Alternativen zum Recht*. Opladen: Westdeutscher Verlag (*Jahrbuch für Rechtssoziologie und Rechtstheorie*, band 6).

———— (1981) "Justice in Many Rooms," 19 *Journal of Legal Pluralism* (forthcoming).

Garth, B. (1982) "The Movement toward Procedural Informalism in North America and Western Europe: A Critical Survey," in R. L. Abel (ed.) *The Politics of Informal Justice*, vol. 2: *Comparative Studies*. New York: Academic Press.

Harrington, C. (1980) "Voluntariness, Consent and Coercion in Adjudicating Minor Disputes: The Neighborhood Justice Center," in J. Brigham and D. Brown (eds.) *Policy Implementation: Choosing between Penalties and Incentives*. Beverly Hills, Calif.: Sage Publications.

Hofrichter, R. (1982) "Neighborhood Justice and the Social Control Problems of American Capitalism: A Perspective," in R. L. Abel (ed.) *The Politics of Informal Justice*, vol. 1: *The American Experience*. New York: Academic Press.

Holloway, J. and S. Picciotto (1978) *State and Capital: A Marxist Debate*. London: Edward Arnold.

Illich, I. (1973) *Tools for Conviviality*. New York: Harper & Row.

Jameson, F. (1979) "Reification and Utopia in Mass Culture," 1 *Social Text* 130.

Keat, R. and J. Urry (1975) *Social Theory as Science*. London: Routledge and Kegan Paul.

Marx, K. (1973) *Grundrisse. Foundations of the Critique of Political Economy (Rough Draft)*. London: Pelican.

———— (1976) *Capital: A Critique of Political Economy*, vol. 1. New York: Vintage.

Mathiesen, T. (1980) "The Future of Control Systems—The Case of Norway," 8 *International Journal of Sociology of Law* 149.

Merry, S. (1979) "Going to Court: Strategies of Dispute Management in an American Urban Neighborhood," 13 *Law & Society Review* 891.

Nader, L. (1979) "Disputing without the Force of Law," 88 *Yale Law Journal* 998.

Nader, L. and L. Singer (1976) "Dispute Resolution . . . ," 51 *California State Bar Journal* 281.

Ong, W. (1971) *Rhetoric, Romance and Technology*. Ithaca, N.Y.: Cornell University Press.

———— (1977) *Interfaces of the Word*. Ithaca, N.Y.: Cornell University Press.

Pashukanis, E. (1978) *Law and Marxism: A General Theory*. London: Ink Links.

Poulantzas, N. (1973) *Political Power and Social Classes*. London: New Left Books.

Reifner, U. (1978) "Rechtshilfebedürfnis und Verrechtlichung am Beispiel einer Berliner Mieterinitiative." Discussion paper, Internationales Institut für Management und Verwaltung, Berlin.

Santos, B. S. (1973) "La loi contre la loi," *Esprit* 67.

———— (1974) *Law Against Law: Legal Reasoning in Pasargada Law*. Cuernavaca: Centro Intercultural de Documentacion.

———— (1977) "The Law of the Oppressed: The Construction and Reproduction of Legality in Pasargada," 12 *Law & Society Review* 5.

———— (1979) "Popular Justice, Dual Power and Socialist Strategy," in B. Fine *et al.* (eds.) *Capitalism and the Rule of Law*. London: Hutchinson.

———— (1980) "O discurso e o poder: ensaio sobre a sociologia da retórica jurídica," *Boletim da Faculdade de Direito de Coimbra* (special issue), Coimbra.

Sarat, A. (1976) "Alternatives in Dispute Processing: Litigation in a Small Claims Court," 10 *Law & Society Review* 339.

Singer, L. (1980) "Non-Judicial Dispute Resolution Mechanisms: The Effects on Justice for the Poor," 13 *Clearinghouse Review* 569.

Wright, E. O. (1978) *Class Crisis and the State*. London: New Left Books.

The Contradictions of
Informal Justice

RICHARD L. ABEL

The chapters in this and the companion volume show that the growth of informal justice is not simply an American fad of the late 1970s. The contemporary reaction against the formal legal institutions of liberal capitalism has significant historical antecedents that are at least a century old (Auerbach, 1979; Wunder, 1979; Hindus, 1980). Nor is it limited to the United States: Informalism is visible in the Third World as well as in industrialized nations, in the Far East as well as in Europe and North America (see generally Cappelletti, 1978–1979; 1981). Because it is a reaction against all formal legal institutions, not just courts, we can understand it only if we examine relationships among changes that may appear quite disparate (see Galanter, 1979; Abel, 1979a). Within the substantive civil law we find reforms in divorce, probate, residential land transfers, and tort that are ostensibly intended to decrease the magnitude and complexity of state intervention in those transactions. Significant segments of the criminal law have been repealed—primarily those concerning "victimless" crimes involving drugs, gambling, sexual behavior, and other sumptuary offenses. Important sectors of the economy have been partly deregulated—such as transportation and communication—and there are calls for a radical dismantling

267

of the governmental apparatus that oversees utilities, natural resources, and many other economic activities (e.g., J. Wilson, 1980). At the same time there are demands that the state abdicate many of the public welfare functions we have come to take for granted—such as education and Social Security. These substantive changes are paralleled by numerous procedural reforms that alter the rules within existing institutions or create new ones (small claims, housing, and family courts on the civil side, juvenile courts on the criminal) (see generally Sander, 1977; Subcommittee on Courts, 1978; 1979) and that foster informal procedures at the edges of or outside formal institutions (e.g., negotiation and pretrial and preappeal conferences) (Rosenberg, 1964; Goldman, 1980; Ross, 1980). Finally, there has been a rapid proliferation of informal alternatives to the criminal process: probation and parole for both juvenile and adult offenders, pretrial diversion, community corrections, restitution, etc. (see, e.g., Nimmer, 1974; Aaronson et al., 1977; Hudson and Galway, 1980).

The proponents of these reforms (and they are often unusually strange bedfellows, even by the promiscuous standards of politics) naturally simplify and glorify them. But only a moment's reflection is needed to reveal their considerable ambiguity. Changes in the substantive civil law do not exempt behavior from state review—if anything no-fault divorce and automobile-accident compensation, simplified probate and land transfers bring more transactions before state institutions (e.g., Halbach, 1976; Widiss et al., 1977). What passes for decriminalization often means a reduction in penalty that permits the state to criminalize more actions (e.g., Aaronson et al., 1978; Cohen, 1979). Deregulation of the economy remains extremely selective and has been accompanied by greater intervention (or calls for increases) in such critical areas as monetary policy and international trade. The same people who argue that the state should abandon health, education, and welfare to the private sector also insist that the state take over failing automobile manufacturers, play an active role as the nation's largest banker, and use the tax code to direct the economy. They call for decontrol of oil and natural gas prices but urge massive government support for the development of synthetic fuels and protection for the nuclear power industry. They favor a more "realistic" attitude toward corporate bribery abroad and the human rights violations of foreign countries but want the state to take a hard line toward abortion and homosexuality. State informal procedures historically have displayed a recurrent, and apparently irresistible, tendency toward reformalization (Stapleton and Teitelbaum, 1972; Rubinstein, 1976). And resort to informal criminal dispositions not only increases the arsenal of state control but also has been accompanied by a substantial expansion of the formal apparatus (prisons, police, prosecutors, criminal judges).

These ambiguities must be the starting point for any attempt to understand the particular manifestations of informal justice that are the primary focus of these volumes and especially of this chapter—those alternative legal institutions that handle conflict, grievances, and deviance. The range of such institutions is broad (see generally Sander and Snyder, 1979; Wilkinson, 1980; Alper and Nichols, 1981; Tomasic and Feeley, 1981): the neighborhood justice centers and metropolitan mediation centers established with the support of the federal government (Cook *et al.*, 1980; *Dispute Resolution*, 1979–1981), comparable forums created by state and local government (Conner and Surette, 1977; Felstiner and Williams, 1978; 1980; Salas and Schneider, 1979; Davis *et al.*, 1980; Palenski *et al.*, 1980; Garofalo and Connelly, 1980a; 1980b; McGillis, n.d.); the expansion of arbitration, either through the choice of the parties (prior to the conflict or as a result of it) or as a prerequisite to state adjudication (Johnson *et al.*, 1977a; *Hastings Law Journal*, 1978); grievance mechanisms created by individual producers and sellers or by trade associations to handle the complaints of consumers (Eovaldi and Gestrin, 1971; Nader 1980a); media ombudsmen in the press, radio, or television (Hannigan, 1977; Palen, 1979; Mattice, 1980); and the dispute institutions of residential, ethnic, religious, and interest groupings (Yaffe, 1972; Doo, 1973; *The Mooter*, 1977–1980).

These institutions are numerous as well as diverse; the number of cases they process is large both absolutely and relative to the caseload of formal legal institutions. Voluntary arbitration, for instance, has been estimated as equivalent to more than two-thirds of all civil litigation (Mentschikoff, 1952), and an increasing number of state and federal courts are offering arbitration as an alternative to litigation or requiring it in a broad range of cases. There are small claims courts in virtually every state (Ruhnka *et al.*, 1978: App. A) that handle between 20 and 65 percent of all civil litigation (Galanter, 1975: 354). There are "action lines" in more than 300 newspapers in the United States and Canada, many of them syndicated, some of which purport to handle tens of thousands of cases a year (Palen, 1979: 803, 810). Federal administrative law judges outnumber the entire federal judiciary and handle more than 100,000 cases a year (Marquardt and Wheat, 1980: 473, 479). More cases are diverted from formal criminal procedures in some European countries than are handled by them (Felstiner and Drew, 1976: 16, 69).

The purpose of this chapter is to assess the social significance of these institutions and processes. Why do we find *these* changes? Why are they occurring *now*? Are they changes at all or have comparable phenomena always existed? If they are changes, are they part of a cycle, or a progression? And what do they signify for the central issues of contemporary capitalist society: the problems of democracy, liberty, oppression, and exploitation? Any answer to these questions will have to be complex and qualified. Because the role of law in advanced capitalism is highly contradictory, the relationship between formal and informal legal institutions is also contradictory. Does the growth of informal institutions represent an expansion or a contraction of the apparatus of state control? Do they grant redress to more individual complaints or do they withdraw state support from grievants? Do they equalize the positions of disputing parties or do they aggravate existing inequalities? Do they provide greater opportunity for popular participation in handling disputes and redressing grievances or do they curtail citizen involvement? Do they introduce new substantive standards for behavior, and if so are these preferable? Do they accelerate dispute processes or do they actually delay outcomes? Do they deprofessionalize this important realm of social interaction, or do they foster dependency on a new category of professionals? Do they reduce conflict or stimulate it? Do they cut public expenditures or enlarge the state budget? Are the procedures truly informal or is a new formality insinuated? Do they close the gap between the promises of liberalism and the reality or do they widen it? Do they enhance or undermine the legitimacy of the state? The answer to virtually every question will be—both. But if this means that informalism is not what its boosters claim, neither is it an unmitigated evil. It must express ideals that are strongly and widely embraced, or it would not be advocated and supported (Santos, 1982). I will try, therefore, to present both sides of this contradictory character: the contribution of informalism to state repression and capitalist exploitation and its potential for liberation.

EXPANDING STATE CONTROL

Sentence first—verdict afterward. [CARROLL, 1946: 132]
The Process Is the Punishment. [FEELEY, 1979]

Informal justice can extend the ambit of state control. Here I am talking only about those institutions that are somehow implicated in the state apparatus (although the boundaries are often amorphous). Informalism permits this expansion, in the first instance, by reducing or disguising the coercion that both stimulates resistance and justifies the demand for the protection of formal due process. Coercion is indeed relaxed: parties are often "referred" to informal institutions rather than arrested; the police are involved briefly, if at all; the symbols of state authority that so dominate the courtroom—a male judge, in black robes, on a raised dais, supported by security personnel—are all banished from the mediation center; and that epitome of force, the prison, is almost never threatened. Even more important, coercion is disguised: In place of prosecution we find the forms of civil litigation, arbitration, or mediation; staff go to great lengths to make participants feel comfortable (Yngvesson and Hennessey, 1975: 270); the mediator is often female (Felstiner and Williams, 1980: 8; Palenski *et al.*, 1980: 43), dressed like the parties, and seated with them round a table; even the language is different, stressing help rather than threats, speaking about a respondent rather than an accused—the velvet glove has largely hidden the iron fist (Center for the Study of Crime and Social Justice, 1979). Penalties are far milder: restitution rather than fines, the promise of behavioral change rather than imprisonment. Because coercion is less extreme and less visible the state can seek to control more behavior: deviance that was too trivial to interest officials (police, prosecutors), justify cumbersome formal procedures, or warrant severe sanctions (Felstiner and Drew, 1976: 46, 73). Because informal justice generally requires lower state expenditures per case, more intervention is possible within the same budget. The lower level of coercion (whether real or apparent) also obviates the need for the full panoply of procedural and constitutional protections, making it both easier and less expensive to extend control (*Ibid.*: 53ff., 64ff.). One index of expanded control is that informal institutions virtually never dismiss a case—everyone needs, and deserves, help (*Ibid.*: 48–49). When comparable behavior is presented to formal institutions—domestic violence, for instance—dismissal is the modal response (Davis *et al.*, 1980: 2). Indeed, a controlled comparison of cases that could have been brought to the neighborhood justice center but were instead prosecuted in formal courts revealed that in half the charges were dropped prior to the hearing and that only a quarter of the remaining half that were tried were found guilty; in other words, seven out of every eight respondents referred to informal institutions would have gone scot-free had they been prosecuted (Cook *et al.*, 1980: 74).

But if coercion is minimized for strategic reasons, it is by no means eliminated. It would be naive to expect otherwise: State action cannot avoid using force; social control cannot function without it (cf. Colson, 1974). Coercion serves to "persuade" parties to submit to informal justice, to "agree" to the outcome, and to comply with it (Harrington, 1980). The modus operandi is similar to the police interrogation in which the suspect is alternately confronted with a "bad" cop, who is large, unpleasant, and threatening, and a "good" cop, who promises to protect the suspect if he will cooperate (Inbau and Reid, 1962: 58–60). Informal justice offers a haven from the formal system: from its lengthy, costly, humiliating process and threat of prison (Palenski *et al.*, 1980). The respondent accepts the referral because he has been arrested or threatened with arrest, prosecuted or threatened with prosecution. Intake personnel in informal institutions stress the duration of the formal process and the number of appearances that will be required—neglecting to mention that a significant number of prosecutions are terminated at the early stages. Informal hearings use a variety of subtle techniques to influence the parties: modes of questioning (in which the mediator is much more active than a judge would be), the alternation of public hearings with private caucuses (in which the adversary is assigned the role of the bad cop), and of course the implicit threat of returning the matter to court (Felstiner and Williams, 1980: 11; Danet, 1980: 514–24). For a while the Kansas City Neighborhood Justice Center warned the parties at the outset that the intermediary would arbitrate if they did not reach a solution (Cook *et al.*, 1980: 36–37); that such arbitration was usually unnecessary does not mean the threat was irrelevant—any more than the rarity of civil or criminal trials makes them irrelevant to settlement negotiations or plea bargaining. The salience of coercion is revealed in a number of ways. Half the disputants who appeared before one mediation program saw no difference between it and a formal court and felt just as coerced by the former (Palenski *et al.*, 1980: 66, 90–91). Successful resolution of disputes in neighborhood justice centers (NJCs) varies directly with the coerciveness of the referral source (criminal justice system versus spontaneous walk-ins) and the threat of arbitration; the Venice NJC, which was the least coercive by both indices, referred out more disputes without resolving them than did either of the other two NJCs (Cook *et al.*, 1980: 27, 39). Since state informal institutions are evaluated by measuring the magnitude of intake and the rate of successful dispositions—each of which is a function of coercion—there is constant pressure to become more coercive.

Because informal state institutions reduce or disguise coercion they can seek to review behavior that presently escapes state control. They are not limited to acting in situations where a party has violated a formal law, civil or criminal. Indeed, whereas the formal institutions of the liberal state punish or reward specified *acts* with the object of channeling behavior that is believed to be governed by a rational, utilitarian calculus, informal institutions engage in covert manipulation that seeks to modify the *character* of a person whose behavior is viewed as an expression of irrational impulses (Mathiesen, 1980). Unlike trial courts of limited jurisdiction, informal institutions often are unconstrained by any upper boundary (amount in controversy, magnitude of crime); instead, their competence is defined by the nature of the relationship between the parties and the type of accusation or claim. If they stigmatize one party less by redesignating the accused as "respondent," they render the other more vulnerable to criticism by recharacterizing the victim as a "complainant." This allows, indeed encourages, informal institutions to ask whether, perhaps, the complainant provoked the conflict or perhaps is being hypersensitive; the parallel to the way formal courts treat rape victims is not coincidental, for informal institutions have a larger number of women complainants than do formal (Cook *et al.*, 1980: Tables C–1, C–4, C–7).

One reason why state control of behavior is relatively ineffective is that it occurs too late: Formal criminal justice (like formal education) acts only after patterns of behavior have been firmly established. Informal institutions are said to be capable of intervening before conflict has escalated (Shonholtz, n.d.). Indeed, in order to achieve the cost savings that are one of their principal justifications, informal institutions must be mobilized before the court has held multiple hearings, before the prosecutor has invested the time in preparation, even before police resources have been expended upon arrest and arraignment (Palenski *et al.*, 1980: 102, 118). In this respect, informal justice appears to reproduce for the entire population what the Gluecks (1950; 1956) advocated with respect to youth some thirty years ago: progressively earlier state intervention to identify and correct situations of predelinquency, predeviance, and pre-conflict. The treatment of family conflict is illustrative. Formal institutions intervene too late. Courts can grant only the imprimatur of divorce; conciliation is either refused or unsuccessful (Foster, 1966; Rheinstein, 1972). Formal intervention is also very costly. Domestic violence stimulates substantial investments by police (Black, 1980: 112–113), prosecutors, and courts, with little visible result. Informal institutions, by contrast, can intervene early, even though no law has been broken; they are given powers that trial courts of limited jurisdiction might lack (over marital dissolution and serious crimes); and they subject the behavior of both parties to scrutiny and discipline.

The creation of informal institutions increases the quantum of state resources devoted to social control—a point that must be stressed because informalism is often promoted as a means of reducing such expenditures. Expansion occurs in two ways. First, formal institutions can be relieved of some of their present burden. Despite the well-deserved American reputation for being overpoliced and overprisoned, certain sectors of our formal legal system—notably the judiciary—are smaller than those of other Western capitalist states (Johnson *et al.*, 1977b: Ch. 9). Since the capacity of any control system can be no greater than that of its smallest component (just as the obstruction of one lane of a highway slows traffic for miles), this is a significant constraint (cf. Nagin, 1978: 344–345). Informal institutions increase the capacity of courts by diverting cases to arbitration and mediation in much the same way that probation, parole, and community corrections increase the capacity of prisons. Reforms can also increase the capacity of formal institutions by reducing the resources they must expend to process a case. Changes in the substantive law that eliminate issues (e.g., recent reforms of divorce, tort, and probate) contribute to this result (Ehrlich and Schwartz, 1974). So do procedures that obviate the need for full-dress trials: on-the-spot fines by the police, prosecutorial fines and convictions, penal orders in lieu of trial, and administrative fines imposed by agencies (Felstiner and Drew, 1976: 8, 16ff., 53ff., 64ff.). Although the rhetoric of informalism initially stressed its superior procedures and increased popular participation, notions of "efficient" case processing quickly predominated. When the original funding for the neighborhood justice centers expired they were shifted to the Law Enforcement Assistance Administration (LEAA) Court Delay Reduction Program, which also funds their successors, the Metropolitan Mediation Centers (*Dispute Resolution*, vol. 6, Fall 1980).

The second way in which informal institutions expand state resources devoted to social control is by supplementing formal institutions. This suggests that the relationship between formal and informal is not cyclical or complementary—one contracting while the other expands (cf. Black, 1976: 107)—but additive. The augmentation attributable to informal institutions is not insignificant. The District of Columbia Complaint Center (one of the new Metropolitan Mediation Centers) heard 8000 complaints in 1979, half the number of minor criminal cases handled by the Superior Court. The Citizen Complaint Desk of the Harris County (Houston) District Attorney received 17,000 complaints in 1979, of which it was only able to prosecute 10 percent; the new Metropolitan Mediation Center in Houston hopes to process *all* such cases (Dispute Resolution, vol. 6, pp. 1–2, 12, Fall 1980). And just as formal institutions experience case overload, which they seek to resolve by diversion, so informal institutions experience case underload and consequently strive to develop higher, more predictable caseloads both to justify their existence and to facilitate their internal operations (Palenski *et al.*, 1980: 66–68).

Informal state social control, like formal, is directed toward the economically, socially, and politically oppressed. Of course, this is not explicit; it is rare for the legal institutions of the liberal state to be openly class biased. Informal justice is available to all complainants and everyone is a potential respondent. Furthermore, the fact that coercion is less extreme and less visible makes it more difficult to comprehend how class bias might be introduced. And there is confusion (often fostered by the advocates of informalism) between facilitative private institutions (e.g., commercial arbitration) and coercive public institutions. Nevertheless, it cannot be denied that the latter, exemplified by the NJCs, are preoccupied with the poor, members of ethnic minorities, and women (Cook *et al.*, 1980: 40, 41, 154). This bias is disguised by evaluations of the NJCs that stress the demographic similarity between disputants and the population of the neighborhoods from which they draw (*Ibid.*). But that characterization conveniently overlooks two critical facts. First, the NJCs are located in neighborhoods that contain disproportionate numbers of the oppressed: Venice (Los Angeles), for instance, rather than Beverly Hills; Harlem rather than the East Side of Manhattan. Second, it is the oppressed who invoke intervention by state institutions, formal or informal, to settle disputes, enhance their authority, or demonstrate conformity to norms (Baumgartner, 1980a). Furthermore, they do so in controversies with equals or inferiors, not against superiors. The privileged classes, by contrast, use law (primarily formal institutions) to control inferiors but protect one another from state intervention. We know, for instance, that wife-beating is distributed fairly equally across class lines but that the police are summoned only by poorer families (Martin, 1977: Chs. 2, 4). The Venice NJC, which served a neighborhood with a large proportion of white middle-class residents and relied less upon coercion, had a lower caseload than the Atlanta and Kansas City NJCs (Cook *et al.*, 1980: 24). One reason for this is that institutions of state control, formal and informal, are staffed by people of relatively low status—police, lay mediators, etc. The privileged classes will not submit to judgment by inferiors; in the rare informal institutions with elite personnel, such as the ÖRA in Hamburg, the privileged classes are well represented (Ford Foundation, 1978b: 48–50; Falke *et al.*, 1978).

Informal justice purports to devolve state authority on nonstate institutions, to delegate social control to businesses, neighborhoods, and other private entities. But in fact informalism expands the grasp of the state at the expense of other sources of authority that appear to be potential competitors. Whether or not "law [*always*] varies inversely with other social control" (Black, 1976: 107), the capitalist state actively seeks to undermine, displace, and coopt other forms of social control (cf. Landes and Posner, 1979). Because the state is the only legitimate source of authority, other forms of social control must either be its creation or exist at its sufferance. The establishment or recognition of informal institutions by the capitalist state bears a striking resemblance to the strategy of indirect rule employed by the imperialist state in the nineteenth and early twentieth centuries. Indirect rule claimed to respect and strengthen indigenous authority, but its actual effect was to subordinate and undermine countervailing power (cf. Abel, 1979b). Indeed a precondition for the survival of informal justice in civil society appears to be the inaccessibility of competing state institutions (Conn and Hippler, 1974: 229–230). When the official state legal system, formal and informal, is highly remote and inhospitable, then true informal justice thrives outside it. Reforms that increase access to state control—of which informalism is an example—draw clients away from nonstate institutions and distort the processes of the latter (van der Sprenkel, 1962; Galanter, 1963; 1972; Engel, 1980: 440–441).

The ideology of informalism expresses a nostalgia inspired by the demise of traditional sources of authority.

> In the past, courts were forums of last resort for disagreements that were severe enough to benefit from the procedural formality of a trial. Numerous less formal public and private institutions were used to settle the relatively minor disputes of everyday life. These institutions included justices of the peace, neighborhood policemen, churches, schools, and the family. In contemporary American life, however, the role of these institutions has diminished [Meador, 1979: 24; see also Snyder, 1978: 740].

Although such institutions are presented as forums for dispute settlement, they performed that role only because they were, preeminently, loci of authority. Yearning for authority also evokes the laudatory, even envious, references to societies whose informal legal institutions are believed to be more effective than those of advanced Western capitalism—e.g., the nations of the Far East (Japan, China, Korea) and of Africa (Burger, 1977: 24, 48; Smith, 1978). What is the common bond between idealized images of nineteenth-century America, Eastern civilizations, and African tribal societies? It is respect for authority, whether embodied in church or political bosses, patriarch or feudal lord, tribal elder or chief.

Yet this nostalgia is hypocritical. Institutional authority in civil society did not decay spontaneously, it was destroyed by the growth of the state, which has assumed many of the functions that used to be performed by family, church, locality, and political party and were the source of their authority. Furthermore, the state has stressed science and rationality as the foundation of its legitimacy and thereby undermined the cognitive basis of alternative authority, which was grounded in tradition, religion, localism, ethnicity, and personal loyalty. The authority of the neighborhood justice center rests, in part, on a claim of technical competence predicated on formal training in psychology, social work, and "mediation skills" (Cook *et al.*, 1980: 20–22; Palenski *et al.*, 1980: 45–46; Davis *et al.*, 1980: 9; Felstiner and Williams, 1980: 8–13)—credentials that most religious, family, and local authorities do not possess. By seeking to subordinate and coopt residual modes of civil authority, the state fosters the growth of corporatism. By offering to resolve disputes and to correct deviance, it penetrates further into civil society. Housing can illustrate a more general pattern. Because the public sector represents such a small proportion of the housing market in the United States (compared to Western Europe) (Winter, 1979), the state has relatively little influence over the behavior of most landlords and tenants. The creation of informal institutions to settle disputes between them can be seen as an extension of state authority into an important sphere of social interaction. Private enterprise—which likes to portray itself as the last bastion of resistance to statism—in fact helps to extend the reach of the state when it invokes the authority of the latter to obtain civil redress against shoplifters, and further expansion would occur if employer punishment of employees received state recognition (Felstiner and Drew, 1976: 90, 100–105). Indeed, informalism can be seen as a means of mobilizing on behalf of the state all forms of civil authority that might engage in opposition (Shonholtz, n.d.)—precisely what Thomas Mathiesen (1980) sees as the crime control policy of social democracy.

The paradigm for contemporary expansion of state informal control is neighborhood justice, for the concept of neighborhood simultaneously fulfills a number of different requirements. It satisfies nostalgia for a mythical past, whether imagined as a small town or an urban ethnic enclave that symbolizes homogeneity, and thus security, in a society whose normative and social conflicts are extremely threatening (Garofalo and Laub, 1978). It locates institutions of social control in residential settings that appear to be as remote as possible from the state, an appearance that is enhanced by the language and forms of decentralization, which conceal the extent of state direction. The Harlem Small Claims Court, generally acknowledged as an exemplar of that institutional form, employs local residents as public relations officers and in other subordinate positions but remains an integral part of the judicial system and thus under state control (Yngvesson and Hennessey, 1975: 269; Ruhnka *et al.*, 1978: 106–107).

If informalism generally conceals the growth of the corporate state under the forms of delegation and devolution, neighborhood justice invokes an even more transparent myth—for there are very few neighborhoods. Where colonial rulers had difficulties identifying loci of authority and comprehending indigenous social structures, the proponents of neighborhood justice have an almost impossible task. Significant interaction in contemporary Western society occurs in the workplace, the community of colleagues, the voluntary association, the dispersed family—not the neighborhood (cf. Sennett, 1977). Residence is chosen for reasons of demography (the neighborhood has the right kind of people, meaning one's own race and class) and physical environment—but with little expectation of, or desire for, intimate association (Buckle and Thomas-Buckle, 1980: 18–19). Nor can neighborhoods readily be created—certainly not by the introduction of dispute institutions. Those ethnic urban enclaves that still survive are a function of the locus of work (a nearby factory), low income, residential immobility, and fear of the outsider (Kidder, 1980). Even if these conditions could be reproduced the cost might be very high—the containment of intraneighborhood disputes at the expense of an aggravation of conflict between neighborhoods divided along the lines of race, religion, ethnicity, and class. This is not likely to happen, however, for informal justice is not organically related to the neighborhood; institutions may be dispersed for the sake of appearances, but they remain centrally controlled. Indeed, few of the informal institutions recently developed are confined to the neighborhood; most have jurisdiction throughout the city or county (Felstiner and Williams, 1980: 6; Davis *et al.*, 1980: 20; Palenski *et al.*, 1980: 2–5; Cook *et al.*, 1980: 13–16).

State informal control does not informalize state control but rather undermines extrastate modes of informal control. The liberal state has always claimed to monopolize violence. Informal justice both perfects this monopoly (by reviewing and disciplining forms of violence that were tolerated or overlooked) and extends it to less coercive forms of control. In lieu of gossip, boycott, self-help, refusal of reciprocity, and the whole range of nonstate sanctions identified by anthropologists, disputants are urged to seek the protection of informal state institutions. Furthermore, the more effective the state monopoly over extreme sanctions, such as violence, the less potent are informal sanctions, whose power ultimately depends on a credible, if implicit, threat of escalation (Engel, 1980: 439–440).

State informalism not only expropriates conflict from the parties (cf. Christie, 1977) but also reduces participation by other citizens in the handling of disputes. State informal institutions substitute paraprofessional state employees for citizen jurors (Yngvesson and Hennessey, 1975: 226; Johnson *et al.*, 1977a: 86, 88 n. 27). This minimizes the threat of jury nullification (Kalven and Zeisel, 1966: Chs. 5–6; Engel, 1980: 444). Whereas voir dire gives parties significant control over the selection of jurors, the state unilaterally appoints mediators and assigns them to particular cases (Sheppard *et al.*, 1978; Palenski *et al.*, 1980: 43; Davis *et al.*, 1980: 9; Felstiner and Williams, 1980: 8). Informal justice has often been used deliberately to minimize citizen participation: arbitration in the United States (Auerbach, 1979: 23, 35–36); lay judges in Poland and Hungary who are carefully selected and readily dominated by the professional judge (Felstiner and Drew, 1976: 106–108; Kurczewski and Frieske, 1978: 164–166).

If I am correct that the growth of informal legal institutions extends state social control, this does not mean that those are necessarily effective. Indeed, there is reason to think that some of the inadequacies and dilemmas of the formal legal system that generate the enthusiasm for informal alternatives will bedevil the latter as well. Just as formal legal institutions fail as deterrence (general or specific) and as rehabilitation, so informal institutions are unlikely to succeed in either conciliation or therapy. It would be naive to expect otherwise. How could a stranger successfully mediate a controversy that, if it is worth resolving, will have a long history, display complex ramifications, and elicit strong emotions (Felstiner, 1974)? How could a lay person change deeply rooted behavior in the space of a few hours and in the presence of the person who is the object of that behavior, if a trained psychotherapist often fails after private meetings that are repeated daily over several years? Nevertheless, contemporary informal institutions devote substantial energies to precisely those situations—conflict between intimates expressing deep-rooted emotions—that they are least able to resolve (Felstiner and Williams, 1980: 24, 30). They tend not to handle problems more susceptible to a quick, superficial remedy—conflict between relative strangers over a narrow issue with a shallow history—for two reasons. First, the pressure to confront such problems is far less strong; because the relationship is relatively unimportant the parties can terminate it, thereby resolving their conflict by lumping it (Felstiner, 1974: 85–89). Second, informal institutions are ill-equipped to handle such problems: They lack sufficient power to compel the parties to participate or to comply with the agreement, and this deficiency is not compensated by informal pressures because the necessary social structure—a true community—does not exist.

The inefficacy of informal social control is virtually preordained by its institutional structure and task, but it is further compounded by other factors. Most elements of the criminal justice system are chronically underfunded. Certainly that is true of courts and prisons; informal institutions will probably be even more severely shortchanged, at least once their initial glamor wears off. They lack the political clout wielded by elite judges and unionized correction officials and do not command the high status that derives from association with serious crimes and dangerous criminals. Furthermore, their capacity to engage in meaningful conciliation and therapy is constantly undermined by the pressure to process caseload. Because state institutions under capitalism are subjected to the criterion of "efficiency" that purportedly governs the private sector, the success of informal institutions will largely be measured by their caseloads (cf. Palen, 1979: 808). But with limited resources, case turnover can be increased only by reducing the time and energy spent on each. Relieving formal institutions of caseload and speeding the processing of disputes have therefore become the principal justifications of the Metropolitan Mediation Centers, at the expense of conciliation and therapy (*Dispute Resolution*, vol. 6, pp. 1–2, 12, Fall 1980). If one index of success imposed by the logic of capitalism is caseload, another is consumer satisfaction. Indeed, the two are closely, if contradictorily, related. High levels of use can be read as an index of satisfaction. But because disputants may not freely "choose" informal institutions, any choice is likely to be poorly informed, and because there is little competition in price or quality, considerable emphasis is placed upon survey research to measure satisfaction.

Yet satisfaction is likely to be a function of individualized treatment, time invested by personnel, and disputant convenience, so that the more "efficient" the institution, the less people will be eager to use it (cf. Abel, 1979b: 185–188). The most frequent response—again in imitation of monopoly capitalism—is a superficial product differentiation that exaggerates the cosmetic and stylistic peculiarities of informal institutions (e.g., Palenski *et al.*, 1980: 23–24). Another problem is that the value of informal institutions—both to the state (for control) (e.g., Davis *et al.*, 1980: 69) and to individuals (for the expression and redress of grievances (e.g., Buckle and Thomas-Buckle, 1980; Nader, 1980b)—varies directly with their coercive resources. Yet the ideology of liberal legalism insists that coercion be accompanied by due process (Rubinstein, 1976). Efficacy may thus lead to reformalization (e.g., Ruhnka *et al.*, 1978: Ch. 7).

These several dilemmas appear to point to a common solution—though, as we will see, it is not really a solution at all. In order to process more cases, conserve state resources, compensate for its lack of coercion, and conceal its inability to conciliate or to engage in meaningful therapy, the informal institution will refer cases out. These referrals could be a means of further extending state social control by mobilizing an ever larger institutional network (Hofrichter, 1982). But I think it is rather a sign of desperation. Both informal state institutions (Johnson *et al.*, 1977a: 53–64, 74) and private institutions like media ombudsmen (Palen, 1979: 818) refer out significant numbers of complaints; the less coercive they are, the more they resort to this course (Cook *et al.*, 1980: 36–37). But most people do not follow up the referrals (*Ibid.*: 65–66), and even when they do the result is often still another referral in an endless, Kafkaesque, circle. Hence the social control functions of informal institutions become indistinguishable from their role in neutralizing conflict by cooling out grievants. The next section looks at that process in greater detail.

NEUTRALIZING CONFLICT

The private strife of man and wife
Is useful to the nation
It is a harmless outlet for
Emotions that could lead to war
Or social agitation.
[Pangloss, in "The Best of All
Possible Worlds," from *Candide*,
lyrics by RICHARD WILBUR]

Informal legal institutions neutralize conflict that could threaten state or capital. Of course, formal legal institutions do this too, but informalism has its own distinctive strengths and weaknesses. Although neutralizing conflict and extending state control may appear to be inconsistent processes, they actually overlap and complement each other in ways I will consider later. Here it is sufficient to observe that whereas informal state control connotes active intervention to suppress or modify specific behavior, informal institutions neutralize conflict by responding to grievances in ways that inhibit their transformation into serious challenges to the domination of state and capital.

Both state and capital create informal institutions so that they can retain control over the handling of those grievances that escape the purview of formal institutions and can continue to influence: which complaints get aired, by whom, to whom, in what form and forum, how they are processed, and what remedy is granted. All these institutions are created and controlled by *respondents*, never by the grievants themselves (but see Weiner, 1976; Wilson and Brydolf, 1980). Frequently, state intervention is unnecessary. The larger capitalists (manufacturers, retailers, service industries) and those that are well organized in trade associations have established numerous, often highly elaborate complaint procedures (see generally Nader, 1980a). Sometimes the state explicitly authorizes or requires them to do so (Magnuson–Moss Warranty Act, 15 U.S.C. §§2301–2312, Supp. V 1975; see Macaulay, 1979) and even delegates to capital the responsibility for establishing the substantive standards of conduct the grievance mechanism will apply (Ford Foundation, 1978b: 59–61). But it is neither efficient nor feasible for every enterprise to construct its own complaint procedure, and those in the competitive sector may be strongly motivated not to do so (just as smaller entrepreneurs have consistently resisted reductions in work hours and improvements in worker health and safety, whereas larger enterprises, especially those in the monopoly sector, more readily accommodated such demands and then turned to the state to impose them uniformly, see Carson, 1974: 118–121; Berman, 1978: 16). Therefore the state assumes this function, performing its traditional role of correcting market failure. Indeed, grievance mechanisms may be seen as the latest service of a constantly expanding welfare state, which thereby socializes another of the costs of reproducing capitalism. In addition, the state must develop mechanisms for responding to grievances directed against itself—and as the state grows, these grievances will multiply.

Enterprises (public as well as private) already control the voicing of grievances by their employees, in which process informal institutions like labor arbitration play a central role (Getman, 1979). But advanced capitalism requires the planning of consumption as well as production; the present economic crisis is in large part a crisis of consumption (Sherman, 1979). Consumer grievances must be satisfied so that consumers continue buying. Consumers must also be kept passive—consumerism has the potential to generate organizations, and even cooperatives, that actively negotiate price and quality. For these reasons it is necessary to generalize to relations of consumption those mechanisms that have been developed to control relations of production. Such mechanisms take a number of forms. A producer or seller may establish a procedure through which consumers can voice grievances (e.g., Karikas and Rosenwasser, 1980). Yet this may create even more discontent if grievances are not satisfied. Some, therefore, take the further step of announcing a policy of unconditional returns of unsatisfactory merchandise. The cost of such a practice is both predictable and small relative to total sales (Nader, 1980b: 12–13). It therefore becomes just another cost of doing business, a cost that is often amply repaid by the enhanced reputation. Maurice Rosenberg (1971a) has proposed that the state implement such a policy with respect to *all* private enterprise: that it reimburse *all* aggrieved consumers in token amounts and then assume the task of seeking redress from the offending businesses. This would enormously extend the state expropriation of citizen grievances that was begun by the state prosecution of crimes (Christie, 1977).

A similar strategy has been adopted with respect to grievances that arise out of injury to the consumer or a third party rather than through disappointed consumer expectations. Here, again, the goal of state and capital is to defuse the anger of those injured and forestall public sympathy by satisfying claims through payment of small, predictable amounts (see Abel, 1981). This strategy is exemplified by workers' compensation (Conley and Noble, 1980), the settlement practice of insurance companies (Ross, 1980), no-fault compensation for automobile injuries (Widiss *et al.*, 1977), the federal "superfund" to clean up chemical wastes (Comprehensive Environmental Response, Compensation, and Liability Act of 1980, §§ 221 et seq., P.L. 96–510, 94 STAT 2767), perhaps the growth of products liability (O'Connell, 1975), and certainly those state welfare schemes that compensate all injuries (Palmer, 1980; Ison, 1980). These responses share several salient characteristics: simplification of the rules of liability and entitlement, an increase in the proportion of claims paid so that almost every claimant gets something, a reduction in the amounts paid to each claimant, economies of scale, and greater predictability in total exposure. They are fundamentally paternalistic, a stance that is justified in the language of technocracy—the paramount rationale for contemporary domination (Ford Foundation, 1978b: 9). In each case an incipient demand for behavioral change (and ultimately for control over that behavior (e.g., Berman, 1978: Ch. 5; Freedman, 1980) is transformed into a claim for money (cf. Johnson et al., 1977a: 82). The notions that consumers should have a say in determining the cost, design, or quality of the products they need, that workers should be consulted about their own safety, or that the public should participate in weighing the externalities of enterprises are effectively foreclosed.

In order to neutralize conflict informal institutions must attract grievants by appearing to champion their interests. The media ombudsman, for instance, seeks to create an image as advocate of the underdog, sometimes going so far as to invent a pseudoperson—"Ombie"—who can be seen as a friend (Johnson et al., 1977a: 73; Palen, 1979). But this is a false friendship, for informal legal institutions do not and cannot have loyalties to particular groups—they are promiscuous friends, like lawyers (compare Fried, 1976, with Simon, 1978: 106–115) or Robert Browning's "last Duchess" (1955). They do not offer the kind of support a worker can obtain from his union or the fidelity of muckraking journalists (Palen, 1979). This can be seen more clearly if we construct a scale of partisanship, from the most partisan (family, friends, fellow workers, others with similar grievances) through professional partisans (lawyer, therapist) to those whose loyalties are divided (social worker). Most informal institutions fall at the far end of this spectrum; some, indeed, are the creatures of one adversary pretending to be the partisans of the other—e.g., government ombudsmen, Better Business Bureaus, or the complaint mechanisms of manufacturers and sellers.

Informal institutions find it difficult to maintain an image of partisanship because they must simultaneously present themselves as neutral. This dilemma is clearest in the case of state institutions, whose legitimacy under the dominant ideology of liberal pluralism requires that they appear to stand above the fray of particular interests. We are familiar with this tension as it occurs in another, and earlier, example of informality—the regulatory agency, which must simultaneously be partisan and neutral. Just as those agencies sought to solve the dilemma by internal distinctions between prosecutorial and adjudicative functions, so the newer informal institutions display incipient differentiation, as we will see later in this chapter. But this solution rarely satisfies anyone. Either the regulated regard the agency as hostile and overly aggressive (industry's view of OSHA, EPA, or the EEOC) or those whom the agency is designed to protect dismiss it as a pawn of the regulated (e.g., the ICC, FPC, or FCC). For the myth of the neutral advocate is necessarily a myth. At best it hides lukewarm advocacy—compromise, delay, and reluctance to use available sanctions. But it also deflects the aggrieved from vigorous pursuit of their grievances by encouraging them to rely on the state (e.g., the Swedish consumer advocate; see Ford Foundation, 1978b: 52–53). And it can easily lead to a situation where the ostensible champion seeks to persuade the aggrieved to moderate his demands—a pattern visible in the protofascist institutions of Germany and Japan in the interwar period (Reifner, 1982; Haley, 1982).

Informal institutions attract disputants not only by claiming to be both partisan and neutral but also by discouraging self-reliance. The offer of help necessarily fosters a sense of personal incompetence (see Illich, 1977; Tomasic, 1978: 22–25). But other factors contribute. The fear of aggression, of expressing anger, and of eliciting the anger sympathetically projected upon an adversary (Moriarty, 1975; Buckle and Thomas-Buckle, 1980: 25; Baumgartner, 1980b) inhibit resort to self-help in redressing grievances. These fears are magnified by media coverage of violence and by the law and order campaigns they encourage (Harris, 1969; Cohen and Young, 1973; Hall et al., 1978; Hall, 1980). Any action outside the protective umbrella of state authority comes to be seen as threatening retaliation and escalation, and this, in turn, justifies the growth of private vigilantism—witness the popularity of courses in self-defense and both offensive and defensive weaponry (New York Times, February 8, 1981: sec. 1, p. 24; Los Angeles Times, February 23, 1981: pt. 1, p. 1).

By inducing disputants to submit voluntarily to the jurisdiction of the institution and by involving them in working out a solution, informal justice enhances their acceptance of the outcome. In the absence of informal institutions, many people "lump" their grievances (e.g., Best and Andreasen, 1977; Burman et al., 1977) and continue to harbor hostility that may ultimately erupt in ways that are less predictable and less readily contained. On the other hand, when complaints are brought to formal institutions many respondents default (Ruhnka et al., 1978: 129), leaving grievants without a remedy or making respondents feel they have been denied a hearing. Informal institutions require participation by both parties (even if they use persuasive rather than coercive means) and thereby secure a better opportunity to convince each of the justice of the result. Some evidence of this may be found in the fact that a large proportion of disputants declare their willingness to return to informal institutions in future conflicts even when those institutions have done virtually nothing to help them (Cook et al., 1980: 78).

Informal institutions neutralize conflict by denying its existence, by simulating a society in which conflict is less frequent and less threatening, and by choosing to recognize and handle only those forms of conflict that do not challenge basic structures. Informal processes moderate the antagonistic adversarial posture of the parties. This is a difficult task because people involved in conflict usually want to win; they seek vindication. For the same reason, they prefer to represent themselves (Foster, 1975); failing that, they invoke the support of an ally or advocate; and as a last resort they appeal to an authority they believe will be sympathetic (Buckle and Thomas-Buckle, 1980: 24–25; Smith *et al.*, n.d.). But informal justice prohibits many forms of aggression, isolates disputants from allies, and refuses to be partisan.

I suggest tentatively that there is a sequence in which conflict is progressively neutralized. In societies without an authority capable of monopolizing force conflict mobilizes opposing groups and is frequently violent (e.g., Fortes and Evans-Pritchard, 1940; Middleton and Tait, 1958). The formal judicial institutions of the state (national or colonial) tend to individualize conflict and to outlaw violence, but they allow, and indeed encourage, verbal conflict. In Western courts, for instance, parties are represented by specialists trained in aggressive advocacy, and the latter are encouraged in their adversarial style by the judge, who is *him*self a lawyer. Informal institutions take the next step of restricting verbal conflict as well; the parties are unrepresented; they are forbidden to make certain accusations. Whereas violent conflict is waged by groups and legal conflict by individuals, informal justice renders conflict *intra*individual—an expression of the personal problems *within* each party. The slogan that mediation offers to disputants was best stated by Pogo: "We have met the enemy, and he is us." The mediator is trained in counseling skills, and *she* (for there are many more women mediators than women judges) seeks to help the parties accommodate.

Conflict is depicted as a failure of communication, a misunderstanding (Palen, 1979: 824). This is certainly the implicit message conveyed when the respondent (government, retailer, manufacturer) itself establishes a grievance mechanism: We are reasonable; our interest and yours are not antagonistic; if you have a complaint, we will listen to it; any disagreement can be sorted out. The Sperry Corporation has gone a step further, equating conflict in the home and at work, attributing both to a failure to listen, and then requiring its employees to take courses in "listening" (*The New Yorker*, February 9, 1981: 82–83). The same theme is echoed by ostensibly impartial informal institutions—e.g., media ombudsmen, regulatory agencies—that refrain from exercising whatever powers they may have (publicity, coercion), thereby suggesting to the complainant and the public that the respondent will listen to reason (Mayhew, 1968; Whitford and Kimball, 1974; Steele, 1975; Johnson *et al.*, 1977a: 67–68, 70, 75; Silbey, 1978; Palen, 1979). Small claims courts are seen by the parties, and even by the judges who staff them, as forums that allow grievants to let off steam, performing an expressive rather than an instrumental function (Sarat, 1976: 345–346, 348). Indeed, mediation is possible only if there never was any real conflict between the parties in the first place (Snyder, 1978: 771), for it purports to offer a solution in which no one wins and no one loses. Furthermore, if the parties can be brought to see their dispute in this light, *both* tend to be pleased with the process and the institution, whereas in zero-sum conflict the losing party is usually much less satisfied than the winner (Ruhnka *et al.*, 1978: 74–76).

If informal justice denies the existence of conflict, its advocates simultaneously (if inconsistently) insist that there is too much controversy. Chief Justice Burger has perhaps been most eloquent on this theme, condemning "our vicious legal spiral," "the inherently litigious nature of Americans," and "excessive contentiousness" (1976: 91; 1977: 23, 24), but many other legal notables have seconded his view, urging (with heavy irony) "let's everybody litigate" (Rosenberg, 1971b) or decrying the legal "explosion" (Jones, 1965; Barton, 1975), "California's colossal legal appetite" (Kline, 1978a; 1978b), "legal pollution" (Ehrlich, 1976), our "Litigious Society" (Lieberman, 1981), or "hyperlexis: our national disease" (Manning, 1976). Formal legal conflict has replaced the "outside agitator" as the serpent in the garden. This attitude sounds reasonable and value-neutral; after all, most of us would prefer peace to conflict (Bohannan, 1967: xi). But it obscures the fact that conflict is necessarily the act of *two* parties, one making a demand and another resisting it. The proponents of informalism seek to reduce conflict by curtailing demands, never acknowledging that just as much conflict would be eliminated if those to whom the demands are addressed would accede—cease discriminating, polluting, exploiting, oppressing.

Advocates of informalism suggest the unreasonableness of the demands of oppressed groups by extolling social settings where those demands would never be made: small towns, nineteenth-century America, the patriarchal family, tribal societies, Far Eastern cultures. I argued earlier in this chapter that these disparate environments were united by their respect for authority. The necessary concomitant of such respect is an acceptance of place, the subordination of women to men, young to old, nonwhites to whites, religious minorities to the majority, consumers to sellers, workers to capitalists. Furthermore, most of those societies were far more homogeneous than contemporary America. Our greater heterogeneity produces not only increased conflict but also conflict that is subversive, rather than supportive, of the social order. Whereas conflict in homogeneous societies reinforces shared norms by creating occasions on which they may collectively be asserted (Durkheim, 1947), conflict in heterogeneous societies threatens norms by highlighting incompatibility and dissensus (Baumgartner, 1980b).

This is the reason why conflict must be suppressed, or at least neutralized. Several social structural features of advanced capitalism are responsive to this imperative (see generally Abel, 1979b). The extreme privatization of American society (Sennett, 1977) has greatly curtailed the opportunities for serious conflict. Kinship relations, a fertile source of contention in tribal societies, have greatly atrophied (though members of the nuclear family may quarrel more often and more seriously as a result). Other relationships, previously multiplex, have become simplex (Gluckman, 1965: Ch. 1); because each partner has invested relatively little, conflict is less likely to arise and is more easily resolved by exit. Property is owned privately, not collectively (cf. Schwartz, 1954), and rights are clearly defined; conflict is more likely to take the form of theft by a stranger than of ambiguous, conflicting claims between intimates. We can sense the magnitude of the conflict that has been eliminated if we reflect on the intensity of controversies sparked by the limited forms of public property that remain—the angry words, fights, even homicides engendered by quarrels over air, water, quiet, parking spaces, turf, streets, and sidewalks (Buckle and Thomas-Buckle, 1980; *Los Angeles Times*, December 30, 1980: pt. 1, p. 2). Indeed, the political program of conservatives and libertarians may be seen as an effort to reduce conflict still further by extending the process of privatization to the few remaining public goods: schools (still a frequent bone of contention), parks, and even the streets.

Our society discourages conflict in another way. To assert a claim is to render oneself vulnerable by admitting that one has been injured or bested and by acknowledging weakness (at least if the adversary is an equal or superior). Many Americans find that very difficult to do (cf. Best and Andreasen, 1977: 720; Menkel-Meadow, 1979: 54), particularly men, which may explain why there is a disproportionate number of women complainants before informal institutions. The claimant also opens himself to further reverses if the claim is denied and may be blamed for initiating the conflict or for advancing the complaint. One way to minimize exposure to such dangers is to blame oneself in the first place (Coates and Penrod, 1981). This tendency to locate the source of unhappiness in oneself rather than in the world is, I believe, a distinctive feature of contemporary American life, another facet of the "me generation." It is visible in the insatiable hunger for self-improvement books and courses, for the myriad forms of psychotherapy, and for the endless variety of practices designed to change the physical self. The alienated, atomistic individual who experiences the world as completely out of control can only hope to control himself. I will argue later in this chapter that informal institutions reflect and accentuate this tendency to attempt to solve social problems by changing oneself.

But informal institutions cannot persuasively deny the existence of conflict or totally suppress it; therefore they selectively emphasize nonstructural disputes that do not threaten social stability. First, advocates of informalism identify culture as the genesis of significant social problems—not capitalism, class struggle, racism, sexism, or autocratic power. The final evaluation of the neighborhood justice centers begins by presenting what it views as a typical case, in which two families are arguing over "differing values and approaches to rearing children" (Cook *et al.*, 1980: 1). Proponents of informalism deny the existence of basic cleavages in American society and seek to restore a consensus they locate in the silent fifties by exhorting grievants to moderate their demands (Barton, 1975). They justify a preference for compromise "or, to use the gentler term, 'accommodation,'" on the ground that today "power is better distributed" (Ford Foundation, 1978a: 6–7).

Second, informal institutions define their jurisdictional limits so as to exclude fundamental structural conflict. Many informal forums are neighborhood institutions, but most significant interaction in contemporary society occurs outside the residential neighborhood. The latter rarely contains the antagonistic dyads of capitalist and worker, producer and consumer, polluter and pollutee; residential segregation separates races and classes, sometimes even age sets, or people with different sexual orientations. Just as the forces of oppression (capital, state) extend across neighborhood boundaries, so must the organizations of resistance that are fighting for distributive justice and social change (women, minorities, unions, environmentalists) (Kidder, 1980). Ignoring such confrontations, the informal institution concentrates, instead, upon conflict between those who are relatively equal: family members, consumer and retailer (visualized as the corner grocery store), tenant and local landlord (not large real estate management organization). It handles intraclass conflict, or at most disputes between workers and petty bourgeoisie. Indeed, it may seek to convince the parties that their interests are really harmonious—for instance, that both tenant and building superintendent are exploited by the landlord—not in order to encourage them to ally against their exploiter but rather to cool out the grievances of each and convince them that nothing can be done (Felstiner and Williams, 1978: 229). Other informal institutions, such as media ombudsmen and consumer protection agencies, also shape conflict by scapegoating the exceptional enterprise that is totally irresponsible, thereby diverting attention from routine business practices and ensuring that regulation and publicity will have only a very limited general deterrent effect (Schrag, 1972; Steele, 1975; Silbey, 1978; Palen, 1979: 824, 832).

The role of informal institutions in channeling conflict can be seen most clearly in those areas that absorb the bulk of their energies: domestic disputes and consumer grievances. The former is the single largest category in most neighborhood dispute institutions, which thereby replicate the preoccupation of virtually all legal aid, legal services, and judicare programs, both in the United States and abroad (Johnson, 1974: 374 n.31; Handler *et al.*, 1978: 52; Royal Commission, 1979: 106–107; Legal Services Corporation, 1980: 73–77). This can hardly be coincidence. Rather (as suggested by the epigraph to this section), it constitutes a diversion of state resources and citizen attention from problems that are relatively insoluble and therefore dangerous—because they oppose the individual to state or capital—to problems that are certainly less dangerous and relatively "soluble," if only by exit (cf. Witty, 1980: 118). Consumerism performs a similar function, if for a different group. Whereas it is the poor and lower middle class whose domestic disturbances reach informal institutions, dissatisfaction with goods and services is more pervasive among the middle class and higher-salaried workers (Best and Andreasen, 1977: 708, 720–721). Consumer grievances are heard (and stimulated) less by neighborhood institutions than by media ombudsmen, state consumer protection agencies, and the complaint mechanisms of producers and sellers. But the latter also serve to distract attention from more fundamental conflict by stressing the quality and performance of consumer goods. Indeed, I see consumerism not as antagonistic to capital but as a corollary of advertising campaigns that seek (with a fair degree of success) to predicate self-image upon consumption—you are what you buy—and substitute brand-name loyalty ("I'd rather fight than switch") for the older loyalties to class, ethnic group, and locality. Informal institutions are able to channel conflict in these ways because they appeal to the basic desire of people to control (or believe they control) their own destinies. Most people, but especially the poor, feel that they exercise more control over their domestic lives than over their relations with the external world (Coates and Penrod, 1981). Most people with significant amounts of discretionary income experience a sense of autonomy and power in spending it (encouraged by superficial product and service differentation)—power they do not expect to exercise in their work lives or over the physical environment. Hence informal institutions allow them to express those grievances that they themselves feel are most likely to be redressed. Informal institutions thus collapse the political into the personal and nurture the commodity fetishism of capitalism.

By mediating conflict, informal justice reduces the potential for social disruption. In this it does not differ from other state dispute institutions, but it is able to reach forms of conflict that may escape the latter for a variety of reasons. Courts and many administrative agencies are organized to process controversies between disputants represented by lawyers; judges do not like to deal with pro se parties, and in any case most lay people feel incompetent to represent themselves in court (Ruhnka *et al.*, 1978: 60–65). Mediators therefore serve to moderate the demands of disputants where no lawyers have been retained and judges are either uncomfortable in performing the task or lack the necessary skills (Ford Foundation, 1978a: 5). Our formal political institutions, both legislative and executive, often shun potentially explosive forms of conflict in the fear that intervention can only make enemies. Mediators and arbitrators, who are not responsible to a constituency, can fill this role with less risk (*Ibid.*: 21–28; see also Goldmann, 1981). Informal institutions can also help to transform conflict so that it is more easily processed by formal institutions. Similar transformations already occur in many other institutional settings (see Bohannan, 1965; Golding, 1969; Felstiner *et al.*, 1981): Lawyers reshape the claims of their clients before presenting them to the judge (Ruhnka *et al.*, 1978: 183–185); courts compel litigants to exhaust their administrative remedies; other third-party agents require grievants to use the conciliatory procedures of those against whom they are complaining (Greenberg and Stanton, 1980); judges send recalcitrant parties out into the corridor to negotiate a resolution, often with the help of their lawyers or a social worker (Mnookin and Kornhauser, 1979: 954–956); colonial courts in Africa required parties to submit their disputes to traditional authorities and to tell the court what the latter recommended (Abel, 1970: 52). Arbitration and mediation, whether mandatory or voluntary, is thus another step in the lengthy process of transforming—and neutralizing—conflict.

One of the most powerful ways in which informal (and formal) legal institu-

tions neutralize conflict is by individualizing grievances. Although neighborhood institutions constantly speak about community, what they actually require
(and reproduce) is a collection of isolated individuals circumscribed by residence.
Informalism appropriates the socialist ideal of collectivity but robs it of its content
(cf. Bankowski and Mungham, 1979). The individual grievant must appear
alone before the informal institution, deprived of the support of such natural
allies as family, friends, work mates, even neighbors. This seems to me a more
subtle form of the very explicit, often brutal, efforts by state and capital to
prevent, undermine, and delegitimate attempts by the oppressed to organize and
take collective action—such as the suppression of strikes and demonstrations, the
subversion of unions and political organizations, or red-baiting (cf. Hall, 1980:
11–12). In one respect, informal institutions actually excel their formal counterparts in individualizing conflict: They operate in total privacy. Although this
guarantee of confidentiality is justifed in the name of process, its effect is to
isolate grievants from one another and from the community, inhibiting the
perception of common grievances. Without the possibility of aggregation, of
some greater impact, even the most committed grievant will burn out and
"lump" the complaint (Nader, 1979: 1017 n. 102).

Advocates of informalism are aware of this objection and stress the capacity of
such institutions to aggregate grievances. Rosenberg (1971a), for instance, proposed that a state agency buy off consumer complaints and then aggregate them;
certainly consumer protection agencies and media ombudsmen are supposed to
look for recurring patterns (see Ladinsky et al., 1979a). But for several reasons
this potential is often unrealized. First, those who hear the complaints may lack
an incentive to aggregate. Enormous caseloads (and the pressure to increase
them) generate pressure to move the cases with the least possible effort (Silbey,
1978; Palen, 1979). The training of mediators focuses their attention on the
unique attributes of the particular disputants (Felstiner and Williams, 1980:
8–10). Informal institutions often lack the records that would permit the perception of common patterns. The use of amateur or paraprofessional mediators, who
handle disputes infrequently and display high turnover, also hinders aggregation,
for they, like the disputants themselves, experience everyone as a first offender
(Baumgartner, 1980b). Indeed, when informal intermediaries perceive and attempt to correct patterns of misconduct, they may be harshly rebuked. An
arbitrator in the Harlem Small Claims Court (widely viewed as one of the best in
the country) was so outraged by a landlord's effort to overcharge an elderly tenant
that he decided for the latter and added on the postcard informing the landlord of
the award: "Judgments are going to continue to go against slum landlords like
you in small claims court so long as you continue to mistreat tenants!" "When
the facts of this case were brought to the attention of the administrative judge, all
hell broke loose . . . and the arbitrator received a severe reprimand and a warning" (Ruhnka et al., 1978: 146). Because community or societal impact is so
much more difficult to measure than case turnover, evaluators of informal jus-

tice tend to stress the latter to the neglect of the former and strongly influence the institutions themselves to adopt similar priorities (Cook *et al.*, 1980: 95). Conflict can result in prospective aggregation through the declaration or modification of general behavioral norms. But informal institutions rarely have this power. Instead they tend to be antinormative: The complainant who protests a normative violation may find himself criticized for making the complaint; the intermediary who is too judgmental (as in the abovementioned case) may be instructed to relax his standards. This hostility to norms is consistent with an ideology that elevates the market over politics and individual choice over collective decision making, and with a pop psychology that urges: "if it feels good, do it."

Informal institutions are able to individualize grievances for the same reason that they were able to divert attention from structural conflict: They offer a remedy that is not unattractive given the limited range of alternatives. The multiplication of specialized institutions—landlord–tenant courts, consumer protection agencies, media ombudsmen, neighborhood justice centers—reflects and reproduces the division of the individual into many discrete roles. In none of these can the individual invest sufficient energy to press a grievance aggressively, whereas his or her adversaries—landlords, merchants, manufacturers, state bureaucrats—*can* concentrate their substantial resources on resisting the claim (Friedman, 1962: 143; Galanter, 1974). As a consequence, the grievant is receptive to the only remedy the informal institution can offer—exit from the relationship (Felstiner, 1974). Informalism thus offers a result, as well as a process, that is individualistic; it fosters labor mobility (exit from employment relationships), residential mobility (exit from landlord–tenant relationships), even interpersonal mobility (exit from intimate relationships). This simply provides normative sanction for the dominant response to grievance and incipient conflict—namely, avoidance (Felstiner, 1974; Baumgartner, 1980b). It puts an official imprimatur on a response already widely accepted as proper (and thus does convey an implicit moral message): Don't interfere, don't meddle, mind your own business (Baumgartner, 1980b). Avoidance, surely, is the ultimate in individualism— severance of a dyadic relationship even before conflict has flowered. One reason it is the preferred response is the fear of escalation and retaliation—hence action, when taken, is anonymous (to preserve the existing anonymity of social interaction) (Baumgartner, 1980a; Dean, 1981; cf. Starr, 1978: 163–167). Informal institutions encourage a limited voicing of grievances in place of precipitate avoidance by offering some continuing anonymity (through privacy) and, more importantly, protection from revenge. Yet the consequence is not to direct anger outward—at the respondent, much less at the more fundamental causes of the grievance—but rather to turn it inwards on the grievant himself. Several of the characteristics of informal institutions converge to foster self-blame: for instance, their lack of authority, their inability to do much about the external world (see

Coates and Penrod, 1981). Individualizing the dispute has a similar effect: Attribution theory asserts that high distinctiveness in the characterization of misfortune—this only happens to me—reduces external blame (*Ibid.*). The very effort by the mediator to help the grievant understand his adversary's behavior tends to convince the former that the latter's conduct was intentional rather than accidental, rectifiable rather than inevitable, idiosyncratic rather than modal; each of these transformations increases self-blame (*Ibid.*). Thus informal institutions perfect the process of individualization: The complainant comes to see himself as his own worst enemy, the solution to his problem as entirely within, "accommodation" as the proper—the only possible—response.

For many of the reasons explored in the discussion of informalism as social control, informal institutions disproportionately neutralize the grievances of the dominated. First, the dominated are relatively uninvolved in the formal legal system: They do not mobilize it proactively, and though they are sued, they frequently default (Mayhew and Reiss, 1969; Curran, 1977: 192–193; Ruhnka *et al.*, 1978: 123, 129). Consequently, formal legal institutions do not serve to cool out their grievances or persuade them to acknowledge and satisfy the claims of others. At the same time, the dominated lack some of the alternatives to law enjoyed by the more privileged. Whereas the latter can often exit from troubled relationships—changing residences, employer, or retailer, or even breaking with an intimate (Felstiner, 1974)—the former are often locked into conflict (Baumgartner, 1980b). Furthermore, the privileged can more readily negotiate with their adversaries, who are likely to be their social inferiors, or at most their equals. On the other hand, the characteristics of informal institutions render them more attractive to the dominated and less attractive to the privileged. Because mediators are of relatively low status (both by origin and by role), the privileged will be reluctant to submit to their authority (Baumgartner, 1980a), whereas the dominated will enjoy a greater sense of control (Coates and Penrod, 1981).

But the relative charms of informal institutions are not enough to attract the dominated; incentives must be supplemented by varying degrees of pressure. This is hardly surprising: most sanctions are ultimately backed by the threat of force, more or less explicit (e.g., Engel, 1980: 439–440). Contemporary American state informalism, however, tries hard to obscure the coercive element by using the forms of individual choice, by miming the market—since buying and selling is the paradigm of freedom under advanced capitalism. (Thus Carl's Jr. spends its advertising budget to persuade the public to associate it with "freedom of choice" between hamburgers and cheeseburgers while its owner, Carl Karcher, spends his profits opposing the freedom of women to choose abortion.) Grievance mechanisms become simply another object of consumption—the commodification of justice is extended from formal to informal institutions. And just as the "freedom to consume" is delusive—producers and sellers stimulate consumer desires and manipulate their satisfaction (Galbraith, 1978)—so the freedom to choose a mode of redress for grievances is strongly shaped by the state. Formal institutions steer grievants to more "appropriate" forums (Cook *et al.*, 1980: 13, 15; Palenski *et al.*, 1980: Ch. 6). Informal institutions hold out a promise of justice—punishment of an adversary, effective use of ostensible power—that is consistently betrayed in practice (as I will argue later in this chapter). At the same time they stress, and even exaggerate, the inaccessibility and inutility of formal institutions. Thus small claims courts "persuade" litigants to arbitrate by pointing out the greater delay, cost, and uncertainty of adjudication (Sarat, 1976: 352). And indeed small claims courts are ineffective: Half the plaintiffs are unable to serve their adversaries, and half the defendants served default (Ruhnka *et al.*, 1978: 123). Hence even when arbitration is not officially an alternative, small claims court judges use the difficulty of enforcement to convince the parties to settle (*Ibid.*: 140–141). Sometimes coercion is even more thinly veiled. Thus arbitration may be mandatory, but the fiction of choice is preserved through a right to appeal or to a trial de novo—rights that are encumbered, however, by a substantial penalty in the form of costs if the applicant does not significantly improve his award (Johnson *et al.*, 1977a: 45 n. 48). Or arbitration may be justified by consent even though the "consent" may be evidenced by a contract of adhesion and the grievant may be unaware of his right to rescind (*Ibid.*: 53).

I have argued in this section that informal legal institutions neutralize conflict. Perhaps the most important way they do so is by denying redress. Sometimes they refrain from using powers they purport to possess: Media ombudsmen decline to name businesses that are the object of complaints (Palen, 1979: 832); consumer protection agencies fail to prosecute (Silbey, 1978; cf. Crowe, 1978; Serber, 1980). Because informal institutions tend to see their role as broker or referral source, rather than as active intermediary, much less champion (Ladinsky *et al.*, 1979; Nader, 1980b), many grievants seek only information, not action (Palen, 1979). Sometimes it is the advocate who holds back: A lawyer representing a client in arbitration may be less vigorous because, in the next case, the lawyer–arbitrator may represent an adversary, or opposing counsel may become the arbitrator (*University of Pennsylvania Law Review*, 1953; Johnson *et al.*, 1977a: 49 n. 74).

But much of the inefficacy of informal institutions is structural, not volitional. Small claims courts present the plaintiff with numerous obstacles: obtaining jurisdiction over an adversary, presenting a threat sufficiently credible to persuade the adversary to appear, avoiding the delays of removal or appeal, adducing enough evidence to prevail, and executing the judgment (Yngvesson and Hennessey, 1975: 251, 254–255; Ruhnka *et al.*, 1978: 123, 139). Sometimes an informal mechanism is transposed from one social setting where it has, at least, a limited effect to another where it may have little or none. An ombudsman may

influence government officials who fear or respect public opinion, whether they
are elected or appointed, but extension of that institution to consumer complaints conflates political and market behavior without persuasive evidence that
the relationship between enterprises and consumers is identical to that between
government officials and citizens (cf. Hirschman, 1970; Lindblom, 1977). Finally, the remedies available in informal institutions—when they award any—
are limited. Small claims courts can grant only money damages, not equitable
relief (Ruhnka *et al.*, 1978: 34), and the judgments are too small to affect the
respondent significantly. Other dispute mechanisms, such as neighborhood justice centers, claim to be interested in changing behavior, but they are incapable
of doing so. Indeed, the heavy caseload, to which they aspire or which is imposed
on them, guarantees this incapacity (Johnson *et al.*, 1977a: 63–64). Consequently, the grievances they are most likely to hear—those between
intimates—are precisely the matters they are least capable of resolving (Felstiner
and Williams, 1980: 45–47).

Informal institutions cannot neutralize conflict if their instrumental inefficacy
is too obvious; they must *appear* to be doing something. If they cannot offer
redress, or are reluctant to do so, the only course is to suggest that the complainant was wrong to complain, to destablize his attribution of responsibility
(Coates and Penrod, 1981). This, then, is one interpretation of what informal
institutions are doing when they claim to explore the full range of grievances on
both sides in order to get to the root of the dispute. Such an approach, together
with the basic powerlessness of the forum, helps prepare the grievant to accept
the solution commonly proposed by informal institutions: compromise. Such an
outcome may actually be invited by the grievant who, deprived of allies, isolated,
fearful of reprisals, and skeptical about success, advances his claim timidly
(Baumgartner, 1980b). But informal institutions do not rely on this; they actively
encourage compromise. If both parties are wrong—as a "full exploration of the
issues" invariably concludes—then neither has a strong normative basis for his
position (Johnson *et al.*, 1977a: 49 nn. 74 and 78, 52). Informalism thus offers a
way out of the impasse created by the clash of inconsistent and irreconcilable
norms that characterize a heterogeneous class society (Baumgartner, 1980b).
The outcome, like the original "choice" of a forum, is clothed in the forms of
consent (Ford Foundation, 1978a: 11–13; Cook *et al.*, 1980: 104). Yet it is
essential to remember that the grievant, strongly influenced by the intermediary,
is relinquishing something valuable and valued by agreeing to the compromise;
60 percent of those who appeal the judgment of mandatory arbitration win their
appeals (Johnson *et al.*, 1977a: 47).

By insisting on a compromise, informal institutions not only fail to give the
complainant the tangible redress he is seeking but also frustrate intangible goals.
It is ironic that institutions publicly justified by the ideal of community and
targeted at disputes arising in ongoing relationships serve instead to dissolve

community and to terminate relationships by facilitating exit (Snyder, 1978: 772; Merry, 1979). Just as compromise preserves the material status quo, so exit reproduces the social status quo. The mediation technique chosen by most programs—communication by the disputants only indirectly, through the mediator, a form of shuttle diplomacy—increases the probability that the relationship will be severed, just as it does in labor disputes (Felstiner and Williams, 1980: 11). Informal justice can be seen as adapting the middle-class response to conflict—exit—to the circumstances of the dominated by surrounding that option with greater physical security and endowing it with authoritative normative approval (Felstiner, 1974; Baumgartner, 1980a; 1980b). And just as informal institutions prepare the complainant for compromise by reversing moral judgment and focusing on the complainant's transgressions, so they reverse the psychological inquiry, seeking to understand rather than to explain the respondent's behavior. Small claims court judges are quite explicit about this: Recognizing they cannot provide the material or intangible relief the complainant seeks, they view the hearing as a form of catharsis (Ruhnka *et al.*, 1978: 21–22). This is another corruption of the anthropological model of informalism. The "full airing" of the complainant's grievances becomes an end in itself, not a preliminary to redressing them. Complainants also appear to be aware of this. They invoke informal institutions as a way to let off steam (Sarat, 1976: 345–346, 348), and though they express satisfaction with the experience, they remain pessimistic about the long-range pay off (Connor and Surette, 1977: 11–15).

None of this should be unexpected. Informalism is simply the latest in a long line of reforms that seek to realize the promises of liberalism. Consistent with liberal ideals, they do so by concentrating on *process* not *outcome*. It is not coincidence that before the Ford Foundation became interested in informal dispute institutions (1978a; 1978b; Cappelletti, 1978–1979; 1981) it supported research and pilot projects on public interest law (e.g., Ford Foundation, 1973; Ford Foundation and American Bar Association, 1976; Weisbrod *et al.*, 1978), legal services (Johnson, 1974: 21–23; Handler *et al.*, 1978), and decentralization. Yet as Marc Galanter has persuasively argued (1974), and as I will discuss further in the next section, changes in process will not alter outcomes as long as the structure of the adversaries remains constant (see also Abel, 1979c). Labor arbitration works (when it works) because capital is opposed by organized labor, not by individual workers (Getman, 1979); if the process is transposed to conflict between slumlords and unorganized tenants, for instance, it will inevitably favor the former (Lazerson, 1982; cf. Goldbeck, 1975). Informalism can respond to such criticism only by trying to evade it, by stressing process to the neglect of outcome, pretending that no one wins or loses, advancing the satisfaction of individual disputants as the only appropriate criterion. Mediators can conclude that they are extraordinarily successful (Felstiner and Williams, 1980: 33), and government and private notables (including the chief justice and attorney general of the United States and the president of the American Bar Association) can lavish uncritical praise on institutions we know to be virtually ineffective (Burger, 1976; 1977; McKay, 1977; Bell, 1978; Ford Foundation, 1978a; 1978b; Tate, 1979).

LEGAL INSTITUTIONS AS RESOURCES

The creation of informal institutions necessarily alters the balance of advantage between parties with opposed interests. This is virtually axiomatic: Legal institutions, formal and informal, are valuable resources for enforcing rights, regardless of whether they are used or merely threatened (Turk, 1976). But the actual impact of any change in legal institutions, substantive rules, or procedures can be determined only by analyzing concrete instances; that is the objective of this section.

Some institutions that are represented as "informal" actually increase the capacity of those who are already advantaged (socially and legally) to enforce their rights. The most notable are small claims courts and, more recently, landlord–tenant courts. The notion that these are intended to benefit individuals or tenants is a contemporary post factum legitimation; small claims courts were explicitly established to facilitate debt collection by merchants (Yngvesson and Hennessey, 1975: 224). The enormous expansion of consumer credit has made them an essential element of the retailing process. Similarly, landlord–tenant courts are an integral part of residential leasing, without which it could not function (Lazerson, 1982). "Informal" alternatives to criminal prosecution are now becoming a significant weapon in the arsenal of sellers. Contemporary retailing mandates open displays and few sales personnel, thereby presenting a substantial temptation to shoplift. Formal prosecution is rarely attempted because it is too expensive and the store stands to gain little (cf. Blankenburg, 1976). But in Canada, a mediation diversion program has been substituted that requires fewer resources and helps the store to secure restitution (The Mooter, p. 9, Fall 1977). In each situation it is argued that the *creditor* cannot be denied a remedy (it is ethically wrong, illegal, and economically undesirable) and will secure it in a formal court if no alternative is offered. This assumption (empirically very questionable) lays the foundation for justifying informal processes on the ground that they are less costly and threatening to the *defendant* (Ruhnka *et al.*, 1978: 41–48, 192; cf. Yngvesson and Hennessey, 1975: 267). This is a variant of the widespread mystification that legal rights and remedies cannot alter economic relationships—the landlord will simply raise the rent, the merchant will deny credit or increase the price of the product (e.g., Hazard, 1969: 707–708)—a form of economic determinism that these same liberal skeptics attribute, disparagingly, to Marxist analysis. The consequence of accepting this argument is a constant increase in the jurisdiction of small claims courts and their like (cf. Galanter, 1975: 354; Ruhnka *et al.*, 1978: 1).

But institutions do make a difference, and the salient characteristic of informal institutions is that they continue to provide advantaged plaintiffs with a sword to enforce their rights while denying disadvantaged defendants an equivalent shield. Those who mobilize a legal institution often begin with a significant advantage over their adversaries. But there are reasons why this is particularly true in informal institutions. Tribunals that are functionally specialized and geograph-ically localized are more easily dominated by a few powerful litigants (Baum, 1977; Palen, 1979: 831, 840; cf. Scheiber, 1980: 706–707). Small claims courts frequently grant continuances to plaintiffs but deny them to defendants; they grant default judgments to plaintiffs, but when the defendant appears alone they refuse to dismiss the case (Ruhnka *et al.*, 1978: 131, 137–138). Corporate plaintiffs frequently choose to sue in a jurisdiction that is inconvenient to the defendant, thereby enhancing the likelihood of default (Yngvesson and Hennes-sey, 1975: 246 n. 19). The plaintiff recovers a higher proportion of his claims when the defendant defaults than when the defendant contests the case (Ruhnka *et al.*, 1978: 135). And when claims are contested plaintiffs are strategically better situated: the prima facie case—plaintiff lent money, extended credit, rented the defendant an apartment—is usually much simpler than the defense—violations of technical protective legislation that "informal" courts typically ignore; fur-thermore, the plaintiff keeps better records and therefore can document his claim (Frierson, 1977; Ruhnka *et al.*, 1978: 27, 112; Lazerson, 1982). Finally, the business plaintiff is not seriously disadvantaged by being denied legal representation—it is still a repeat player with the strengths of that status— whereas the individual defendant feels, correctly, that he needs a lawyer (Sarat, 1976: 250–251; Ruhnka *et al.*, 1978: 60, 112; Abel, 1979c). The consequence is that plaintiffs are disproportionately successful in small claims courts—they win half of all cases by default and three-quarters of all contested cases (Yngvesson and Hennessey, 1975: 243, 246)—a much better record than they achieve in courts of general jurisdiction (Wanner, 1975). Perhaps aware of the hopelessness of the situation, individual defendants simply admit 60–80 percent of all claims (Ruhnka *et al.*, 1978: 149). Thus small claims courts display the combination of formal equality and substantive inequality that characterizes other legal institu-tions of liberal capitalism: Although individual plaintiffs win almost as large a proportion of their claims as do business plaintiffs, the latter so greatly out-number the former that small claims courts are primarily a mechanism for enforcing the rights of business (*Ibid.*: 110–112).

Not all informal institutions are as coercive as small claims and landlord–tenant courts. But those that lack effective power are simply shunned by business claimants. Thus enterprises refuse to arbitrate controversies with debtors (Johnson *et al.*, 1977a: 52) or to mediate their claims in the neighborhood justice centers (Harrington, 1980; Cook *et al.*, 1980: 23, 38). Business can do so because it is well equipped to use the coercive alternatives the state provides; indeed, it can invoke the mandate of due process to require that coercion be made available. Business uses noncoercive means only when those are *more* effective in gaining its ends, when persuasion is more likely to secure compliance, e.g., to convince a tenant to pay back rent rather than simply wait for eviction and leave, or to induce a debtor to reschedule the debt rather than default (Sarat, 1976: 356–357; Johnson *et al.*, 1977a: 96). Sometimes coercive institutions incorporate persuasive processes for just this reason (Yngvesson and Hennessey, 1975: 226; Ruhnka *et al.*, 1978: 167–168) or refer the plaintiff to a less coercive institution (Cook *et al.*, 1980: 23, 38). Even if an enterprise has no intention of submitting to the jurisdiction of a noncoercive institution, it may threaten to do so in order to secure a better settlement from an individual who is concerned about the cost and inconvenience of mediation or unable to distinguish it from adjudication (Snyder, 1978: 765).

If informalism grants additional offensive weapons to those already endowed with disproportionate legal resources while depriving the legally disadvantaged of the protection of formal defenses, it also denies the latter the sword of formality while assuring the former that they can continue to invoke formality as a shield. For the disadvantaged, informal institutions are a substitute, not a supplement. To use Galanter's concepts: informal institutions tend to be an arena in which one-shot plaintiffs make claims against repeat players, or against other one-shot defendants (whereas repeat players prefer formal institutions when they act offensively) (1974). Thus arbitration is often substituted for adjudication when insured are claiming against insurers, consumers against sellers, students against teachers, tenants against landlords, welfare recipients against the government, patients against physicians or health plans, prisoners against prison administrators, and employees against employers (Johnson *et al.*, 1977a: 50–58). This is not because the legally disadvantaged *prefer* informal institutions; they would like the leverage of state coercion (Merry, 1979). Informalism is not a grass roots movement; rather, informal institutions are imposed from the top down, typically by the state or by capital. Small claims court litigants rated neighborhood justice very low when asked to rank a number of proposed reforms of those courts (Ruhnka *et al.*, 1978: 185). What individual grievants want is an authority with adequate resources (Baumgartner, 1980a; Palenski *et al.*, 1980: 65–66). They are particularly aware of the need for coercion when confronting a more powerful adversary (e.g., Engel, 1980: 440–444); even the mediators recognize their own inadequacy and seek to avoid such disputes between unequals (Felstiner and Williams, 1980: 5).

Informal institutions do not satisfy this need for coercive authority for several reasons. First, they often cannot obtain jurisdiction: Sellers and producers refuse to submit to arbitration when consumers complain (Eovaldi and Gestrin, 1971:

310–311); more than a third of the respondents failed to appear in one mediation program (*The Mooter*, vol. 1, no. 3, p. 35, Spring 1978). Second, they deny legal representation: Some specifically exclude lawyers on the ground that the institution is informal and the grievant has a right to a formal rehearing (Stanley, 1977); others simply fail to provide lawyers. Although the unrepresented plaintiff does better in arbitration than in adjudication (Yngvesson and Hennessey, 1975: 250; Sarat, 1976: 567), in neither situation does he do as well as the litigant who is represented in court. Individuals are more disadvantaged by being denied representation than are businesses. And the claimants themselves sense this: They affirm their need for representation in small claims court (Ruhnka *et al.*, 1978: 60); of all the referrals by neighborhood justice centers, they found referrals to lawyers most helpful (Cook *et al.*, 1980: 66). Third, individual grievants confronting more powerful adversaries want an authority that is sympathetic, predisposed toward their plight—e.g., an administrative agency or jury—mediators and arbitrators do not help to right the scales. Fourth, informal institutions deprive grievants of substantive rights. They are antinormative and urge the parties to compromise (Sarat, 1976: 364–365; Witty, 1980: 115–117); although this appears evenhanded, it works to the detriment of the party who is *advancing* a claim—typically the individual grievant. Informalism may ensure that more claimants get *some* redress, but the relief is almost always less adequate—that is certainly the history of workers' compensation, no-fault divorce, and no-fault compensation for automobile accidents (Johnson *et al.*, 1977a: 49 n. 74). Laws designed to protect and benefit the disadvantaged, such as those protecting the consumer, are ignored in informal tribunals (Ruhnka *et al.*, 1978: 27, 50). We can see the differential resources conferred by formal and informal institutions if we look at a particular disadvantaged category—women—and note that informal institutions offer them less protection against spousal violence and worsen their chances of obtaining custody after divorce (*Dispute Resolution*, no. 6, p. 7, December 1980). Fifth, the success rate for individual plaintiffs in informal institutions is frequently less than 50 percent and thus much lower than the success rate of business and governmental plaintiffs in formal institutions (Wanner, 1975; Palen, 1979: 817). Sixth, the claim that informal institutions are speedier than their formal counterparts is often based on a false comparison with full-scale trials; if informal processes are compared, instead, with the abbreviated proceedings by which the vast majority of cases are disposed in formal courts, they are no quicker and may even be slower (Cook *et al.*, 1980: 74, 76). Seventh, informal institutions are ineffective in ensuring the performance of agreed outcomes. Unrepresented individual plaintiffs have much more difficulty executing judgments than do unrepresented corporate plaintiffs (Yngvesson and Hennessey, 1975: 254–255). Given all this, evidence that individual grievants are "satisfied" hardly proves that they are benefited by informal institutions, especially since those grievants appear to be just as "satisfied" when the informal institution *fails* to hold a hearing and even when the institution itself labels the dispute as "unresolved" (Cook *et al.*, 1980: 59, 63). By the time the informal institution measures satisfaction, it has so depressed the expectations and shaped the wishes of the grievant that any outcome will be satisfactory (Crowe, 1978; Palen, 1979: 816–818; see generally Nader, 1980a). Indeed, even the advocates of informalism acknowledge that it is ineffective in redressing the grievances of individuals against powerful entities (Cook *et al.*, 1980: 28, 31–32). This inefficacy is neither accidental nor rectifiable but is rather essential to another function (discussed later in the chapter) that informal institutions share with the other legal institutions of liberal capitalism—legitimating that social system by publicly declaring rights and remedies while simultaneously ensuring that they are systematically unenforced or underenforced.

Notwithstanding this powerlessness, respondents before informal institutions still retain the protections of formality. They can transfer cases to formal courts or obtain a formal trial de novo by way of appeal (Ruhnka *et al.*, 1978: 157). They have a right to retain counsel, either in the informal institution or in the formal alternative (*Ibid.*: 69). They can even refuse to submit to the jurisdiction of most informal tribunals. None of this should be surprising: If formality, either as sword or as shield, can sometimes help to redress the balance of advantage, it will usually benefit the powerful.

The creation of informal institutions generally increases the quantity of state coercion available to the advantaged, in two ways. First, *all* legal institutions under liberal capitalism necessarily favor the advantaged unless they aggressively champion the interests of the disadvantaged—something that liberal ideology severely constrains. Such favoritism is not primarily the result of bias on the part of the decision maker (so that studies seeking to measure individual bias are misguided and, by demonstrating its absence, simply contribute to the legitimation of liberalism; see Abel, 1978). Rather, inequality infiltrates the legal system through the less visible behavior of nonofficial actors, principally the disputants themselves (cf. Goldstein, 1960). Informal institutions that confer significant resources on complainants display patterns of use quite similar to those found in formal courts (Galanter, 1975: 348; cf. Wanner, 1974). Surely it would be naive to expect that those who consume disproportionate amounts of all other goods and services, private and public, would make an exception for informal justice. As long as other resources are unequally distributed—wealth, power, knowledge, social networks, access to lawyers—these will strongly influence the mobilization of law (Ruhnka *et al.*, 1978: 85–88). And just as those with prior legal experience use formal legal institutions more frequently than those who are legally inexperienced (Galanter, 1974; Marks *et al.*, 1974: 63–64; Curran, 1977: 190–194), so they also resort to informal alternatives more often (Salas and Schneider, 1979: 178). Similarly, the number of middle-class complainants is greater when the informal institution functions as a resource rather than a means of state social control (Cook *et al.*, 1980: 23). This simply reflects the general pattern in a class society: The privileged mobilize institutions they can control, whereas the disadvantaged appeal to superordinate authority (Baumgartner, 1980a; see also Palenski *et al.*, 1980: 90).

Variation in use is itself a function of the benefits that can be anticipated from the institution. Here, too, less visible differences are likely to be crucial. I have already noted that the probability of executing a small claims court judgment is greatly enhanced by legal representation (Yngvesson and Hennessey, 1975: 254–255; Ruhnka *et al.*, 1978: 165–166) and that business plaintiffs are much more likely than individuals to be legally represented (Yngvesson and Hennessey, 1975: 251). Another low-visibility hurdle that is both critical and difficult is service of process: Half of all complaints initiated in small claims court are never served, and this is the single most frequent cause of litigant dissatisfaction (Ruhnka *et al.*, 1978: 175). Although the studies have failed to investigate bias at this stage, it seems likely that business plaintiffs are more successful than individuals in perfecting service. Sometimes coercive informal institutions consciously accommodate large-volume business users, and thereby foster their dominance, by establishing special collections dockets that reduce the plaintiff's cost per case (*Ibid.*: 130). But such deliberate preferential treatment is generally unnecessary: The distribution of public resources, such as law, naturally mirrors the allocation of private resources (*Serrano* v. *Priest*, 5 Cal. 3d 584, 1971; Abel, 1979c: 32–36; Baumgartner, 1980a). And the consumption of legal resources, in turn, enhances not only power and wealth but also social status: Litigants seek to appeal to the Supreme Court as much for the symbolic affirmation of the importance of their claims as for any material advantage they are likely to gain.

Informalism not only broadens the spectrum of state coercion but also reallocates legal resources in a way that confirms and strengthens the status quo. This can be seen if we contrast those who mobilize the more coercive small claims court—disproportionately businesses—with those who resort to less coercive processes such as conciliation and mediation—disproportionately individuals. Situations in which the same adversaries confront one another in inverted positions illustrate this proposition more dramatically. When a seller asserts a claim against a consumer—accuses the latter of shoplifting, for instance—the full coercive power of the state is mobilized, although this may be cloaked within an informal process that effectively deprives the accused of the shield of formal due process (Grau and Kahn, 1980). When the consumer complains against a seller—about defective goods, poor service, or unfair prices—the former is relegated to a remedy that is noncoercive and largely ineffective (Friedman, 1977). Although reforms at both the top and the bottom of the judicial hierarchy seek to maintain a semblance of evenhandedness, even a superficial analysis reveals that resources are being lavished on formal, coercive legal institutions used almost exclusively by business (Kastenmeier and Remington, 1979), whereas the infor-

mal alternatives offered to individuals are relatively inexpensive and systematically underfunded and may actually make a net contribution to the state treasury
(Ruhnka *et al.*, 1978: 89–91, 106). Just as colonial regimes expected the judicial
systems they conferred on indigenous populations to pay their own way (e.g.,
Patterson, 1969)—although courts in the metropolitan countries were heavily
subsidized (Abel-Smith and Stevens, 1967: Chs. 4–5)—so informal justice—a
mode of internal colonialism—is to be self-financing.

This disparity is defended in a variety of ways. The state invokes a need for
"conservation," for budget reductions, arguing that there is "too much law"—
but these jeremiads are always directed at the meager legal resources of the
disadvantaged, not at the conspicuous consumption of business, just as budget
cuts invariably affect welfare recipients, not the military. Proponents of informalism maintain that individual claimants must relinquish some precision, that
due process for welfare recipients is an expensive indulgence (Johnson *et al.*,
1977a: 78; Ford Foundation, 1978b: 14); yet no one suggests that business should
make similar sacrifices, although its claims are frequently smaller in magnitude
than those of welfare recipients in the aggregate. Advocates of legal informalism
draw a misleading analogy to the groundswell of resentment against our over-
medicalized society, suggesting that because some women may prefer to give
birth at home assisted by midwives (Smith, 1978: 210) or that Warren Burger's
mother once offered a more accurate diagnosis than a specialist in dermatology
(1977: 24), the disadvantaged would also rather pursue their rights without the
aid of trained lawyers and formal courts. Finally, informalism is said to be *just* a
change in process (Ford Foundation, 1978b: 42ff.). What this obscures is that
every change in process, substance, or institutional access alters outcomes
(Mnookin and Kornhauser, 1979). The efforts of poverty lawyers in the 1960s to
secure due process safeguards for welfare recipients were motivated not by an
enthusiasm for the process itself but by the belief that it would mean more money
for more poor people (Johnson, 1974: Ch. 8; Lazerson, 1982). Because the vast
majority of disputes are resolved by the disputants themselves anticipating the
behavior of legal institutions (formal or informal), the consequences of any
change in that behavior is greatly amplified in extrainstitutional social life. All
processes are outcome influential, if not outcome determinative (cf. *Guaranty
Trust Co.* v. *York*, 326 U.S. 99, 1945).

INFORMALISM AND
OCCUPATIONAL SELF-INTEREST

Thus far I have concentrated on the significance of informal institutions to
those who use them—the state, capital, and individuals—and have argued, first,
that such institutions possess distinctive advantages for some participants and

disadvantages for others, and, second, that this in turn helps to explain institutional structure. A similar analysis can be applied to those actors within legal institutions (both formal and informal) who are not disputants but are rather specialized functionaries—judges, police, lawyers, and mediators. On the one hand, because law is not merely a subject of sporadic concern to them but is rather their occupation, they have a much larger stake in the shape of legal institutions. On the other, they are neither autonomous nor particularly powerful—they can do more to obstruct change than to implement it. Yet they are certainly not a negligible influence.

Judges appear to have a number of reasons for favoring the creation of informal institutions. Elite state appellate and federal judges (those involved in policymaking and in national professional associations) see informalism as a means of legitimating the judiciary—the subject of the next section. Trial judges at the base of the judicial hierarchy share this enthusiasm but for different reasons. First, informal institutions offer a repository for what they regard as "junk" cases—matters that fail to use their legal skills and may even resist legal resolution, that appear politically, economically, or socially insignificant, or that have become highly repetitive (Beresford, 1977). Second, trial judges enhance their own status when they establish a new stratum of subordinate employees, just as family court judges did by employing social workers and juvenile and criminal court judges by institutionalizing probation officers (cf. Larson, 1977: 214–215). At the same time, those who presently occupy subordinate positions—primarily court clerks—may feel threatened by such reforms, which deprive them of jurisdiction over deferential disputants and challenge their competence by elevating therapeutic technique over legal skills (Snyder, 1978: 764; Felstiner and Williams, 1980: 16–17). The police are also ambivalent about informalism. On the one hand, it allows them to dispose of cases, primarily family fights, that they find dangerous, messy, and unsatisfying (Parnas, 1967; Black, 1980: Ch. 5). But on the other, the police see their job as catching and punishing criminals; they feel their unique role is trivialized when they must refer a good "collar" to mediation (Felstiner and Williams, 1980: 17–18). And no one, whether police, judge, or clerk, is eager to relinquish institutional authority or resources (Erickson, 1978: 282).

Most lawyers are moved by different considerations. Like nonelite judges and police, those few lawyers in the public sector who handle cases that might be diverted to informal institutions—the 1 percent of the bar who practice in public defender and legal services offices—may be interested in divesting themselves of responsibility for matters they view as trivial or routine, such as misdemeanors or divorce (cf. Katz, 1978; Singer, 1980). But private lawyers commonly want more business, not less. Yet here, too, the situation is actually more complex. Elite lawyers lose no business through such reforms and are, in any case, more concerned with the capacity of informalism to legitimate the legal system from which they derive extraordinary benefits. Most lawyers at the base of the profession feel threatened by informalism, which they correctly perceive as expressing a strong, if implicit, animus against lawyers. Consequently, they tolerate informalism only when the parties would have been unlikely to retain a lawyer, for instance, in some uncontested divorces (Mnookin and Kornhauser, 1979) and in penny-ante personal injuries—but not in the six-figure claim (Henderson, 1977: 292–294). They oppose the provision of lay advice in small claims court where that might obviate the need to hire a lawyer (Ruhnka et al., 1978: 104). Yet this attitude is shortsighted. Prior reforms that sought to eliminate lawyers by creating informal alternatives simply generated more legal business: Lawyers frequently represent parties in workers' compensation tribunals (Conley and Noble, 1980: Table 6–1) and small claims courts (Ruhnka et al., 1978: 60–65); their advice is sought in 25 percent of all no-fault claims against automobile insurers in Massachusetts (Henderson, 1977: 314); and though they appeared in only 36 percent of all arbitrations in 1927, they were involved in 91 percent by 1947 (Auerbach, 1979). Informalism also interacts with formal legal institutions along complex boundaries, and these become the subject of endless litigation in the latter—workers' compensation is again a good example (California Citizens' Commission, 1977: 38–40). Furthermore, informalism tends to simplify disputes and to increase their numbers, making them more amenable to mass processing and permitting lawyers to increase their profits (Yngvesson and Hennessey, 1975: 227; Johnson et al., 1977a: 88, n. 24). Not all lawyers can exploit these opportunities, which require a capacity for innovation, entrepreneurial skills, the use of word processing and subordinate paraprofessionals, etc. (Muris and McChesney, 1979). Therefore informalism may intensify divisions within the profession, contributing to the obsolescence of the sole practitioner and the growth of legal clinics.

If those occupations with a stake in the formal legal system have an ambivalent attitude toward informal justice, the latter spawns its own specialists who, not surprisingly, become its strongest boosters. They ensure that informal institutions foster dependence on paraprofessional mediators, counselors, and advocates, notwithstanding the rhetoric of disputant participation and self-reliance (Yngvesson and Hennessey, 1975; Sarat, 1976; Johnson et al., 1977a: Chs. 5–6; Ruhnka et al., 1978). They also exaggerate their own success—most of the evaluations of recent programs have been performed by people dedicated to the cause of informalism, who tend to give considerable weight to the mediators' own estimates of their efficacy (Conner and Surette, 1977: 11, 13; Felstiner and Williams, 1980: 31–34).

Mediators, like all other categories of service providers, will seek to professionalize, i.e., to control entry into the occupation and to enhance its status and perquisites (Larson, 1977). Academic credentials in social work, psychology, or law may come to be required (Snyder, 1978: 751; Bridenback et al., 1979: 572):

The Boston Mediation Program intends to use volunteer attorneys, the Houston Metropolitan Mediation Center employs law student interns (*Dispute Resolution*, vol. 6, pp. 12–14, Fall 1980), and the San Jose Neighborhood Small Claims Court and the Small Claims Court of New York City both use lawyer arbitrators (Sarat, 1976; Beresford and Cooper, 1977). Indeed, we have already seen substantial progress toward the professionalization of arbitrators and, more recently, the founding of a Society of Professionals in Dispute Resolution (with an acronym—SPIDR—that is, perhaps, embarrassingly evocative), which presently has 900 members (*Dispute Resolution*, vol. 6, p. 11, Fall 1980). The emerging occupational category will differ significantly from existing legal professions: Since it defines its task as helping rather than controlling, focuses on managing people rather than manipulating technical concepts, and deals with low-status clients, it is likely to be recruited from socioeconomic strata lower than those that furnish judges and lawyers and to attract a larger number of women than do the police. Given these characteristics, it will more easily be subordinated to those legal professionals who already dominate formal institutions. The result will be yet another layer of professionals—relatively unthreatening to the existing constellation, eager to handle (and ultimately to monopolize) cases the latter do not want—who increase the dependence of citizens on occupational specialists.

INFORMALISM AND
THE LEGITIMATION OF STATE AND CAPITAL

Although informalism has important instrumental consequences—extending state control, neutralizing conflict, redistributing state resources, and advancing the interests of professionals—it is also significant as symbol, as a means of legitimating state and capital. The concept of legitimation, as I am using it, has two essential ingredients. First, it is an attempt to offer a moral account, a justification, for some activity or institution. Whether anybody is listening or is convinced are empirical questions that speak to the success of the legitimation but not to the characterization of the behavior as legitimation. Second, the account is not acceptable on its own terms—the institution or activity are not what they claim to be. Formal legal institutions constantly advance such myths: that substantive laws achieve their declared purposes; that the criminal justice system deters crime; that promulgating and inculcating ethical rules alters behavior (see Abel, 1977). Informal institutions propagate similar myths: that a stranger with minimal training can, in the course of an hour's meeting, resolve deep-rooted, long-standing conflicts between intimates; that an intermediary without coercive authority can secure redress for a grievant against a powerful adversary. That these accounts are mythic is indicated not only by their facial implausibility but also by the fact that the institutions assigned these ambitious tasks are systematically denied the resources that would be necessary to perform them. Despite the current surge of enthusiasm for informalism there are relatively few programs, and those are underfunded and little used (Johnson *et al.*, 1977a: 20, 52, 60). The infrequency of evaluations and their lack of rigor also suggest that the ostensible goals are more a form of legitimation than a motivating force. Notwithstanding the transparency of the claims for informalism, or perhaps because of it, those claims are reiterated with fervor and exaggeration. Informal institutions are characterized as a fundamental reform (Burger, 1976: 83), a remarkable, dramatic development (Smith, 1978: 205) that can reduce the caseload of civil courts by 50 percent (Johnson *et al.*, 1977a: 96). And the institutions themselves indulge in this kind of self-promotion, employing public relations officials (Palenski *et al.*, 1980: 25–26) and engaging in market research in order to identify potential consumers (*Dispute Resolution*, no. 6, p. 7, December 1980). It is noteworthy that formal legal institutions—whether courts or legal services lawyers—feel little need to advertise their services and rarely seem to lack for clients (e.g., Handler *et al.*, 1978: 60–63).

Those informal institutions that belong to the state apparatus serve to legitimate the state. Authority always seeks legitimation by settling disputes among its constituents and championing their grievances. The tribal elder, feudal lord, and urban machine politician (Karikas, 1980) all illustrate this. Informal institutions are thus an attempt to revive faith in the beneficence of the state and hope in the possibility of justice at a time of widespread cynicism and apathy (see *Dispute Resolution*, no. 6, p. 7, December 1980). At the same time, informalism responds to public hostility toward and mistrust of the state by simulating its withdrawal from civil society, purporting to relieve citizens of oppressive regulation and to expand their freedom of choice.

Informalism is obviously most relevant to the legitimation of the legal system. There is considerable evidence that public confidence in legal institutions is low (Sarat, 1977; Curran, 1977: Ch. 6; Yankelovich, Skelly and White, Inc., 1978). Litigants find formal courts forbidding, impersonal, indifferent, but there is little that judges can do about this because they are concerned to preserve the aura of impartiality that is the core of their legitimacy (Ruhnka *et al.*, 1978: 18–19). Informal institutions, by contrast, subordinate neutrality to an image of paternalistic concern (Spence, 1982). They also anticipate and allay litigant suspicions by offering a choice of forums and remedies, since disputant satisfaction correlates strongly with the belief that the procedure has been chosen (Coates and Penrod, 1981). A central ingredient in public cynicism is the belief that the legal system fails to provide equal justice for poor and rich, individuals and corporations (Curran, 1977: Ch. 6). Formal institutions respond by claiming to correct inequalities within the forum through requirements of due process and the subsidization of legal representation. Informal institutions, by contrast, try to exclude the more egregious instances of inequality. Formal institutions are legitimated by reference to an adversarial ideal according to which the parties not only have been equalized but also assert their claims vigorously before an impartial adjudicator. In reality, however, most outcomes are negotiated privately by the parties and simply approved by the formal authority: Plea bargaining (*Law & Society Review*, 1979) and the settlement of civil disputes (Mnookin and Kornhauser, 1979; Ross, 1980) are notorious examples. Formal institutions address this dissonance between ideal and practice by seeking to judicialize negotiation. Informal justice offers a different solution: It legitimates and institutionalizes two-party negotiation as an appropriate means of dispute resolution, and it reinvigorates an adversary process within informal institutions by fostering disputant participation. If familiarity with formal legal institutions breeds contempt (Sarat, 1976: 347; 1977: 441; Curran, 1977: 234–239), then the innovative appearance of informalism may revive interest and rekindle enthusiasm (Weller *et al.*, 1979). In each of these respects, informalism helps to legitimate the legal system by distracting attention from the problems of formal institutions. These, it is argued, are not defective; they are simply being asked to do too much and to do the wrong kinds of things (Sander, 1976). The solution, therefore, is not to reform the core of the legal system—formal courts and administrative agencies—but rather to create alternative institutions at the periphery (cf. Santos, 1982). To the extent that this strategy succeeds, pressure for fundamental change in the legal system will be dissipated.

Capital also employs informalism as a means of legitimation. Grievance mechanisms allow capitalists to appear to care for their consumers, thereby responding to the loss of confidence that occurs as manufacturers and sellers increase in size and grow more remote. Consumer hot lines become a mode of product differentiation in an oligopolistic market (compare the emphasis on caring, personal service, and friendship in corporate advertising). By conceding the individual claim presented by the unusually aggressive consumer, capital denies the structural disparity in power between itself and its customers (cf. Ross and Littlefield, 1978). But it is difficult for capital to do these things by itself or even through a trade association or Better Business Bureau because few consumers are willing to believe in the neutrality of such institutions (Eovaldi and Gestrin, 1971: 304–305; Johnson *et al.*, 1977: 52; Eaton, 1980; Greenberg and Stanton, 1980).

The following incident vividly illustrates this dilemma, although the instrument of corporate disguise is private philanthropy and education rather than the state. Nestlé S.A. was very concerned to nullify widespread criticism of its aggressive marketing of infant formula in Third World countries. The corporate vice-president recognized, however, that "third-party rebuttals of the activists' case" were critical because of "the lack of credibility in the United States for any company to overtly sell itself when it has been attacked." Therefore the Ethics

tate cannot monopolize political power or physical force, whatever it may pre-
end, and its claim to do so enjoys only a tenuous legitimacy.

Yet if the goals of informal justice are contradictory, and if it is incapable of
alizing them because of contradictions inherent in advanced capitalism, in-
malism should not simplistically be repudiated as merely an evil to be resisted,
be dismissed as a marginal phenomenon that can safely be ignored. It is
ocated by reformers and embraced by disputants precisely because it expresses
ues that deservedly elicit broad allegiance: the preference for harmony over
flict, for mechanisms that offer equal access to the many rather than unequal
lege to the few, that operate quickly and cheaply, that permit all citizens to
cipate in decision making rather than limiting authority to "professionals,"
re familiar rather than esoteric, and that strive for and achieve substantive
e rather than frustrating it in the name of form. Those ideals must, and
continue to inspire the struggle to create the institutions—and the
y—that can realize them.

RENCES

David E., Bert H. Hoff, Peter Jaszi, Nicholas N. Kittrie, and David Saari (1977) *The New
e: Alternatives to Conventional Criminal Adjudication*. Washington, D.C.: National In-
of Law Enforcement and Criminal Justice.
David E., C. Thomas Dienes, and Michael C. Musheno (1978) "Changing the Public
enness Laws: The Impact of Decriminalization," 12 *Law & Society Review* 405.
rd L. (1970) "Case Method Research in the Customary Laws of Wrongs in Kenya, Part II:
al Analysis," 6 *East African Law Journal* 20.
7) "From the Editor," 11 *Law & Society Review* 747.
8) "From the Editor," 12 *Law & Society Review* 333.
Da) "Delegalization: A Critical Review of Its Ideology, Manifestations, and Social Con-
s," in E. Blankenburg, E. Klausa, and H. Rottleuthner (eds.) *Alternative Rechtsfor-
Alternativen zum Recht*. Opladen: Westdeutscher Verlag (*Jahrbuch für Rechtssozi-
Rechtstheorie*, band 6).
) "Western Courts in Non-Western Settings: Patterns of Court Use in Colonial and
nial Africa," in S. B. Burman and B. E. Harrell-Bond (eds.) *The Imposition of Law*.
Academic Press.
"Socializing the Legal Profession: Can Redistributing Lawyers' Services Achieve
ce?" 1 *Law & Policy Quarterly* 5.
Critique of American Tort Law," 8(2) *British Journal of Law and Society* (Winter).
n and Robert Stevens (1967) *Lawyers and the Courts: A Sociological Study of the
l System, 1750–1965*. London: Heinemann.
and Lawrence T. Nichols (1981) *Beyond the Courtroom: Programs in Community
onflict Resolution*. Lexington, Mass.: Lexington Books.
. (1979?) "Informal (In)justice? The Legalization of Informal Dispute Settlement
erica. Part I: Conciliation and Arbitration" (unpublished).
and Geoff Mungham (1979) "Law and Lay Participation," 1978 *European
w and Sociology* 17.
75) "Behind the Legal Explosion," 27 *Stanford Law Review* 567.

---

and Public Policy Center, a conservative foundation, commissioned a *Fortune*
editor to write an article on the subject, paying him $5000 on condition that the
draft be reviewed by a panel of three, chosen by the foundation, one of whom
would be an industry representative. When the article appeared, smearing the
activists as "Marxists marching under the banner of Christ," Nestlé reprinted and
distributed it widely since, the vice-president noted, "there must be maximum
exploitation of the opportunities presented by the *Fortune* article"—a purportedly independent journal publishing an ostensibly disinterested author. It also
made a $25,000 contribution to the Center, though the president of Nestlé USA
was "somewhat concerned that Nestlé should not be seen to be the dominant
subscriber to the . . . center" (*Los Angeles Times*, January 6, 1981: pt. 4, p. 4; cf.
Weinstein 1975; Berman, 1978: 29). In the same way, capital looks to the state to
create grievance mechanisms that are structurally incapable of damaging the
power of capital but nevertheless share the reputation of the liberal state for
"relative autonomy," and thus acquire an aura of impartiality.

CONCLUSION

State informal justice under advanced capitalism is a very difficult phenomenon to understand and evaluate because it is constructed out of contradictions
(*compare* Longmire, 1981a, 1981b, *with* Brady, 1981). It appears to be simultaneously more and less coercive than formal law, to represent both an expansion
of the state apparatus and a contraction. For the same reason it is peculiarly
resistant to criticism: When accused of being manipulative it can show its noncoercive face; when charged with abandoning the disadvantaged it can point to
ways in which informal justice extends state paternalism. It is essential to unravel
these contradictions if we are to grasp the full significance of recent legal innovations.

On the one hand, contemporary informal legal institutions clearly do increase
state control, although they seek to appear to withdraw it, and are just as clearly
coercive, although they try to disguise coercion in the forms of volition. Formal
law, by contrast, limits the substantive reach of state intervention—when certain
behavior is specifically proscribed as illegal all other behavior is protected as legal.
Formal law also constrains the procedures by which the state intervenes—
explicit coercion requires the safeguards of due process. This expansion of state
control through informal means is necessary both to maintain order—the minimum requirement of any social system—and to meet those requirements peculiar
to advanced capitalism—imposition of the commodity form upon both the labor
process and the process by which human wants are defined and satisfied.

On the other hand, those same informal institutions represent a withdrawal of
state intervention that assumes the guise of concerned paternalism, a denial of

state coercion that purports to hold out a helping hand, a reallocation of legal resources that deprives those it claims to benefit, a neutralization of conflict that presents itself as a new and better mode for expressing conflict. Formal law, by contrast, is less accessible but may be more worth striving for; if it is harder to mobilize, it is less tolerant of the excuses offered by the object of the grievance; the aggrieved can *demand* state redress as of right rather than depend on a paternalistic construction of what is best. This erosion of formal rights is a necessary concomitant of the progressive penetration of state and capital into areas of personal autonomy: The individual must be given the illusion that his dissatisfactions will be heard and redressed as he surrenders more and more actual control over his life.

The contradictory nature of informal justice can be appreciated better, perhaps, through concrete illustrations. Earlier I gave an example of disputes between the consumer and the producer or seller—a category of conflict that informal justice emphasizes over the struggle between labor and capital in one of the mystifications of oppression typical of advanced capitalism. I argued that in such situations informal justice extends state control by concealing the coercion necessary to enforce the contract of purchase: rendering the small claims court a more efficient collection device through the use of installment payments, employing informal procedures and sanctions to extract restitution from shoplifters. At the same time, informalism diminishes the ability of the regulatory agency to protect the consumer from fraud and overreaching and persuades the dissatisfied purchaser to compromise his complaint of excessive price, poor quality, or dangerous design. This same duality can be discerned in the response of legal informalism to the oppressions of patriarchy, as well as to those of capitalism. On the one hand, informal procedures allow the state to increase its surveillance and control over the domestic sphere: Family disputes that previously would have been overlooked are now subjected to mediation; failing marriages that would have ended in de facto separations are now scrutinized by the state before they are granted the imprimatur of de jure divorce; and the process itself, though it goes under the name of *no*-fault, quickly tends toward an *all*-fault regime in which the behavior of the petitioner (almost always a woman) is examined as closely as that of the respondent. On the other hand, state coercive resources are withdrawn from the disadvantaged party: The threat of criminal prosecution for domestic violence becomes less credible, and women are denied the leverage of fault-based divorce—the power to deny the divorce unless the woman is the complaining party and the rights to custody and to alimony that such a position confers. Thus what appears as help may often be coercion, and what appears inefficient coercion may actually be the neutralization of conflict.

If the contradictory nature of informal justice is one obstacle to interpretation, another pitfall is the danger of confusing its goals, self-proclaimed accomplishments, or tendencies with its actual consequences, particularly its long-term

10. The Contradictions of Informal Justice

effects. Informal legal institutions cannot expand the control of t indefinitely or neutralize conflict once and for all; their rea resources inevitably will be challenged by the oppressed, and legitimacy will evoke renewed skepticism. The forms of conse never succeed in completely concealing coercion. Instead, ever more subtle modes of control has invariably drawn nipulative nature of those institutions, and this has eventu tance to them, either through active opposition or passive history of public schools (e.g., Katz, 1968; Tyack, 197 1976), mental hospitals (e.g., Rothman, 1971; 1980; S measures (e.g., Platt, 1969; Foucault, 1977; Igna nineteenth and twentieth centuries repeatedly illustra Donzelot, 1979). The state responds to resistance b coercive, and this, in turn, compels a reformaliza control; schools, hospitals, and punishment agair juvenile and small claims courts and arbitration.

By the same token, informal legal institutions temporarily, at most. Complainants who invoke inutility; other potential users will see through th tion of novelty has worn off. One response will be American electorate cast a vote of no confiden during the 1980 presidential election, so gri mechanisms, as they have already done in oth 1976: 78, 80–81, 104). But apathy is not th satisfactory to those who choose it. Because with, rather than eliminate, formal alterna and often successfully, to escape from the workers' compensation and no-fault comp favor of tort remedies, reintroduce fault c place under divorce regimes that are os comes of mediation, arbitration, and s formal trial de novo. Just as the oppr defending themselves against state co asserting grievances. Alternatively, gri cesses, formal and informal, choosin their adversaries. Thus workers comp are not content to sue for damage grievances to arbitration, or to invol simply walk off the job (*Whirlpoo* And citizens who suffer from pol the courts to correct such outra demand with violence. As these

REFEI

Aaronson
    Justi
    stitut
Aaronson,
    Drun
Abel, Rich
    Statisti
——— (197
——— (197
——— (197
    sequenc
    men un
    ologie un
——— (1979
    Neo-Colo
    New York
——— (1979c
    Social Just
——— (1981) "
Abel-Smith, Bri
    English Leg
Alper, Benedict S
    Justice and C
Auerbach, Jerold
    in Modern A
Bankowski, Zenon
    Yearbook of L
Barton, John H. (1

Baum, Lawrence (1977) "Judicial Specialization, Litigant Influence, and Substantive Policy: The Court of Customs and Patent Appeals," 11 *Law & Society Review* 823.

Baumgartner, M. P. (1980a) "Law and the Middle Class: Evidence from a Suburban Town." Presented at the joint meeting of the Law and Society Association and the ISA Research Committee on Sociology of Law, Madison, Wisconsin (June 5–8).

—— (1980b) "Aspects of Social Control in a Suburban Town." Presented at the annual meeting of the American Sociological Association, New York (August).

Bell, Griffin (1978) "The Pound Conference Follow-Up: A Response from the United States Department of Justice," 76 Federal Rules Decisions 320.

Beresford, Robert (1977) "It Takes a Big Judge to Handle Small Claims," 16 *Judges' Journal* 14.

Beresford, Robert and Jill Cooper (1977) "A Neighborhood Court for Neighborhood Suits," 61 *Judicature* 185.

Berman, Daniel M. (1978) *Death on the Job: Occupational Health and Safety Struggles in the United States*. New York: Monthly Review Press.

Best, Arthur and Alan R. Andreasen (1977) "Consumer Response to Unsatisfactory Purchases: A Survey of Perceiving Defects, Voicing Complaints, and Obtaining Redress," 11 *Law & Society Review* 701.

Black, Donald (1976) *The Behavior of Law*. New York: Academic Press.

—— (1980) *The Manners and Customs of the Police*. New York: Academic Press.

Blankenburg, Erhard (1976) "The Selectivity of Legal Sanctions: An Empirical Investigation of Shoplifting," 11 *Law & Society Review* 109.

Bohannan, Paul (1965) "The Differing Realms of Law," in L. Nader (ed.) "The Ethnography of Law," 67 (6) (pt. 2) *American Anthropologist* (special issue).

—— (1967) "Introduction," in P. Bohannan (ed.) *Law and Warfare*. Garden City, N.Y.: Natural History Press.

Bowles, Samuel and Herbert Gintis (1976) *Schooling in Capitalist America: Educational Reform and the Contradictions of Economic Life*. New York: Basic Books.

Brady, James P. (1981) "Sorting Out the Exile's Confusion: Or Dialogue on Popular Justice," 5 *Contemporary Crises* 31.

Bridenback, Michael L., Kenneth R. Palmer, and Jack B. Planchard (1979) "Citizen Dispute Settlement: The Florida Experience," 65 *American Bar Association Journal* 570.

Browning, Robert (1955) "My Last Duchess," in R. P. Warren and A. Erskine (eds.) *Six Centuries of Great Poetry*. New York: Dell.

Buckle, Leonard G. and Suzann R. Thomas-Buckle (1980) "Bringing Justice Home: Some Thoughts about the Neighborhood Justice Center Policy." Presented at the meeting of the Law and Society Association and the ISA Research Committee on Sociology of Law, Madison, Wisconsin (June 5–8).

Burger, Warren E. (1976) "Agenda for 2000 A.D.—A Need for Systematic Anticipation," 70 Federal Rules Decisions 83.

—— (1977) "Our Vicious Legal Spiral," 16 *Judges' Journal* 23.

Burman, S. B., H. G. Genn, and J. Lyons (1977) "The Use of Legal Services by Victims of Accidents in the Home—A Pilot Study," 40 *Modern Law Review* 47.

California Citizens' Commission on Tort Reform (1977) *Righting the Liability Balance*. Los Angeles: California Citizens' Commission.

Cappelletti, Mauro (gen. ed.) (1978–1979) *Access to Justice*, 4 vols. Alphen aan den Rijn: Sijthoff and Noordhoff; and Milan: Giuffrè.

—— (ed.) (1981) *Access to Justice and the Welfare State*. Alphen aan den Rijn: Sijthoff.

Carroll, Lewis (1946) *Alice in Wonderland and Through the Looking Glass*. New York: Grosset & Dunlop.

Carson, W. G. (1974) "Symbolic and Instrumental Dimensions of Early Factory Legislation: A Case

Study in the Social Origins of Criminal Law," in R. Hood (ed.) *Crime, Criminology, and Public Policy.* London: Heinemann.

Center for the Study of Crime and Social Justice (1979) *The Iron Fist and the Velvet Glove,* 2d ed. San Francisco: Synthesis Publications.

Christie, Nils (1977) "Conflicts as Property," 17 *British Journal of Criminology* 1.

Coates, Dan and Steven Penrod (1981) "The Social Psychology of Disputing," 15 (3) *Law & Society Review* (forthcoming).

Cohen, Stan (1979) "The Punitive City: Notes on the Dispersal of Social Control," 3 *Contemporary Crises* 339.

Cohen, Stan and Jock Young (1973) *The Manufacture of News: Deviance, Social Problems and the Mass Media.* London: Constable.

Colson, Elizabeth (1974) *Tradition and Contract: The Problem of Order.* Chicago: Aldine.

Conley, Ronald W. and John H. Noble, Jr. (1980) *Workers' Compensation Reform: Challenge for the 80s.* Washington, D.C.: Office of the Assistant Secretary for Planning and Evaluation, U.S. Department of Health, Education, and Welfare.

Conn, Stephen and Arthur E. Hippler (1974) "Conciliation and Arbitration in the Native Village and the Urban Ghetto," 58 *Judicature* 228.

Conner, Ross F. and Ray Surette (1977) *The Citizen Dispute Settlement Program: Resolving Disputes outside the Courts—Orlando, Florida.* Chicago: American Bar Association.

Cook, Royer F., Janice A. Roehl, and David I. Sheppard (1980) *Neighborhood Justice Centers Field Test: Final Evaluation Report.* Washington, D.C.: National Institute of Justice.

Crowe, Patricia Ward (1978) "Complainant Reactions to the Massachusetts Commission against Discrimination," 12 *Law & Society Review* 217.

Curran, Barbara A. (1977) *The Legal Needs of the Public.* Chicago: American Bar Foundation.

Danet, Brenda (1980) "Language in the Legal Process," 14 *Law & Society Review* 445.

Davis, Robert C., Martha Tichane, and Deborah Grayson (1980) *Mediation and Arbitration as Alternatives to Prosecution in Felony Arrest Cases: An Evaluation of the Brooklyn Dispute Resolution Center (First Year).* New York: Vera Institute of Justice.

Dean, Paul (1981) "Information Please: The Public Gets Involved in Crime Detection: Hot Lines for Informants," *Los Angeles Times* (January 7) pt. 5, p. 1.

Dispute Resolution (1979–1981). Washington, D.C.: American Bar Association Special Committee on Resolution of Minor Disputes (quarterly).

Donzelot, Jacques (1979) *The Policing of Families.* New York: Pantheon.

Doo, Leigh-Wei (1973) "Dispute Settlement in Chinese-American Communities," 21 *American Journal of Comparative Law* 627.

Durkheim, Emil (1947) *The Division of Labor in Society,* Simpson (trans.). Glencoe, Ill.: Free Press.

Eaton, Marian (1980) "The Better Business Bureau: 'The Voice of the People in the Marketplace,'" in Nader (1980a).

Ehrlich, Thomas (1976) "Legal Pollution," *New York Times Magazine* (February 8) 17.

Ehrlich, Thomas and Murray L. Schwartz (1974) *Reducing the Costs of Legal Services: Possible Approaches by the Federal Government.* Washington, D.C.: Government Printing Office.

Engel, David M. (1980) "Legal Pluralism in an American Community: Perspectives on a Civil Trial Court," 1980 *American Bar Foundation Research Journal* 425.

Eovaldi, Thomas L. and Joan E. Gestrin (1971) "Justice for Consumers: The Mechanisms of Redress," 66 *Northwestern University Law Review* 281.

Erickson, William H. (1978) "The Pound Conference Recommendations: A Blueprint for the Justice System in the Twenty-First Century," 76 *Federal Rules Decisions,* 277.

Falke, Josef, Günter Bierbrauer, and Klaus-Friedrich Koch (1978) "Legal Advice and the Non-Judicial Settlement of Disputes: A Case Study of the Public Legal Advice and Mediation Center in the City of Hamburg," in M. Cappelletti and J. Weisner (eds.) *Access to Justice,* vol. 2:

Promising Institutions. Milan: Giuffrè; and Alphen aan den Rijn: Sijthoff and Noordhoff.

Feeley, Malcolm (1979) *The Process Is the Punishment.* New York: Russell Sage Foundation.

Felstiner, William L.F. (1974) "Influences of Social Organization on Dispute Processing," 9 *Law & Society Review* 63.

Felstiner, William L.F., Richard L. Abel, and Austin Sarat (1981) "The Emergence and Transformation of Disputes: Naming, Blaming, Claiming...," 15 (3) *Law & Society Review* (forthcoming).

Felstiner, William L. F. and Ann Barthelmes Drew (1976) *European Alternatives to Criminal Trials and Their Applicability in the United States (including an appendix surveying non-European alternatives).* Los Angeles: University of Southern California Social Science Research Institute and Law Center.

Felstiner, William L.F. and Lynne A. Williams (1978) "Mediation as an Alternative to Criminal Prosecution: Ideology and Limitations," 2 *Law and Human Behavior* 223.

────── (1980) *Community Mediation in Dorchester, Massachusetts.* Washington, D.C.: U.S. Department of Justice, National Institute of Justice.

Ford Foundation (1973) *The Public Interest Law Firm: New Voices for New Constituencies.* New York: Ford Foundation.

────── (1978a) *Mediating Social Conflict.* New York: Ford Foundation.

────── (1978b) *New Approaches to Conflict Resolution.* New York: Ford Foundation.

Ford Foundation and American Bar Association Special Committee on Public Interest Practice (1976) *Public Interest Law: Five Years Later.* Chicago: American Bar Association; and New York: Ford Foundation.

Fortes, Meyer and E. E. Evans-Pritchard (eds.) (1940) *African Political Systems.* London: Oxford University Press.

Foster, Henry (1966) "Conciliation and Counseling in the Courts in Family Law Cases," 41 *New York University Law Review* 343.

Foster, Ken (1975) "Problems with Small Claims," 2 *British Journal of Law and Society* 75.

Foucault, Michel (1977) *Discipline and Punish: The Birth of the Prison.* New York: Pantheon.

Freedman, Eric (1980) "'Dear Mr. Nader': A Study of Consumer Complaint Letters," in Nader (1980a).

Fried, Charles (1976) "The Lawyer as Friend: The Moral Foundations of the Lawyer–Client Relationship," 85 *Yale Law Journal* 1060.

Friedman, Aryeh (1977) "The Effectiveness of Arbitration for the Resolution of Consumer Disputes," 6 *New York University Review of Law and Social Change* 175.

Friedman, Milton (1962) *Capitalism and Freedom.* Chicago: University of Chicago Press.

Frierson, James G. (1977) "Let's Abolish Small Claims Courts," 16 *Judges' Journal* 18.

Galanter, Marc (1963) "The Displacement of Traditional Law in Modern India," 24 *Journal of Social Issues* 65.

────── (1972) "The Aborted Restoration of 'Indigenous' Law in India," 14 *Comparative Studies in Society and History* 53.

────── (1974) "Why the 'Haves' Come Out Ahead: Speculations on the Limits of Legal Change," 9 *Law & Society Review* 95.

────── (1975) "Afterword: Explaining Litigation," 9 *Law & Society Review* 347.

────── (1979) "Legality and Its Discontents: A Preliminary Assessment of Current Theories of Legalization and Delegalization," in E. Blankenburg, E. Klausa, and H. Rottleuthner (eds.) *Alternative Rechtsformen und Alternativen zum Recht.* Opladen: Westdeutscher Verlag (*Jahrbuch für Rechtssoziologie und Rechtstheorie,* band 6).

Galbraith, John K. (1978) *The Affluent Society,* 3d rev. ed. New York: New American Library.

Garofalo, James and Kevin J. Connelly (1980a) "Dispute Resolution Centers, Part I: Major Features and Processes," *Criminal Justice Abstracts* 416 (November).

———— (1980b) "Dispute Resolution Centers, Part II: Outcomes, Issues, and Future Directions," *Criminal Justice Abstracts* (December).

Garofalo, James and John Laub (1978) "The Fear of Crime: Broadening Our Perspective," 3 *Victimology* 242.

Getman, Julius G. (1979) "Labor Arbitration and Dispute Resolution," 88 *Yale Law Journal* 916.

Gluckman, Max (1965) *The Ideas in Barotse Jurisprudence*. New Haven, Conn.: Yale University Press.

Glueck, Sheldon and Eleanor Glueck (1950) *Unraveling Juvenile Delinquency*. New York: Harper & Row.

———— (1956) *Physique and Delinquency*. New York: Harper & Row.

Goldbeck, Willis B. (1975) "Mediation: An Instrument of Citizen Involvement," 30 *Arbitration Journal* 241.

Golding, M. P. (1969) "Preliminaries to the Study of Procedural Justice," in G. Hughes (ed.) *Law, Reason, and Justice*. New York: New York University Press.

Goldman, Jerry (1980) *Ineffective Justice: Evaluating the Preappeal Conference*. Beverly Hills, Calif: Sage Publications.

Goldmann, Robert B. (ed.) (1981) *Roundtable Justice: Case Studies in Conflict Resolution*. Boulder, Colo.: Westview Press.

Goldstein, Joseph (1960) "Police Discretion Not to Invoke the Criminal Process: Low-Visibility Decisions in the Administration of Justice," 69 *Yale Law Journal* 543.

Grau, Charles W. and Jane Kahn (1980) "Working the Damned, the Dumb and the Destitute: The Politics of Community Service Restitution." Presented at the joint meeting of the Law and Society Association and the ISA Research Committee on Sociology of Law, Madison, Wisconsin (June 5–8).

Greenberg, David I. and Thomas H. Stanton (1980) "Business Groups, Consumer Problems: The Contradiction of Trade Association Complaint Handling," in Nader (1980a).

Halbach, Edward C., Jr. (1976) "Toward a Simplified System of Law," in M. L. Schwartz (ed.) *Law and the American Future*. Englewood Cliffs, N.J.: Prentice-Hall.

Haley, John (1982) "The Politics of Informal Justice: The Japanese Experience 1922–1942," in R. L. Abel (ed.) *The Politics of Informal Justice*, vol. 2: *Comparative Studies*. New York: Academic Press.

Hall, Stuart (1980) *Drifting into a Law and Order Society*. London: Cobden Trust.

Hall, Stuart, *et al.* (1978) *Policing the Crisis: Mugging, the State, and Law and Order*. London: Macmillan.

Handler, Joel, Ellen Jane Hollingsworth, and Howard S. Erlanger (1978) *Lawyers and the Pursuit of Legal Rights*. New York: Academic Press.

Hannigan, John A. (1977) "The Newspaper Ombudsman and Consumer Complaints: An Empirical Assessment," 11 *Law & Society Review* 679.

Harrington, Christine B. (1980) "Voluntariness, Consent and Coercion in Adjudicating Minor Disputes: The Neighborhood Justice Center," in J. Brigham and D. Brown (eds.) *Policy Implementation: Choosing between Penalties and Incentives*. Beverly Hills, Calif.: Sage Publications.

Harris, Richard (1969) *The Fear of Crime*. New York: Praeger.

Hastings Law Journal (1978) "Compulsory Judicial Arbitration in California: Reducing the Delay and Expense of Resolving Uncomplicated Civil Disputes," 29 *Hastings Law Journal* 475.

Hazard, Geoffrey C., Jr. (1969) "Social Justice through Civil Justice," 36 *University of Chicago Law Review* 699.

Henderson, Roger C. (1977) "No-Fault Insurance for Automobile Accidents: Status and Effect in the United States," 56 *Oregon Law Review* 287.

Hindus, Michael Stephen (1980) *Prison and Plantation: Crime, Justice, and Authority in Massachusetts and South Carolina.* Chapel Hill, N.C.: University of North Carolina Press.

Hirschman, Albert O. (1970) *Exit, Voice and Loyalty: Responses to Decline in Firms, Organizations, and States.* Cambridge, Mass.: Harvard University Press.

Hofrichter, Richard (1982) "Neighborhood Justice and the Social Control Problems of American Capitalism: A Perspective," in R. L. Abel (ed.) *The Politics of Informal Justice,* vol. 1: *The American Experience.* New York: Academic Press.

Hudson, Joe and Burt Galaway (eds.) (1980) *Victims, Offenders, and Alternative Sanctions.* Lexington, Mass.: Lexington Books.

Ignatieff, Michael (1978) *A Just Measure of Pain: Penitentiaries and the Industrial Revolution.* New York: Pantheon.

Illich, Ivan, *et al.* (1977) *Disabling Professions.* London: Marion Boyars.

Inbau, Fred E. and John E. Reid (1962) *Criminal Interrogation and Confessions.* Baltimore: Williams and Wilkins.

Ison, T. G. (1980) *Accident Compensation: A Commentary on the New Zealand Scheme.* London: Croom Helm.

Johnson, Earl, Jr. (1974) *Justice and Reform: The Formative Years of the OEO Legal Services Program.* New York: Russell Sage Foundation.

Johnson, Earl, Jr., Valerie Kantor, and Elizabeth Schwartz (1977a) *Outside the Courts: A Survey of Diversion Alternatives in Civil Cases.* Denver: National Center for State Courts.

Johnson, Earl, Jr., Steven A. Bloch, Ann Barthelmes Drew, William L.F. Felstiner, E. Wayne Hansen, and Georges Sarbagh (1977b) *A Comparative Analysis of the Statistical Dimensions of the Justice Systems of Seven Industrial Democracies.* Washington, D.C.: Law Enforcement Assistance Administration.

Jones, Harry Wilmer (ed.) (1965) *The Courts, the Public, and the Law Explosion.* Englewood Cliffs, N.J.: Prentice-Hall.

Kalven, Harry, Jr. and Hans Zeisel (1966) *The American Jury.* Chicago: University of Chicago Press.

Karikas, Angela (1980) "Solving Problems in Philadelphia: An Ethnography of a Congressional District Office," in Nader (1980a).

Karikas, Angela and Rena Rosenwasser (1980) "Department Store Complaint Management," in Nader (1980a).

Kastenmeier, Robert W. and Michael J. Remington (1979) "Court Reform and Access to Justice: A Legislative Perspective," 16 *Harvard Journal on Legislation* 301.

Katz, Jack (1978) "Lawyers for the Poor in Transition: Involvement, Reform, and the Turnover Problem in the Legal Services Program," 12 *Law & Society Review* 275.

Katz, Michael B. (1968) *The Irony of Early School Reform: Educational Innovation in Mid-Nineteenth-Century Massachusetts.* Cambridge, Mass.: Harvard University Press.

Kidder, Robert L. (1980) "Down to Earth Justice: Pitfalls on the Road to Legal Decentralization." Presented at the joint meeting of the Law and Society Association and the ISA Research Committee on Sociology of Law, Madison, Wisconsin (June 5–8).

Kline, J. Anthony (1978a) "Curbing California's Colossal Appetite," *Los Angeles Times* (February 12) pt. 4, p. 1.

—————— (1978b) "Law Reform and the Courts: More Power to the People or the Profession?" 53 *California State Bar Journal* 14.

Kurczewski, Jacek and Kazimierz Frieske (1978) "The Social Conciliatory Commissions in Poland: A Case Study of Nonauthoritative and Conciliatory Dispute Resolution as an Approach to Access to Justice," in M. Cappelletti and J. Weisner (eds.) *Access to Justice,* vol. 2: *Promising Institutions.* Milan: Giuffrè; and Alphen aan den Rijn: Sijthoff and Noordhoff.

Ladinsky, Jack, Stewart Macaulay, and Jill Anderson (1979) "The Milwaukee Dispute Mapping

Project: A Preliminary Report." Madison: University of Wisconsin Law School (Disputes Processing Research Program Working Paper 1979–3).

Landes, William M. and Richard A. Posner (1979) "Adjudication as a Private Good," 8 *Journal of Legal Studies* 235.

Larson, Magali Sarfatti (1977) *The Rise of Professionalism: A Sociological Analysis.* Berkeley, Calif.: University of California Press.

Law & Society Review (1979) "Plea Bargaining," 13 *Law & Society Review* 189 (special issue).

Lazerson, Mark H. (1982) "In the Halls of Justice, the Only Justice Is in the Halls," in R. L. Abel (ed.) *The Politics of Informal Justice,* vol. 1: *The American Experience.* New York: Academic Press.

Legal Services Corporation (1980) *Delivery Systems Study.* Washington, D.C.: Legal Services Corporation.

Lieberman, Jethro K. (1981) *The Litigious Society.* New York: Basic Books.

Lindblom, Charles E. (1977) *Politics and Markets: The World's Political–Economic Systems.* New York: Basic Books.

Longmire, Dennis R. (1981a) "A Popular Justice System: A Radical Alternative to the Traditional Criminal Justice System," 5 *Contemporary Crises* 15.

——— (1981b) "Cutting the *Gordian Knot:* Continuing the Dialogue on Popular Justice," 5 *Contemporary Crises* 39.

Macaulay, Stewart (1979) "Lawyers and Consumer Protection Laws," 14 *Law & Society Review* 115.

McGillis, Daniel (n.d.) *Dispute Processing Projects: A Preliminary Directory.* Cambridge, Mass.: Harvard Law School Center for Criminal Justice.

McKay, Robert B. (1977) "A New Look for Lady Justice," 16 *Judges' Journal* 39.

Manning, Bayless (1976) "Hyperlexis: Our National Disease," 71 *Northwestern University Law Review* 767.

Marks, F. Raymond, Robert P. Hallauer, and Richard R. Clifton (1974) *The Shreveport Plan: An Experiment in the Delivery of Legal Services.* Chicago: American Bar Foundation.

Marquardt, Ronald G. and Edward M. Wheat (1980) "Hidden Allocators: Administrative Law Judges and Regulatory Reform," 2 *Law & Policy Quarterly* 472.

Martin, Del (1977) *Battered Wives.* New York: Pocket Books.

Mathiesen, Thomas (1980) "The Future of Control Systems—The Case of Norway," 8 *International Journal of the Sociology of Law* 149.

Mattice, Michael C. (1980) "Media in the Middle: A Study of the Mass Media Complaint Managers," in Nader (1980a).

Mayhew, Leon H. (1968) *Law and Equal Opportunity: A Study of the Massachusetts Commission against Discrimination.* Cambridge, Mass.: Harvard University Press.

Mayhew, Leon and Albert J. Reiss, Jr. (1969) "The Social Organization of Legal Contacts," 34 *American Sociological Review* 309.

Meador, Daniel J. (1979) "Statement," in Subcommittee on Courts (1979).

Menkel-Meadow, Carrie (1979) *The 59th Street Legal Clinic: Evaluation of the Experiment.* Chicago: American Bar Association.

Mentschikoff, Soia (1952) "The Significance of Arbitration—A Preliminary Inquiry," 17 *Law & Contemporary Problems* 698.

Merry, Sally Engle (1979) "Going to Court: Strategies of Dispute Management in an Urban American Neighborhood," 13 *Law & Society Review* 891.

Middleton, John and David Tait (eds.) (1958) *Tribes Without Rulers.* London: Routledge and Kegan Paul.

Mnookin, Robert H. and Lewis Kornhauser (1979) "Bargaining in the Shadow of the Law: The Case of Divorce," 88 *Yale Law Journal* 950.

The Mooter (1977–1980) Pittsburgh: Grassroots Citizen Dispute Resolution Clearinghouse.

Moriarty, Thomas (1975) "A Nation of Willing Victims: Urban Danger and Urban Insult," *Psychology Today* 44 (April).

Muris, Timothy J. and Frederic S. McChesney (1979) "Advertising and the Price and Quality of Legal Services: The Case of Legal Clinics," 1979 *American Bar Foundation Research Journal* 179.

Nader, Laura (1979) "Disputing Without the Force of Law," 88 *Yale Law Journal* 998.

―――― (ed.) (1980a) *No Access to Law: Alternatives to the American Judicial System.* New York: Academic Press.

―――― (1980b) "Alternatives to the American Judicial System," in Nader (1980a).

Nagin, Daniel (1978) "Crime Rates, Sanction Levels, and Constraints on Prison Population," 12 *Law & Society Review* 341.

Nimmer, Raymond T. (1974) *Diversion: The Search for Alternative Forms of Prosecution.* Chicago: American Bar Foundation.

O'Connell, Jeffrey (1975) *Ending Insult to Injury: No-Fault Insurance for Products and Services.* Urbana, Ill.: University of Illinois Press.

Palen, Frank S. (1979) "Media Ombudsmen: A Critical Review," 13 *Law & Society Review* 799.

Palenski, Joseph E., Nancy Wohl, Deirdre Shea, and Joseph Aponte (Evaluation Group Inc.) (1980) *An Evaluation Report on the Suffolk County Community Mediation Center.* Glendale, N.Y.: Evaluation Group.

Palmer, Geoffrey (1980) *Compensation for Incapacity: A Study of Law and Social Change in New Zealand and Australia.* New York: Oxford University Press.

Parnas, Raymond I. (1967) "The Police Response to the Domestic Disturbance," 1967 *Wisconsin Law Review* 914.

Patterson, K. David (1969) *The Pokot of Western Kenya, 1910–1963: The Response of a Conservative People to Colonial Rule.* Syracuse, N.Y.: Maxwell School (Program in East African Studies, Occasional Papers No. 53).

Platt, Anthony M. (1969) *The Child Savers.* Chicago: University of Chicago Press.

Reifner, Udo (1982) "Individualistic and Collective Legalization: The Theory and Practice of Legal Advice for Workers in Prefascist Germany," in R. L. Abel (ed.) *The Politics of Informal Justice,* vol. 2: *Comparative Studies.* New York: Academic Press.

Rheinstein, Max (1972) *Marriage Stability, Divorce and the Law.* Chicago: University of Chicago Press.

Rosenberg, Maurice (1964) *The Pretrial Conference and Effective Justice: A Controlled Test in Personal Injury Litigation.* New York: Columbia University Press.

―――― (1971a) "Devising Procedures that Are Civil to Promote Justice that Is Civilized," 69 *Michigan Law Review* 797.

―――― (1971b) "Let's Everybody Litigate?" 50 *Texas Law Review* 1349.

Ross, H. Laurence (1980) *Settled Out of Court: The Social Process of Insurance Claims Adjustment,* 2d rev. ed. Chicago: Aldine.

Ross, H. Laurence and Neil O. Littlefield (1978) "Complaint as a Problem-Solving Mechanism," 12 *Law & Society Review* 199.

Rothman, David (1971) *The Discovery of the Asylum.* Boston: Little, Brown.

―――― (1980) *Conscience and Convenience: The Asylum and Its Alternatives in Progressive America.* Boston: Little, Brown.

Royal Commission on Legal Services (1979) *Final Report,* vol. 1. London: Her Majesty's Stationery Office.

Rubinstein, Leonard (1976) "Procedural Due Process and the Limits of the Adversary System," 11 *Harvard Civil Rights–Civil Liberties Law Reporter* 48.

Ruhnka, John C. and Steven Weller with John A. Martin (1978) *Small Claims Courts: A National Examination.* Williamsburg, Va.: National Center for State Courts.

Salas, Luis and Ronald Schneider (1979) "Evaluating the Dade County Citizen Dispute Settlement Program," 63 *Judicature* 174.

Sander, Frank E.A. (1976) "Varieties of Dispute Processing," 70 Federal Rules Decisions 111.

———— (1977) *Report on the National Conference on Minor Disputes Resolution*. Chicago: American Bar Association.

Sander, Frank E.A. and Frederick E. Snyder (1979) *Alternative Methods of Dispute Settlement—A Selected Bibliography*. Washington, D.C.: American Bar Association.

Santos, Boaventura de Sousa (1982) "Law and Community: The Changing Nature of State Power in Late Capitalism," in R. L. Abel (ed.) *The Politics of Informal Justice*, vol. 1: *The American Experience*. New York: Academic Press.

Sarat, Austin (1976) "Alternatives in Dispute Processing: Litigation in a Small Claims Court," 10 *Law & Society Review* 339.

———— (1977) "Studying American Legal Culture: An Assessment of Survey Evidence," 11 *Law & Society Review* 427.

Scheiber, Harry N. (1980) "Federalism and Legal Process: Historical and Contemporary Analysis of the American System," 14 *Law & Society Review* 663.

Schrag, Philip (1972) *Counsel for the Deceived: Case Studies in Consumer Fraud*. New York: Pantheon.

Schwartz, Richard (1954) "Social Factors in the Development of Legal Control: A Case Study of Two Israeli Settlements," 63 *Yale Law Journal* 471.

Scull, Andrew (1979) *Museums of Madness: The Social Organization of Insanity in Nineteenth Century England*. New York: St. Martin's.

Sennett, Richard (1977) *The Fall of Public Man*. New York: Knopf.

Serber, David (1980) "Resolution or Rhetoric: Managing Complaints in the California Department of Insurance," in Nader (1980a).

Sheppard, David I., Janice A. Roehl, and Royer F. Cook (1978) *Neighborhood Justice Centers Field Test: Implementation Study*. Reston, Va.: Institute for Social Analysis.

Sherman, Howard (1979) "Inflation, Unemployment, and the Contemporary Business Cycle," 44 *Socialist Review* 75.

Shonholtz, Raymond (n.d.) *A Justice System that Isn't Working and Its Impact on the Community*. San Francisco: Community Board Program.

Silbey, Susan S. (1978) *Consumer Justice: The Massachusetts Attorney General's Office of Consumer Protection, 1970–1974*. Ph.D. Dissertation, Department of Political Science, University of Chicago.

Simon, William H. (1978) "The Ideology of Advocacy: Procedural Justice and Professional Ethics," 1978 *Wisconsin Law Review* 29.

Singer, Linda R. (1980) "Nonjudicial Dispute Resolution Mechanisms: The Effects on Justice for the Poor," 13 *Clearinghouse Review* 569.

Smith, David N. (1978) "A Warmer Way of Disputing: Mediation and Conciliation," 26 *American Journal of Comparative Law* 205 (supplement).

Smith, Alan, John Bryant, and Deborah Bond (n.d.) *A Pilot Study of Dispute Treatment in Leamington: A Report*. Coventry: University of Warwick School of Law.

Snyder, Frederick E. (1978) "Crime and Community Mediation—The Boston Experience: A Preliminary Report on the Dorchester Urban Court Program," 1978 *Wisconsin Law Review* 737.

Spence, Jack (1982) "Institutionalizing Neighborhood Courts: Two Chilean Experiences," in R. L. Abel (ed.) *The Politics of Informal Justice*, vol. 2: *Comparative Studies*. New York: Academic Press.

Stanley, Justin A. (1977) "The Resolution of Minor Disputes and the Seventh Amendment," 60 *Marquette Law Review* 963.

Stapleton, W. Vaughan and Lee E. Teitelbaum (1972) *In Defense of Youth: A Study of the Role of Counsel in American Juvenile Courts.* New York: Russell Sage Foundation.

Starr, June (1978) *Dispute and Settlement in Rural Turkey: An Ethnography of Law.* Leiden: E. J. Brill.

Steele, Eric H. (1975) "Fraud, Dispute, and the Consumer: Responding to Consumer Complaints," 123 *University of Pennsylvania Law Review* 1107.

Subcommittee on Courts, Civil Liberties, and the Administration of Justice of the Committee on the Judiciary, House of Representatives, 95th Cong., 2d Sess. (1978) Hearings on S.957: Dispute Resolution Act. Washington, D.C.: Government Printing Office.

Subcommittee on Courts, Civil Liberties, and the Administration of Justice of the Committee on the Judiciary and Subcommittee on Consumer Protection and Finance of the Committee on Interstate and Foreign Commerce, House of Representatives, 96th Cong., 1st Sess. (1979) Joint Hearings on Resolution of Minor Disputes. Washington, D.C.: Government Printing Office.

Tate, S. Shepherd (1979) "Access to Justice," 65 *American Bar Association Journal* 904.

Tomasic, Roman (1978) *Lawyers and the Community.* Sydney: Law Foundation of New South Wales.

Tomasic, Roman and Malcolm M. Feeley (eds.) (1982) *Neighborhood Justice.* New York: Longman.

Turk, Austin T. (1976) "Law as a Weapon in Social Conflict," 23 *Social Problems* 276.

Tyack, David B. (1974) *The One Best System: A History of American Urban Education.* Cambridge, Mass.: Harvard University Press.

University of Pennsylvania Law Review (1953) "Note: The Administration of Divorce: A Philadelphia Study," 101 *University of Pennsylvania Law Review* 1204.

Van der Sprenkel, Sybille (1962) *The Legal Institutions of Manchu China: A Sociological Analysis.* London: Athlone Press.

Wanner, Craig (1974) "The Public Ordering of Private Relations, Part One: Initiating Civil Cases in Urban Trial Courts," 8 *Law & Society Review* 421.

_____ (1975) "The Public Ordering of Private Relations, Part Two: Winning Civil Court Cases," 9 *Law & Society Review* 293.

Weiner, Max (1976) "Consumer Alternative: Redress of Grievances," 1(7) *New Directions in the Delivery of Legal Services* 105 (November).

Weinstein, Henry (1975) "Defending What? The Corporation's Public Interest," 5(6) *Juris Doctor* 39 (June).

Weisbrod, Burton A., Joel F. Handler, and Neil K. Komesar (1978) *Public Interest Law: An Economic and Institutional Analysis.* Berkeley: University of California Press.

Weller, Steven, John A. Martin, and John C. Ruhnka (1979) "Litigant Satisfaction with Small Claims Court: Does Familiarity Breed Contempt?" 3(2) *State Court Journal* 3.

Whitford, William C. and Spencer L. Kimball (1974) "Why Process Consumer Complaints? A Case Study of the Office of the Commissioner of Insurance of Wisconsin," 1974 *Wisconsin Law Review* 639.

Widiss, Alan I., *et al.* (1977) *No-Fault Automobile Insurance in Action: The Experiences in Massachusetts, Florida, Delaware and Michigan.* Dobbs Ferry, N.Y.: Oceana.

Wilkinson, Philip J. (1980) *The Social Organisation of Disputes and Dispute Processing and Methods for the Investigation of their Social, Legal and Interactive Properties. A Bibliography in Three Parts.* Oxford: Centre for Socio-Legal Studies.

Wilson, James Q. (ed.) (1980) *The Politics of Regulation.* New York: Basic Books.

Wilson, Gregory and Elizabeth Brydolf (1980) "Grass Roots Solutions: San Francisco Consumer Action," in Nader (1980a).

Winter, Gerd (1979) "Housing for the Poor in West Germany: Legal Instruments and Economic Structure," in M. Partington and J. Jowell (eds.) *Welfare Law and Policy.* London: Pinter.

Witty, Cathie J. (1980) *Mediation and Society: Conflict Management in Lebanon.* New York: Academic Press.

Wunder, John R. (1979) *Inferior Courts, Superior Justice: A History of the Justices of the Peace on the Northwest Frontier, 1853–1889.* Westport, Conn.: Greenwood Press.

Yaffe, James (1972) *So Sue Me! The Story of a Community Court.* New York: Saturday Review Press.

Yankelovich, Skelly and White, Inc. (1978) "Highlights of a National Survey of the General Public, Judges, Lawyers, and Community Leaders," in T. J. Fetter (ed.) *State Courts: A Blueprint for the Future.* Williamsburg, Va.: National Center for State Courts.

Yngvesson, Barbara and Patricia Hennessey (1975) "Small Claims, Complex Disputes: A Review of the Small Claims Literature," 9 *Law & Society Review* 219.

About the Authors

RICHARD L. ABEL is Professor of Law at the University of California, Los Angeles. He has been editor of *African Law Studies* and of the *Law & Society Review* and has written on African legal systems, dispute institutions, and the sociology of family law, of American and British lawyers, and of the legal protection of health and safety. He is currently working on the comparative sociology of lawyers.

JONATHAN GARLOCK is Assistant Director of the Office of Grants and Funded Projects and Assistant Professor at Monroe Community College in Rochester, New York. A labor historian, he has focused on U.S. developments in the late nineteenth century, especially the Knights of Labor. As director of a 3-year project in community history, an important second interest, he published a researchers' handbook, edited a newsletter, participated in numerous conferences, and generally promoted the involvement of citizens in discovering and comprehending their past.

CHRISTINE HARRINGTON is Assistant Professor of Political Science at Rutgers University. She has been doing research on lower court reforms in the twentieth century, the ideology of liberal legalism, and the institutionalization of minor dispute-processing programs, in conjunction with her dissertation research at the University of Wisconsin–Madison.

RICHARD HOFRICHTER is a research associate for the Committee on Behavioral and Social Aspects of Energy Consumption and Production of the National Academy of Sciences. He has been senior research associate for the Criminal Justice and the Elderly Program, National Council of Senior Citizens, and has published a number of articles on victim compensation, restitution, and neighborhood justice, most recently "Techniques of Victim Involvement in Restitution Programs," a chapter in Joe Hudson and Burt Galway (Eds.), *Victims, Offenders, and Alternative Sanctions*. His current interests include democratic social planning, alternatives to conventional legal institutions, and class struggle in American cities.

MARK H. LAZERSON received his J.D. from New York University Law School and is a member of the New York bar. He is presently a Ph.D. candidate in sociology at the University of Wisconsin–Madison, and engaged in research in Italy on the Workers Charter, supported by a Foreign Area Fellowship. His publications include "Cops and Prosecutors: Cleavages Within the 'System,'" a chapter coauthored with Malcolm Feeley in *Empirical Theories of Courts*.

BOAVENTURA DE SOUSA SANTOS is Professor of Sociology at the School of Economics, University of Coimbra, where he also teaches sociology of law at the Law School. His primary interests are popular justice, legal pluralism, and the theory of the state, and he has conducted field research in Rio de Janeiro and Recife (Brazil) and Angola, as well as in Portugal.

ANDREW SCULL teaches sociology at the University of California, San Diego. His primary research interest is the historical sociology of social control. He is the author of *Decarceration: Community Treatment and the Deviant: A Radical View* and *Museums of Madness: The Social Organization of Insanity in Nineteenth Century England*, as well as numerous essays. His new book is *Madhouses, Mad-doctors, and Madmen: The Social History of Psychiatry in the Victorian Era*. He is presently at work on a study of Durkheim's sociology of law (with Steven Lukes) and on a book on English concepts of insanity between the mid-eighteenth and the end of the nineteenth centuries.

STEVEN SPITZER is Associate Professor of Sociology at Suffolk University in Boston. In 1979–1980 he was a Fellow in Law and Sociology at Harvard Law School. He is interested in the historical and comparative study of law, punishment, and policing, particularly the political economy of social control. He is coeditor (with Rita J. Simon) of the annual series *Research in Law, Deviance and Social Control*.

PAUL WAHRHAFTIG received his J.D. from the University of California, Berkeley. He helped to pioneer the concept of community-based dispute resolution in 1972, and established the Grassroots Citizen Dispute Resolution Clearinghouse in Pittsburgh, under the aegis of the American Friends Service Committee, and directed it until its demise in 1980.

Subject Index